PATHWAYS TO NUMBER
Children's Developing Numerical Abilities

PATHWAYS TO NUMBER
Children's Developing Numerical Abilities

Edited by

Jacqueline Bideaud
Université Charles de Gaulle, Lille III
Claire Meljac
Centre Henri-Rousselle, Paris
Jean-Paul Fischer
Institut Universitaire de Formation des Maîtres de Lorraine:
Site de Montigny-lès-Metz

Selected chapters translated by
Constance Greenbaum

LEA 1992 LAWRENCE ERLBAUM ASSOCIATES, PUBLISHERS Hillsdale, New Jersey   Hove and London

Originally published by Presses Universitaires de Lille, Copyright © 1991.
Constance Greenbaum translated from the French Edition the Introduction and Chapters 2, 3, 9, 10, 11, 12, 14, 17, and 18.

BF
723
N8
C4513
1992

Lawrence Erlbaum Associates, Inc., Publishers
365 Broadway
Hillsdale, New Jersey 07642

Library of Congress Cataloging in Publication Data

Chemins du nombre. English
   Pathways to number / edited by Jacqueline Bideaud, Claire Meljac,
Jean-Paul Fischer.
     p. cm.
   Translation of: Les chemins du nombre.
   Includes bibliographical references and indexes.
   ISBN 0-8058-0866-3
   1. Number concept in children. I. Bideaud, Jacqueline.
II. Meljac, Claire. III. Fischer, Jean-Paul. IV. Title.
BF723.N8C4513 1992   92-9448
155.4'13 — dc20   CIP

Printed in the United States of America
10 9 8 7 6 5 4 3 2 1

Table of Contents

−IV−
DIFFICULTIES AND REMEDIATION

CONCLUSION

Introduction

Jacqueline Bideaud
Université Charles de Gaulle, Lille III

In 1941, now half a century ago, *La Genèse du Nombre* by Jean Piaget and Alina Szeminska was published by Delachaux and Niestlé (Neuchâtel, Switzerland). The work was of obvious importance. It was the first time a coherent theoretical explanation for the developmental construction of number, based on rigorous observation, had been put forward. It was the first time that Piaget's already abundant list of publications contained an experimental study of concrete operations founded on the ingenious tasks that were destined to become the famous and now classic "Piagetian" tasks. It was also the first time that a formal model of the cognitive structures thought to underpin behavior observed during these tasks and their outcomes was formulated in terms of subjects' logico-mathematical groupings of operations or interiorized actions. Interest in *La Genèse du Nombre* has never waned, despite (or perhaps due to) both criticism on the theoretical level and new empirical data. This testifies to the extraordinary richness of both the tasks themselves and their interpretation. It would be impossible to inventory the total number of studies that have used either the standard forms or variants on the small numerical set conservation task, the rod seriation task, or the famous inclusion question, either to challenge operational theory or to confirm it. *Pathways to Number* attempts to continue this tradition.

Yet, 50 years after *La Genèse du Nombre*, why bring out *Pathways to Number?* One single and self-sufficient reason is to honor Piaget and Szeminska and, via these two authors, to pay tribute to the Geneva school as a whole—in particular, Barbel Inhelder who co-authored *Le Développement des Quantités chez l'Enfant* with Piaget (1961), which also appeared in 1941. For nearly three-quarters of a century the Geneva school has been a mecca of cognitive development, and an unparalleled meeting place of the minds, which has fostered inter-

1

national endeavors in all fields of knowledge. It is my hope that the flame kindled by Piaget did not die with him in 1980 and that Piagetian theory will not stagnate, but rather will be re-invigorated by the extensions and restructurations Piaget himself introduced in the 1970s, which are presented even more clearly in his posthumous publications (Piaget, 1981, 1983; Piaget, Henriques, & Ascher, 1990).

My purpose in this Introduction is to pay homage to these great pioneers and to commemorate their achievements by bringing the past back to life. This is why, before turning to a brief overview of *Pathways to Number,* I would like to set these two authors, Piaget and Szeminska, within the scientific context of their time.

THE SCIENTIFIC CONTEXT OF THE FORTIES

The decades between the two World Wars, in retrospect, were periods of intense intellectual activity in all fields of science, but in particular in the science of the mind, a field that today is covered by the cognitive sciences.

This was the time when triumphal behaviorism was waging constant war against the unobservable from its foothold in Anglo-Saxon countries. It was the era of victory of physics-inspired pragmatism over a form of idealistic psychology based on outlived introspection. Functional stimulus–response (S–R) relationships between observables were thought to account fully for behavior, and the various mediational amendments to the theory were basically to change very little. The key words were *environment, conditioning* and *learning. The animal—the Cartesian prototype of the machine—was the model of psychological activity.* The contribution of behaviorism to methodological objectivity and the discovery of certain principles of learning was acknowledged immediately, as was the failure of the S–R model to account for any except the most elementary psychological mechanisms in man and animal. In this respect, Hull's 1943 *Principles of Behavior,* which stressed the limitations of the theory, was to be the high point of behaviorism and at the same time—in Tiberghien's (1985) words—its swan song. The psychology of behavior was fiercely attacked by the Gestalt movement, as shown by the heated debate in 1923 opposing Watson to McDougall, the American spokesman for Gestalt theory.

Gestalt theory flourished between the 1920s and 1940s. Like behaviorism, it shared a goal of objectivity, but rejected the explanatory power of association and repetition. The specificity of Gestalt theory stemmed from three sources: the phenomenology of Husserl, which led to the idea that there is a basic interaction between subject and object; the experimental psychology of Wundt, whose locus of investigation was behavior; and the psychophysics of Fechner, and even physics (Kohler had a solid background in physics), which sparked interest in the "structured wholes" of force fields. *The model of psychological activity became the physical field model,* such as the electromagnetic field, where the composition of forces takes its specific shape from its directions and intensities.

The field model was thought to capture the rapid adaptation of man and animal to the environment. As early as 1912 Wertheimer argued that stroboscopic motion exhibited features that demonstrated the independence of shapes with regard to the sensory substrate. In his major work on intelligence in chimpanzees, Kohler (1921) considered insight to be proof of the emergence of structured connections that were not associative.

The classic demonstrations in Gestalt theory were all in the field of perception. These experiments were to result in the famous laws of "perceptual wholes," and in particular, two basic principles: (a) the principle of nonadditive composition—the whole has properties of its own such that the value of the whole is not equal to the sum of its parts), and (b) the tendency for perceptual wholes to take on the best form possible through mechanisms of adjustment and self-regulation. The pregnance of "good shapes," which appear electively in a specific subject–object setting, is the manifestation of self-regulatory abilities of the organism. Pregnance, as a totality, is not produced, but, rather, is a given. The explanatory power of Gestalt concepts was extended to cover all forms of behavior, from perception ("structured and non-structuring") to higher mental operations (the theory of isomorphisms). The work of the Gestalt school rapidly revealed the shortcomings of S–R mechanisms by showing organization to be a basic concept of psychology, but the claim that good Gestalt was, *sui generis,* the somewhat forced objectivation of certain phenomena plus the lack of importance attributed to individual behavior paradoxically led Gestalt theory to commit the physics-based excesses it criticized in behaviorism. The individual vanished despite the basic postulate of subject–object interaction. Kohler's efforts to restore the place of the individual in his work *The Place of Value in a World of Facts* (1939) was both the ultimate point and the upper limit of Gestalt theory.[1]

This same 20-year period between 1920 and 1940 was to mark the rise of two major movements: burgeoning Piagetian structuralism and the debut of Anglo-Saxon cognitivism. Anglo-Saxon cognitivism grew out of upheavals in logic and mathematics dating back to the end of the 19th century. In the footsteps of Frege, Russell (initially in the *Principles of Mathematics,* 1903) attempted to "found" mathematics by demonstrating that mathematical concepts are derivable from a small number of logical notions (entities, predicates, propositions). On the basis of the concept of *relation,* Russell's aim was to reconstruct mathematics (and in particular arithmetic) through assignment of an explicit logical definition to whole numbers. From 1910 to 1913, Whitehead and Russell's volumes of the *Principia Mathematica* extended this demonstration, which derives cardinal and

---

[1]Note that application of Gestalt theory to the study of social relations enabled Lewin and his students to lay the foundation for a social psychology that was to develop considerably in the United States in the 1950s.

ordinal whole numbers from class structures governed by equivalence classes. The English edition of the Austrian philosopher Wittgenstein's *Tractacus Logico-philosophicus,* which defined the truth tables for propositional calculus, appeared in 1922. It was interpreted by the positivists of the time as the basis for a rigorous technique of reduction of scientific concepts to a combination of logico-mathematical formulas and empirical facts.

Doubts as to the limits of the formalist approach were soon to be expressed, however. During a meeting in 1928, the German mathematician David Hilbert iterated his famous questions: "Is mathematics complete?" (Can every statement necessarily be proved or disproved?); "Is mathematics consistent?" (Can we ever arrive at $2 + 2 = 5$ by a sequence of valid steps of proof?); and "Is mathematics decidable?" (Is there a definite method that can be applied to any assertion that can lead to a correct decision as to whether it is true or false?).

In 1931, a young Czech mathematician, Kurt Gödel, presented his solution to the first two questions. His famous theorem of the incompleteness of mathematics revealed that there is no necessary correspondence between truth and demonstratability: A formal system can be constructed in which a true assertion can be represented by an undemonstratable expression. Completeness, and hence the consistency of arithmetic, cannot be proven within the axiomatic system of arithmetic. In Great Britain, another mathematical genius, Alan Turing, working at Cambridge on group theory, decided to tackle Hilbert's third question, on decidability, which in fact encompassed the question of the determinism of a formalized approach in science. Turing (1937) generalized the issue even further to that of the inherent properties of a determinism fixed in advance, which excludes all new elements—a property that he then applied to the mechanical manipulation of numerical symbols in his famous Turing machine. An in-depth exploration of "calculatable numbers" (i.e., any number defined by rules of calculation) led him to distinguish operations that generate numbers with an infinite number of decimal points, which he called *satisfactory numbers,* from *nonsatisfactory numbers,* which could not be identified by any existing method. This was Turing's unresolvable mathematical problem, which responded to Hilbert's question of decidability in the negative. In addition, however, Turing showed that by formalizing the concept of algorithm, his machine could calculate any number likely to be found through mathematics and could generate any demonstrable assertion. By determining the class of decidable problems in this way, Turing's machine formed the basis for contemporary theories of robotics. His set of concepts as a whole was published in an article entitled "On Computable Numbers with an Application to the Entscheidungs Problem," which appeared in 1937 in the *Proceedings of the London Mathematical Society.*

At the same time, a host of physicists and mathematicians fled Nazi persecution and emigrated to the United States. Many were given positions at the Princeton Institute for Advanced Study, which became a true scientific "melting pot." The Hungarian mathematician Janos von Neumann (soon to be known as

"John") arrived at Princeton in the 1930s. Albert Einstein joined him in 1933. Turing lived in Princeton from 1936 to 1938. He was in contact with von Neumann and the logician Alonso Church, who had answered Hilbert's third question in another way. In 1941, during his second stay in the United States, he began what was to be a fruitful series of exchanges with Claude Shannon. After working at MIT, Shannon began to apply the fundamental principles of communication theory in the Bell Laboratories in New York. Turing and Shannon focused on one of the key themes of "On Computable Numbers": A Mechanical Representation of the Brain. This idea took shape and was presented in a major article by McCulloch and Pitts (1943), "A Logical Calculus Immanent in Nervous Activity," which analyzed neural activity in logical terms and described electronic connections in these same terms, referring to a new experimental epistemology in which *the model of psychological activity becomes the electronic robot.* Slightly later, in 1948, Wiener laid the foundation for cybernetics, which directly paved the way for computer science, artificial intelligence, and cognitivism. The electronic robot became the now "classic" computer.

THE BIRTH OF PIAGETIAN STRUCTURALISM: JEAN PIAGET, ALINA SZEMINSKA, AND THE OTHERS

Piagetian structuralism was in the eye of this storm of new ideas and theories. Attentive to all movements, it set out on its own path in 1920, a path which was to be fruitful from its inception.

The climate was one of epistemological interrogation, logico-mathematical formalization, structuralism, and a need for interdisciplinary work. With the passing of time, Piaget emerged as a thinker who encompassed all of the conceptualizations of his time, to shape and mold them into his own perspective.

The first of these was epistemology, the theory of the limits and validity of knowledge. Its most basic concern (Is knowledge possible?), which was one of the prime concerns of philosophers and even logicians, was of little interest to Piaget. His epistemology, like that of McCulloch at another level entirely, was empirical. Piaget believed that knowledge was never static. Rather, evolutions in mathematics, logic and physics show that knowledge is a process in constant growth, reflecting a continual transition from weaker to stronger validity. Constant change was emblematic of the process of development. True analysis of its laws thus called for investigation at the source of the mechanisms underpinning the growth of knowledge: that is, the child. Genetic psychology thus became the experimental terrain for developmental, historico-critical epistemology. Although Piaget's constant aim was to establish norms, his epistemological method differed from Hilbert's, which was oriented toward the validity of established mathematics.

Piaget's fascination with "becoming," as well as his interest in a science of formative phases rather than states of knowledge explains why he was one of the people who interpreted Gödel's theory of incompleteness positively, as a demonstration of the dynamism of knowledge rather than its finitude. The fact that a demonstration that is impossible in one system can become possible in another by using a more robust method leads directly to the notion of the relative strength of structures and then to the notion of the transformation of structures. It is this structural constructivity that Piaget was later to apply to the study of normative intelligence. He was later to write that, in fact, the idea of structure as a system of transformation becomes synonymous in this way with a constructivism of never-ending, continual learning. (Piaget, 1968, p. 31).

The 1930s can be characterized by the emphasis on structure and theories of structure. Gestalt psychology still reigned and the Bourbaki, as of 1939, were to argue that mathematics was a science of structures. Piaget obviously adopted the Gestalt concept of organization and its firm rejection of behaviorist associationism. His rejection of an innate Gestalt and the evanescence of the individual were equally strong. He was to write later that the subject is not a mere theater on which plays are acted out independently of him and regulated beforehand by automatic physical laws of equilibrium. (Piaget, 1968, p. 51). Piaget saw the epistemic subject as the actor, the author, and the builder of objects. The normative structures of knowledge, which simultaneously form the groundwork for objectivity and subjectivity constitute the subject's operational structures. The model of psychological activity was no longer the animal, or physical fields of force, and was not destined to become the calculator. *The child "expert in development" and the adult "scientific expert" were to account for each other mutually: The explanatory model was the human.* Naturally, Piaget drew momentarily on cybernetics as a connection between logic and psychology in his explanations of equilibration and the self-regulation of structures. These "mechanical" features, however, never preceded individual action, which was seen as primordial.

The logico-mathematical formalization used by Piaget to account for the stages of states of transitory equilibrium during development was again to reflect his originality. Mathematics in the 1930s took a strong interest in "groups," which Piaget viewed as the paramount tool for constructivity. A *group* is a system of transformations, which are, in a certain sense, "regulated" by differentiation of groups into subgroups and the possibility of shift from one to another. (Turing was working at the same time on the Theory of Groups.) According to Piaget, the mathematical notion of group had its psychological counterpart in the basic mechanisms of intelligence: reversibility and association. However, Piaget "invented" the *grouping,* an incomplete group or semi-network, which was better suited to an axiomatic description of the structures-of-the-whole corresponding to psychological entities observed in naturalistic settings over the course of development of thought in the child. Papert, in his Foreword to the most recent posthumous volume by Piaget (Papert, 1990, p. 10) drew attention to a little-known article by Piaget "La Réversibilité des Opérations et l'Importance de la Notion de 'Groupe'," which appeared in 1938 in the *Rapports et Compte Rendus du XIeme Congrès International de Psychologie,* where there is a definition of *grouping.* However, as I pointed out at the start of this Introduction, it was not until 1941—in *La Genèse du Nombre*—and in *Le Développement des Quantités* that grouping, in a more elaborated form, was applied to observed behavior. In the same Foreword just mentioned, Papert also stressed the originality of Piaget's approach, which moved from entities like "number" to mathematical systems and emphasized more elementary systems. The study of the development of number was to become a study of operations *on number,* and the study of the seriation and classification subsystems that underpin them. Slightly later, in a perspective similar to the one adopted by Bourbaki, Piaget was to point to the relationship between the foundations of mathematical architectures and the coordination of intelligence at its inception.

This brief historical sketch illustrates to what extent Piaget's work reflected the scientific context of the years between 1920 and 1940, and to what extent his work was original. The picture would be incomplete without mentioning Piaget's belief in interdisciplinarity, which he shared with other theorists of his time. Turing not only had an interest in mathematics but explored philosophy and biology as well. Shannon was equally versed in neurology and in mathematics. Piaget was a typical example of the productivity of a man with vast competencies applied to domains other than his own theory. This was due, first, to his background; he described himself in his autobiography as ". . . a former zoologist, hostile to logic and mathematics, [who] was transformed into a psychologist of logical operations while at the same time believing he could remain faithful to his biological past" (Piaget, 1959, pp. 9–10). He was acquainted with a host of fields from zoology (he had a doctoral degree in malacology) to biology, logical philosophy, mathematics, physics, and chemistry, and all nourished his epistemological vision of a connection between forms of life and forms of thought, mechanisms in the growth of knowledge in the child, and mechanisms in the growth of scientific knowledge. Second, Piaget's approach was interdisciplinary, in that historico-critical genetic epistemology calls for a certain amount of interdisciplinarity and the awareness of the interrelationships among the sciences, the famous "scientific circle." If there is a psychogenetic explanation for mathematical operations, and if logic is the axiomatic basis for thought mechanisms, then a gap can be bridged between the life sciences and the physical and mathematical sciences. Piaget (1970) wrote that he had put forward these ideas as early as 1929 in his introductory lecture to a course entitled "History of Scientific Thought," which he taught at the Geneva Faculty of Sciences and which was published in 1929 in the *Archives des Sciences Physiques et Naturelles.*

Piaget was also interdisciplinary and multicompetent by predilection and because of his insatiable scientific curiosity. He encountered many of the major thinkers of his time. For example, Einstein suggested to him to explore whether intuition of time preceded intuition of speed, or the reverse, over the course of development, and was highly entertained reading about nonconserving behavior in 4- to 6-year-olds. In his biography of Turing, A. Hodges (1983) reported that Piaget gave a lecture in Manchester in 1952 on the learning of logical structures and used arguments that astonished Turing because, although they were in fact Turing's own, they came from another area of experience entirely. These interdisciplinary encounters increased with the founding of the International Center for Genetic Epistemology in 1955, including McCulloch's participation in one symposium.

But, I am anticipating here. Between the two World Wars, Piaget continued to work and publish. He became Claparède's assistant in 1921 at the Institut Jean-Jacques Rousseau. At the same time he taught in Geneva and Lausanne, and was named director of the Bureau International de l'Education (B.I.E.) and director of the Institut after Claparède's death in 1940. From 1920 to 1932, in addition to other publications, he published four works which, in Piaget's own words, were "groundbreakers" and which would give him an international reputation: *Le Langage et la Pensee chez l'Enfant, La Representation du Monde chez l'Enfant, La Causalité Physique chez l'Enfant,* and *Le Jugement Moral chez l'Enfant.* His three children, Lucienne, Jacqueline, and Laurent were born in 1925, 1927, and 1931, respectively. Piaget conducted on them his remarkable observations of development in the first 2 years of life, and published *La Naissance de l'Intelligence* (1936), and *La Construction du Réel chez l'Enfant* (1937). He began collecting the experimental material for the study of the child's construction of number, physical quantities, time, speed, and space in 1929. His aim was to gain insight into these processes from the start of cognitive operations, but these publications were not the exclusive product of Piaget's fertile mind. They were also the result of the work of an extraordinary team, including Alina Szeminska.

ALINA SZEMINSKA

Alina Szeminska spent her childhood in Sweden and Poland and went to secondary school in Warsaw. She received her bachelor's degree in 1926, but because of the discrimination of the time against women, she was not admitted to medical school and went, instead, to study child psychology in Berlin with Kohler, Lewin, and Wertheimer. In an interview she had in 1983 with Christiane Gillièron, she recalled that, in 1928, she told Kohler she wanted a change. His suggestion was the following: "There are three places I would advise you to go: the first, but I don't know if that would please you, is Decroly and Belgium. The second is Kofka in the United States, but it's a little too far away. There is a third possibility but I don't know where he is: He's very young, he's just starting out, but he is going to be the psychologist of the century. His name is Piaget. . . . I am not sure what his first name is and I don't know where he teaches. He's somewhere in Switzerland, but you can find out at the Jean Jacques Rousseau Institute." Szeminska located Piaget in Geneva in 1928.

During the first year of her stay in Geneva, she worked with Meili on a study of stroboscopic movement. The next year she chose to study the correspondences between "primitive" peoples' numerical notions and those of the child, which Piaget described in his course on the history of scientific thought. Szeminska discovered nonconservation of small numerical sets in the young child and de-signed a series of experiments which, when brought together, formed the mate-rial for *La Genèse du Nombre*. She completed almost all of the experimentation in 1935.

In 1932 she received her first degree and passed the preliminary examinations for enrollment in a doctoral program. In the same year Barbel Inhelder arrived in Geneva and started her first study on the dissolving of sugar. Edith Meyer, fresh from a doctorate in Leipzig, was working on the construction of space. At the same time, André Rey set up a psychology consultancy at the Jean Jacques Institute and Marc Lambercier ran the laboratory under the direction of Claparède. The team was lively, young, and spirited, as shown by the group picture (Fig. 15.1) of a picnic on the slopes of the Salève.

In 1935, Alina Szeminska published "Essai d'Analyse Psychologique du Raisonnement Mathématique" in *Cahiers de Pédagogie Expérimentale et de Psychologie de l'Enfant*. In the same year, in the same journal, Edith Meyer published "La Représentation des Relations Spatiales chez l'Enfant," and in 1937 Barbel Inhelder published "Observations sur le Principe de Conservation dans la Physique de l'Enfant." In 1938, Inhelder left for Zurich to finish her clinical training, and Meyer finished her research program just before leaving for the United States.

In Europe, war was threatening. In the summer of 1939 Szeminska, who wanted to go back to Poland, took the last plane leaving Switzerland for Warsaw, where she arrived on August 31. On Friday, September 1, at 5:45 a.m. the first German Panzer tank division crossed the Polish border, although war had not yet been declared. On September 3, France and Britain declared war on Germany. Devastating air raids destroyed Warsaw and Cracow and caused over 2,000 casualties. Szeminska worked first at the Polish Red Cross as director of the Missing Persons Bureau. She also immediately joined an active resistance net-work. She was arrested in 1942, spent 9 months in prison, and was then deported to Auschwitz. Night and fog . . . She was freed in 1945 by the Russian army. The French version of *La Genèse du Nombre* appeared in 1941, just before her arrest.

During the first postwar years, Szeminska founded a clinic for orphans in a children's shelter in Warsaw and taught, at the same time, at the Institute for

FIG. 1. Picnic on the slopes of the Salève, 1936. From left to right: André Rey, Marc Lambercier, Alina Szeminska, and Barbel Inhelder (in the foreground). Barbel Inhelder collection.

FIG. 2.   Jean Piaget, 1976. Christiane Gillièron collection.

FIG. 3.   Alina Szeminska, 1976. Howard Gruber collection.

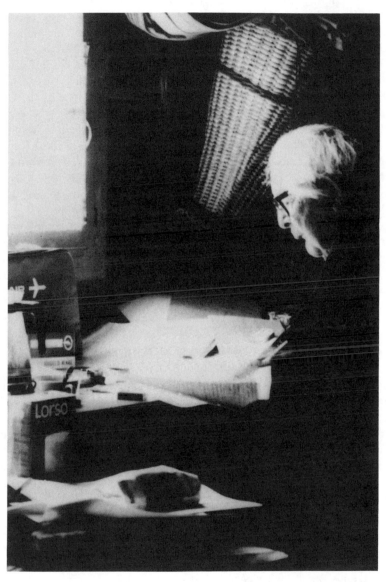

FIG. 4.   Piaget's desk in his summer home. Jean-Remy Berthoud collection.

Teacher Training. In 1949 she became director of a psychological clinic for schoolchildren. In 1952 she worked at the Pedagogical Institute of Warsaw where she was head of the psychology department while simultaneously conducting numerous experiments on the teaching of mathematics. She was granted professorial rank in 1956. She was subjected to the pressure of Marxist, Pavlovian psychology up to the 1960s: She translated Wallon but was not authorized to translate Piaget. In 1967 she was allowed to travel and made several trips to Geneva where, in 1979, she was awarded an honorary doctorate by the University. She died in 1986, 6 years after Piaget.

The picture of Alina Szeminska (Fig. 2) was taken in 1976, during Piaget's 80th birthday festivities. It shows the vitality and brilliance of this exceptional woman. During the festivities, a film by Christiane Gillièron and Howard Gruber entitled *What a Team!* was presented, which corrected the omission of her name from the English version of *The Child's Concept of Number* (Piaget, 1952a).

The forties were marked by the terrible upheaval caused by World War II. On the scientific level, and particularly in psychology, it was also a turning point. Behaviorism and Gestalt theory, despite their last death throes, were to recede into the background. Cognitivism was born. *La Genèse du Nombre, Le Développement des Quantités,* and other works on geometry, time, and space that appeared between 1941 and 1950,[2] made Piagetian structuralism a dominant trend, and heralded its reign in the field of cognitive development.

PATHWAYS TO NUMBER

In this Introduction, I have made little reference to number, and even less reference to *La Genèse du Nombre chez l'Enfant,* which is too well known to need summarizing here. I have deliberately chosen to stress how Piagetian structuralism fit into the logico-mathematical movement of its time, to ensure a clearer, and perhaps renewed, understanding of the theoretical positions of the two co-authors. Times change and contexts with them. I have hinted at the changes that were to come. *Pathways to Number* reflects these changes. In the conclusion to this volume, I compare contexts and the specific avenues of exploration they led to an attempt to measure how far we have come, and the distance remaining to be covered. In the final analysis, however, whether pathways depart from the initial road or adhere to it, they clearly illustrate what Remy Droz (this volume) termed "the incredible heuristic impetus" of the work of Alina Szeminska and Jean Piaget.

---

[2]The experimental material for these works was devised before 1940. Publication was held up by the War.

The goal Claire Meljac, Jean-Paul Fischer, and I, as the three co-editors of this volume, set out to accomplish—in addition to commemorating the 50th anniversary of the publication of *La Genèse du Nombre*—was to present the new paths that have since been charted. To do so, we solicited contributions from international experts on the subject with no restriction as to school of thought, but with directives to produce thought-provoking material for a readership including researchers, teachers, practicing psychologists, and those in the remedial fields.

The book is divided into four sections, which are not watertight: Topics found in one section could have been located in another. The main topic of each chapter guided its location in its most appropriate section.

Section I is devoted to initial encounters with number, and the processes underlying these encounters. Catherine Sophian (chap. 1) introduces this section with an overview of studies on 3- to 5-year-olds not yet enrolled in school. She shows that counting, as well as some mathematical operations, can be grasped early and that instead of being repressed when children are exposed to mathematics in school, these skills need to be integrated into a contextualized form of pedagogy. In chapter 2, Rémi Brissiaud presents a detailed description of the pathway of a child whose first contact with number arose from finger-symbol sets and not from the more classic pathway of counting. The comparison of these two pathways helps pinpoint certain key features concerning the concepts of quantity and number. The importance of the development of the notion of "half" is explored in the next chapter by Silvia Parrat-Dayan and Jacques Vonèche, and is related to issues regarding number conservation.

The remaining three chapters in this section deal with two topics: the integration of early acquisitions into the developmental progression, and the mechanisms underlying them. Leslie Steffe (chap. 4) provides a finegrained analysis of steps in the construction of numerical sequences and transition processes, and stresses the importance of an initial unitizing operation. Arthur Baroody (chap. 5) presents a critical examination of R. Gelman's position on early counting principles examining the related methodological issues, and arguing for a modification of nativist theory. Karen Fuson (chap. 6) studies the changes between ages 2 and 8 in the relationships between counting and cardinality and shows the importance of empirical procedures and one-to-one correspondence.

Section II centers on the structuration of the numerical field. Linda Tollefsrud-Anderson, Robert Campbell, Prentice Starkey, and Robert Cooper (chap. 7) tackle the complicated problem of the conservation of small numerical sets. They argue that investigation of this type of conservation should be placed within the study of a complex developmental sequence where its prerequisites—quantifiers and operators—are located. Rochel Gelman and Elizabeth Meck show, in chapter 8, that the use of "principles" guiding the early numerical abilities of the young child may hinder later mathematical growth and, in particular, operations on fractions. Rather, they claim that the mastery of mathematical language goes hand in hand with the acquisition of "alternative" conceptualizations. In chapter 9, Jean-Paul Fischer provides evidence for the discontinuity between numbers 3 and 4 in apprehension and analyzes the mechanisms involved. He accounts for this discontinuity by suggesting that there is a different counting mechanism for 3 that derives from declarative knowledge primitives or is based on prior experience of counting. Michel Fayol (chap. 10) presents an overview of additive problems and shows to what extent problem difficulty is dependent on both conceptual and linguistic factors. In the last chapter in this section, Gerard Vergnaud argues for the richness and complexity of the development of number concepts and shows that development is dependent on the context, operations, and relationships authorized by this context.

Section III is entitled "Theories and Methods: Critical Approaches." The term *critical* deliberately reflects the two meanings of the word: critical in the sense of challenging, and critical in the sense of calling for a systematic investigation leading to better knowledge. This section begins with chapter 11, by Rémy Droz, who argues for a polymorphous psychogenesis of number and criticizes Piaget's epistemological position and overly experimental approaches to the genesis of number. The three remaining chapters in this section present new approaches to the study numerical ability. Xavier Seron, Gérard Deloche and Marie-Pascale Noël describe a study of transcoding (the transition from a phonological code to a number code) in 7- to 8-year-olds in chapter 12. Madelon Saada-Robert presents the methodological advantages of breaking down sequences of behaviors observed during the microgenesis of numerical and protonumerical procedures (chap. 13). In a cross-cultural study, Karen Fuson and Youngshim Kwon (chap. 14) report on the different outcomes of using conventional number words and tags in a variety of Asiatic language systems and irregular number words in Indo-European languages.

The last section of this volume deals with mathematical learning disabilities and remedial work. Arthur Baroody (chap. 15) provides an inventory of the problems many children face during oral counting, the counting of objects, and numerical comparisons. An analysis of the psychological bases of counting is followed by remedial strategies for each specific difficulty. Finally, Claire Meljac speculates, in chapter 16, on the processes used by children in number acquisition, and looks at instances of dysfunction. These assumptions are tested against observations of children with severe learning disabilities in the learning and application of numerical sequences.

In the conclusion, I chart the changes in the Piagetian perspective since the publication of *La Genèse du Nombre* and describe the context in which the later studies took place. This comparative (and prospective) assessment suggests that in the end, much remains to be accomplished and the unresolved issues are numerous.

ACKNOWLEDGMENTS

The editors extend their thanks to C. Afchain of Lille III University, and the trainees at the Centre Henri Rousselle (Paris) for their invaluable assistance in the production phases of this volume. We also take this opportunity to express thanks to Christiane Gillièron, of the University of Geneva, who provided the details of Alina Szeminska's life described here. Christiane Gillièron and her acquaintances were also kind enough to supply the photographs reproduced in the Introduction.

ENCOUNTERS WITH NUMBER AND FIRST ACQUISITIONS

1
Learning About Numbers: Lessons for Mathematics Education From Preschool Number Development

Catherine Sophian
University of Hawaii

An important issue both for cognitive-developmental theory and for educational practice concerns the relationship between the development of mathematical concepts and the acquisition of numerical procedures. In developmental work, discussion of this issue has focused on the relationship between counting and the development of mathematical concepts, particularly cardinality. Piaget (1941/1952a) viewed these two developments as quite independent. Because he was mainly interested in conceptual development, he had little to say about children's counting, but the attention he did give it was merely to make the point that counting does not play an important role in the development of conceptual knowledge about number. Recent research, in contrast, has put a lot of emphasis on children's counting, taking it both as an indication of the richness of even very young children's mathematical knowledge (Gelman & Gallistel, 1978) and also as a potentially important factor in the development of conceptual knowledge about number (Gelman, 1982a; Klahr, 1984b).

An important ramification of the research on counting has been to emphasize that it is as much a theoretical problem to account for the development of counting as to account for the development of numerical concepts like cardinality. In characterizing counting as merely "verbal," Piaget suggested that it fell outside the bounds of the conceptual development that he was interested in explaining. It seems incompatible with his general theoretical position, however, to view it as wholly independent of children's conceptual development. Whereas Piaget allowed for figurative aspects of development, he always viewed them as subordinate to operative development. An integrated account of conceptual development and the development of counting seems all the more critical insofar as we accept the characterization of counting as based on principles that represent substantial, albeit implicit, knowledge about number (Gelman & Gallistel, 1978; Gelman & Meck, 1983). At the same time, however, this characterization presents a challenge to Piaget's account of conceptual development, because he did not believe that children achieve a conceptual understanding of number until the concrete-operational period of development, several years after they have learned to count.

Questions concerning the relationship between procedural and conceptual aspects of mathematical development are as important practically as they are theoretically. Accumulating evidence of conceptual deficits in children's mathematics learning has led educators to recognize that schools must teach more than computation. There is little satisfaction in having taught children how to perform calculations when they are unable to use those procedures to solve any but the most routine problems (Cockcroft, 1982; National Assessment of Educational Progress, 1983), and even purely computational errors often reflect inadequate conceptual understanding (Resnick, 1984). At the same time, most educators seem to agree that children need to learn computational skills as well as concepts (Hughes, 1986; Resnick, 1989; Resnick & Ford, 1981); the question they face is how best to combine the two. Should schools teach the concepts first, and then the procedures that build on those concepts? Or is it better for children to begin with the procedures and then reflect on what they are doing once they are able to do it? Clearly, developmental questions about the causal relationships between procedural and conceptual knowledge have important ramifications for these educational issues.

In this chapter I begin by reviewing a series of studies I have conducted on preschool children's knowledge about counting and cardinality, and then present a theory of number development that accounts for the findings. I conclude by discussing the implications of my theoretical position for early mathematics education. Although the content of school mathematics is clearly different from the early numerical developments that I have studied in my research with preschool children, the parallel issues concerning procedural and conceptual knowledge in the two domains provide a basis for drawing instructional conclusions from the developmental research.

It should be noted that different definitions of cardinality, and different methods for studying it, have been used in different lines of research. Piaget's original work was based on the classical mathematical definition of cardinality in terms of one-to-one correspondence: Two sets have the same cardinal number if and only if their elements can be put into one-to-one correspondence. Piaget combined this definition with his theoretical interest in transformations in his research on conservation: He did not credit children with understanding cardinality until they knew that the equivalence between two sets is unchanged when the perceptual alignment between them is destroyed by spreading out or condensing one of the sets. In the portion of my own research that I discuss here, I maintain a focus on correspondences between sets but not the emphasis on transformations that characterized Piaget's work. Instead, I focus on children's ability to use counting or single number words to reason about equivalences between sets that are never presented in a perceptually aligned way. A useful feature of this approach is that it can be examined both in relation to counting and in relation to children's understanding of numbers as they are used in natural language.

In research on children's counting, cardinality has also been inferred from children's behavior in relation to just a single set (e.g., Fuson & Hall, 1983; Gelman & Gallistel, 1978; Schaeffer, Eggleston, & Scott, 1974). Certainly it is an important achievement for children to realize that when they count a single set, the last number in their count represents the numerosity of the whole set, although it may not necessarily follow that they can use that representation to reason about its relationship to other sets (Sophian, 1987). Although I do not discuss research on this aspect of cardinality in any detail here, I do take it into account when I discuss theoretical ideas about the relationship between counting and cardinality.

THE DEVELOPMENT OF CARDINAL ASPECTS OF COUNTING

In several studies, I have examined young children's understanding of counting as a source of numerical information that can be used to reason about relationships between two sets. These studies address the question of the relationship between counting and cardinality by investigating the development of cardinal aspects of children's counting. If a concept of cardinality precedes children's counting and guides them as they learn to count, then cardinality should be an integral part of children's counting from the earliest phases of its development. On the other hand, the conclusion that cardinal aspects of counting are a relatively late achievement in the development of counting would imply that counting is not initially learned as a cardinal activity but only gradually becomes integrated into children's developing understanding of cardinality.

Experiment 1: Counting to Compare Two Sets

In the first study I conducted on this issue (Sophian, 1987, Experiment 1), I asked 3-year-old children questions about the relationship between two sets that were presented either in a pairwise fashion or in different spatial configurations (see Fig. 1.1). The sets contained between three and seven objects, and the pairs of sets were either equal in number or differed by one. Children were not asked to count the objects; they were simply asked about the correspondence relation between the two sets, for example, "Are there enough lids so that every jar can have a lid?". (There were never more lids than jars.) Of course, when the sets were paired, children did not need to count in order to answer the question. I

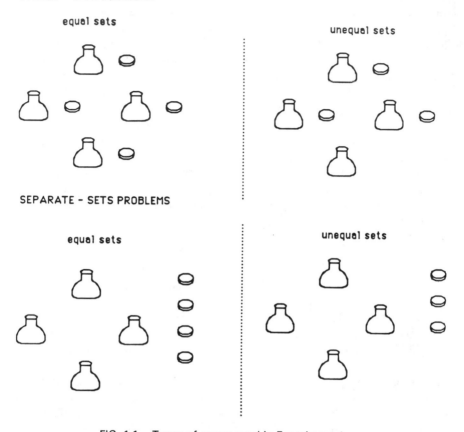

FIG. 1.1.   Types of arrays used in Experiment 1.

included these trials in order to make sure that the children understood the
questions I was asking. On the separate-sets trials, counting was a potentially
useful way of comparing the two sets. The results are summarized in Table 1.1.
Children did show a good understanding of the comparison questions, in that
they performed well on the paired-set problems. As expected, it was more
difficult for them to compare the sets without counting on the separate-sets trials;
nevertheless, they seldom counted on those trials, although counting was somewhat more prevalent among the older children.

To ascertain that the problem was not just lack of counting skill, I asked the
children explicitly to count single sets of the same sizes on a posttest. Although
some children did have very limited counting skills (eight of eighteen 3-year-olds
and four of eighteen 3½-year-olds failed to count sets of four or more items

TABLE 1.1
Patterns of Performance on Paired-Sets and Separated-Sets Problems
(Experiment 1)

	Problem Type/Set Size			
	Paired-sets		Separated-sets	
	3–4	6–7	3–4	6–7
3-year-olds				
% of problems on which children counted	03	0	01	01
% correct given child did not count*	80	61	76	52
3½-year-olds				
% of problems on which children counted	0	0	25	14
% correct given child did not count*	92	75	87	60

*Chance = 50%.

correctly), many others were able to count at least the smaller set sizes accurately on the posttest and yet did not even once attempt to count on the comparison problems (nine 3-year-olds and eight 3½-year-olds fit this pattern).

Interestingly, even when children did count on the separate-sets comparison problems, they were not very likely to arrive at a correct answer to the question. While this may be due in part to errors in children's counting, it is also at least in part a reflection of their lack of understanding of how to use counting to solve the problems. On several trials, children counted only one of the two sets; and on others they counted both sets yet subsequently gave an answer that did not correspond to the results of their counting. Similar observations have been made in other studies of children's use of counting to compare two sets (Saxe, 1977).

Experiment 2: Counting to Generate Equivalent Sets

In a second study (Sophian, 1987, Experiment 2), I asked children to construct a second set that had the same number of objects as a set I presented. As in the previous study, I used sets that contained three to seven objects, and I asked children either to put the new objects in a separate grouping and a different spatial configuration than the original set or to put them with the original set. The children in this study were 3½-year-olds (comparable to the older group in the previous experiment), 4-year-olds, and 4½-year-olds. The results, which are presented in Table 1.2, were similar to those of the first experiment. On the separate-sets trials, where children could not use a simple pairing strategy, 3½-year-olds seldom counted either set whereas the 4½-year-olds often counted. Yet children at all ages did show a good understanding of what they were asked to do, performing well on the paired-set problems.

TABLE 1.2
Patterns of Performance on Paired-Sets and Separated-Sets Problems
(Experiment 2)

	Problem Type/Set Size			
	Paired-sets		Separated-sets	
	3–4	6–7	3–4	6–7
3½-year-olds				
% of problems on which children counted	03	06	18	09
% correct given child did not count	91	69	14	06
4-year-olds				
% of problems on which children counted	11	12	40	26
% correct given child did not count	85	91	39	14
4½-year-olds				
% of problems on which children counted	17	11	31	42
% correct given child did not count	97	91	68	33

Experiment 3: Judgments About Counting to Compare Two Sets

A third study examined children's understanding of counting as a way of comparing two sets when they did not have to do the counting themselves (Sophian, 1988). In this study, 3- and 4-year-old children observed a puppet who was asked about a set of objects comprised of two subsets (e.g., on some trials there would be three baby horses and three big horses). The puppet was asked either about the total number of objects ("how many?" task) or about the relationship between the two subsets (compare task). In both cases the puppet responded sometimes by counting all of the objects together (e.g., "one, two, three, four, five, six") and sometimes by counting the two subsets separately (e.g., "one, two, three, three baby horses; one, two, three, three big horses"). Before the puppet had a chance to draw any conclusion from his counting, the child was asked to judge whether or not the way the puppet had counted was a good way to find out the answer to the question he had been asked. (Warm-up trials with non-numerical problems were used to familiarize children with this judgment task.)

The results are summarized in Fig. 1.2. Both age groups performed better on the how-many task than on the compare task, but the specific patterns of performance that they showed differed. The 3-year-olds tended to judge both types of counting as *good* regardless of the puppet's task, but in the "how-many?" task they judged counting of all the objects together as *good* more often than counting of the two subsets separately; the 4-year-olds, by contrast, were much less likely than the 3-year-olds to say that the puppet had counted properly when he counted the two sets separately—even on the compare task. Thus, like the 3-year-olds, on the "how-many?" task they appropriately judged counting of all the objects together as *good* more often than counting of the two subsets separately; how-

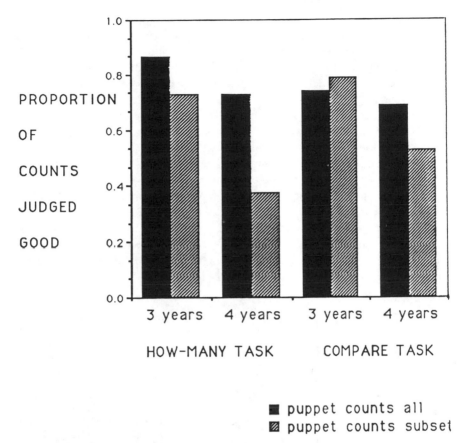

FIG. 1.2. Mean proportions of puppet's counts that were judged
"good" in Experiment 3.

ever, they showed the same pattern on the compare task, where it was not appropriate.

These findings indicate that the limitations on children's use of counting are not just a production problem. Children show the same limitations in their understanding of counting as a way of comparing two sets whether they are doing the counting themselves or evaluating counting that they have observed.

Experiment 4: Inferring the Numerosity of a Corresponding Set

Finally, (Sophian, 1989) I examined children's ability to make inferences about the number of objects in a set that was presented in one-to-one correspondence with another set that they were instructed to count (Sophian, 1989). In this study the question was not whether children would count spontaneously, but rather whether they could use the results of a count to reason about two sets that were in one-to-one correspondence with each other.

To establish the correspondence between the sets, the experimenter presented objects in pairs (e.g., trucks and elephants, nests and birds). She put one member of each pair (e.g., the trucks) on the table in front of the child and the other member (e.g., the elephants) into a box. After she had presented all the objects, she asked the child to count the set that was on the table, and then asked how many objects were in the set in the box (where they were out of sight). (For methodological reasons, on half the trials she added an extra object to the box before having the child count; for present purposes, however, let us consider just the data from the same-number trials, which provide a simpler test of children's understanding of the cardinal significance of their counting.)

The accuracy of numerical responses the children made on these trials, and on corresponding control trials on which the children did not have the opportunity to count the set on the table, are summarized in the left and middle sections of Fig. 1.3. As in the other studies I have described, the 3-year-olds were less successful

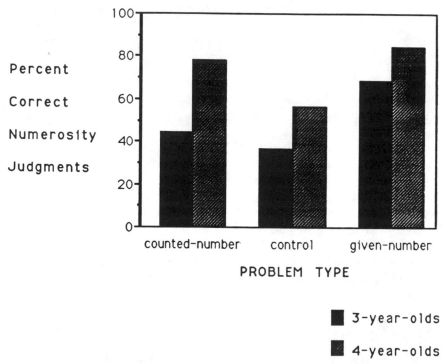

FIG. 1.3.   Mean proportions of problems on which children made correct numerosity judgments in Experiment 4.

in using counting to reason about corresponding sets than were the 4-year-olds. Their performance on the trials on which they had counted was not significantly better than on the control trials. The 4-year-olds' performance, in contrast, was significantly better on the count trials than on the control trials.

Cardinal Aspects of Early Counting: Conclusions

In sum, the consistent finding across these studies is that 3-year-old children do not connect counting with problems concerning the numerical relationship between two sets. They do not spontaneously count to compare two sets or to construct equivalent sets; they cannot distinguish between appropriate and inappropriate forms of counting for comparing two sets; and they do not use the information they obtain by counting one set to infer the number of objects in a second set that is in one-to-one correspondence with that set. By 4½ years of age, performance is much better on all of these problems. These results suggest that cardinality, at least that aspect of cardinality that has to do with the relationships between two sets, is a relatively late achievement in the development of children's counting.

THE CARDINALITY OF COUNTED
AND NONCOUNTED NUMBERS

Although counting is an important source of information about cardinality, it is not the only one. Even before children begin to count, they use number words to describe collections of objects (Wagner & Walters, 1982). Do children understand the cardinality of these number words that are used without counting? How does their understanding of cardinality in relationship to these noncounted numbers compare with their understanding of cardinality vis-à-vis counting? If children develop a concept of cardinality through counting, then they should show an understanding of cardinality in relation to counting earlier than—or at least no later than—they show the same kind of understanding in relation to noncounted numbers. On the other hand, to the extent that cardinality emerges in children's use of noncounted numbers before it emerges in children's counting, it would suggest that children acquire a concept of cardinality that is initially independent of their counting but gradually integrate the two.

I addressed this issue in the study of numerical inferences that I have already described (Experiment 4) by including a set of problems on which children were told the number of objects in one set instead of being asked to count them. These given-number problems were identical to the counted-number problems in all other respects. Children's performance on them can be seen in the right-hand section of Fig. 1.3. Here the 3-year-olds as well as the 4-year-olds gave evidence of understanding cardinality, performing significantly better on the given-number trials than on the control trials. There was still an improvement in performance with age, but it was not as great as in the counted-number condition.

These results suggest that children understand cardinality in relation to non-counted numbers before they show comparable understanding in relation to counting. Taken together with the evidence that cardinal aspects of counting are a relatively late achievement in the development of counting, they present a picture of cardinality and counting as initially separate developments that become integrated with development. Thus, 3-year-olds show considerable knowledge about how to count, and also considerable knowledge about cardinality, but they do not yet use their counting to reason about cardinality. Over the following year, this limitation is overcome and children begin to use counting as well as other sources of numerical information to reason about cardinality.

A THEORY OF NUMBER DEVELOPMENT

These findings place several important constraints on a theory of number development. First, we need to account for the presence of cardinality as early as 3 years of age, much earlier than Piaget suggested. Second, we need to account for the dissociation between cardinality and counting early in development. Third, we also need to account for the integration of cardinality with children's counting just a short time later. The theoretical account I offer is a synthesis of a Piagetian perspective on conceptual development with a theory of socially transmitted procedural knowledge, including an account of how the socially transmitted procedures become integrated with the child's conceptual knowledge.

Origins of Cardinality

The finding that children show an early concept of cardinality in their comprehension of number words simultaneously supports Piaget's contention that cardinality is not a result of counting and raises in its stead the question of how children do attain a concept of cardinality at such an early age. Some researchers have argued that, at least for very small numbers, this kind of knowledge may be innate (e.g., Starkey, Spelke, & Gelman, 1983). In my view, a nativist account cannot be adequate because cardinality is inherently a representational concept, and representation—in Piaget's sense—is a major cognitive-developmental construction. This point is often overlooked or misunderstood in discussions of infant numerical abilities.

It is now well-known that infants within the first year of life can discriminate between sets of different small numerosities; for instance, after having been habituated to displays of three objects, they will attend more to sets of two or four objects (Starkey & Cooper, 1980; M. S. Strauss & Curtis, 1981). This kind of behavior is often taken to indicate a preverbal "concept" of number, and it has played an important role in nativist theories of number development. However, from a Piagetian perspective a concept is far more than discrimination: It implies the representation of some commonality that has been abstracted from a set of exemplars. Although we know that infants see displays of three items as different from displays of two or four, we don't have any reason to believe that they have a representation of numerosity as an abstracted dimension that unites the displays of three and differentiates them from the displays of two or four. Even simple physical systems perform discriminations analogous to those the infants make. For instance, a simple pan balance will discriminate between objects that have the same weight as a standard and those that differ. Nevertheless, we do not attribute to the balance a concept of weight, because we have no reason to think that it realizes that weight is what unites the objects to which it responds the same way or what differentiates them from objects to which it responds differently. Infants' discriminations cannot be based on a continuous physical dimension (such as length or density), because the numerical displays used in many of the discrimination studies have been carefully designed to vary number orthogonally from such physical dimensions. Thus, we cannot account for the evidence of numerical discriminations without crediting infants with some sort of specifically numerical processes that enable them to apprehend small numbers. Although these numerical processes may even be innate, infants' ability to use them to discriminate small numerosities does not indicate that infants know that number is the basis for the discriminations they are making, any more than the scale knows that it is discriminating by weight.

The distinction between discrimination and conceptual knowledge corresponds to the major theoretical difference between the information processing view of representation as encoding and Piaget's interactive notion of representation (Campbell & Bickhard, 1987). Infants must encode the numerical properties of displays in order to discriminate between displays containing different numbers of objects; however, that is very different from a representation of number in Piaget's sense. For Piaget, representation is closely connected with the capacity to carry out mental transformations: The development of representation enables the child to envision actions or transformations without actually carrying them out. In a classic example, Piaget (1952b) described how his daughter, Lucienne, by opening and closing her mouth, represented the action of opening a matchbox before she actually carried it out. This dynamic sort of representation is essential for a concept of cardinality because it allows infants to abstract the numerical properties of the sets they encounter from all the other characteristics of those sets and use them as a basis for classification.

An important source of evidence concerning the development of this kind of dynamic representation of number in preverbal infants lies in research on babies' understanding of the effects of numerical transformations, such as adding another object to a set or taking one away. Indeed there is evidence that babies as young as 14 to 18 months of age can respond appropriately to numerical transformations (Sophian & Adams, 1987; Starkey, 1987). Although these studies do not directly implicate cardinality, in that they do not involve reasoning about equivalences between sets, they do suggest that infants have the capacity to represent number and to operate mentally on that representation by 14 months of age. Although that is earlier than Piaget believed representation to emerge, it is compatible with other evidence concerning the emergence of Piagetian representational abilities (Haake & Somerville, 1985; Sophian, 1985).

In Piaget's view, cardinality is not merely a representational concept but an operational one. Piaget argued that number is not equivalent to other everyday concepts because number is not inherent to objects: It depends on the child's structuring activity in bringing the objects together into a set and enumerating them. Piaget illustrated this idea by recounting an incident in which a friend of his, as a child, counted a set of pebbles first in one order and then in another, discovering that the number was always the same. In this example, the regularity or commonality was not inherent in the objects but in his own counting activity. There is a sense, however, in which number, though not inherent in objects, is a property of sets, and a set may function like a physical object if it is composed of like elements in a coherent spatial arrangement. Moreover, when the numerosity is very small, it can be detected perceptually in much the same way that children detect the color or shape of an object. In my view, babies do form perceptually based concepts of sets of two or three just as they form concepts of red things or square things, and these early number concepts are the foundation for a primitive concept of cardinality (see also Wagner & Walters, 1982). Of course, children cannot abstract the commonality among larger sets so easily; however, they may understand that large numbers represent the numerosity of large sets in the same way that small numbers represent the numerosity of small sets, even before they can determine precisely which large number goes with which large set.

There is certainly much more than this to Piaget's research on cardinality. In arguing that children form a representational concept of cardinality from an early age I do not mean to suggest that the kinds of abilities that Piaget studied at the concrete-operational level are unimportant or uninteresting. I do think, however, that they go beyond the classical definition of cardinality in terms of equivalence relations between sets. In my research, children as young as 3 were able to reason about equivalences between sets in ways that could not have been based on perceptual mappings between the sets, because the children never saw the two sets aligned with each other. This is an important intermediate achievement between the infant's perceptual apprehension of number and the 6- or 7-year-old child's ability to grasp the reversible operations that make it possible to understand concrete-operational quantitative comparisons. It amounts to the acquisition of a representational concept of cardinality.

The Development of Counting

Counting is clearly a socially transmitted activity. People count in very different ways in different cultures (e.g., Saxe, 1982), yet, at least in its mature form, counting cannot be considered strictly a rote, imitative performance. It is a goal-directed activity, and the goal is closely tied to the concept of cardinality: We count to find out how many objects are in a set, to compare one set to another, or to generate a set that has a particular numerosity.

The strong implication of my research on counting is that this goal-directed quality of mature counting is a cognitive-developmental construction. Very young children may well have goals in their counting, but they do not appear to be these goals; more likely, they are social-interactive goals such as to participate in a familiar routine with a parent. The striking thing about this phase in the development of counting is that the same children who seem to attribute no notion of cardinality to their counting use the very same number words as representations of cardinality in noncounting contexts (Sophian, 1989); and of course, within just a couple of years they begin to use counting in the same ways (Sophian, 1987).

How does this transition take place? It is a matter of discovering that the new counting procedure the child has learned corresponds in important ways to other things he or she knows about numbers. There is no reason for the child to make that assumption from the outset. After all, we often use numbers in ways that do not preserve their cardinal properties. There is no three-ness to the size 3 shoes a child may buy with his or her parent; there is no correspondence between his or her house or apartment number and the number of rooms (or anything else) it contains, and so on. Furthermore, children's activities often use the counting numbers in ways that bear no relationship to their cardinal meaning. Consider, for example, this nursery rhyme, which is widely known among American children:

> One, two, buckle my shoe.
> Three, four, close the door.
> Five, six, pick up sticks.
> Seven, eight, close the gate.
> Nine, ten, a big fat hen.

Here the objects that are mentioned bear no cardinal relationship to the numbers in the rhyme; they are not necessarily even plural for numbers above *one*. Clearly, they are chosen on the basis of rhyme and not for any cardinal properties.

The child, then, has to discover that counting is one of those uses of number that in fact does have an important cardinal aspect. How does he or she make that discovery? No direct evidence about this issue is available, but it seems to me that the notion of *agreement,* or *convergence,* is a promising one. Bryant (1982) used the notion of agreement to explain how children come to understand another new mathematical procedure, measurement. He showed that the spontaneous use of measurement to compare two objects increased when children had the opportunity to observe that the results they obtained by measuring corresponded to the results they got when they had the opportunity to compare the objects directly. In an analogous way, children may come to appreciate cardinal aspects of counting by observing that it produces the same results as more familiar procedures for comparing two sets or for arriving at a representation of the numerosity of a single set.

It seems likely that the first thing children have to realize in order to discover relationships between counting and other numerical procedures is that the last number in the count is special: It is the result of the count, which provides the basis for comparing counting to other processes. Children do, in fact, give special emphasis to the last number in their counts from an early age (Gelman & Gallistel, 1978; Walters & Wagner, 1982). While Gelman and Gallistel interpreted this observation as evidence that children understand the cardinal aspect of their counting from a very early age, it seems at least as likely that children initially learn this pattern of emphasis as part of the counting procedure and only later discover its cardinal significance. One source of evidence for this view is Walters and Wagner's (1982) longitudinal observation that, developmentally, children adhere to the *cardinality principle* in their counting (treating the last counting number as representing the set as a whole) before they adhere to the one-to-one principle (one number word for each object), although conceptually the meaning of the last number depends on adherence to the one-to-one principle. This observation fits with the idea that children initially learn about the special status of the last counting number in a procedural way, because they adhere to it before they have the logical foundation to understand it conceptually. Further evidence for the procedural origins of giving special significance to the last number in counting comes from research on children's responses to questions about the number of objects in a set they have just counted. Whereas children as young as 3 respond to such "how-many?" questions with the last number from their count, they are often unable to indicate that this response refers to the whole collection of objects (Fuson, 1988; Fuson & Hall, 1983). Thus, Fuson and Hall suggest that children often learn a last-number response rule on a procedural level before they understand its cardinal implications. For present purposes, the important thing about such a last-number response rule, and an analogous last-number emphasis rule, is that it focuses the child's attention on the last number and so provides a basis for comparing the results of counting to other activities.

Once the child has a grasp of the last number as the "result" of the count, there are several kinds of comparisons that could help him or her to discover its conceptual significance. Probably the most basic is a comparison between the number obtained by counting and a number ascribed to the set without counting—by either an adult or an older child, or, for sets small enough to subitize, by the young child him- or herself. Because these noncounted numbers already have cardinal meaning for the child, observing that they correspond to the result obtained by counting enables the child to realize that counting has the same cardinal meaning. A second comparison might be between counting and the putting of two sets into one-to-one correspondence through a pairing process. Indeed, activities in which children are encouraged to notice that two sets that have been paired with each other give the same result when counted, have been found to increase children's spontaneous use of counting to compare two sets (Michie, 1984).

The account I have presented of the development of counting and its relationship to cardinality bears a close correspondence to Vygotsky's (1962) account of the developmental relationship between language and thought. Counting, like language in Vygotsky's analysis, is a socially transmitted activity, and cardinality is, of course, a specific form of thought. Just as Vygotsky argued that language and thought have separate origins but, with development, become integrated, I have argued that cardinality and counting are dissociated early in development but later become integrated.

Vygotsky's theory emphasized the internalization aspect of this process: As language becomes internalized it gives rise to "inner speech," which becomes an important aspect of thinking. In the same way, although I have argued that counting is not the basis for the initial construction of the concept of cardinality, it does seem likely that counting contributes to later mathematical-cognitive developments. Once counting has gained a cardinal meaning, children can use it to explore the numerical effects of conservation transformations (Gelman, 1982a), to learn addition and subtraction facts (Siegler & Shrager, 1984), and to support basic arithmetic problem solving (Carpenter & Moser, 1984).

INSTRUCTIONAL IMPLICATIONS

Probably the most important instructional point to be made from these results is that a new procedure does not automatically take on all of the conceptual substance of the domain in which the procedure is used. Mathematics teachers, particularly at the elementary level, are very often involved in the teaching of new procedures, and the biggest concern in mathematics education today is that children too often seem to learn these procedures without acquiring any meaningful understanding of why they work or even what their results mean. In my view these problems derive in large part from insufficient attention to explaining the connections between a new procedure and the knowledge the child already has.

The counting research shows that children are sense-makers. They may be happy to learn a new procedure in an imitative way at first, but once they are using it they try to make sense of what they are doing. They look for ways to connect it with things they already know, and in doing so they quickly move from what I have called *recitative* counting (Sophian, 1987) to *cardinally oriented* counting.

In the same way, I think children try to make sense of what they are learning in school, at least at first. The difference is that as the procedures children learn become more abstract and symbolic, it becomes less likely that opportunities to discover their interconnections with other numerical activities will arise spontaneously. Therefore more deliberate instructional planning is needed to ensure that the new procedures do not become detached from the familiar world of numbers and sets within which children are able to function as sense-makers. Too often children seem to learn school arithmetic as a world all its own, a world in which it is difficult to make sense of new procedures, and so they often resort to trying just to learn the rules by rote. Indeed, I think we need to be sensitive to the danger of unintentionally teaching children to give up sense-making when it comes to school mathematics, to view it as a world of its own, with its own kinds of problems and its own tricks for solving them, that may have neither a meaningful basis in everyday experience nor any apparent applicability to real-world problems. Children are likely to be deterred from tying to make sense of school mathematics when instructional activities are presented without any explanation of their purpose, when lessons consist of a rapid succession of unrelated activities, and when the emphasis in the classroom is on getting work done quickly rather than on reflection (Stigler & Perry, 1988).

The results of children's efforts to learn without making sense of what they are doing, of course, are both procedural errors and severe limitations on their ability to apply what they have learned to novel problems. We find children making computational mistakes that make no sense at all from a conceptual standpoint but that are syntactically similar to the correct procedures (Resnick, 1984), and we find children performing computations on the numbers presented in word problems without giving any though to whether or not the results make sense in relation to the problem situation (National Assessment of Educational Progress, 1983). Of course, once children have started on the path of learning without sense-making, the process is difficult to reverse because new material will be all the more difficult to make sense of without having understood the earlier lessons.

For younger children, what is meaningful mathematically is their interaction with sets of objects in the world. A young child who can count sets and compare them, who can even say that one brick and one brick make two bricks, may be completely baffled by the more abstract question, "What does one and one make?" (Hughes, 1986). When children enter school, they are likely to encounter many arithmetic lessons that involve working with actual objects or at least pictures of objects, and so provide a valuable point of contact with familiar ways of thinking about numbers. In my view, however, this is not sufficient. In order to build on existing knowledge, children need to see how the results of new procedures fit with the results of old ones, not just to apply the new procedures to familiar contents. In general, this idea means that children need opportunities to solve the same problem in two ways, as Bryant's children did when they first measured two objects they were comparing and then set them side by side to compare them directly (or vice versa). In order to clarify how this idea can be applied to instructional design, I consider an example involving elementary arithmetic problem solving.

Arithmetic operations are familiar even to preschool children as activities that are carried out with sets. Children can think about the numerical consequences of putting more objects into a set or taking some away even in infancy (Sophian & Adams, 1987; Starkey, 1987). Preschool children can reason about numerical differences between two sets by thinking about pairing the elements of one set with elements of the other and seeing what will be left over (Hudson, 1983). Although these action-oriented ways of reasoning provide a rich intuitive basis for arithmetic learning, they are also limited in important ways. For instance, they do not lend themselves well to thinking about "initial-unknown" problems, which require a reversal of the action described in the story (Briars & Larkin, 1984). The ability to solve these and other problems that are not easy to translate into actions on sets is one of the major arithmetic achievements children display in the first few years of school (Carpenter & Moser, 1984). However, it is worth considering the possibility that many children achieve this "more advanced" problem-solving only at the cost of abandoning their efforts at sense-making. It may be possible to prevent such an unfortunate progression through instructional methods that explicitly build connections between the new problem solving methods and the old.

One reason for suspecting that sense-making may get lost along the way is that even as children are expanding the range of arithmetic problems they can solve, they seem to be losing their appreciation of the actions and objects in arithmetic problems as a point of contact with the real world and the numerical relationships that make sense in that world. Thus, whereas preschool children reason intelligently about story problems that involve concrete objects and events, but have little or no idea of how to think about purely symbolic problems, for elementary school children the situation has become just the reverse: purely symbolic problems pose little difficulty, but story problems are often anathema.

Cognitive analyses of the generalized arithmetic problem-solving abilities that characterize the older elementary school child focus on the use of a "part–whole" schema that enables the child to reason about the relationships between the sets in problems (e.g., Riley & Greeno, 1988). A part–whole schema is clearly more than a rote procedure, and yet there is something very rote-like in the keyword strategies children often use for mapping arithmetic problems into that schema. Keywords like *altogether* have the potential for guiding children to an understanding of the relationships among the sets in a problem, but they also have the potential for cuing shortcuts that enable the child (usually) to pick the right operation to perform without thinking about the relationships among the sets at all (Schoenfeld, 1988). In my view, this latter approach to keywords is likely to arise when the part–whole schema is not firmly enough grounded in the child's experience with actions of joining, separating, and pairing sets.

Some recent research from my laboratory suggests that children do have the conceptual basis for understanding the part–whole relations in arithmetic problems even before they begin formal schooling. In our research (Sophian & McCorgray, 1991), we gave 4-, 5-, and 6-year-old children a series of story problems, corresponding to the initial-unknown and final-unknown "change" problems used in previous research. The initial-unknown problems were of particular interest because they are thought to require a part–whole schema (e.g., Riley & Greeno, 1988); the final-unknown problems are conceptually simpler because the action in the story directly parallels the arithmetic operation that is required (i.e., joining implies addition, separating implies subtraction).

In order to make the problems as meaningful as possible for young children, we always illustrated the story with sets of toys. However, one set (the set that would be asked about or a subset of it) was kept out of sight in a covered box, so that the children could not simply count the relevant objects in order to solve the problem.

Not surprisingly, considering how young the children were, children's accuracy in this study was rather poor (see Fig. 1.4). What interested us, however, was the pattern of their answers, not their precision. Specifically, we were interested in whether children's answers to the initial-unknown problems were in the correct direction relative to the number given for the final set. If children

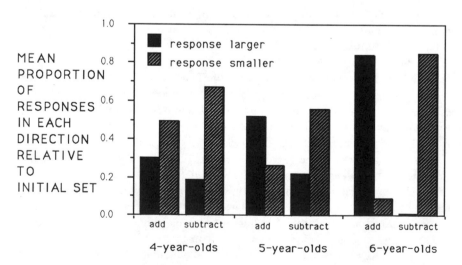

FIG. 1.4. Mean proportions of correct responses to final-unknown and initial-unknown arithmetic problems.

understood the part–whole relationships in the problems, their responses should have been larger than the number given for the final set when the problem called for addition and smaller than the number given for the final set when the problem called for subtraction. (The problems were carefully constructed so that the same numerical values were mentioned in the addition and subtraction problems to prevent the children from differentiating between them on the basis of the size of the numbers given in the problem.)

Both the 5-year-olds and the 6-year-olds did successfully differentiate between the addition and subtraction initial-unknown problems, although the 4-year-olds did not (see Fig. 1.5). The 4-year-olds tended to choose a smaller number than that given for the final set regardless of the type of action in the problem and hence the arithmetic operation required for correct performance. The 5- and 6-year-olds, on the other hand, generally responded with a smaller number on subtraction problems but with a larger number on addition problems.

The 4-year-olds did a little better on the final-unknown problems, as did the older age groups (Fig. 1.6). Although the 4-year-olds again favored small-number responses, they were somewhat more likely to respond with a number larger than that given for the initial set on addition than on subtraction problems. This correct differentiation strengthens the conclusion that their lack of differentiation on the initial-unknown problems was at least partly due to the conceptual difficulty of those problems and not just to their limited facility with larger numbers.

The finding that 5- and 6-year-old children were able to differentiate between addition and subtraction on the initial unknown as well as the final unknown

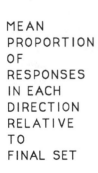
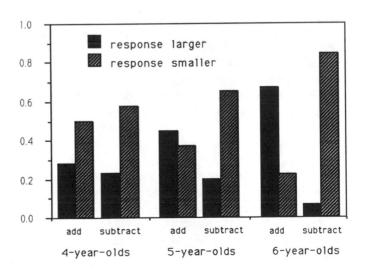

FIG. 1.5. Mean proportions of responses in each direction on final-unknown arithmetic problems.

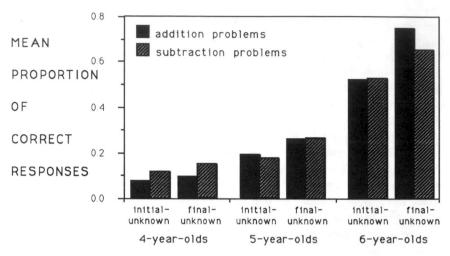

FIG. 1.6.   Mean proportions of responses in each direction on initial-unknown arithmetic problems.

problems suggests that children have a grasp of the part–whole relations in arithmetic problems even before they begin formal instruction. (The 5-year-old children in this study were all in kindergarten, whereas arithmetic instruction generally begins in first grade.) An important question, of course, is why elementary school children have so much trouble with initial-unknown problems and other kinds of word problems, if the necessary conceptual knowledge is already in place. Obviously a major difference between our research and the typical arithmetic work in school is that in school children are expected to get the right answer, not just one that is in the right direction. Thus, it is tempting to conclude that schoolchildren's difficulty is not a conceptual one, but one of mastering the necessary addition and subtraction facts. This answer is too simple, however, for it does not account for why children have a degree of success with those facts as long as the problem is one of the easier types (like the final-unknown problems), but have trouble marshalling the same arithmetic facts to solve the more difficult types of problems (like the initial-unknown problems).

Perhaps the problem again lies in coordinating a new computational skill (in this case, arithmetic computation) with the children's existing conceptual knowledge (knowledge of part–whole relations); just as in the research I described earlier on preschool children's counting, children had difficulty connecting their new counting procedures with what they already knew about cardinality. Thus, as children are beginning formal schooling, they can reason about part–whole relationships among sets (as the 5- and 6-year-olds–kindergarteners and first-graders–did in differentiating appropriately between addition and subtraction problems in the Sophian and McCorgray, 1991, study), and they can demonstrate computational proficiency (in accurate performance on final-unknown problems, e.g., in Carpenter and Moser's, 1984, study), but they cannot put the two together to perform accurately on the initial-unknown problems.

This analysis suggests that the solution to children's difficulties with arithmetic problem solving may lie in providing opportunities for children to integrate the computational skills they are learning in school with their existing conceptual knowledge. One way to do that would be to encourage children to interrelate different ways of thinking about arithmetic problems. Basic number facts are generally learned through action-based computation, as when children are taught to count out a set of three objects and then a set of two and then count all the objects together to verify that $3 + 2 = 5$. Because children cannot use an action-based approach with problems like the initial-unknown change problems, they never have an opportunity to directly connect their new computational knowledge with those kinds of problems. Not surprisingly, then, they have difficulty using the number facts they have learned (or the counting-out strategies by which they have learned to derive them) to solve these problems. A possible solution to this difficulty is to help children interrelate their computational skills with their understanding of part–whole relationships by drawing their attention to the correspondence between the two approaches on final-unknown problems and other simple problems that can be conceptualized both in terms of the action schemas that underlie computational instruction and in terms of part–whole relationships. Most analyses of children's problem solving assume that children use the part–whole schema only to solve problems that are not amenable to simpler, action-based, problem-solving strategies. In principle, however, part–whole analysis is a very general problem-solving approach that can be applied to all kinds of problems. Analyzing the part–whole relationships in the same problems that they are solving through action-based computational strategies would enable children to discover the relationship between their new computational knowledge and their understanding of part–whole relations. Thus, children's computational knowledge would gain a broader conceptual foundation that would make it more readily generalizeable to problems on which it could not be directly verified through action.

CONCLUSION

In conclusion, there are three lessons for early arithmetic instruction that I want to highlight in my discussion of the implications of research on young children's numerical development. First, newly acquired mathematical procedures are not necessarily well integrated with children's conceptual knowledge. In early development, we see this in children learning to count without attributing to their counting the kind of cardinal meaning that they ascribe to the very same numbers in other contexts. In education, we see it in the widespread concern over children's lack of flexible problem-solving skills even when computational performance and performance on routine kinds of problems is quite good. Second, in spite of the frequent gaps between children's conceptual knowledge and their procedures, children are basically sense-makers. In early development, they move from recitative counting to cardinally based counting without explicit instruction. In school I believe they will likewise seek to make sense of what they are learning if they are given the opportunity. Third, and on a more speculative note, I have suggested that convergences between the results of a new procedure and a more familiar one are central to the process of sense-making. In early development, these convergences arise when children have the opportunity to count sets that they can also subitize or map into a one-to-one correspondence relation. In the classroom, I believe teachers can promote sense-making by taking care to give children an opportunity to validate new problem-solving methods against familiar ones. By allowing children to use the new method first in conjunction with a familiar one on problems the child can already solve, the teacher can strengthen the child's grasp of the conceptual meaning of the method so that later applications to more difficult kinds of problems are not beyond the reach of the child's sense-making capabilities.

ACKNOWLEDGMENTS

Preparation of this chapter was supported in part by National Research Service Award # 8F3HD07338A from the National Institutes of Health, and by a research grant from the Spencer Foundation. I thank Ann Brown, Kate McGilly, and Jack Smith for helpful comments on this chapter.

2 A Tool For Number Construction: Finger Symbol Sets

Rémi Brissiaud
I.U.F.M. de Versailles

The first method one thinks of for testing a young child's numerical knowledge is to give him or her a set of objects (tokens, for example) and ask, "How many tokens are there?". This type of question almost always triggers counting responses (see Fuson, 1988, for a recent overview of studies using this type of approach). Counting, however, is not the only available procedure for describing a given quantity of objects. Descoeudres (1921/1946) reported on one 4-year-old who did not know how to count beyond *two*. When presented with a collection of three objects, he spontaneously set up a one-to-one correspondence between his fingers and the objects; he held up three fingers and said, "That's more than two; it's like that!"[1] Few studies in the literature have focused on this type of behavior, in which children represent numerosities by a gesture after having formed a corresponding finger symbol set by a one-to-one matching procedure.

In their discussion of counting, Piaget and Szeminska (1941) stated that this verbal factor plays almost no role in acquisition. Most later works on early acquisitions departed from the Piagetian position in the sense that they argued, to the contrary, that counting *is* a major factor in mathematical learning (see Baroody, 1987; J.-P. Fischer, 1984; Fuson, 1988; Gelman & Gallistel, 1978; Gréco, 1962; Meljac, 1979; Steffe, von Glaserfeld, Richards, & Cobb, 1983).

Piaget took the same position for one-to-one matching as he did for counting and stated that it is not "truly numerical" if the child fails on the conservation task. Although many theorists have ascribed more importance to counting in early mathematical learning, performance on the conservation task still leads

---

[1]This example is described more fully further on.

many to consider that numerical one-to-one correspondences are acquired late (Gelman & Gallistel, 1978; Klahr, 1984b; Klahr & Wallace, 1976).

Nevertheless, since the pioneering work of Piaget and Szeminska (1941), one-to-one correspondences have been studied almost exclusively in comparison situations (as is the case for the conservation task), where the subject is asked to compare two numerosities (when the question, for example, is, "Are there as many, more, or fewer red tokens than green tokens?") and not in situations where the child is asked to describe a *single* quantity ("How many tokens are there?," and the child answers, "There are like that," while holding up the corresponding number of fingers). Gréco (1962) pointed out that the "how many?" question is more likely to elicit quantification. Frydman and Bryant (1988) reported that in sharing situations, one-to-one correspondence can result in numerical equivalence judgments in children as young as 4. It may even be the case that one-to-one correspondence is a numerical procedure in children under 4 because sharing is already a complex procedure, more complex than one in which the child forms a finger symbol set by one-to-one matching to answer a question of the "how many?" type.

Use of finger symbol sets has been described elsewhere (Fuson, 1988), but is probably rare. In most cases parents teach their children to count early and a question beginning with, "How many . . . " is a cue for counting. However, counting and forming finger symbol sets by one-to-one correspondence are two competing modes of quantification. For this reason, the comments in this chapter draw on observations of a child who learned to count late because his parents encouraged him to use finger symbol sets. This example will be used to describe a different "pathway to number" than the ordinary one, a pathway whose point of departure is one-to-one finger symbol sets and not counting. Comparing these two pathways helps clarify certain features of the concepts of numerosity and number. In particular I show that use of the fingers in this way is a genuine *analog* mode of quantification, and that it constitutes one of the basic stepping stones in the construction and acquisition of conventional representations of numerosity.

DIFFERENT PATHWAYS TO NUMBER?

One Pathway: Counting-Word Tagging to Number

When children learn to count early, their first attempts at counting generally do not yield a numerical representation of the corresponding numerosity. What typically happens is:

Adult: How many tokens are there?
Child (counting the tokens): One, two, three, four, five.

Adult: Yes, so how many tokens are there?
Child (re-counts the tokens): One, two, three, four, five.
Adult: That's right, but how many tokens are there?
Child (re-counts again): One, two, three, four, five.

This child is clearly putting number words and the tokens in the set in one-to-one correspondence, but does not differentiate the last number word spoken as the response to the question the adult asks. Some writers consider that this type of child does not use the *cardinality principle* (Gelman, 1983; Gelman & Gallistel, 1978) or the *cardinality rule* (Schaeffer et al., 1974), whereas others more cautiously refer to the *last-word strategy* (Frye, Braisby, Lowe, Maroudas, & Nicholls, 1989; Fuson, 1988; Fuson & Hall, 1983; Fuson, Pergament, Lyons, & Hall, 1985), in which the child repeats the last word in the sequence to comply with adult expectations, although the word has not taken on true cardinal meaning.

The adult–child dialogue just presented can be interpreted in several ways. The simplest is the observation that when a child counts, each of the number words (*one, two,* etc.) is said while pointing to an object with a finger. From the child's point of view, each number word is associated with the object pointed to: there is "the one," "the two," "the three," "the four." The last number word spoken, *four,* is a sort of tag: It refers to the object pointed to. In other words it refers to a single object and not to the *quantity,* which is a property of the objects taken as a whole. I have suggested (Brissiaud, 1989) calling this type of counting *word tagging* because when children answer "how many?" questions, they tend to treat number words like tags, so that the last number word in a sequence does not differ in status from the preceding ones. Children use number words as they would for any other word: to designate objects in a qualitative way. When saying a sequence of different words such as *eraser, pencil case, pen, notebook,* the last word spoken (*notebook*) refers to that object only, and never to the entire set of objects.

This interpretation is congruent with findings reported by Fuson (1988, p. 216) in an experiment in which she interviewed children (ranging from 3 years, 2 months to 4 years, 9 months) who counted x soldiers and used the last-word strategy. The question, "Are these the x soldiers?" was asked three times while she pointed respectively, to all the soldiers, all the soldiers except the last one, and only the last one. Of 20 children, only 5 answered correctly, and the most frequent answer from the other children was the last soldier pointed to as the referent for the number word x. This occurred despite the syntactic form of the questions, which explicitly used the plural: "Are *these* the x soldiers?"

In summary, when children are taught to count early, this form of counting is in fact a counting-word tagging procedure; access to cardinalized counting is not acquired this early (where cardinalized counting is defined as counting where the last word spoken refers explicitly to a property of the set of the objects). This is clearly a first phase in the acquisition of number concepts. A full description of this process cannot be made here, although some of the steps are commented upon in later sections.

A Rarely Investigated Pathway: From Finger Symbol Sets to Number

Descoeudres (1921) studied children's ability to hold up as many fingers as there were objects in a given set. She made a detailed description of the behavior of one child (G.) whom she observed:

> One day, I was giving arithmetic tests to a smart little four-year-old boy. The next day he came to see me to finish, and while waiting began to play with his tokens so he wouldn't be bored. Spontaneously he began to use the finger procedure to say the number of tokens[2]; in terms of vocabulary he only knew the names of the first two numbers. G. has three tokens in front of him and says, while lifting three fingers, "That's more than two, it's like that"; he adds a token and raises four fingers, "one more token," and then lifts his whole left hand. He then adds a sixth token and raises the thumb of his right hand, the seventh token and raises the thumb and the index finger. I said to him "Really? All those tokens and you're only showing me that many fingers!" He takes his left hand out from under the table as though to say "Obviously, don't you see?" (p. 219)

This description is particularly striking because it shows that this child had discovered a means to represent the numerosity of objects in a set, although he did not know how to name the different quantities (he only knew the words *one* and *two*). This procedure, like counting, makes use of one-to-one correspondence, but here, quantity is represented by the *set* of fingers in correspondence. In counting, numerosity is represented by the last number word in one-to-one correspondence. This suggests that there can be two types of modes of representation of numerosity: The first, as in the case of the construction of a set of fingers in one-to-one correspondence, is an analog mode, because manyness is represented by another, equivalent, manyness. In contrast, the second mode of representation of numerosity, which is customarily termed *numerical* is a conventional mode, in that it is based on a system of count labels through the use of a conventional sequence of number words.

The analog representation of number was found in ancient civilizations. The shepherds of Mesopotamia, who needed to recall the number of sheep in their herds, built up sets of pebbles using a one-to-one correspondence between animal and pebble. All analog representations of quantity are thus not gesticular, but when small numerosities are involved, the fingers seem to be particularly appro-

---

[2]Because this child does not use number words, the term "enumerate" would have been better.

priate for this form of representation perhaps because they are always readily available.

The example of Descoeudres' subject, who did not know the number words beyond *two* shows that in this case, at least, use of fingers is not a by-product of counting. The one-to-one correspondence between fingers and objects directly enables quantification. This usage of the fingers should not be confused with the one described by Steffe and von Glasersfeld (1985; von Glasersfeld, 1982), where a child associated a number word with a finger configuration in the way he or she would associate a number word with a domino, without having performed a unit-by-unit analysis of the set, but basing the comparison exclusively on its overall shape. This is why I use the term *finger symbol sets* in this context and not patterns or configurations. Depending upon the child, use of fingers can be interpreted in either of these ways, and I will reserve the term *symbol sets* for instances when it is clear that the basis for finger use is one-to-one correspondence.

Descoeudres' example also shows that a child may initially represent quantities in an analog fashion, using finger symbol sets, and that number words to name these symbol sets can be taught to him or her later. In the case of a pathway to number of this type, the first meaning of number words is not the tag and thus counting is not the only language activity that can be associated with the first numerical acquisitions in the child.

Numerous authors have observed that certain children show finger sets when they say number words (Baroody, 1987a; Decroly & Degand, 1912; Fuson, 1988; Hughes, 1986), however, they do not make the distinction between symbol set and pattern. To my knowledge, Descoeudres' account is the only one in which it is clear that the child is using symbol sets before having learned to count, sure evidence that this skill is not a by-product of counting. The case I present in the following sections is that of my son, Julien, who followed this same pathway: He also began by using finger symbol sets before knowing how to count.[3] The description of the main stages of his pathway to number are detailed.

JULIEN'S FINGERS: FROM SYMBOL SET TO NUMBER

At 2 years, 11 months, Julien knew how to name and form sets of two objects, but no one had taught him to count a set of two objects, that is, to point to objects while saying *one, two*.[4] At this time, the decision had not been made to postpone

---

[3]Observations of one's own child obviously create methodological problems, but I see no other way to be sure that up to a certain age a child does not learn to count.

[4]Anglo-Saxon readers, in particular, may be surprized that a child of almost 3 years does not know how to count beyond 2 or 3. This is still common in France because, for a long period of time and until very recently (Julien was born in early 1983), the teaching of counting had fallen into disrepute (J.-P. Fischer, 1981) especially in the eyes of nursery school teachers.

teaching him to count. It was made after the following attempt, in which I tried to
teach him to count up to three.

> Father: See, there is one, two, three; there are three tokens. Go ahead, do
> what I did.
> Julien (pointing to each token successively): one, one, one.

Julien felt no inclination to use number words as tags. This is why I initiated a
teaching session in which I tried to get him to understand the meaning of the
word *three* by using finger symbol sets. I gave him the following two tasks to do:

From gesture to a set of objects:
Father (raising two fingers: the thumb and the index): How many fingers
do I have there?
Julien: Two.
Father: You give me that in tokens: two.
Julien gives the correct set of tokens.
Father (raising three fingers: the thumb, the index, and the middle fin-
ger): Now give me that in tokens; you see, like that, it's three.
Julien gives me the right number of tokens. (He probably broke the set
down into 2 + 1.)
Father (using two other fingers, the index and the middle finger): Now
give me that.
Julien succeeds.
Father: How many are there like that?
Julien: Two.
Father (shows three with the index, middle finger, and ring finger): Now
you give me that in tokens.
Julien succeeds.
Father: How many is that like that?
Julien: (No response.)
Father: Like that it's three, see?

From object sets to gesture:
Father (displaying a set of two tokens): Show me with your fingers how
many tokens there are.
Julien raises the thumb and the index finger of the right hand. (He doesn't
have too much trouble keeping the other fingers bent.)
Father: Good! What do you call that in tokens?
Julien: Two.
Father (displaying a set of three tokens): Show me with your fingers how
many tokens there are.
Julien looks at the set of tokens and then at his fingers. He holds up his
thumb, his index finger, and the middle finger of his right hand while
holding down the ring finger and little finger with his left hand.

Father: Yes! What do you call that in tokens?

Julien: (No response.)

Father: Like that, it's three.

I display a set of four objects and ask Julien to perform the same task. He looks at the set and makes a mistake: He shows all five fingers. The session ends.

Julien thus knew how to represent the first three numerosities in analog form, using finger symbol sets (I didn't think of using the numerosity 1 on this first session but I saw later on that 1 presented no particular difficulty). Note that Julien did not know how to name a set of three fingers (gesture → number word), but finger symbols enabled him to communicate about this numerosity by saying "There are like this." Gesture replaced verbal communication. This session convinced me not to teach him to count immediately, but to encourage him to use an analog representation of numerosities on his fingers, and to record the associations he made. The aim was extremely simple: to continue to talk about sets in this way so that he would learn the word *three* and then *four* as names for symbol sets.

This teaching project would have not worked if Julien had been taught to count in nursery school, but as I have already pointed out, the teaching of counting had been virtually outlawed in French nursery schools for quite a while. The context, thus, was particularly important: His nursery school teacher could vouch for the fact that up to age 4½, all of his numerical learning was acquired at home. Julien did not take part in any number-related activities in school before this age: His teachers did not teach him to count and there were no numbers hanging up in the classroom. In addition, Julien was an only child, so that everything he was taught about number he learned from me, as part of the process described in this chapter.

Before Teaching to Count: From 2 Years, 11 Months to 3 Years, 8 Months

At the age of 2 years, 11 months, Julien knew how to represent numerosities less than or equal to 3 by gesture (he knew how to name a finger set of 2 but not of 3). I wondered if it would be a good idea to teach him a gesture corresponding to larger sets, for example, to prompt him to put his thumb on one token, the index finger on the next, the middle finger on the following one, and so on, and then to raise the fingers corresponding to them to show the matching set of fingers. Up to 3, Julien used a one-to-one correspondence, which was based on visual analysis of the array. In this case, the one-to-one correspondence is implicit, and teaching of this type would help make it more explicit.

An alternative teaching strategy would be to work with gradually larger numerosities without teaching him the general rule for finger–object correspondence. For example, Julien's knowledge about numerosities under 3 could be enhanced so that he would become able to name finger symbol sets of three; then, with further work, he would be able to construct a set of fingers equal to a set of four objects, then name this finger symbol set, and so on. In this alternative strategy, gesture would only slightly precede verbal communication: He would not be taught to represent large numerosities in analog form that he did not know how to name. In the end, this strategy was selected. The rationale is discussed further on.

Julien, then, was not given a general rule for object–finger correspondence, and initially we only worked with the first three numbers. For example, "I am going to give you three cookies; show me "three" with your fingers." Julien holds up three fingers. I continue, "Here are your three cookies (only giving him two); O.K.?" This did not preclude presenting Julien with larger numerosities, but that was done only in context. For example, I might say "Eight days from now, we'll go see Grandma," and then add "See, *eight* is like this." The aim was not necessarily to enable Julien to differentiate a reference set of eight from another finger symbol set of nine for example, but rather to have him realize that the mode of analog representation he had mastered for small numerosities was applicable beyond these numbers, to teach him to estimate the quantitative meaning of corresponding gestures (when shown eight fingers, he would say, "That's a lot"), and to show him that these gestures could be used to identify the verbal label for these quantities.

For sets of three objects, acquisition took place as shown in Fig. 2.1. As is always the case for language acquisition, understanding of the number word *three* (number word → gesture) preceded use in labeling a set of fingers (gesture → number word). Julien's third birthday had a catalyzing role in his learning *three:* "You're 3 years old: like that" (holding up three fingers).

Note, here, the lack of direct association between "set of objects" and "number word." This should be interpreted in the following way: When Julien was asked how many objects there were in a set, he first answered with a

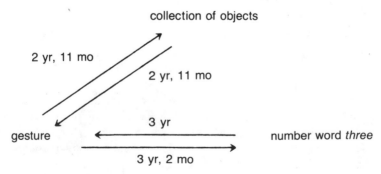

FIG. 2.1.   Julien's use of number-word and finger symbol set for "three."

gesture ("There are that many") and only replied with the number word after the adult had asked again ("How many is that many?"). At 3 years, 2 months, Julien knew the number of objects in a set of three (set of objects → number word), and knew how to construct a set of three objects (number word → set of objects), but he carried out each of these tasks via gesture, by an analog representation of the quantity.

At 3 years, 4 months, I asked him once again (as in the first session) to tell me on his fingers how many objects there were in a set of 4 tokens. (object set → gesture). He began by holding up 3 fingers while saying "Like that," then corrected himself immediately, without any comment on my part: "No, like that," while holding up an additional finger. I went on to ask him to make the sets corresponding to their gestures, (gestures → object sets), first with two, and then with four fingers. He succeeded but obviously did not know the name for the latter finger set. Here, again, the analog representation of numerosity preceded the ability to name this quantity.

At 3 years, 8 months Julien had roughly the same degree of ability for a set of four objects as for a set of three (see Fig. 2.1), except that he did not systematically succeed in naming a finger symbol set of four (gesture → number word). In contrast, he knew how to raise four fingers directly (number word → gesture) without counting, and he knew how to do this in several ways. One day when he had shown me 4 by keeping his thumb down, I asked him if he could do it another way. He said, "Yes, because you can do it this way," (showing me his whole hand except the little finger) but explained that he did not do it "because it hurts."

This account of Julien's performance for numerosities of 3 and 4 does not cover the entire range of his abilities. It is likely that he had deeper knowledge. First, he knew the rule for one-to-one correspondence as a general-purpose rule: For example, at 3 years, 7 months, he used the following procedure to represent the set of heros in the "Masters of the Universe" game: He held up his thumb and said "HeMan," his index finger and said "Skeletor," and the middle finger saying, "Stridor," and so on, through to the index finger of his other hand, and then showed the symbol set and asked, "That's how many, like that?" No one had taught him this procedure and it is hard to determine whether he invented it or whether he adapted it after seeing an adult use it in a non-teaching situation.

In addition, he had developed the ability to detect linguistic cues related to numerosity. When an adult used a sentence containing a number word x as a modifier, he could pinpoint the adjective and ask "How many is x?". For example if he heard that a family had six children, he could ask, "That's how many, six?". At 3 years, 8 months, Julien apparently had encountered an obstacle that hindered his progress: He had trouble memorizing the names for numerosities. This is why I finally decided to teach him to count: The conventional order of the number words probably acts as a mnemonic device. To take the example of another type of verbal material that children need to memorize, it is clear that if the letters of the alphabet were not in alphabetical order, letter memorization would be extremely difficult. When there is no conventional order, all rote recitations will contain repetitions and omissions.

First Attempts at Counting: From 3 Years, 8 Months to 4 Years, 6 Months

This period started at 3 years, 8 months with the acquisition of counting, and ended at 4 years, 6 months, when Julien entered a class where the teacher used numerical activities. "Graduation" to this class was likely to lead to interactions between school-based learning and home learning, which is why I have divided up the time period in this way.

The teaching of counting, at 3 years, 8 months took place in the following way:

> Father (takes three tokens, shows them to Julien and counts them): "Here; there are one, two, three tokens (holding up three fingers).
> Father (takes four other tokens): "How many tokens are there? Do like me: Count them."
> Julien puts his thumb on a token, and says *one*, the index finger on another and says *two* . . . I interrupt.
> Father: "No, wait; look."

Previously Julien relied on visual analysis of the array to construct a finger collection by one-to-one correspondence. Thus, when he was encouraged to make direct use of his hand, he naturally tended to set up a one-to-one finger–object correspondence, and did not resort to pointing with the index finger. I wanted to avoid this behavior, which explains the rest of the sequence. The reasons for this are discussed later.

> I put the four tokens together, then move one toward Julien while saying *one*. I then move another token in Julien's direction and say *two*. I then move yet another so that there are three tokens together before he says *three*, and again, in the same fashion, for *four*. When I have finished I address Julien.
> Father: "How many tokens are there?"
> Julien: Four (raising four fingers).
> Father: Your turn: Start and I'll help you (I take six tokens out of the pile). You count to know how many tokens there are (I guide Julien's index finger to get the first token out.)
> Julien: One (he goes on moving tokens by himself), two, three, (takes another token out but glances at me . . .)
> Father (as Julien takes out new tokens): "Four, five, six."

Julien: "That's how many, six?"

Father (counting on his fingers one by one): One, two, three, four, five, six. Six; it's like this (holding up one hand and the thumb of the other hand).

During this first counting session, Julien thus isolated the last word spoken, *six,* and asked me to specify the corresponding quantity using an analog representation of this quantity: "That's how many? Six?"). He thus knew that the word *six* represented a quantity, and he applied the cardinality rule on his first experience with counting. There was no period of time when counting was purely counting word tagging.

During this session, I started to teach Julien three new skills:

- Knowing the sequence of number words in the correct order.
- Knowing how to count a set of objects (object set → number word). (Prior to this session, Julien went through gesture and through visual analysis of the array for small sets; see Fig. 2.1).
- Knowing how to count on his fingers up to x to know which gesture corresponded to x (number word x → gesture).

Julien did not immediately become a good counter, in the sense of being able to count "high": at 4 years, 6 months he could not count beyond *six.* However, his counting always accurately reflected the one-to one correspondence between objects and number words, and he was one of the few children (Fuson, 1988) who, when he did not know the right number word, stopped pointing to objects and said, "I don't know any more" or "What is it after *four?*," rather than continuing to count with other number words. When reciting the number words, there was no distinction between an unstable portion and a stable portion, or between a stable conventional portion and a stable non-conventional portion (Fuson, Richards, & Briars, 1982): He used a stable, conventional portion and then stopped and said, "I don't know any more."

Counting did not have the expected effect as a mnemonic device with respect to counting on his fingers up to x (number word x → gesture). When Julien finished a counting sequence with an adult on the number word *five,* for example, and asked, "What is that like, five?," suggestions to count on his fingers (which would have consolidated memorization of the verbal number sequence) were met with signs of impatience; he clearly wanted the adult to show him the corresponding set of fingers. Thus, at the start he was only autonomous on sets of four objects; prior to having been taught to count, Julien knew how to hold up four fingers via visual analysis of the collection, but after teaching he began to count the sets of four objects before making the related gesture. To quantify a collection of four objects, he adhered to the sequence shown in Fig. 2.2.

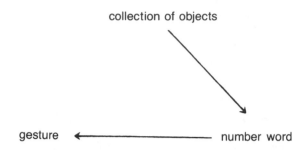

FIG. 2.2. Julien's use of number-word and finger symbol set for "four" after the age of 4.

In this new diagram, the arrows are missing from the left-hand portion, between "object set" and "gesture," whereas before (for 3 and 4) Julien went through a gesture phase to be able to label a numerosity. For 4 and higher he would now go through the number word, which he possessed through the teaching of counting, to produce the gesture. (For 3 and under, he never counted.)

The number *four* was thus a turning point for a change in the order of production of gesture and number word. Counting, however, did little to help Julien memorize new number words. What apparently worked best for learning the number *five* and the analog finger representation was a nursery rhyme involving finger movements: In this rhyme, the right hand pushes on the little finger of the left hand as though shoving the other fingers in the hand while reciting:

> There were five in the big bed
> And the little one pushed his brothers
> Push your brothers!
> And the thumb falls out (fold under the thumb)
> There were four in the big bed
> And the little one pushed his brothers
> Push your brothers!
> And the index falls out (fold under index finger), and so on

Julien never learned to recite the sequence of number words by rote during this period. He was encouraged to do so but was not interested. Thus, at age 4½ he could show up to six fingers directly without counting (number word → gesture), which corresponded precisely to the upper limits of his counting ability. He knew how to show 2, 3 and 4 in different ways. In contrast, the opportunity never arose for 5 and 6, and since we did not create a situation, I do not have the corresponding information.

At 4 years, 6 months, before Julien became involved in numerical activities in nursery school, we decided to test his mathematical abilities on a series of addition and subtraction tasks. I discuss the results further on and continue here presenting the sequence of observations concerning the memorization of number words.

After 4 Years, 6 Months: Counting as a Mnemonic Device

Counting at school probably whetted Julien's interest. He learned to count to 7, 8, 9, 10, and beyond before being able to show the corresponding quantities directly on his fingers, and at roughly 4 years, 9 months, he behaved the way we tried to teach him at 3 years, 8 months. When asked how many objects were in a set of eight, for example, he counted them to reach the corresponding number word *eight,* and then started to count on his fingers until he heard *eight* to make the corresponding finger set.

Similar to his earlier approach to counting, when he asked adults what *six* was "like," obtaining the number word *eight* was apparently not enough for him to grasp the corresponding numerosity. In other words, he felt the need to have an analog representation of the quantity in the form of a finger symbol set to know what *eight* was "like." In contrast to the previous stage, he counted on his fingers until he heard the target number word to construct this finger symbol set.

Recall that Julien knew how to show 2, 3, and 4 in different ways on a single hand. Beyond 5, however, he always represented 6 by one whole hand and the thumb of the other. Similarly, he represented 7 by a whole hand and the thumb and the index finger of the other. One plausible explanation is that he never used a finger other than the thumb to represent 1—which accounts for the representation of 6—and this raised thumb governed the rest of the procedure: Hold up the index after the thumb, then the middle finger, and so on. In a certain way, the hand is a "naturally" oriented set. The use of this order had a major effect: during this period, Julien began to use his fingers as numerals to represent their rank in the series of entities belonging to an ordered sequence (ordinal use of number). For example, at 4 years, 8 months, he counted from 1 to 6 by holding up his fingers successively, and continued by holding up the index of the right hand and saying, "This is the one I never remember." At 4 years, 10 months, he lifted his right-hand ring finger and said, "That's the last one all alone" to indicate that 9 (which goes with this finger) is the last number that is written with a single numeral. At 4 years, 11 months when I told him that in 10 days we were going to see his grandmother, he looked at his fingers, counted silently, designated his left hand little finger and said, "In 10 days, when we get there, we'll go see Grandma."

At about 5 years, 3 months, he was able to produce finger symbol sets for 7, 8, and 9 on his fingers directly without counting: Finger counting certainly played a major role in this memorization.

Characteristics of This Pathway

Julien thus took an extremely different pathway to number than the one ordinarily described when parents teach their children to count early. He was able to represent numerosities of 3 and 4 by using finger symbol sets before being able to use the matching number words, that is, before being able to name these numerosities.

For sets of four objects or less, analog representation through gesture preceded the naming of a quantity ("There are like that"). For numerosities of 4 and over, gestures still apparently preceded labeling of the quantity in Julien's mental representations: He always tried to interpret the outcome of his countings over 4 in analog form either using finger symbol sets, or by asking an adult about the corresponding set or by recounting on his fingers to form this set. Gesture was thus the resultant end-state of the counting procedure and the last word spoken was the way of reaching this goal. This suggests that before having been taught to count, Julien had constructed a genuine conceptualization[5] of numerosity, a conceptualization that *held true over 4* and was based on the use of a gesticular system of analog signs (finger symbol sets) and not on a verbal system, such as number words. If so, simply encouraging the construction of one-to-one finger matches to represent numerosities up to 4 and including the use of finger sets in discussions with him beyond 4, was enough for his conceptualization of numerosity to generalize beyond 4 and thus precede his learning how to count.

Numerous observations lend weight to this interpretation. The use of one-to-one correspondences to represent quantities of objects each of which has a different name (He Man, one finger; Skeletor, another finger) was perhaps an invention. Similarly, Julien behaved during the first counting sessions in a way that suggested he was trying to coordinate an emergent system of signs, a system of number labels, and an initial and better elaborated system of signs: the analog system of finger symbol sets. This explains why his early counting was cardinalized and why he was one of the few children to stop counting when he was no longer sure of recalling the right number word. Thus, when Julien counted on his fingers at 4 years, 8 months, and said while designating his index finger, "I never remember that one," he was deliberately deciding not to guess a number word for the next number because he knew that the word he should say was the one that matched the symbol set of seven fingers he is holding up. What could be interpreted as evidence for superior metacognitive skill was in fact nothing more than the need to coordinate two systems of signs: a word sequence and a gesture sequence that conveyed the same meaning. Because Julien first encountered number words as words for symbol sets, he controlled the use of these number words during counting.

---

[5]The use of the term *conceptualization* is explained more fully further on. I use it to refer to an explicit representation, in contrast to representations that are encapsulated in procedures.

It is worthwhile stressing the specific status that finger counting can have in the case of a child who progresses in the way Julien did, and who knows that the sequence of number words is also the sequence of labels for a series of nested symbol sets. When a child like Julien counts on his fingers, each new finger he holds up allows him to make a one-to-one correspondence between the number word spoken and the current finger symbol set. He can view counting on his fingers as a counting of number words because of the enumeration of the sequence of finger symbol sets (in this case, the sequence of symbol sets is the "incrementer"). The gesticular system of representation of numerosities could serve as a starting point for reflection on verbal counting. This can be seen clearly when Julien used his fingers to describe the irregularity of written numbers, for example, describing 9 as "the last one all alone." More generally, finger counting probably helped Julien develop ordinal usage of number words on the basis of their cardinal usage.[6]

This progression is partially the result of teaching methods and partially the result of Julien's resistance to them (in particular, the fact that he would not count higher than what he knew). Other progressions are obviously possible with the same point of departure, in particular, one in which the child would be systematically taught a one-to-one correspondence between fingers and objects by having the child practice putting his thumb on one object, the index finger on another, so that when he lifted his finger he would have a matching finger symbol set. This type of teaching would probably allow the child to have an ordered sequence of symbol sets at his disposal quickly (thumb, thumb-index, thumb-index-middle finger, and so on). Julien took a long time to be interested in oral counting. He might have been less so if we had proceeded in this way. Would his rote acquisition of number words then have been in the conventional order or would there have been gaps (for 7, for example, which Julien had a hard time learning)? What would have ensued for finger counting as an underpinning for numerical thought? I have no straightforward answer, and it would be worthwhile to observe a child who learned in this way.

THE USE OF FINGER SYMBOL SETS IN SOLVING ADDITION AND SUBTRACTION PROBLEMS

At 4 years, 6 months, Julien had an analog system of signs at his disposal that enabled him to talk about numerosities up to 6, and that fit into his parents' conversations (because we used both number words and finger symbol sets). At

---

[6]My account of the construction of the meaning of ordinal number words on the basis of their cardinal meaning is similar to one found in Klahr (1984a). However, in Klahr's model, the child relies on cardinal representations, which use one-to-one correspondence in an implicit way, whereas matching was explicit for Julien.

this age, before being exposed to any numerical activities at school, could this system be used to solve addition and subtraction problems?

The use of fingers to solve addition and subtraction problems on a general level has received ample documentation (Fuson, 1982), but the use of finger symbol sets has rarely been differentiated from the use of fingers as a marker system. The exceptions are Siegler and Robinson (1982), and then Siegler and Shrager (1984), who gave 4- and 5-year-olds addition and subtraction problems orally and reported two types of finger use: finger counting, and the use of the fingers without counting (*finger strategies*). Siegler and Robinson (1982) suggested that children find the answer without counting because the answer is associated with a kinesthetic sensation.

These investigators showed that finger strategies are faster than counting. Thus, in certain cases the strategies that implement finger symbol sets may derive from enhanced (advanced) counting strategies. In these cases, children count first and then switch to a finger strategy, because it saves time. My differentiation between two possible pathways to number raises an additional question: Does pathway to number affect the choice of counting versus finger strategies for problem solving? Certain children who were not exposed early to the use of finger symbol sets may become counters, whereas children who were encouraged to use finger symbol sets may preferentially choose finger strategies. This motivated me to test Julien, who at 4 years, 6 months only rarely counted on his fingers.

First Solutions to Addition and Subtraction Problems: 4 Years, 6 Months

The design was an adaptation of Starkey and Gelman (1982). The experimenter shows the child x objects in his hand. He or she then adds or takes away y objects and hides them in his fist. The child is asked to say how many objects are hidden in the experimenter's hand (the child counts the number of objects in the initial set and counts the number of objects that are added or taken away). Because at 4 years, 6 months, Julien only knew how to count up to 6, only operations that used numerosities equal to or less than 6 were given to him as problems. These included $1 + 1$, $1 + 2$, $1 + 3$, $1 + 4$, $1 + 5$, $2 + 1$, $2 + 2$, $2 + 3$, $2 + 4$, $3 + 1$, $3 + 2$, $3 + 3$, $4 + 1$, $4 + 2$, and $5 + 1$; and for subtraction: $6 - 1$, $6 - 2$, $6 - 3$, $6 - 4$, $6 - 5$, $5 - 1$, $5 - 2$, and so on. In all, Julien was tested on 30 operations in three sessions of 10 operations each (5 additions, 5 subtractions) selected in such a way that there were both easy and difficult problems (in terms of magnitude) in each session.

This was the first time Julien had encountered problems of this type. The only addition or subtraction situation he was familiar with was the nursery rhyme with the finger movements described earlier. That rhyme is more like a story than a problem, and only one finger is taken away each time. Thus, both the form and content of the problems were new to him. However, the results are straightforward: He succeeded on all of them. The only mistake he made—and this was in the first session—was for the $6 - 4$ problem (he answered 3), and he answered this same problem correctly when it was given to him again in the last session. As soon as I closed my hand over the unknown set, Julien concentrated and thought: Neither his lips nor his fingers moved until he was ready to produce the answer, which he announced verbally while producing it on his fingers. When I asked him how he found the answer, he said, "in my head." The finger configurations he uses to display the answers shed no light on the problem-solving procedure he used because they were common configurations (the thumb out for 1, the thumb in for 4, etc.) and the choice seemed to depend on the answer and not on the givens of the problem. Did Julien only use his fingers to *show* the answer or did he also use them to *find* the answer? Although up to 4½ he had only counted objects and never fingers, was he nevertheless resorting to counting on his fingers to solve these problems? One observation strongly suggests that there was no finger counting: On two occasions, although the answer was 6 (4 + 2 and 2 + 4) he held up a finger symbol set and was unable to produce the corresponding number word. When an answer is obtained through counting, the number word is available immediately, if for no other reason than by a recency effect.

Another observation made a week later (described in Brissiaud, 1989) helps clarify how Julien proceeded: He was doing an anomaly game ("Find what's wrong in this picture.", e.g., a man smoking a pipe upside down), and had already circled 4.

Father: Do you remember how many mistakes there are?
Julien: Six (holding up six fingers).
Father: How many have you found?
Julien (counting on the picture with his index finger): Four.
Father: So how many more do you have to find?
Julien immediately holds up his two thumbs and says, "*Two*" (see Fig. 2.3).

This confirms that Julien not only used his fingers to produce the answer. If this had been the case, he would simply have raised two fingers on the same hand (probably the thumb and the index finger), because he never used both hands before. Although Julien did not move his fingers at any time to form a configuration of 4, his problem solving strategy can doubtless be schematized as shown in Fig. 2.4.

Julien did not form configurations with motor movements, but most likely used proprioception or a visual representation (mental image) of his fingers. This

FIG. 2.3.   Julien's gesture while saying "two."

procedure is not a counting procedure—the number words are not recited one by one—and more global processing is used. At first glance, success in the use of this procedure apparently depends on a variety of skills:

- The ability to associate the number words *four* and *six* with the elements in a special sequence of symbol sets.
- The ability to quantify finger sets when they did not belong to the special sequence of symbol sets, when Julien used fingers on both hands, for example. Another likelihood is that in this case, Julien used mental counting for numbers over 2 or 3.

Recall that at this point in time, Julien had never counted on his fingers. Later, between 4 years, 6 months and 5 years, 3 months, during the phase when he counted on his fingers to construct sets having between 7 and 10 elements, he continued to use this type of procedure in which the symbol sets are used globally. This was the context for the following exchange:

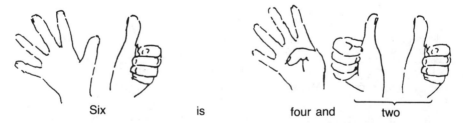

Six   is   four and   two

FIG. 2.4.   Probable finger's set combination that results in the gesture for "two."

Father: How much is 5 and 4? (a question Julien understood at this age)

Julien: That's too easy (holding up nine fingers).

Father: How much is 7 and 3?

Julien: I don't know . . . oh, yes: two whole hands (without holding up the corresponding symbol set).

This example also shows that the use of symbol sets belonging to a special sequence (here, for 7, one hand and the thumb and index finger of the other) would be insufficient: Julien needed to know how to quantify novel finger sets (here, 3 with the middle finger, the ring finger, and the little finger). This example underscores the importance of finger symbol sets as a problem solving tool: By saying that 5 + 4 was "too easy," Julien showed that the easiest numerical relationships to verbalize were those that were favored by his gesticular model.

- The use of the gesticular model ("two whole hands") when he did not know the name for the outcome (*ten*).

To sum up, the use of finger symbol sets enabled Julien to communicate about numerosities. In addition, this analog numerical reference system was also the tool he opted for spontaneously to solve addition and subtraction problems. This use of finger symbol sets can thus emerge without prior exposure to counting on the fingers. Thus the finger strategies observed by Siegler and Robinson (1982) should not always be interpreted as mere enhancements of counting procedures.[7]

COMPARING THE TWO PATHWAYS

There has been frequent reference in preceding sections to both representations, such as finger symbol sets, and to problem solving. These two features are connected. The two pathways not only differ because children construct different representations, but also because these different representations are associated with different processing modes for problem solving. It is perhaps more appropriate to refer to different *representation and processing systems* (Hoc, 1987) for an identical set of tasks, or different *specialized action schemas* (J.-F. Richard, 1990), because the notion of schema refers to a knowledge base that reflects how

---

[7]The strategies Siegler et al. term "finger strategies" are not exactly the ones used by Julien. For 4 + 3, for example, their subjects represented 4 on one hand and 3 on the other, and then gave the answer without counting. It is likely however that they completed the first hand mentally to form a known symbol set: one hand and two fingers. This procedure is grounded in the same knowledge bases as the ones used by Julien.

knowledge is structured (system of representations) and how this knowledge is used (processing system).

Explicit Representations (Conceptualizations) or Representations Encapsulated in Procedures?

Take the case of a child who, after having counted, does not know that the last word spoken represents a quantity, that is, a child who employs counting word tagging. Surprisingly, some children use these successfully. For example when asked to compare two numerosities of four and five objects, respectively, a child might proceed in the following way: "Here there are one, two, three, four and here there are one, two, three, four, five, so here there are more because here it's one, two, three, four, five." This child is using what Vergnaud (1982) termed *theorems in action* and in a certain way has constructed a representation of quantity, but this representation differs from the ones constructed by Julien. This child uses number words to regulate action, and the words have no meaning outside of this action. At best, the sequence *one, two, three, four* as a unit "represents" the corresponding numerosity. When a child who uses number tags employs representations, these representations are not initially explicit but rather are "encapsulated" in the procedures.

Most theorists believe that the use of number words to label patterns (dominos, dice, playing cards, finger patterns) or very small quantities (subitizing) plays a major role in the construction of explicit representations (Fischer, 1984; Klahr & Wallace, 1976; von Glasersfeld, 1982). However the Fuson (1988) data described earlier in this chapter, in which children were asked "Are these the x soldiers?," when only the last soldier was being pointed to, suggest that in early teaching of counting, number words are not immediately construed as linguistic signs designating quantities. In contrast, they had this status immediately for Julien.

In early learning of counting, another factor affecting the acquisition of explicit representations is experience in solving addition and subtraction problems when the real sets corresponding to the problem statements are not in view. Children begin by solving these problems by recreating the problem statement with objects or fingers (Carpenter & Moser, 1983). To solve a problem where two numerosities of 4 and 3 objects are united, for example, the child creates 4 on one hand, and 3 on the other, and re-counts the total number of fingers while monitoring his counting by pressing in sequence on the table or on his cheek. Even when children begin learning with counting, they still resort to symbol sets, that is, analog representations (which were the first that Julien used). There is, nevertheless, a difference between Julien's approach and this one: In the previous example, fingers are employed like tokens and the seven fingers are counted one by one. There is no use of the hand as a special grouping and no special sequence of symbol sets. The child forms unspecified, unstructured symbol sets on his fingers, in contrast to the ones formed by Julien.

Unspecified Symbol Sets and Structured Symbol Sets

In preceding sections I have almost exclusively stressed the analog features of finger symbol sets in the representation of numerosities. However, finger symbol sets differ in two fundamental ways from unspecified symbol sets, such as the sets of pebbles used by the shepherds of Macedonia to recall the number of sheep in their herds. First, finger symbol sets open up possibilities for dual sensory (visual and kinesthetic) coding of finger sets. Second, the hand physically forms a special grouping. Finger symbol sets thus constitute an imaginal system that privileges the number 5 and thus favors recognition and rapid labeling of numerosities over 5. Note that many teaching devices imitate this imaginal system (Brissiaud, 1989; Flexer, 1986; Hatano, 1982).

The special status of the hand groupings also explains why children tend to organize symbol sets of more than five fingers into a sequence of *nested sets:* When asked to show an increasingly higher number of fingers, the gesture that comes naturally is to use all the fingers of one hand before starting on the fingers of the other. Thus, special symbol sets tend to come in chunks of five: the first five numbers use only one hand (although those less than five can be represented in different ways on this hand) and the next five numbers are displayed by this full hand plus fingers on the other hand. Julien at times used a more constraining sequence, representing 1 by his thumb, 2 by the thumb and index finger, 3 by the thumb, index, and middle finger, and so on, but finding the mistakes in the "what's wrong?" picture shows that he also knew how to free himself from this constraint.

The "what's wrong?" game also shows that the special symbol sets that Julien used were both nested and seriated[8] and that he knew how to quantify the differences (two thumbs held up, for example). This is obviously the result of the conceptualization process corresponding to the use of symbol sets, but it is likely that the kinesthetic coding and special grouping of 5 made the quantification of differences easier. To find the difference between 6 and 8, for example, use of a sequence of special symbol sets calls for "activating" one hand and finding the difference between 1 and 3 on the other hand while the first remains activated. The special grouping of 5 also enabled Julien to find all the relationships between 1 and 5 in the 6 to 10 range, which are unchanged by the translation of 5.

Sensory dual coding, the special status of the grouping of 5, and the naturalness of the 5 gesture all favor the emergence of a general system or richly organized finger symbol sets. Simply saying that these symbol sets are analog representations of numerosities does not do justice to them. The key issues are

---

[8]This is a specific ability, which is not "operational" in the Piagetian sense of the word. It is not because finger symbol sets form a system of nested and seriated sets that Julien has class logic knowledge that would allow him to succeed on any inclusion or seriation task. Rather, symbol sets apparently serve as categories that are structured in a schematic way (i.e., based on schemas as knowledge architectures; see Bideaud & Houdé, 1989).

(a) that the natural grouping of 5 favors rapid labeling of finger symbol sets, and (b) that children tend to organize these finger symbol sets into a sequence of nested, seriated sets with differences they can quantify. Because, in the end, children learn to match a given number word (*seven* for example) with a finger symbol set immediately (by displaying seven fingers, visualizing them "in their heads" or feeling seven fingers without moving them), this tool makes rapid processing possible. This is why a child may opt for finger sets as a preferential means for the representation of quantities. This was true for Julien at 5½ when given the following problem:

> A picture shows six pencils in a case (this picture can be seen as an unspecified symbol set), and the problem statement says it can contain up to nine pencils. The task is to draw the number of missing pencils and write the number on the pencil case.

Julien works backwards: He first calculates the number of missing pencils and then draws three pencils. His representation system was so well adapted to problem solving that when he was provided with an (unspecified) symbol set to solve the problem (the pencils in the picture) he preferred to reason with his system of organized symbol sets (finger symbol sets).

Thus, as Julien proved when saying, "5 and 4, that's too easy," use of this gesticular system helped him structure the verbal system (number words) into an arithmetic system.

CONCLUSION

In 1962 Gréco made a strong plea to restore the importance of one-to-one correspondences in the genesis of number. In his article entitled "Quantité et quotité," which is subtitled "Nouvelles Recherches sur la Correspondance Terme-à-Terme et la Conservation des Ensembles," he criticized Piaget for not assigning one-to-one correspondence more than a secondary and non-essential role in the construction of numerical concepts. He argued that situations in which children are asked to find the answer to "how many?" questions should be differentiated from situations, like the conservation task, in which they must compare (when the question is "How many more?"), because children tend to count on the former and this implicit use of one-to-one correspondence is, as Gréco showed, part of the acquisition process.

The present study is one extension of Gréco's work. A child who uses finger symbol sets to answer a "how many?" question makes more explicit use of one-to-one correspondence, and Julien is an example of how this practice, even when restricted to small numerosities, can play a decisive role in the future construction of numerical concepts. I have shown that the use of symbol sets is a genuine and analog mode of quantification, and that a pathway to number that diverges from the traditional route can, indeed, be worthwhile.

When a child follows this type of pathway (from finger symbol set to number) he or she starts out having two systems of signs available for representing quantity: a gesticular, analog system, which emerges first; and a verbal system, which is built up like an analog labeling system. In the case of early teaching of counting, the child learns the sequence of number words as he would a series of numerals and initially has neither gestures nor words to represent numerosities. If this type of child has representations, they differ in nature from Julien's and are "encapsulated" in the procedures in which they are used.

This comparison of the two pathways can be better understood in terms of the notion of "unitization." Dewey (cited in von Glasersfeld & Richards, 1983, p. 9) described the notion of "three" in the following way:

> In simple recognition, for example, of three things as three the following intellectual operations are involved: The recognition of the *three* objects as forming one connected whole or group—that is, there must be a recognition of the three things as individuals, and of one, the *unity*, the whole, made up of the three things.

I take a similar position. The "representation of a quantity" calls for both one-to-one correspondence to "recognize the things as individuals," and a "unitization" (or unification) of the different elements that one to one correspondence made it possible to differentiate. This allows a child to be able to recognize them as forming a whole. I share Dewey's belief that both unitization and one-to-one correspondence are fundamental operations. Initial use of symbol sets favors this "unitization" because the child is prompted to produce one gesture and one word to designate a quantity. In contrast, initial use of counting is likely to create an obstacle because the word that designates the numerosity also refers in an ambiguous way to one of the objects pointed to. At the start of this chapter I mentioned the debate over Gelman's cardinality principle. Fuson and her co-workers have argued (correctly, in my opinion) that some children count and use the last-word strategy without having carried out the unitization process described by Dewey. I go one step further: Some children count and do not repeat the last word spoken although they have carried out a certain type of unitization. They have an implicit representation of numerosity, a representation that is "encapsulated" in their procedures. Early teaching of counting, because it is weakly explicit, puts children on extremely different levels of representation (either no representation, or implicit representations or conceptualizations) and whether they do or do not repeat the last word spoken during a counting sequence may not be an optimal indication of their level of attainment.

The Construction of Arithmetic Units

In my opinion, the first form of unitization described by Dewey is sufficient to be able to represent a numerosity, but a second form of unitization is called for to determine to represent it by a number. When a Macedonian shepherd put his last sheep in one-to-one correspondence with a pebble, he had clearly formed *one* set of pebbles thus forming a unit, which served to represent the quantity of animals. However, this is simply the action binding the extension of this unit (the shepherd stops because there are no animals left). This first form of unitization, which can be termed *pragmatic unitization,* needs to be distinguished from another, more formal one: the constitution of complex informational units (arithmetic units) that are characterized by the relationships they can form with other units of the same type (9 is 1 more than 8; it is 5 + 4 but also 6 + 3). It is worthwhile pointing out (a) that counting, even when it is cardinalized, only initially authorizes pragmatic unitization, and (b) that the ensuing representation of numerosity is no richer than the one corresponding to the symbol set.

This becomes clear if you try to label numerosities with an unusual verbal system, such as the letters of the alphabet, rather than with figures or number words. You can form a set of H tokens, by counting A, B, C . . . up to H. However, the label H is a poor representative of the corresponding numerosity. H is not an arithmetic unit because there is no relationship such as H is E plus C. Regardless of pathway, there is a need to differentiate two forms of unitization: an initial one, which corresponds to the representation of the numerosity (the construction of a symbol set and certain forms of counting), and a second one, which corresponds to number.

We have seen that Julien constructed these arithmetic units over the course of his numerical development. To represent numerosities over 5, he set up finger symbol sets by exploiting the natural grouping formed by the hand and the natural order that is induced by the naturalness of the gesture (complete one hand before using the other), until he had constructed a sequence of nested and seriated symbol sets. He thus had a gesticular system at his disposal that, when it operated on the analog level, allowed him to solve addition and subtraction problems by re-creating the problem statements with symbol sets. Each element in this gesticular system could be labeled rapidly, which facilitated the emergence of the other system in ongoing development: the arithmetic system of number word designations ("5 and 4; that's too easy").

When a child first learns to count he or she still solves early arithmetic and subtraction problems by simulation, using symbol sets (Carpenter & Moser, 1983), but these sets are not necessarily organized in the way Julien's were. It is likely that this type of organization is a prerequisite for the acquisition of number. This is because counting unspecified symbol sets is an instance of sequential processing that serves to form proximity relations, such as 9 is 8 + 1, or 9 is 7 + 2. In contrast, relations such as 9 is 5 + 4 and, probably, 9 is 6 + 3 are likely to be extremely hard to memorize without global processing, which is made possible by a representation system such as the gesticular one. All adults know how to display a given number on their fingers directly, without counting the fingers one by one. This proves that whatever the teaching method chosen by parents and teachers, we all construct two systems of representations of numerosity: a gesticular system and a verbal system. My basic hypothesis is that the gesticular system, which we all construct, is almost never a byproduct of the verbal system of number designation. The grouping of 5 has probably always played a major role in the construction of numerical relationships that are not relations of proximity. It is, thus, likely that an analog system, such as the gesticular one developed by Julien, is, regardless of pathway, a necessary underpinning for the construction of a logico-mathematical system, such as number.[9]

What emerges from the present case study is that very early teaching of counting can be fairly costly: Counting in this case is almost always counting word tagging and the number words are used in a way that does not lay the groundwork for either the first or the second forms of unitization ("3 and 2 makes 5" is meaningless when 3, 2, and 5 are tags). When they are used differently, number words help construct a gesticular system that can successfully buttress these two forms of unitization and that probably needs to be constructed anyway. In some cases initial teaching of number tags may be detrimental in the long term. One of the common characteristics of learning-disabled children in the United States is their difficulty in memorizing number facts, and hence, in constructing arithmetic units (Allardice & Ginsburg, 1983; Geary, Widaman, Little, & Cormier, 1987). In contrast, their counting performances are unaffected. What would have happened if these children had taken another pathway? In general, children construct number regardless of path, but in some cases, the long-term consequences of initial choices may weigh heavily in the balance.

ACKNOWLEDGMENTS

I extend my thanks to J. Bideaud, J.-P. Fischer, C. Meljac, G. Mottet, A. Ouzoulias, and J.-F. Richard for their helpful comments on the preliminary version of this chapter.

---

[9]This type of system is necessarily propositional. My claims concerning number are compatible with the more general theoretical framework developed by Lautrey (1987), who argued that all propositional systems need analog underpinnings.

3 Conservation and the Notion of "Half"

Silvia Parrat-Dayan
Jacques Vonèche
Université de Genève

This chapter offers an in-depth exploration of one of the central topics in the works of Jean Piaget: part–whole relationships. Part–whole relationships were the focus of one of Piaget's first "psychological" publications (1921), which bears the hallmarks of what was to become operational theory.

From 1921 to 1941, Piaget's works dealt primarily with the logic of the young child, logic characterized by the absence of operational structures. *Le Jugement Moral chez l'Enfant* (Piaget, 1932), which sheds light on the cognitive prerequisites for internalization of social norms, is also associated with this period. In addition, it was during this time that Piaget was writing his well-known studies drawn from his daily observations of his own three children (Piaget, 1936, 1937, 1945). However, part–whole relationships only really came to the forefront in Piaget's "major" era, starting in the early 1940s. (Piaget & Inhelder, 1959; Piaget & Szeminska, 1941). At this point, the Geneva studies took two complementary tacks: a systematic investigation of the ontogenesis of operations in the major areas of understanding, and the elaboration of formal models of groupings and groups. This explains why the ontogenesis of number is considered to be the synthesis of class inclusion (additive grouping of classes) and seriation (grouping of asymmetrical relations): Number is elaborated as a seriated class. This constitutes a profound change in the notion of number itself through attribution to it of an exclusively logical meaning. This conception contrasts with the classical Greek view of number, which gave as much weight to *eidos* (image) as to *logos*. This shift towards *logos* is due to both the perspective adopted by Piaget, and to the misinterpretations that later arose concerning the abstraction and generalization of part–whole relationships.

The purpose of this chapter is to rectify these misinterpretations through

67

examination of issues connected to the conservation of the part and the whole in a series of partitioning and bi-partitioning experiments that depart considerably from standard conservation tasks. We define our theoretical position by comparison with two conflicting trends in research: the structuralist, Piagetian trend, and the contemporary pragmatic trend, which, in our opinion, places undue stresses on skills. Our position is structuro-functional, in that we contend it is the function that creates the structure and not the reverse. This position integrates the subject's current cognitive organizations, the context (material, instructions, and problem situation), and behavior. Earlier studies in this perspective (Parrat-Dayan, 1980) on the development of the notion of half (bi-partitioning) have shown that young children (4 to 5 years old) consider a half to be any (but preferably a small) part of an object, whereas older children (6 to 8 years old) consider that half must recreate a whole—an object—and not a unit. This whole is not necessarily the initial whole, but can be formed subsequent to partition activities. Still older children (9 to 11) have grasped the reference to the initial unit, but get lost in the maze of parts of parts, and heteromorphic and homomorphic parts. In other words, there is, in fact, no conservation of the part and the whole in the strict sense of the word until the stage of formal operations.

Piaget's point of departure can be traced to a fundamental intuition put forward by Pierre Janet, whose courses Piaget attended at the Collège de France: "Do children who use the word "part" so badly know how to serve themselves a piece of pie?" (Janet, 1936, p. 33).[1] Studying thought in action led Piaget to restrict himself to the most elementary facets of conservation of the part and the whole, and to investigate its specific logic. In doing so, Piaget neglected the study of elementary intelligence, for which Janet chided him: "Mr. Piaget . . . clearly shows what we can learn about intelligence of initial operations of the young child. But Mr. Piaget merely examines the child in terms of slightly more advanced intelligence: He has not studied elementary intelligence." (Janet, 1928, p. 259).

Today, a new generation of psychologists refers to skills in challenging the Piagetian structuralist model of development. The interest generated by the study of cognitive operations (e.g., Inhelder et al., 1976), the controversy around the precocity of Piagetian acquisitions (e.g., Bovet, Parrat-Dayan & Deshusses-Addor, 1981; Bryant, 1974; Gelman, 1982a; McGarrigle & Donaldson, 1975; Parrat-Dayan & Bovet, 1982; Van den Brink & Streefland, 1979), and the problem of décalages (Bideaud, 1988; Gillièron, 1977; Markman, 1973; Markman & Siebert, 1976; Parrat-Dayan, 1980, 1985; Retschitzki, 1978) all indicate converging evidence for a model of cognitive development that is less systematic than the Piagetian description would have us believe.

---

[1]This contains excerpts from lectures at the Collège de France in 1920 which dealt with the "origins of intelligence." For the relationship between Piaget and Janet, see the interview with Piaget in Broughton and Freeman-Moir, 1982.

Second, because the study of the ontogenesis of concepts is often equated with the identification of structural aspects of thought, it has been assumed that the study of functional aspects should challenge the notion of structure, relegate it to the background, or lead to a revised definition. It is sometimes claimed that abandoning the study of concepts would facilitate efforts to grasp the mechanisms of cognitive development. This claim is based on Bresson's idea that "nothing authorizes us to state that our conception of science is the one that drives our cognitive acquisitions" (quoted in Puche Navarro, 1983, p. 5), and on the recognition that one of the difficulties in cognitive development lies in the fact that analysis of the successive forms of development is conducted in terms of a final, adult state (Bresson & Schonen, 1979). Some investigators have therefore chosen to ignore, and even to reject, the study of notions, while at the same time questioning children *about* these same notions, as does Puche Navarro (1983) vis-à-vis partitioning: "Abandoning this conception implies *rejecting* [emphasis added] the study of partition as a concept and rejecting the final model generated by the logical systems in which this knowledge is organized" (p. 5), and even more clearly: "The study of the practice of "cutting" *replaces* [emphasis added] the study of partitioning as a notion" (p. 6).

We do not challenge the idea that the functional aspects of development lead more specifically to the study of cognitive processes. Rather, we would like to show that the study of the ontogenesis of notions can, when certain methodological precautions are adhered to, relate functional and structural aspects of thought. We would also like to show the focusing on pragmatic aspects (in terms of cognitive skills) does not necessarily negate the study of concepts.

The notion of *half* (as defined in Parrat-Dayan, 1980) has a number of (empirical) advantages. First, it is part of the child's everyday life: What child has never asked for half an apple or half a chocolate bar? What child has never given up half of something or been asked to share (half) with friends? In addition, the content (discontinuous or continuous) of these halves is extremely varied. This notion can, therefore, be incorporated into a series of different sharing, sampling, and fractioning contexts. The notion of half, then, is connected to operations of sharing and union, and to fractions and proportions, as well as to geometric concepts, such as the center of an object, or physical concepts, such as the center of gravity, and so forth. It entertains a particularly well-defined relationship with part and whole, and because of this, is connected to notions of conservation.

In addition, in contrast to other studies, whose point of departure is a complex notion (for example, fractions), studies that attempt to analyze behavior and more elementary structurations, the aim here is to understand how an apparently simple notion, which does not appear to create major problems for children (Piaget, Inhelder, & Szeminska, 1948), becomes gradually more complex. The present study, thus, differs from works aimed at showing that there is early elaboration of complex notions; it has more in common with studies that show that there are empirical, non-conceptual solutions to logical problems (Bideaud, 1988; Markman, 1973; Markman & Siebert, 1976.)

HALF AND CONSERVATION

A quantity can be conserved because the whole is the sum of its parts. As Piaget et al. (1948, chap. 12) put it, to the extent that there is a permanent totality, there is subordination of the parts to the whole and hence, operational conservation. However, examination of Piaget's works on this topic, from 1921 to his last writings, leads to the inevitable conclusion that his ideas of totality and part were fairly limited. In the Piagetian perspective, segmentation apparently always operates on a single object whose parts can be reassembled to its original form. Moreover, transformations are transformations on one and the same object: a ball of clay, a given quantity of liquid, and so forth.

However, studies by Bruner (1964) and Elkind (1961), for example, show that in Piagetian conservation situations, the conservation or the identity of the transformed object precedes conservation of the equality between the transformed test object and the unmodified reference object. In other words, instead of raising the question of the invariance of the test object through the ingenious transformation situations devised by Piaget and his co-workers, the child could, in fact, be asking whether the test objects and the reference objects are comparable. This is obviously a different question. In these conditions, it is clearly Piaget's experimental methodology on the notion of totality that prevents dissociation of the factors involved in the experiment: conservation, comparativity, and partitioning/union of totalities.

These considerations prompted us to raise the issue of the limits of totality, which, in turn, led to the hypothesis that the part–whole relationship is a relationship that is gradually modified as a function of the different meanings assigned to it by the child. These meanings are themselves a function of level of the subject's knowledge, his or her conception of a totality, and the representation of the target problem, which is dependent on the subject's point of view as well as on the nature of the problem situation. As Reuchlin (1973) pointed out:

When new content is incorporated into natural thinking, it conveys several pieces of information in an indissociable (or virtually indissociable) way. The existence of these rigid associations can, in particular, be seen in cases where the unfolding of natural thinking does not adhere to the expectations of the logician. "Natural" inferences do not only use information derived from operations on the content that is relevant to the problem at hand. These inferences draw on other pieces of information derived from this content, which are foreign in logical terms from the problem: Certain logically correct deductions are considered to be invalid because of the effect of this information or side effects; this information can also trigger sequences of formal though that, without having a necessary connection with the problem, interfere with appropriate problem solving reasoning. (p. 395)

This is shown in an experiment in which 4- to 12-year-olds were asked to divide a rectangle of cardboard in half (Parrat-Dayan, 1980, chap. 5). The children did so using a vertical section, a horizontal section, or two subtypes of diagonal section.

Each section yields halves that differ in shape: The vertical section yields two squares, the horizontal section yields two elongated rectangles, and the diagonal section results in two triangles. Whereas 6-year-olds agree fairly easily that two initial (uncut) rectangles are equal (either by overlaying them or by visual inspection), children up to age 10 reject the suggestion that the two halves are equal. This is even more striking given that they readily agree that the two homomorphic halves form a whole. These children do not conserve the part–whole relationship when the initial totalities are equivalent but produce halves with different shapes. In contrast, when the initial totalities are different, children tend to conserve the part–whole relationship to a greater extent, but not in all cases. To conserve this relationship, there is a constant need to refer to the abstract unit of reference, which authorizes the comparison of two different totalities. Thus, the more the halves differ, the more arduous is conservation.

The Notion of Part and Unit

In his study on the origins of intelligence, Janet (1936) wrote that the most elementary intellectual behavior consists of combining two perceptual acts into a single synthetic act. He illustrated this by analyzing certain forms of behavior, using a task he called the "apple basket." The apple basket is one of the numerous "intellectual objects" constructed by the subject through his or her first intellectual acts. In the case of the apple basket, the intellectual acts are related to quantity, and give rise to the complex intellectual operation of regrouping. For regrouping to take place, Janet believed the subject must show that he or she can differentiate objects, consider them independently from each other, and perform specific behaviors on each (for example, the subject must be able to pick an apple, eat one, put the apples into the basket, etc.) The subject must demonstrate the ability to produce a new external action that can transform these multiple objects into a single object (once the basket is full, the subject must be able to treat it as a single object). Then, the subject must perform a new action with the set formed in this way—a single action with only one form despite the quantity of objects united (e.g., emptying the basket and carrying out a different behavior with each apple, filling the basket with other multiple objects, etc.).

Intellectual objects always have the potential for two types of action. The apple basket covers two sorts of actions, neither of which are related, per se, to the basket or to apples: the action of filling and the action of emptying.

By referring to the notion of part, Janet drew attention to the fact that the part is always a part of something. This something, this total and complex object, which is transformed by partition, nevertheless preserves characteristics of its own. How is it possible to conserve the notion of entity when only dealing with pieces? Janet claimed it is impossible to refer to parts of an object if this object is seen as singular. *Part* implies that there is a transition from what Janet termed the *individual* to the *unit*. The *individual* is an object that differs from other objects, which can be grouped together with objects of the same type, but which cannot be divided into parts. Why is it that some objects can be divided and some not? Sheep can be united into a herd, but the shepherd does not cut up his animals, claimed Janet: If a sheep is cut in two, it disappears.

> The idea of unit is similar to the idea of individual. It is also an object (sic), which can be grouped with other objects of the same kind to make sets. We add units of measure, meters, to make sums. When we carry out this operation, we do not divide the meter, we take it all together and at this point in time it acts like an individual. (Janet, 1936, pp. 52–53)

The meter is thus taken as an individual, in the etymological sense of the word, and is indivisible. However, by switching standpoints, we can make both the sheep and the meter divisible. A live sheep is an indivisible individual for the shepherd; a dead sheep, from the butcher's point of view, is a unit that can be divided into parts: It is thereby seen as a unit and not as an individual. Thus, indivisibility is not an absolute characteristic for either the individual or the unit. In addition, individuals, while conserving their indivisible characteristics, can differ from each other. Units, however, are all equal, as though they were indistinguishable from each other. The idea of unit is much more general than the idea of individual; it can apply to the life sciences, astronomy, physics, and chemistry, and is the point of departure for the mathematical sciences. It raises different problems in science and in philosophy: for example, the distinction between continuous and discontinuous, of infinitely large and infinitely small.

When we divide an object, the object undergoes changes. Sometimes an object can be divided easily, but always, only up to a certain point. If we cut an apple in two, each half still looks like an apple. We can also cut a sheep in two, but this calls for a change in perspective and, hence, object transformation. It is no longer the shepherd's sheep, which cannot be divided, but rather the butcher's.

Dividing operations are related to combinatory operations that form sets. An object (a totality) can be seen as a unit of an individual or a unit of a set. An apple, for instance, becomes an individual when we realize that it is the final state of the intellectual act of dividing up a basket of apples. The apple transforms itself into a unit of a set when we consider it from the point of view of the parts that make it up. In Janet's terms, then, "The unit (an important problem in science and philosophy) is not something that exists in the word such that we only have to see or feel it. It is not a given in things or in itself; it is, like most things, a construction of the human mind" (p. 70).

Partition and union activities are complementary. The transition from one to the other is dependent on one's point of view; this is the source of numerous errors. Despite these difficulties, humankind has preserved these operations of partition and union; they have even been stretched to enable combination and partition beyond the limits of the object. Through an appeal to abstraction, even the individual can be transformed into an abstract unit.

THE NOTION OF HALF

The construction of the notion of half thus presents a whole host of difficulties. These difficulties can be delineated in a number of ways. A child who is able to produce half a ribbon by folding the two ends together may have considerable difficulty producing half of a rigid object, such as a length of uncooked spaghetti. The nature of the material prevents the child from implementing elementary cognitive skills because the inequalities created when the pieces of spaghetti breaks are handled differently by children as a function of age and level of cognitive development (Parrat-Dayan, 1985).

Similarly, a child who is incapable of following instruction to give half of six apples to a doll may be able to carry out this sharing task perfectly with two dolls. The presence of the second doll allows the child to refer to the scheme of sharing without having to abstract the notion of half of the number 6.

Space prevents us from fully developing the findings of studies by Parrat-Dayan (1980, 1985); it is worth stressing, however, that numerous difficulties related to the material or to the instructions hinder full development of the apparently simple notion of half. Second, the concept of half is at the crossroads of the logical and what Piaget termed the *infralogical,* because it involves both classification and rigorous seriation.

Late Development of the Notion of Half

Studies by Piaget et al. (1948) on fractions showed, in contrast to what is claimed here, that children acquire the notion of half early. What accounts for this difference?

First, Piaget et al. did not focus on the notion of half in the strict sense, but rather on the notion of sharing. Sharing is more precocious, as we saw in the previous section. Giving others their share is relatively simple for children. It is sufficient to set up a one-to-one correspondence between the elements to distribute and the individuals (real or imaginary) to allocate them to. Maurice-Naville (1988) has shown that very young children can set a table properly, even when there are several table settings and glasses for each guest. In our case of six apples, the fact of doling them out to two dolls, as Piaget et al. did, is carrying out iterative one-to-one correspondence between apples and dolls. The overview by Frydman and Bryant (1988) shows that 3-year-olds do extremely well in distributing discontinuous quantities in equal parts by using one-to-one correspondence.

In contrast, asking a child for half of six apples forces him or her to think of the six apples as a totality, such that the union of the parts forms a whole, where the two parts are disjuncted (i.e., with no parts in common) and none of the parts forms an empty class. Clearly the task is not an easy one, even through action. This accounts for the wide variety of behaviors such requests elicit from youngsters.

It is tempting to attribute the difficulties children experience to a simple question of vocabulary. Asking for half of something is apparently ambiguous. It would be highly instructive in this respect to conduct a psycholinguistic study of *half*. It is known that very young children consider half of a bar of chocolate to be some piece—even a tiny one—of the bar. However, it is obvious that this is a question of semantics: The differences observed between children of different ages is related to their understanding of the problem, because the question the experimenter asks is always the same. An alternative explanation for these difficulties is related to the nature of the material. Our own observations indicate that, initially, taking half of a set of elements is more difficult than carrying out this same operation on a continuum. The complexity of the problem of the unit and its division, as revealed by the history of arithmetic (Peet, 1923; Taton, 1957), tends to support this hypothesis. An analysis of the experimental situations we have used (Parrat-Dayan, 1980, 1985) shows that, contrary to expectations, the nature of the material is not the fundamental source of difficulty. This is because, through their actions on the material, children can at times arrive at results that surprise them, and may make them hesitate, depending on their level of comprehension. We have shown that there is age-related heterogeneity in the behavior of children who succeed on these tasks, and that the nature of success differs as well, in that identical behavior can have a different meaning as a function of age.

For purposes of illustration consider the following general instruction: "Give me half of the five apples." The instructions are clear: The experimenter asks the child to give him half of all the apples he or she has in front of him, and makes a gesture encompassing all the apples. Children's responses to these instructions vary considerably. This diversity can be accounted for by different features of the experimental design, aspects that are not always dissociated by the child. Young children (4- to 5-year-olds), when they fail to view the set of five apples as a divisible continuum, do not centrate on the totality but rather on each unit in the totality, which is viewed as a specific whole (or rather an object): The child gives either half of one apple or half of each apple. One source of ambiguity, then, is a lack of sufficient differentiation between the unit and the whole (the set). Because each apple is a whole in itself, the unit is the apple. On the other hand, a child can, in addition, dole out all the apples, and hence, the set of apples. At this point, two referents coexist in an indifferentiated way for the child. First, the apple, seen as a unit, is cut into two halves and each half is evocative of the unit (the apple the halves were obtained from), but there is also a remainder (the four other whole apples, i.e., the rest of the set the apple that was cut in half was taken from), that the child can dole out. Furthermore, if the child cuts each apple, he or she is acting on the set of apples, but this eliminates the whole (the starting set). Suppose, for example, that the child is asked to share the apples between two dolls. He or she will give each doll five apple halves, but what is half of five apples? The same child could waver and state: "half an apple," or "two half apples" (everything that was in one apple is "broken"), or "all the halves of apples" (everything that has been "broken," but that makes a lot of halves). Thus, from one half (one half of an apple) the child moves to half of all the apples and *one* becomes *ones* because the instructions are to give half of all the apples. Reiterating the instructions, "You are not supposed to give all the apples, but to give half," can prompt the child to say or indicate that half of five apples is half an apple (new centration on the apple as a unit) or several apple halves (hence part of the set). In other words, one of the main reasons for ambiguity is the fact that the child does not know what the referent is: the unit (the apple) or the whole (the set).

Another source of ambiguity for young children is the relationship between action and outcome. Depending on what the child is centrating on, there are two possible outcomes: Either the apple halves become "elements," which are doled out, and the half is justified by the equality of the parts (the child gives the "same thing of things" to each of the dolls), or there is a new centration on the unit, where half becomes half an apple, something that is not whole, that is, an incomplete apple. Note, as well, that in all cases, behaviors are linked to the action of cutting, and once the apples have been cut, the outcome of the action orients the child either toward half of an apple or to the equality of the parts. In the latter case half is justified as "the same thing" in apple halves.

Between the ages of 6 and 8, another series of behaviors are observed. These are characterized by sharing of the set. Different types of behaviors can manifest themselves: sharing by symmetrical iteration of the elements and elimination of the apple in the middle; sharing by symmetrical iteration, which leads to two unequal subsets, followed by restoration of equality by adjunction or elimination of an element; sharing by iteration, then adjunction or elimination of an element; elimination or adjunction of an element, then sharing by iteration; or sharing by iteration or separation, yielding two unequal subsets.

These approaches, which avoid units of one-half, eliminate ambiguity. "Half" consists of doling out the whole into two equal parts, and it is "a half" precisely because "they are equal," or in two unequal parts, and it is a half because they form the whole. Or again, when the child has split the whole into two unequal parts, half is the smaller subset. The experimenter can then re-introduce the ambiguity methodologically by proposing a situation where units and half-units appear simultaneously. This situation not only places the child in front of apples that have already been cut, but also gives him the idea of cutting. The ambiguity resurfaces, either in the same form as that found in younger children through confusion between the two referents (the unit and the set), or by the difficulty of splitting different "classes" of elements (whole apples and apples that have been cut). For example, a child asked to dole out four apples (one of which has been cut in half) to two dolls may make mistakes because he or she does not allot elements of the same class to each doll (either whole apples or cut apples). Each doll will get one apple and one half, and the child will leave the remaining whole apple aside. This same child, when asked to split five apples (one of which is cut in half) will naturally reach the right conclusion, whereas we know how difficult it is to find half of an odd number, either when the apples are whole, or when a child who has had the idea to cut each apple in half no longer knows what *half* corresponds to.

Thus, 6- to 8-year-olds are responsive to two types of ambiguity: reference to the whole, like younger children, and the difficulty of splitting elements belonging to different classes.

At about the age of 9, a new source for ambiguity emerges when the child tries to assign a value to the half-unit. Because the child does not differentiate between number and object, he does not know what value to ascribe to the half-unit: one half or one and a half. The confusion between number and object gives rise to another ambiguity in children who cut all the apples and try to consider the whole. Because the whole has been multiplied (by division), each element becomes the half "added on" in relationship to the half "taken away." In the set of rational numbers, where should the whole number 5 be located in terms of double and half? This problem ceases to be a factor of confusion when the child realizes that half of 5 is $2\frac{1}{2}$, because 5 divided by 2 is equal to $2\frac{1}{2}$, or because $2\frac{1}{2}$ plus $2\frac{1}{2}$ is 5.

To conclude, similar behavior can be observed at 5 and at 10. Through a splitting and one-to-one correspondence procedure, children arrive at satisfactory answers: They split each apple in two and distribute the whole in two equal parts, but in both cases conceptual difficulties related to the subject's knowledge base subsist. For a 5-year-old who cuts all the apples in two, half can be half an apple, all the apple halves, or some apple halves, because of confusion between the unit and the whole. For a 10-year-old who proceeds in the same fashion, half is either each apple half (five halves) by lack of coordination of the whole and the unit, or all of the apple halves, through confusion between the number and the unit, between half and double. A 6-year-old may say that half of five apples is four apples, because these can be split and that the remainder is the "token" for the whole (the "whole" one), by juxtaposition of the whole and the part. An older child will speak of four halves (the two halves of four whole apples and the two halves of the fifth apple cut in half) through an effort to coordinate the whole and the unit. Similarly, a young child will find it easy to treat the apples and apple halves as object and will thus dole out the elements of different classes, whereas an older child will be troubled in an analogous situation. Thus, what must be taken into account simultaneously is the nature of the material, the child's action on this material, and the outcome of this action on the cognitive schemes of the child, in addition to the general level of cognitive development of the subject and the interaction between logical and infralogical schemes inherent to all measurement.

Interaction Between Logical and Infralogical Schemes

We must now deal with two new issues: the interaction between logical and infralogical schemes over the course of development as a whole, and the absence of a décalage between conservation—with respect to the half—between discrete (logical) and continuous (infralogical) elements.

Interaction Between Schemes. As we have just seen, logical and infralogical schemes are always present in the notion of half. There is no décalage between the discrete (logical) and the continuous (infralogical) in the ontogenesis of half, in contrast to the advances observed for other notions. These two types of schemes may interact in a dialectical fashion at the outset, in that they can first amalgamate and fuse, and subsequently differentiate. We have shown that this interaction can be an obstacle to the construction of the notion of half as a numerical fraction. The comments made by Piaget in 1921 on the notion of part are particularly appropriate here. Referring to an analysis of children's reactions to collective terms, Piaget wrote:

> There is thus confusion between two schemes, which are distinct for adults, a confusion between a homogeneous collection, like a herd, etc. . . . and in general all collective terms, and an individual object, which can be doled out in pieces like a pebble or a table, rather than as individuals. All collection judgments presuppose, however, that the enumeratibility of the individuals in the collection has been grasped. In other words, these individuals need to be viewed as discrete units. A scheme such as the one the child uses for collective terms (to prevent mental fusion of individuals) . . . seems on the contrary to contain the space occupied by the collection instead of the number. . . . When not forced to make a precise calculation, there is nothing more natural for the child's mind to schematize the collective terms not on the enumerable set but rather as an object that can be split into pieces. This is enough to create confusion, or rather a lack of differentiation between the two schemes mentioned above. (pp. 468–469)

By examining changes in behavior, we have observed that when children are asked to give half of something, they can activate logical or infralogical schemes, regardless of whether the material is of discrete or continuous elements. From this point of view, we agree with Inhelder, Blanchet, Sinclair, and Piaget (1975) that, at the start and over the course of the preoperational period, there is relative undifferentiation of the two systems of schemes,[2] either because one system is based on the other or because they mutually deform each other until their gradual differentiation allows for more fruitful interactions. In this way, we believe that the development of the notion of half is characterized by the gradual transition from initial undifferentiation to progressive differentiation.[3]

In addition, the interaction between these schemes can sometimes give rise to confusions that occur at different points in development. Children confuse the notions of half and middle, for example: The youngest children, when attempting to give half of five apples, give the apple in the middle; the older children, when given the same problem, ask, for example, where to locate the number to be divided up in relationship to the double or to the half. Thus, although the interaction between logical and infralogical schemes can hinder the construction of the notion of half, this hypothesis should be formulated in developmental terms. The difficulty created by associating each part in terms of the unit and each part in terms of the set is coupled with a confusion between logical and infralogical schemes. Nine-year-old Nadine, for example, who responded correctly by giving 1½ apples for half of 3 apples, needed to realign the apples in order to separate (i.e., cut) them with her arm, by saying, "That should make two halves."

Décalages Between Logical and Infralogical Schemes. Analysis of different types of behavior yields the following correspondences between children's behavior on discrete and continuous material, which hold for a given point in development:

Discrete
- construction of two unequal subsets
- construction of two equal subsets with a remainder
- construction of two equal subsets with division of the remainder into halves:
    a. only the apple halves are considered to be halves
    b. the subject states that there are four halves
Continuous
- construction of two unequal parts

---

[2]that is, logico-mathematical operations or preoperations based on similarities and differences between elements; and infralogical operations or preoperations based on nearness or distance between parts of a given element at all scales.

[3]It is worth noting that in the beginnings of geometry there is relative undifferentiation between space and number. "In early geometry, the separation between a concrete object and the rule that determines it is imprecise. . . . The square spatial figure and the square of a number are so tightly linked that they are considered to be equivalent" (Vonèche, 1988, p. 105).

- equalization of two pieces with a remainder
- equalization of the two equal pieces and splitting of the remainder in two:
  a. only the larger part is considered to be a half
  b. the subject states that there are four halves

Construction of the Notion of Half

In this concluding section, we distinguish three problems in the construction of the notion of half: (a) splitting and fractions, (b) conservation and the fraction of the object, and (c) construction of the unit and relational fractions.

Splitting and Fractions. Whereas splitting consists of dividing a whole into two or several parts for purposes of distribution, distribution does not imply splitting as an operation. A 5- and 6-year-old can distribute a number of elements between two or more people (or dolls). He or she will succeed in doling out the elements if there are an equal number of items for each individual, but will not know whether the apples allotted to one doll form half or not. The child who can distribute in this way, however, may not be able to share. If a child can divide the whole into two parts, it is because he or she has the appropriate schemes that permit it. By activating the one-to-one correspondence scheme, the child can distribute the whole into correct halves. However, one-to-one correspondence does not imply the conservation of the whole or even the equality of the shared quantities (Frydman & Bryant, 1988), and as long as there is not conservation, it is impossible to speak of a true sharing operation. Similarly, as long as sharing and fraction-making are not operational, we cannot speak of fractions. The partition of a totality (sharing) and the union of the parts into hierarchized totalities are only possible if there is conservation of the whole. The issue we raise, then, is whether the notion of half (and hence, the notion of fraction) is dependent solely upon notions of conservation.

Conservation and the Fraction of an Object. The notion of half presupposes the coordination of operations of sharing and union. A number of relations are involved: $B = A + A'$, $A + A' = B$, $A = B - A'$, $A' = B - A$, $A = A'$. An operational transformation is always relative to an invariant: "This invariant of a system of transformations constitutes what I have termed up to now a conservation notion or scheme" (Piaget), and further, "Notions of conservation can thus serve as a psychological index for the completion of an operational structure" (Piaget & Inhelder, 1966b, pp. 76–77).

In this framework, it can be assumed that the notion of half is directly dependent on notions of conservation. If the partition operations involved in making fractions are likely to be reversed in carrying out the corresponding operations in the other direction, the conservation of the whole could ensure the notion of half as a fraction: Piaget et al. (1948) remarked in this respect:

> To the extent that operational partition becomes finer (with metric or simply intensive quantification) the conservation of the whole and the equivalence between it and the sum of the sectioned parts gradually becomes emerge as a necessity. (p. 420)

> The notion of fraction arises from elementary correspondence between the parts themselves; this is possible as soon as they are subordinated to the whole. (p. 424)

Nevertheless, our observations show that children who exhibit conservation of the whole (length, elementary number, area) have not necessarily mastered conservation of the *part*, that is, of the *half*. This can be accounted for by the distinction we have made between the *fraction of an object* and the *relational fraction*. The fraction of an object presupposes the coordination of the operations of sharing and union relative to a whole. These operations are, thus, applied locally. In this way, the fraction of an object is driven by the conservation of the whole, because it allows for anticipation on the possible associations between the whole and its parts. However, as we shall see now, the conservation of the whole is not sufficient for understanding the fraction system. The notion of totality needs to be extended to the conservation of the relation independently of each totality. This is what we will term the relational fraction.

The Relational Fraction and the Construction of the Unit. The relational fraction presupposes generalized coordination of the operations of sharing and union. Thus, half of a cookie is not only equal to the other half, but is also, as a half, independent of the size of the cookie. To understand this, it is necessary to relate a dual system of units: the conservation of the relation that each fraction has with its respective unit of reference. Similarly, when a child is asked to find half of five elements (five apples, for example), he or she needs to coordinate the partition into halves of an element with the partition of the set. Thus, two types of behavior can be observed: Either the child cuts the apple into halves and doles out 2½ apples twice, or he or she cuts each apple into halves and doles out 5 apple halves each time. In both cases the totalities must be handled simultaneously (each unit and the set), the fraction part in relationship to the whole and the fraction part in relationship to each unit.

Notions of conservation, restricted to the conservation of an object or a totality, although necessary, cannot ensure comprehension of these relationships. In addition to conservation of the whole, there needs to be conservation of an abstract reference unit that makes comparison of the two relationships possible (in relationship to different totalities). This presupposes the construction of the notion of unit, a change of standpoint, and a coordination of different points of view. We have shown that the notion of unit, which needs to be constructed in the domain of the continuous, is not a given in the domain of the discontinuous either. We have shown that the status of the unit changes as a function of the problem and the child's level of development. This demonstrates, once again, the nonlinearity of development. In this way, the notion of unit, which is constructed in the area of natural numbers by equalization of differences at about the age of 7 or 8, needs to be differentiated in the area of fractions. Consider the behavior of a 10-year-old who has divided the five apples to obtain half; this is characterized by an attempt at relating conservation of the whole and conservation of the part. To do so, the child tries, for example, to make each unit correspond to the two halves obtained, and the two halves with the respective reference unit. This system results in errors during the comparison of the whole (the set taken as a unit) and the half. To correct these errors, it is not only necessary to conserve the totality, but also the operations corresponding to each unit with respect to this totality and to the whole. This is similar to problems of distribution, which are known to be mastered late in development. The presence of a division that modifies both the whole and the parts in numerical proportions involves a dual relationship, which calls for formal operations. This is the framework for our hypothesis that there needs to be generalized conservation for construction of the notion of half as a relational fraction. The child, thus, no longer needs to make a distinction between equivalence classes arrived at through a series of bi-unequivocal congruence, comparison, or folding—correspondence operations elicited by Piaget et al.'s (1948) instructions—but rather needs to establish a relationship where what is conserved is the relationship that the part has with the whole.

The construction of the notion of fraction, therefore, presupposes an evolution from distribution to sharing, from comparison (for example by congruence) to comparativity, from the establishment of local relations to generalized relations, from the fraction of the object to the relational fraction.

CONCLUSION

The topic on which we have reported here has two orientations: the ontogenesis of bipartition and the construction of part–whole relations with discrete and continuous material. These orientations intersect in a variety of ways, as we have seen.

With respect to the ontogenesis of bipartition, we believe we have identified a progression in the domain of the discontinuous that goes from simple distribution (give a piece of something to everyone) to sharing (equal splitting and union of the parts relative to a whole, i.e., sharing operations and union applied locally). In the continuous domain, the progression (when children do not cut off little bits and dole them out) goes from comparison (by congruence) to comparativity (with respect to the whole). In both domains this progression moves from local association to generalized association, from the fraction of the object to the relational fraction. From a psychogenetic standpoint, children first proceed stepwise before generalizing to the purely abstract relationship of the relational fraction.

From the standpoint of the part–whole relationship, we believe we have begun to show its complexity. Restricting this relationship to one of distribution or sharing, or even comparison or comparativity, limits it in both extension and intension. Doing so also creates many artificial, if not artifactual, difficulties in experimentation, such as horizontal and vertical décalages. These contradictions resolve themselves spontaneously when conservation is only considered to be mastered with the emergence of the relational fraction. In doing so we run the risk of challenging the internal logic of cognitive development reported by authors who claim its precocity, its lateness in psychogenesis, or its complexity. If under the pretext of studying skills or actions, notions are simplified and partition is reduced to sharing or distribution, this can lead to even greater simplification. The issue of the conservation of conservation is not purely rhetorical, and the literature on precocity only exists because of the conceptual and methodological fuzziness of this notion.

Moreover, the notion of number itself, if it is reduced to its two dimensions of classification and seriation as single components of the concept, may be disconfirmed experimentally by children who have classification without seriation or the reverse, or number without one of its components or the other. Thus, we need to go beyond simple logic and introduce a network of supplementary concepts such as *eidos,* measurement, and the binary nature of bipartition, which is central to the notion of number.

4 Learning Stages in the Construction of the Number Sequence

Leslie P. Steffe
University of Georgia

To those individuals interested in the construction of mathematics by children, *The Child's Conception of Number* (*La Genèse du Nombre chez l'Enfant*) by Piaget and Szeminska (1941) will always be a classic work in genetic epistemology. The finding that human beings can construct a rational system of numerical operations in early childhood using their conceptual operations and the sensory material that is available to them is even more relevant today than it was in 1941 because of the international search for improvements in the mathematical education of children (Steffe & Wood, 1990). My enthusiasm for this classic work has not waned, but I now view the picture of the child's numerical concepts as painted by Piaget and Szeminska as serving more to help solve the problems in genetic epistemology than those in mathematics education. This is no criticism because any model of the knowledge of the child is formulated to meet certain goals of the investigators. However, after working for a period of ten years within the framework of Piagetian stage theory to understand how it might be used to foster mathematics education of children (e.g., Steffe, Hirstein, & Spikes, 1976), I developed an internal necessity to formulate a model of the child's conception of number that would be compatible with the Piagetian model, but would also account for experiential phenomena that seemed to be inexplicable within that model.

When teaching 6- and 7-year-old children in teaching experiments,[1] it became evident to me that the counting scheme was one of their fundamental numerical

---

[1]The term *teaching experiment* does not mean an investigation of teaching a predetermined or accepted way of operating. Instead, it is primarily an exploratory tool, derived from Piaget's clinical interview but aimed at investigating children's constructive processes (Cobb & Steffe, 1983).

schemes. In some cases, it was a manifestation of a number sequence, and in other cases it was a sensorimotor or figurative scheme. The nature of the counting scheme varied widely within a particular child over time as well as across children of the same age. Having established regularity in this variability, I isolated five learning stages[2] in the construction of the number sequence: the perceptual counting scheme, the figurative counting scheme, the initial number sequence, the tacitly nested number sequence, and the explicitly nested number sequence. These learning stages are distinguished by the assimilatory operations that are available to the child prior to counting and were established following the initial work in the project Interdisciplinary Research on Number (IRON; Steffe et al., 1983).[3]

The learning stages can be characterized by a progressive decrease in children's dependence on their immediate experiential world when creating countable items. In the stage of the *figurative counting scheme,* children can count perceptual unit items that are not in their range of perception or action by creating substitute countable items during counting that were implicit in the counting acts of the preceding stage. Willfully creating such substitute countable items is a step away from the child's immediate experiential world. The next step occurs when the child constructs the *initial number sequence.* Number words in that stage symbolize the operations used in creating and counting countable items. It is no longer necessary for the child to believe that there are perceptual items of any kind available to count, as the symbolized operations can be used in the creation of figurative representatives of countable items at the level of interiorization; in the preceding learning stage of the *figurative counting scheme,* the child could create figurative representatives of countable items only at the level of internalization. The operations symbolized by the lexical items of the *tacitly nested number sequence* can be used to remove children even further from their experiential world because number words here symbolize the operations involved in making a unit of units. These operations are a step toward the construction of part-to-whole operations, operations that are completed by the construction of the *explicitly nested number sequence.*

THE PERCEPTUAL AND FIGURATIVE COUNTING SCHEMES

Piaget (1937) provided a powerful model for the complex process that results in the child's conception of objects as internalized, permanent entities that are considered to have an existence of their own in space and time independent of the

---

[2]A learning stage of a scheme is taken to be the result of an accommodation of a particular kind. For the result to be a stage, four criteria must be satisfied (see Steffe & Cobb, 1988, p. 7ff).

[3]Without the contributions of my colleagues, the model of children's construction of the number sequence summarized in this chapter would have been more descriptive than explanatory.

experiencing subject. In our model (cf. von Glasersfeld, 1981), these object concepts emerge as the result of unitizing operations of the subject. The child compounds (unitizes) co-occurring sensorimotor signals in the stream of experience into experiential objects. These experiential objects occur in the immediate here-and-now, and there may be no element of recognition in their establishment. However, if the child recognizes an experiential object as having been experienced before, this is an operation of assimilation that involves activation of the records of operating that produced the previous experiential object. Because these records are activated, the child focuses on the sensory material that the activated records point to in immediate experience and compounds this sensory material together using the unitizing operation. This act of abstraction is a step in the creation of an object concept as Piaget described it, in that it creates a more or less stable unitary item.

Still another act of abstraction is involved in the child eventually being able to imagine an experiential object in the absence of the relevant sensorimotor signals, which is what we mean by the conception of an object as an internalized permanent object; this act of abstraction involves a review of more than one experiential item. Let us say, for example, that a child recognizes a perceptual situation as an instantiation of the unitary item he or she has associated with what an adult would call *cup*. The child may continue to explore his or her visual field, assimilating another combination of sensory signals, and then another. The result of this activity can be three separated, individual experiential items. If the child "steps back" and successively applies the same unitary item[4] to each experiential item that was used in its establishment, this is an act of categorization that introduces repetition into the unitary item and an awareness of using the unitary item more than once. It is also an act of abstraction in that it "strips" the sensorimotor items of sensory qualities and creates a *template* (an abstracted unitary item) containing records of experiential discreteness. That is, the child views the reprocessed items from the point of view of their unitariness and creates a sequence of *perceptual unit items*. Using the template is still dependent on some experiential situation, but the child has made progress because he or she can now establish *pluralities* and collections of perceptual unit items in its experiential field.

A plurality is formed by the repeated use of a template, because this use creates a sequence of perceptual unit items. When the process that generates a plurality terminates, the beginning and end of the process may constitute boundaries of the plurality. The experiential items may also be a part of a broader experiential field that forms a boundary, like the houses on the hill. In either case, the experientially bounded items form a collection of perceptual unit items. Repeatedly using a template in an experiential situation is sufficient to isolate a property of the resulting collection that has been introduced by the repeated use

---

[4]Applying a unitary item means using the activated unitizing operation that was used in establishing the unitary item.

of the template: an awareness of repetition or of more than one perceptual unit item. I would not call this awareness a sense of number; rather, it is an awareness of plurality.

Although I am not certain of all the processes involved in establishing the ability to recreate an experience of an object in its immediate absence—a re-presentation of the object—the categorizing act of reprocessing the items of a collection must be involved. The experience of reprocessing distances the child from the reprocessed collection because an awareness of more than one perceptual unit item is created. Having just been used in categorization, the template is in a state of activation. There is at least an incipient visualization of the common sensory material used in categorization because what the activated records point to is also in a state of having just been used more than once in the immediate past. This would seem at least to initiate the internalization[5] of the template, but it may not complete it.

Whatever the process is that is involved in internalization, we can describe its results (cf. Steffe et al., 1983, pp. 50–54). The child's template must come to serve in the creation of a *figurative representative* that replicates certain sensory characteristics, as well as the discrete oneness, on the level of imaginary experience. The figurative representative becomes an item of awareness and serves as a substitute for the original perceptual unit item. When the child can use the template to create more than one figurative representative without the relevant sensory signals being immediately available, this produces a figurative plurality. If an experiential context bounds the process, the conceptual structure that is created is called a *collection of figurative unit items,* or a *figurative collection.* An awareness of figurative plurality is an awareness of more than one figurative unit item; it is a property that is introduced by the acting subject as a result of repeatedly using a template in re-presentation.

Counting as a Perceptual Scheme

The Components of Counting.   The operations that produce collections of perceptual unit items are the assimilating operations of a perceptual counting scheme. As a perceptual scheme, counting is a complex consisting of three component activities. The first is the ability to produce a perceptual collection of units that can be counted; the second is the ability, vocally and later subvocally, to produce a sequence of number words; and the third is the ability to coordinate the first two productive activities so that they accompany each other in such a way that each vocal production experientially corresponds to the production of a

---

[5]Internalization is the process that results either in the ability to re-present a sensory item without the relevant sensory signals being available in actual perception or in the ability to re-enact a motor activity without the presence of the kinesthetic signals from actual physical movement. It leads to visualization in all sensory modalities.

unit item. The first component of counting is the first part of a perceptual counting scheme and the third component, the activity of counting, is the second part. An awareness of plurality drives counting activity: The goal is to make what is indefinite definite. It is this definite awareness of a bounded plurality of counted unit items that constitutes the results of counting perceptual unit items, the third part of the perceptual counting scheme.

Two 6-year-old children whose counting schemes were classified as being perceptual in October of first grade remained as counters of perceptual unit items for at least 6 more months. A third 6-year-old child, whose counting scheme was found to be perceptual in March of first grade remained in that learning stage until the end of the school year (cf. Steffe & Cobb, 1988, pp. 22–47). These children had no object concepts associated with their number words except for *one, two, three,* and possibly *four,* and their number words referred to the transitory experience of counting collections. The activity of counting was not a meaning of number words, but it served in creating an experiential meaning: *a proto-numerosity.*

Patterns. There are experiential roots of numerosity that do not involve counting. First, there are the arrangements of dots or other discrete items that form the "twos," "threes," "fours," and so on, on dice or dominoes. They are stable geometric patterns that are readily recognized as items whose names are number words. Furthermore, there is another type of pattern that is usually overlooked in discussions of the patterns children normally connect with number words: finger patterns. Finger patterns are neither purely spatial nor purely motor, as children usually put up fingers simultaneously to form finger patterns. In this sense, the finger patterns are motor programs whose result can appear in the visual (or tactile) field of the child. There are also certain sequences of experiential events—visual, tactual, auditory, or kinesthetic—that are perceived, recorded, and recognized as temporal patterns, like the chimes of a clock. Because temporal patterns consist of a sequence of discrete "beats"—rarely more than three or four—they may, like spatial patterns, be associated with number words. The association, however, does not mean that if a child recognizes a pattern by saying a number word, the child makes the pattern into a numerical pattern.

Patterns of all three types can be associated, *qua* patterns, with names that are number words without counting (cf. von Glasersfeld, 1982). The child who is in the stage of the perceptual counting scheme can establish (or re-establish) connections between patterns of discrete elements and number words by first establishing the pattern as a collection of perceptual unit items. If the child counts these perceptual unit items, say, one, two, three, connecting the specified collection with the last number word said is an act of pseudo-empirical abstraction (Piaget, 1980, p. 92) because the child abstracts a property of the pattern—a proto-numerosity—introduced by counting. The counted pattern provides an opportunity for the child to isolate a proto-numerosity because the elements of the pattern seem to co-occur as a unitary but composite entity. The pattern provides an "object" for reflection and abstraction without which counting would not be curtailed.

If a child isolates a pattern in his or her visual field on some future occasion, the assimilation could lead the child to utter the number word previously connected to the pattern without any intervening counting activity. All of this can occur without the child being able to re-create an experience of the pattern in the absence of the relevant sensory signals. In this case, the pattern the child has established to give meaning to the involved number word is analogous to the templates the child established earlier on in childhood before transforming them into object concepts.

Transition to the Figurative Counting Scheme.   The child makes two major advancements when he or she achieves the learning stage of the figurative counting scheme. First, the items of figurative collections are established as countable items. What this means is that the child's counting scheme can be activated when the items to be counted are not in the child's range of action or perception. The second major advance is that the child can create sensory items to count in the activity of counting that serve as substitutes for the figurative unit items that are only imagined. The figurative unit items are countable, but the child still needs to create experiential unit items to count.

Lack of Figurative Collections

Creating figurative collections is much more difficult for some children than adults might suspect. These children may have constructed object concepts, but they are yet to use them to create figurative collections. Although they might know that there are, say, cookies in a cookie jar because they can imagine what a cookie might look like, they might not have an awareness of a figurative plurality of cookies because they do not use their cookie template to "run through" a production of more than one cookie.

My experience with these children is that they can use finger patterns to create a figurative collection of countable items (cf. Steffe & Cobb, 1988, pp. 98–147). For example, a child might be asked to determine how many perceptual items were placed in two separate locations after the items have been screened from view, one of four items and the other of three. A child who cannot produce figurative collections would not be able to count in this situation. However, in the case where the two number words that refer to the screened items also refer to finger patterns, the child might introduce a novelty in a search for perceptual unit items to count. Because *four* and *three* are connected to counted finger patterns, the child might activate the respective finger patterns, which in turn might activate the curtailed counting activity. In my experience, this can lead to the finger patterns being internalized and becoming object concepts associated with number words.

The change in status of the finger patterns from perceptual to internalized finger patterns is indicated when the child sequentially puts up fingers to complete the finger patterns synchronous with uttering number words. That is, the child might utter "one, two, three, four (pause) five, six, seven" synchronous with putting up four fingers on one hand and then three fingers on the other. This is quite distinct from a child simultaneously putting up four fingers and then three fingers as *replacements* for the hidden items, and then taking the fingers as a collection of perceptual unit items for counting. This latter coordination of finger patterns and the counting scheme is within the province of children with perceptual counting schemes.

Creating finger patterns as object concepts for number words opens up a path for these children eventually to transform their counting schemes into a figurative scheme, but this is not an immediate achievement, because for a counting scheme to be truly figurative, both the activity of the scheme and the items that are to be counted must be internalized. The path that is opened up includes the child creating a figurative plurality of fingers and an awareness of such a plurality concomitant with creating finger movements as countable items in the activity of counting. These two achievements, especially the first, encourage the production of figurative pluralities other than fingers and the establishment of finger movements as substitutes for the elements of these more general figurative pluralities.

Lack of Internalized Counting Acts

Some children with perceptual counting schemes can produce figurative collections, but their counting scheme remains perceptual because they cannot independently create countable items in the activity of counting that are substitutes for the figurative representatives they intend to count. For example, a child was shown a row of 12 checkers where the first 7 were screened from view. The child was told that there were 12 checkers in the row and was requested to find how many were covered. She first counted the visible checkers, subvocally uttering "one, two, three, four, five" and continued "six, seven, eight, nine, ten, eleven" while synchronously fixing her gaze on and pointing to successive locations on the cover under which she thought checkers might be hidden. She stopped fortuitously when reaching the end of the cover and said that 10 were covered. What she counted was what she intended to count because it was as if she was trying to look through the cover to see the checkers.

For this child, counting figural unit items was context-dependent, and there was no novelty involved from her point of view because she simply continued counting checkers. She did not create substitute countable unit items of a different kind than checkers. However, from my point of view, what she was counting did constitute a novelty because she counted figural representatives of the checkers rather than the checkers. This opens a path to isolating the involved pointing acts, first as experiential items and, second as substitutes for the figural representatives.

It also opens up one of several paths for the internalization of the sequence of involved counting acts because the pointing acts co-occur with the production of number words, and both co-occur with the production of a figural unit item. What this means is that the sensory material generated in the counting acts can feed into the activated template used in re-presentation and be recorded as a new but constitutive part of the object concept, changing it from a "checker" template to a "counted checker" template.

Other possibilities for internalization of counting acts have also been observed (Steffe et al., 1983, p. 52). Because counted spatial patterns are object concepts for children, they can be used as substitute figural collections in a counting context. For example, when counting a partially covered collection of seven checkers, a child was told that there were three covered. She placed the tips of three fingers on the cover but did not count them, and then counted the visible checkers "four, five, six, seven." Counting the three checkers had been curtailed, but in a different sense than explained before because that explanation only dealt with patterns that could not be re-presented. Here, we see a finger pattern for three being used as a surrogate spatial pattern and as an object concept for three. Because the child simply uttered "four, five, six, seven" in counting the visible checkers, we see that the counting acts corresponding to "one, two, three" were embodied in the finger pattern and had thereby been internalized.

The Figurative Counting Scheme

Internalized finger patterns are not universal among children who are in the perceptual stage and cannot be used to explain the process of internalization of counting acts in all cases. For example, a child who had not developed finger patterns except for the words *two* and *ten* counted in such a way that solidly indicated internalized counting acts (Steffe, in press). When counting a collection of felt squares hidden by two covers, one covering six and the other five, the child sequentially moved fingers on his left hand, moving his index finger twice, as he synchronously uttered, "1, 2, 3, 4, 5, 6." He then continued moving his middle finger and ring finger on his left hand—"7, 8"—then his index finger and middle finger—"9, 10"—then no fingers—"11, 12."

Given that the child had no finger pattern for *six,* the interpretation of the first part of his counting episode becomes interesting. Did he have an object concept associated with *six* other than a finger pattern, or is there another way to explain his behavior? My choice, for reasons to be explained later, is to attribute an awareness of a figurative plurality of squares to him and an intention to count them. Given that he wanted to count, a lack of perceptual material (i.e., squares) to make countable items could leave him in a state of activation, searching for something to count. It seems reasonable that he would "call up" records of his past counting acts if *six* referred to counting the squares. That the child was successful in counting to "six" indicates that at least the auditory records of his past counting acts were internalized and could be re-presented in the absence of actual sensorimotor material.

The *image of a number word sequence* refers to a more-or-less permanent record of the kinesthetic or auditory aspect of saying the number words in the standard order (Steffe et al., 1983, p. 26). When these records can be used in re-presentation, the number word sequence is internalized. This can occur independently of counting figural unit items. In the case where the number word sequence is internalized, counting figural unit items could lead to rapid progress because the sensory material generated in counting could feed into the activated sound images of number words (de Saussure, 1959). As a result, creating a figurative collection could activate an internalized number word sequence and, conversely, activating the image of an internalized number word sequence could signify counting figurative unit items.

Before the child counted to six, I assume his counting scheme was in a state of activation, but he had no squares in his visual field to count. If the child's internalized image of his number word sequence was activated, this would signify the sensorimotor items of moving fingers as countable items. I assume that *six* was a source of activation of the internalized number word sequence. However, more than the number word was involved in activation, because the child tried to continue to count five more times beyond *six* and *five* could not possibly activate saying, "7, 8, 9, 10, 11, 12" for this particular child because the child had no object concept for *five*. The figurative collection had to signify counting, and this was the result of past counting experiences like those explained for counting figurative unit items.

I can see no reason to believe that the child needed an object concept of *six* in order to count as he did, and it was not a necessary part of my explanation. I already mentioned that he had no object concept he could use to monitor counting five more times beyond counting to *six,* so there is no reason to believe that he had constructed an object concept for *six.* I do believe that *six* referred to a figurative plurality, but there was no necessity that he "see" six individual figurative unit items that appeared to him to co-occur in some pattern. Nevertheless, it was essential for the figurative collection to signify counting for the search of something to count to be completed and for counting to be successfully actualized to create an experiential meaning for *six*. The explanation of counting to *six* is what I mean by a counter of motor unit items.

We have to wonder why the child continued on counting beyond *six;* why didn't he simply start counting all over again with *one?* My explanation is based on what the child intended to count: the hidden squares. Being aware of a figurative collection of squares that were experientially separated by two cloths was sufficient to propel him on counting after reaching *six*. The number word *five* served as a goal for when to stop counting. He attempted to keep track of counting five more times by using his two-pattern, but he critically failed to monitor the use of this pattern.

THE INITIAL NUMBER SEQUENCE

It is interesting to speculate on whether the child's awareness of a figurative plurality in the counting episode just described was indicative of a number sequence. In other words, should the results of counting to *six* be interpreted as an instantiation of a numerical concept of "six"? A counterargument has been presented, but this is certainly a possible interpretation, and I can imagine someone making it because there was a time when I interpreted equivalent counting behavior in that way (Steffe, Richards, & von Glasersfeld, 1979). Since that time, I have become aware of a more essential criterion for imputing numerical concepts to a child. Had the child monitored his continuation of counting, creating a concept for "five" on the spot, then I would be willing to attribute to him the execution of the operations that are necessary to make numbers: the operations of re-presentation and unitizing.

Monitoring a Continuation of Counting

What monitoring might consist of was illustrated by a child with a figurative counting scheme who counted a collection of items covered by two cloths, one covering seven and the other five items, in the following way (Steffe, 1991): He touched the first cloth seven times synchronous with subvocally uttering "1, 2, 3, 4, 5, 6, 7" and then proceeded by touching the second cloth six times in a row while whispering "8, 9, 10, 11, 12, 13." As a result of touching the second cloth, he had an awareness of plurality, but he realized he had not made it definite; he had not reached his goal. So, he independently started over from *one*. In the midst of touching the second cloth again, he lost track, so he started over once again. This time he deliberately touched the second cloth five times in a row and then looked at me and said "13, 14," indicating that he still was not sure that he had touched the second cloth five times. After he uttered "13, 14," I asked him how many there were hidden under the second cloth; he said, "5," and proceeded to count one more time. This time he stopped at 12 with conviction, and while continuing to count past 7, he stared into space while touching the cloth synchronous with uttering number words.

The act of simply recognizing a row of five dots does not require an intentional monitoring of the activity that produces the pattern. When the child was producing a pattern consisting of the records of his points of contact of his finger on the second cloth, he had to establish what pattern he produced after each touch because there were no visible traces. The explanations offered up to this point concerning the internalized counting scheme are not sufficient to explain this child's monitoring behavior, because he independently reinitialized counting after producing an ambiguity and he created a pattern for "five" in the activity of counting. Either of these aspects of the counting episode is not possible for children who have only constructed the figurative counting scheme.

To monitor counting activity intentionally in the way described, there has to be a re-presentation of the results of counting. That is, after saying, "8, 9," and making two pointing acts, the child must have re-presented these counted items and "held them at a distance" while reflecting on them, but distancing oneself from the figurative pattern requires an operation not provided by re-presentation. The child must "run through" or reprocess the items of the figurative pattern using the unitizing operation. This operation strips the figurative unit items of their sensorimotor quality and creates a pair of abstract unit items that contain the records of the counting acts. It begins the process of *interiorization* of the internalized counting acts. The concept the child finally created for "five" was a numerical pattern that contained the records of counting: "8, 9, 10, 11, 12."

Monitoring as Feedback.   An internalized counting act is a template containing the records of a perceptual counting act that can be used in re-presentation. An interiorized counting act is an abstract unit item that contains the records of an internalized counting act. It, too, can be re-presented by re-presenting what the records point to, but on a higher level than the internalized level. Application of the unitizing operation to the re-presentation of the internalized counting acts "eight, nine" *disembedded* them from the rest of the internalized sequence of counting acts and recorded them at the level of interiorization. This disembedding operation made it possible for the child to take the two counted items— "eight, nine"—and reconstitute them as being a part of the items that he was counting: the countable items. In other words, the counted items, or the result of using the counting scheme, fed back into the countable items, or the first part of the scheme. This feedback system is what I mean by monitoring counting, in this case.

Autoregulation of Feedback.   We should not expect one or two disembedding operations executed in experiential contexts to complete the interiorization of the internalized counting scheme, if for no other reason than that interiorized records can decay. But more importantly, it would be implausible that monitoring counting in experiential contexts would be sufficient to explain how the child just described reorganized his counting scheme.

This monitoring activity occurred on October 15 of the child's first year in school; by January 8 of the same school year he could use his counting scheme as follows: A partially hidden collection of squares were in the child's visual field. He was told that there were 16 squares in the collection and was requested to find how many were hidden (9 were visible). He counted the 9 visible square and then estimated that 8 would be hidden "because 9 and 8 make 16." In justification of his estimate, he counted up to "16" from "9" and said, "7."

I had never observed him use counting-up-to prior to winter vacation. Up to that point, he simply could not solve my "missing items" situations. Rather, he reorganized his counting scheme over the holidays, when it was very unlikely that he solved anyone's missing items situation. I certainly had not modeled counting-up-to for him and his independently reorganized counting scheme was truly a novelty. It would not be too much to say that his counting scheme had undergone a metamorphosis over the holidays because he also independently counted-off-from to solve what an adult would call subtraction situations (cf. Steffe & Cobb, 1988, p. 71).

To explain the metamorphosis, I hypothesize that a disturbance was created by having part of his internalized sequence of counting acts interiorized while the rest of it was only internalized. It existed on two levels. I further hypothesize that this perturbation was neutralized by autoregulation of the monitoring activity that was set in motion in experiential situations. The only assumption I make about this process is that the unitizing operation was applied enough times to neutralize the perturbation. Although autoregulation might terminate before the interiorization process is completed, in the case of completion, a sequence of abstract unit items is constructed that contain records of counting: the initial number sequence.

The Counting Scheme as a Numerical Concept.   When the interiorized records of counting are used in re-presentation, a verbal number sequence can be produced. A lexical item of a verbal number sequence symbolizes an initial segment from *one* up to and including the lexical item. These symbolized segments, in turn, symbolize sequences of abstract unit items as well as the activity and results of counting: numerosities.

A symbolized segment of the initial number sequence should be thought of as an elaborated numerical pattern. To use it means to instantiate the records that compose it, or more simply, to count. When counting, the child is aware of the counting acts between the beginning and the end of counting. After counting, the child is aware of what is inside the boundaries of the counted items, but the counted items are not taken as one thing even though counting is a connected activity for the child. A lexical item of the verbal number sequence symbolizes these operations and activities, and refers to the individual lexical items up to and including the given lexical item. It does not, however, refer to a unit containing these lexical items.

An *extensive meaning* (an object concept) of a lexical item is provided by its initial segment of the verbal number sequence and an *intensive meaning* is provided by the symbolized counting acts (Thompson, 1982). Because of the symbolizing function of the words of a verbal number sequence, the meaning of such a word can be said to be *an intention to act* (Van Engen, 1949), and the possibility of acting provides a dynamic quality to the child's numerical concepts. It provides a source of confidence on the part of children that they can act to solve a variety of numerical situations, a source of confidence that is often actively discouraged when adults stress visual patterns in work with number (cf. Easley, 1983). Both counting and patterns are crucial material of operation in the construction of the initial number sequence by children, and for adults to stress one at the expense of the other can only delay this important construction.

When a child uses the initial number sequence in assimilation, the results are easy to observe. Consider, for example, the following task:

> There are seven marbles in this cup (rattling marbles in the cup). Here are four more marbles (placing four marbles in another cup). How many marbles are there in all?

If the child says there are 7 in the cup, and proceeds to count on "8, 9, 10, 11— 11!," this suggests that in uttering *seven* the child knows that the number word stands for a collection of perceptual unit items that satisfy the "template" called "marble" and that, if counted, they would be coordinated with the number words from *one* to *seven*. The child knows this and therefore does not have to run through the counting activity that is implied.

The operations available to the child are symbolized and are not necessarily carried out in assimilation, but the child can very well create a figurative collection of marbles and then reprocess this figurative collection using the unitizing operation, creating a sequence of abstract unit items and an awareness of more than one abstract unit item: an *awareness of numerosity*. This also creates an interiorized concept of marbles and is why I used quotes above when referring to the child's template called "marble." This sequence of abstract unit items has been called *arithmetic lot* by von Glasersfeld (1981). Whatever it is called, it differs in nature from a figurative collection in that it is an *interiorized figurative collection*. The child still establishes perceptual and figurative collections, but these collections can now symbolize the abstract unit items that the child is capable of creating.

TACITLY AND EXPLICITLY NESTED NUMBER SEQUENCES

Two further number sequences have been observed in children's itinerary of constructive activity: tacitly and explicitly nested number sequences (cf. Steffe & Cobb, 1988, pp. 284ff). The principal advancement in the tacitly nested number sequence is that a number word now symbolizes the operations used to take an initial segment of its verbal number sequence as a unit. *Seven,* for example, refers to the verbal number sequence from *one* up to and including *seven* as constituent unit items of a composite unit. The ability to create units of units is a crucial step in the construction of whole numbers and is a step toward the construction of an inclusion relation for numbers. As a unit of units, *seven* can be distinguished in, say, *nine* but the child is yet to disembed *seven* from *nine* and treat it as a number separate from *nine* while leaving it *in nine*. In other words, the child is yet to take *seven* as a number apart from other numbers in which it is included while simultaneously viewing it as being in those other numbers. The construction of an inclusion relation for numbers involves another use of the disembedding operation and a reorganization of the tacitly nested number sequence. When a child becomes aware of part–whole numerical relations, I call the child's number sequence explicitly nested because now a lexical item of the sequence, say *seven,* refers to a unit that can be iterated seven times as well as to a unit containing the verbal number sequence up to and including seven.

SUMMARY

An itinerary for the child's construction of the number sequence has been isolated that includes the child's counting scheme and patterns as necessary components. The constructive process is portrayed as starting with the child's object concepts and the pluralities and collections the child can make using these object concepts, and culminating in the iterable unit of one that is characteristic of the explicitly nested number sequence. The child's number sequence begins as a perceptual counting scheme and then is constructed as a figurative counting scheme as a result of the process of internalization of the object concepts and of the activity of counting. From here, the child constructs an initial number sequence as a result of the process of interiorization of the object concepts and the activity of counting. Re-interiorization yields the tacitly nested and then the explicitly nested number sequence.

The unitizing operation is the critical operation that produces the items of experience, including numbers. Alone, however, it is insufficient to produce number sequences. Using the unitizing operation to re-process the products of past operating is necessary, but it is insufficient because, for the child to make progress from the perceptual to the figurative counting scheme, the pluralities and collections that were established in experience must be re-presented and then used as the situations of counting. When the items of these collections occur in patterns, internalization can be facilitated.

The internalized counting scheme prepares the way for the construction of the initial number sequence. When that monumental event occurs, the child creates a feedback system between the results of counting and the situations of counting by reprocessing re-presentations of the results of counting. Patterns play a crucial role because the items of re-presented sequences of counting acts that occur in patterns appear to co-occur in experience and thereby can be reprocessed and taken as countable items. If the feedback system that initiates the process of interiorization is sustained by autoregulation, a metamorphosis of the counting scheme can occur, and the initial number sequence can be produced. The initial number sequence is the first interiorized counting scheme, but it is unstable due to its incompleteness. Occasions arise in its use for the child to disembed part of the sequence from the sequence and re-interiorize the elements of these parts. This process eventually leads to the production of the tacitly nested number sequence. Another re-interiorization can follows that produces the explicitly nested number sequence and an iterable unit of one.

DISCUSSION

Each learning stage has its own inadequacies that lead to further constructions. One of the most important of these is the possibility of composite units becoming countable in the stage of the explicitly nested number sequence. This can lead in various directions, one being the construction of a generalized number sequence and another being the decimal system of numeration for whole numbers.

Mathematics teaching in the early years of schooling essentially ignores children's number sequences and the further constructions they make possible, and proceeds as if there were no rational systems of numerical operations available to children. The reasons for this rejection, other than a lack of awareness, are at least two-fold. The first is the belief that educational experiences provided by the mathematics programs of the schools are the major determiners of children's progress in mathematics. The second, related, reason is the belief that mathematical experiences are essentially the same for all individuals. With regard to the first, the IRON model does not deny the crucial role played by experience in cognitive constructions, just as the seminal work of Piaget and Szeminska (1941) did not deny the necessity of experience. Quite the contrary, children's mathematical experiences are taken to be the results (or possible results) of operating in environments and, as such, are essential in their mathematical progress, but these experiences cannot possibly be determined by the mathematics programs of the schools. No longer can we take the mathematical experiences of two human beings as being essentially the same even though they might appear to an observer to be using the same scheme. Max Born (1965) put it quite succinctly when he said, "It dawned on me that fundamentally everything is subjective, everything without exception. That was a shock" (p. 162). A shift to focusing on the mathematics of children as it is constructed in learning environments is needed in mathematics education, where the learning environments are established as a result of interactive communication in consensual domains of experience.

The differences between the IRON model and the Genevan model of the child's construction of number do not reside in epistemological differences.

Rather, the differences reside in the specific operations used in the creation of the models as well as the purposes for which they were created. For example, Piaget (1970a) characterized the concept of a unit by a negative description: "Elements are stripped of their qualities and become arithmetical unities" (p. 37). This might indicate what has to be done, but Piaget and Szeminska essentially took the construction of the arithmetical unity for granted. I have posited a unitizing operation as a mechanism of construction and have shown how this mechanism is the basis for the construction of unitary items of all kinds.

5

The Development of Preschoolers' Counting Skills and Principles

Arthur J. Baroody
University of Illinois at Urbana-Champaign

Researchers have taken dramatically different positions on preschoolers' mathematical competence. Earlier in this century, psychologists portrayed young children's knowledge in terms of its deficiencies: what preschoolers cannot do. Some even implied that before the "age of reason," children are mathematically incapable. For example, E. L. Thorndike (1922), the famous association theorist, concluded: "It seems probable that little is gained by using any of the child's time for arithmetic before grade 2, though there are many arithmetic facts that can be learned in grade 1" (p. 198). Later, Piaget's (1941/1952a) theory of cognitive development reinforced this judgment of the young child as mathematically incapable. More specifically, his theory proposed that preoperational children could not understand number or arithmetic, because they had not developed the prerequisite logical structures.

More recently, a number of psychologists have noted the limitations of such a perspective (Briars & Siegler, 1984). For example, Gelman and Gallistel (1978) contended that an accurate picture of early mathematical knowledge requires an examination of preschoolers' capabilities: what they *can* do. Indeed, there is now a considerable amount of empirical evidence that suggests children just beginning school have many mathematical strengths (see Baroody, 1987b; Fuson, 1988; Gelman, 1982b; Ginsburg, 1982; Hiebert, 1986; Resnick & Ford, 1981). However, in reacting to views that underestimate young children's mathematical knowledge, perhaps some researchers have overestimated the quality of early mathematical knowledge (cf. Siegler, 1979).

This chapter focuses on a key aspect of preschoolers' mathematics: the development of counting skills and principles. More specifically, it examines the developmental relationship between counting procedures and understanding.

Some researchers (e.g., Briars & Siegler, 1984) have proposed a skills-first position. In this view, the development of skills is *not* principle-driven: Counting procedures are acquired without an understanding of their underlying rationale. In contrast, Gelman (Gelman & Baillargeon, 1983; Gelman & Gallistel, 1978; Gelman & Meck, 1983, this volume) proposed a some-principles-first model. In this view, the development of counting skills is principle-driven: The construction of counting skills is "directed by the implicit knowledge of some counting principles" (Gelman & Meck, 1986, p. 29). In reality, the development of counting may be more intricate than either of these two views suggest. A mutual-development view (Baroody & Ginsburg, 1986; Fuson, 1988) suggests that the development of counting principles and skills is intertwined. This chapter begins with a summary of these three views, then evaluates some of the research supporting the some-principles-first and the mutual-development perspectives, and ends with some conclusions about the evidence for these views and the issue of counting principles.

THREE MODELS OF COUNTING

Skills-First View

According to the skills-first position, the development of counting skills precedes principled understanding of counting. Gelman and Cohen (1988) noted that this position is based on the association theory of British Empiricists. In this view, counting skills are learned by rote through imitation, practice, and reinforcement. This means skills are learned piecemeal. For example, children essentially must learn a different procedure for each counting context: one procedure for objects in a linear array, another for objects in a circular array, and so forth. "Once they have learned many such routines, children eventually generalize over all these routines, abstracting out what all have in common—namely, the counting principles. Only after this has happened do children have principled knowledge" (Wynn, 1990, p. 158).

Children's variable performance within and across counting tasks (see Fuson, 1988; Fuson & Hall, 1983) is consistent with the skills-first position. In this view, the inconsistent use of a skill on a particular task is due to a weak habit, and the use of a skill in only limited situations is attributable to a task-specific habit and a lack of understanding. As children strengthen their habits and induce counting principles, both the consistency and the generalization of skills improve.

Some-Principles-First View

Gelman and Meck (this volume) grant infants a skeletal set of counting principles, which guide interaction with the environment and the development of counting skills. In their view, the development of counting within the preschool period involves "the perfection of [counting] procedures rather than the emergence of new or firmer principles" (Gelman & Meck, 1983, p. 352). They caution that children will not exhibit perfect skill or understanding, because they must learn how and when to apply the skeletal counting principles.[1]

The Skeletal Counting Principles.   Gelman and Gallistel (1978) adduced three how-to-count principles (procedural rules for counting) and two permissibility principles (statements concerning what can be counted and how items can be counted):

1. The *stable-order principle* decrees that count tags must be generated in the same sequence on every count.
2. The *one-to-one principle* specifies that every item in a collection must be marked with one and only one unique tag.
3. The *cardinality principle* dictates that the tag used to mark the last item in a collection represents the total number of items in the collection.
4. The *abstraction principle* states that various kinds of items may be collected together for the purpose of counting.
5. The *order-irrelevance principle* specifies that the items of a collection can be marked in any order and, as long as the one-to-one principle is observed, the outcome (the last tag) will be the same.

It is important to note that count tags need not be number words or even verbal. Gelman and Gallistel (1978) pointed out that a number of languages have used the alphabet as tags. They also suggested that a set of unique mental markers of some type might be used by preverbal children and some animals to determine numerosities. Thus, the counting principles just described apply to any counting system, whether it involves number words (what we commonly think of as counting) or other types of tags (e.g., the electronic-based counting of a computer).

It is the five principles just described or some subset of these principles that Gelman and Meck (1986) proposed as children's initial or *skeletal* conceptual competence—the understandings that children bring to the task of acquiring

---

[1]Gelman and Meck (this volume) noted that they are rational-constructivists and that their some-principles-first model does not imply infants have a fully developed understanding of counting and number. They have allowed that, once acquired, counting skills can lead to the discovery or construction of new understandings: "The initial competence guides the development of initial procedures. Once the system is on its way, it is inevitable that there will be an interaction between procedural and conceptual competence" (Gelman & Meck, 1986, p. 30). Gelman and Meck (1983, 1986, this volume) have described various examples of this interactive learning: an understanding of ordinal number, rules for counting to one hundred and beyond, an understanding that the number sequence is infinite, and an understanding of fractions.

counting skills. For example, Gelman and Gallistel (1978) argued that an order-irrelevance principle underlies the development of different-order skills like (a) arbitrarily designating any item in a set as "one" or (b) counting sets in different ways (e.g., from left to right or from right to left).[2]

The Need for Skeletal Counting Principles. Gelman and Meck (1986) argued that some principled understanding must precede skilled counting: "A fundamental reason for postulating principles is to capture the proposition that the acquisition of early knowledge can be aided by the availability of domain-specific mental structures" (p. 35). They pointed out that at a very young age, children seem attuned to number-relevant information, such as the number words. They observed that Piaget (e.g., Inhelder & Piaget, 1964b) regularly argued that children assimilate information of a particular kind only if there is a mental structure available to support the assimilation. Without a suitable structure, young children may fail to notice certain information altogether or rely on rote memorization. Gelman and Meck noted that it is difficult to imagine how children could learn to count by rote, because skilled counting involves complex behaviors, and knowing when and how to apply them is complicated. They also pointed out that positing skeletal counting principles accounts for self-initiated learning on novel tasks, a phenomenon that is difficult to explain in terms of the association-based, skills-first model.

In this volume, Gelman and Meck have further argued that early numerical competencies are better explained by positing a counting process than a pattern-recognition (subitizing) process. For example, they have cited infants' ability to discriminate among small collections (e.g., Starkey & Cooper, 1980; Strauss & Curtis, 1981), noted that it is unclear how a subitizing model can account for such a phenomenon, and have concluded that infants probably have a nonverbal counting mechanism.

Conceptual, Procedural, and Utilization Competence. Gelman (e.g., Gelman & Meck, 1986) argued that the variable performance of young children is not inconsistent with a some-principles-first position and, indeed, can be predicted by the model. She pointed out that understanding can be masked because principles do not dictate how they are put into practice in any given setting.

To account for performance variability, Greeno, Riley, and Gelman (1984) distinguished among conceptual, procedural, and utilization competence. In this model of counting, *conceptual competence* refers to an understanding about

---

[2]Although Gelman and Meck (1986) did not make clear whether they believe that children's skeletal conceptual competence consists of all five principles or not, they clearly implied it does. They have defended the position that preschoolers understand—at least implicitly—all the principles. Likewise, Gelman and Cohen (1988) and Gelman and Meck (this volume) implied that infants' skeletal counting knowledge entails all five principles.

counting, namely, a counting principle that establishes a guideline for counting procedures. That is, principles here define the requirements for a procedure. *Utilization competence* refers to the ability to understand a question or the requirements of a task. *Procedural competence* refers to the ability to plan a course of action that takes into account the guidelines of the counting principles and the requirements of the task. If children fail a particular task, it may be because they lack the conceptual, the utilization, or the procedural competence. In other words, it is not necessarily evidence that children do not understand a principle, because the difficulty may be due to inadequate procedural or utilization competence.[3]

A Mutual-Development View

A mutual-development view suggests that an understanding of number-word counting evolves gradually and in conjunction with counting-skill development. Based on Piaget's schema theory, as adapted by R. C. Anderson (1984), it provides a middle ground between the skills-first view and Gelman's some-principles-first view (Baroody & Ginsburg, 1986).

I agree that it makes sense to grant infants some innate basis for number competencies; I am not convinced that this innate knowledge informs and governs all aspects of counting-skill development. The development of counting within the preschool period probably involves the perfection of counting procedures *and* the emergence of new or, at least, firmer principles. Lastly, variable performance and self-initiated learning are not unambiguous evidence for a some-principles-first model, because there are plausible alternative explanations for these phenomena (cf. Gelman & Cohen, 1988).

Strong and Weak Schemata. To explain comprehension, R. C. Anderson (1984) distinguished between strong and weak schemata. A *strong schema* implies that comprehension is principle-driven and that predictions can be derived. It involves generalizations broad in scope. Moreover, it implies well-structured or well-integrated knowledge—knowledge that is interconnected and internally consistent. Thus, answers to novel problems can be deduced with a measure of certainty and reliability. A *weak schema* implies that comprehension is precedent-driven and that predictions are not so much derived but looked up. It involves generalizations local in scope. Moreover, it implies disconnected knowledge that is internally inconsistent. Thus, it provides an uncertain and unreliable basis for a priori reasoning.

---

[3]The constructs of procedural and utilization competence make it difficult, if not impossible, to disprove the some-principles-first position empirically. They are analogous to Piaget's notion of décalage, which has been used to account for variable performance across groups of related tasks, such as conservation of number, length, volume, and so forth.

Applied to the development of mathematical thinking, Baroody and Ginsburg (1986) suggested that the weak versus strong schema distinction should be thought of as a continuum rather than as a dichotomy. We observed, moreover, that a relatively weak schema aptly describes the state of children's initial mathematical knowledge in various mathematical domains, including counting: disconnected, task specific, and logically incoherent. In this view, children only gradually construct relatively strong schemata: well-connected, highly generalizable, and logically coherent knowledge.

Initial Competence.   It makes sense to grant infants organizing tendencies and even skeletal domain-specific knowledge. Shipley and Shepperson (1990), for instance, have described how innate general predispositions may underlie the construction of counting principles. Whether children have an innate subitizing mechanism or an innate nonverbal counting mechanism,[4] the mental structures underlying this mechanism might best be described as weak schemata: incomplete and disconnected. Even if children had an innate nonverbal counting mechanism, it might not require all five principles adduced by Gelman and Gallistel (1978), and the principles might be severely limited in scope.

To discriminate among oneness, twoness, threeness, and "other," an infant would need only the stable-order, one-to-one, and abstraction principles and weak forms of the cardinality and order-irrelevance principles. The tag of the last item marked might simply name the *end item* (end state) of the counting process, not necessarily the number of items in a collection.[5] In effect, the infant could compare collections qualitatively: displays with the same last tag are alike, those with a different end item are different. Although a qualitative tag could be obtained by scanning a collection of any arrangement in any order, skeletal

---

[4]The evidence against attributing early number competence to subitizing is not as strong as Gelman and Meck (this volume) claim. First, it is not clear that oneness is always learned before twoness, twoness before threeness, and so forth. Although the verbal label for twoness is typically learned before that for threeness and the verbal label for threeness is often learned before fourness, there is no evidence that infants learn to discern such numerosities in sequential order. Second, reaction times and error rates may increase on "subitizing tasks" as function of collection size, because scanning time and effort increase or because data are averaged over subjects using different strategies. Furthermore, although evidence that children 12-months or older can order collections by size or take into account surreptitious changes of a collection appears inconsistent with a subitizing account, it is not clear evidence for an innate nonverbal counting mechanism. Some parents begin counting with children as early as 12 or even 6 months. Nevertheless, it is troubling that no subitizing-based account has been advanced to explain the infant number-discrimination data.

[5]A weak cardinality principle is all that is needed to account for animal behaviors like that of the solitary wasp, described by Dantzig (1930/1954): Some species of the wasp provide each egg with five caterpillars; others provide twelve; and some provide up to twenty-four. Wasps do not need a mechanism to abstract number, they need a mechanism to stop a repetitive behavior after a specified number of repetitions. Although a cardinality principle is required by the first mechanism, a weak cardinality principle is sufficient for the latter mechanism.

knowledge might not include an implicit understanding that differently ordered counts of a collection must result in the same last tag.

Furthermore, the principles underlying an innate counting mechanism might initially be task specific: apply only to the use of the three nonverbal tags necessary to discriminate among small collections. Such knowledge might be disconnected from children's first efforts to acquire number-word counting skills.

The Development of Number-Word Counting. Connecting the structures underlying number-word counting skills with innate structures might represent a major advance in the development of meaningful counting: By applying initially meaningless counting routines to collections they can innately subitize or nonverbally count, children may come to associate number words with those numerosities they can naturally recognize and come to relate counting activities with their concept of numerosity (cf. Klahr & Wallace, 1976; Wynn, 1990). This knowledge can lead to further discoveries about the nature of number-word counting specifically, and a deeper understanding of counting generally.

A mutual-development view, then, differs from the some-principles-first model in three important ways:

1. It suggests that Gelman and Gallistel's five counting principles do not direct all skill-learning efforts. Children may *begin* to construct some skills or skill components piecemeal by imitation, practice, and reinforcement, through what Piaget (1964) called "social transmission." For example, a child might memorize the term one-two by rote, because of parents who take special delight in using this utterance and in the child's imitation of it.

2. A mutual-development view suggests that relatively *incomplete* principles may be sufficient to inform and govern *some* skills. For example, children might have a different-order schema that specifies: A collection can be counted in any order, and any item may be labeled *one, two,* and so forth. This partially complete understanding of the order-irrelevance principle may underlie the development and use of different-order skills.

3. It suggests that a deeper understanding of counting can evolve from the application of skills. That is, a relatively complete understanding of counting might spring, in part, from reflection on counting actions. Thus, at least some basic counting principles, such as the order-irrelevance principle, might evolve *after* the development of skilled counting.

In brief, a mutual-development view proposes that children are endowed with inchoate mental structures, first learn and use some counting skills or skill components in a relatively mechanical manner, construct counting skills and at least some counting principles in tandem, and only gradually construct a principled understanding of number and number-word counting (cf. Frye et al.,

1989; Fuson & Hall, 1983; Sophian, this volume; Steffe et al., 1983; von Glasersfeld, 1982; Wynn, 1990).

Accounting for Variability.   Clearly, children may fail a counting task because they lack *any* conceptual competence or because they lack procedural or utilization competence, even though they comprehend the relevant counting principles (Gelman & Meck, 1986). Failure may also be attributable to a relatively weak schema. That is, children may have adequate conceptual, utilization, and procedural competence to respond correctly to familiar tasks, but their understanding of counting may not be sufficiently complete to deduce the correct response to a novel task. For example, a different-order schema is adequate for the construction of different-order skills but is not adequate to foresee (predict) the outcome of differently ordered counts. With the construction of relatively strong schemata, counting knowledge becomes less error-prone and context-bound and can be correctly applied to a variety of situations with less hesitation.

Self-Initiated Learning.   A mutual-development view also accounts for spontaneous corrections, sudden insights, or other forms of self-initiated learning. For example, some children appear to understand the order-irrelevance principle after only one or two demonstrations of re-counting. Consider the case of 4-year-old Alison. After she had counted a collection of things, her father covered the array with his hands and asked how many she would get if she counted in the opposite direction. Alison smiled sheepishly and then tried to pry her father's fingers away from the collection. When asked again to make a prediction, Alison insisted on counting. This scene was repeated a second time with another collection. On the third trial with yet a new collection, she smiled broadly and announced that the re-count would yield the same number as her original count.

It might be argued that to achieve competence so quickly, Alison must have understood the order-irrelevance principle all along. A mutual-development view suggests that, although her existing mental structures were not adequate to make the prediction initially, they were adequate to understand her father's question, to choose a strategy (counting) for answering it, and to profit from the re-counting experiences. That is, Alison's incomplete schemata were sufficiently developed that she was ready to discover the order-irrelevance principle.

RESEARCH ON COUNTING KNOWLEDGE

This section evaluates some of the research that bears upon the some-principles-first and the mutual-development views. Gelman and Gallistel (1978) suggested that their evidence of young children's counting reflected at least an implicit understanding of the five skeletal counting principles. Indeed, this and other research on early counting (e.g., Fuson, 1988) does suggest that before they begin school, children—by and large—do understand or at least behave in a manner consistent with the five basic principles. However, extant research does not unambiguously support a some-principles-first view of development. Because of space limitations, the following literature review presents an overview of the research on Gelman and Gallistel's (1978) five counting principles; for a more detailed discussion, see Fuson (1988).

The Stable-Order Principle

Gelman and Gallistel (1978) found that preschoolers used the standard sequence ("one, two, three . . .") or a nonstandard sequence (e.g., "one, two, nine, ten")[6] on repeated trials and concluded that they understood the stable-order principle. Unfortunately, such results do not provide unambiguous evidence that children understand—even implicitly—a stable-order principle, or that such a principle directs the learning of number-sequence terms, particularly the initial acquisition of counting terms.

Wagner and Walters (1982) argued that Gelman and Gallistel's evidence provides support for only a weak form of the stable-order principle, for a localized phenomenon in which a particular sequence is used consistently with one collection at one given time. In their longitudinal study, Wagner and Walters found no evidence for a strong form of the stable-order principle, such as consistently using a nonconventional segment over different collections or over time. Fuson et al. (1982) found that an initial conventional portion was followed by a stable nonconventional portion (usually consisting of terms from the conventional sequence with some omissions, such as "five, eight, nine, eleven") and a final nonstable portion ("spew"). Contrary to Wagner and Walters' evidence, Fuson et al. found that the stable nonconventional portion persisted without change in some subjects for up to 5 months. Similarly, Baroody and Price (1983) found that children used nonconventional sequences consistently for up to 10 weeks. The discrepancy may be due, in part, to the ages of children studied. Wagner and Walters' sample included children from 1 to 5 years of age, whereas that of Fuson et al. ranged from 3 to 5 years and that of Baroody and Price included only 3-year-olds.[7]

It may be that children *initially* do not realize that numbers must be produced

---

[6]Apparently, not all children begin learning the number sequence with one. This can lead to such nonstandard sequences as two, three, four or eight, nine, ten, even among children of well-educated parents (Baroody, 1987b; Fuson, 1988). Consider the case of Mark, a Caucasian boy from a middle-class family whose parents were enrolled as undergraduates at a major midwestern university in the U.S.A. Mark's mother volunteered to my interviewer (Sara E. Scoville) that, initially, her son did not begin his counts with *one,* and that she had had to work with him on this.

[7]Wagner and Walters (1982) found no evidence for the strong form of the stable-order principle for children even in the 3- to 5-year age range. This discrepancy with the findings of Fuson et al. (1982) and Baroody and Price (1983) might be due to methodological differences, such as the way stable nonconventional portions were scored. Unfortunately, Wagner and Walters did not specify their scoring procedures.

in the same order, as Wagner and Walters suggest. Even if a nonverbal counting mechanism was governed by a stable-order principle, this does not mean that the acquisition of the number-word sequence is immediately linked to this principle and governed by it. On the other hand, an inability to produce a stable sequence may be due to an inability to remember previously used sequences (Baroody, 1986a). For example, a child who knows the stable-order principle might count "one, two, four" and then count "four, two, three" subsequently, because he or she cannot remember (a) all the terms used earlier or (b) their previous sequence.

However, even if children did produce stable sequences from the start, it would not necessarily mean that acquisition of this knowledge was principle driven. Children might acquire the first portion of the standard sequence ("one, two, three . . .") or parts of it (e.g., "two, four . . .") through rote memorization. Merely producing a stable sequence, then, is not evidence that children understand—even implicitly—that the number-word sequence must be produced in a stable order (Fuson & Hall, 1983).

Another line of evidence has yielded results no less equivocal. Gelman and Meck (1983, 1986) used an error-detection task and found that 3- to 5-year-olds identified as incorrect lists with reversed number words (e.g., "one, two, four, three"), random lists (e.g., "two, one, four, three"), and lists with skipped number words (e.g., "one, two, four"). These researchers reasoned that children could not identify such sequence errors unless they understood the stable-order principle. However, given the age of their subjects, Gelman and Meck's results may "reflect knowledge *learned* about counting rather than knowledge *underlying* the learning of counting" (Wynn, 1990, p. 159). Alternatively, a relatively weak schema seems adequate to account for such results: Children might recognize that the puppet's sequence does not match their well-learned portion of the sequence, but they may not recognize that—in principle—the number words continue in a particular order.[8] Furthermore, other research contradicts Gelman's results. Briars and Siegler (1984) and Frye et al. (1989) found that counting skill and an ability to detect examples of correct counting developed before an ability to detect examples of sequence errors.

A variety of factors could account for the discrepant findings. Gelman and Meck (1986) argued that utilization competence might be at issue. They found that using an interactive interview technique, best-response scores were higher

---

[8]Gelman and Meck (1983) had children evaluate counts to 5, 7, 12, and 20. A child who did not know the number sequence beyond *five*, say, might evaluate the correctness of the sequences to 7, 12, or 20 by comparing the *first portion* of these sequences against his or her known sequence. If it matched, the child would conclude the sequence was correct, whether or not there was an error beyond this known sequence. *If* the error occurred in the first five terms, the child could correctly identify the sequence as incorrect. This would explain why nearly all the correct sequences were identified as correct and the fewest number of errors occurred in identifying random lists. Future research should gauge each subject's level of sequence knowledge and evaluate his or her error-detection skill for familiar and unfamiliar portions of the sequence separately.

than immediate-response scores.[9] Thus, studies that permit only one judgment per trial may underestimate children's conceptual competence: Children may fail error-detection tasks because of the high degree of attentiveness they require (Fuson, 1988).

On the other hand, an interactive interview may provide children an opportunity to learn and may overestimate their pre-existing conceptual competence. Even preschoolers may sense that when an adult repeats a question, it implies they have not responded correctly and need to rethink their answer. If sufficiently ready, a child might reflect on the situation and construct the understanding tapped by the task. In other words, for a child whose zone of proximal development includes the conceptual competence gauged by the task, the selective feedback of an interactive interview might create cognitive disequilibrium, insight, and improvement.

Other methodological differences might also help account for the discrepant findings (see Frye et al., 1989). For example, some children apparently feel it is impolite or hurtful to point out another's—even a puppet's—mistakes. My graduate assistant, Janice Hume, reported that one 4-year-old child denied that a muppet had made an error, patted the muppet on the head, and said sympathetically, "It's O.K. Cookie Monster." In the same vein, Saxe, Becker, Sadeghpour, and Sicilian (1989) found that a majority of 4-year-olds failed to identify sequence errors as obvious as "one, one, two" or "one, three, four." However, when the error-detection task was changed so that children had to mediate a dispute between two puppets, 75% of the 4-year-olds successfully identified sequence errors with three terms and 69% did so with six terms. Saxe et al. concluded that arbitrating an argument apparently produces a greater willingness to reject incorrect counts. Even so, it is not clear why a substantial number of 4-year-olds did not identify obvious sequence errors; nor is it clear how younger children just beginning to master the number sequence would fare on the arbitration task. In summary, the available error-detection studies do not provide clear-cut evidence about the order in which number-sequence skill and the stable-order principle develop.

Fuson (1988) concluded that children at an early age realize that number-word counting requires a special list of unique number words. A mutual-development view suggests that children gradually construct such an understanding by discovering, in turn, each of the three component elements noted by Fuson. Children may first discover that the list is composed exclusively of number words; they may then discover that the list has a particular order; and they may last realize that each number word in the list is unique and thus appears only once in the list (Baroody & Price, 1983).

---

[9]In an interactive interview, a question is repeated if a child responds incorrectly to an initial question. Children are given credit if they then respond correctly *and* justify their new response.

Although Gelman and Gallistel (1978) included the uniqueness element in their definition of the one-to-one principle, there is ample justification to include it as an element of the stable-order principle as well. Because one function of counting is to assign cardinal values to collections so as to distinguish among them or compare them, it is important that children not only generate a stable sequence and assign one and only one tag to each element of a collection, but also that they use a sequence of *unique* tags (Baroody & Price, 1983). Even when a child has to resort to using nonconventional terms, an appreciation of the uniqueness requirement (the differentiating function of counting) would preclude choosing previously used terms. This element may not only develop later than other aspects of understanding comprising the one-to-one and stable-order principles underlying number-word counting (Baroody, 1987b), it may serve as a connecting point between the two schemata.

The evidence relating to when the uniqueness requirement develops is ambiguous. Some research (Baroody, 1986; Baroody & Price, 1983) suggests that an understanding of the uniqueness requirement does, in fact, develop relatively late. However, children who appreciate this requirement might repeat a term if they did not remember using it previously in a count. Nevertheless, some children repeat terms they had just used (e.g., "one, two . . . fourteen, *fourteen,* sixteen) or recycle to *one* (e.g., "one, two . . . nine, *one,* two . . ."). Such errors are not likely to be due to memory failures. Fuson (1988) pointed out, however, that children who understand the uniqueness requirement may make such errors for several reasons: For example, they may be more concerned about continuing a count and pleasing an adult than adhering to counting principles. In brief, evidence for the early development of the stable-order principle, in general, and the uniqueness requirement, in particular, are inconclusive.

Saxe et al. (1989) noted, "Gelman and Meck's early-competence model suggests that even very young children shouted be able to demonstrate knowledge that cultural symbols used to represent number are a matter of convention. Furthermore, based on the Gelman and Meck model, there is no compelling reason to expect differences between bilingual and monolingual children in their understanding of this distinction" (p. 470). Saxe and colleagues found, however, that children only gradually construct an understanding of number-word conventions. For example, a majority of their 8- and 11-year-olds recognized the arbitrariness of our counting sequence terms but relatively few of their 4-year-olds did so. Moreover, bilingual children, who have had experience with two different standard sequences, recognize earlier the arbitrariness of counting sequences. Such evidence is consistent with the view that children move from precedent-driven to principle-driven counting knowledge.

The One-To-One Principle

Gelman and Gallistel (1978) found that although children did not perform flawlessly, those as young as 2½ tend to tag each item of a collection only once, thus honoring the one-to-one principle. Again, this is not unambiguous evidence that a principle governs the acquisition of counting skill.

Children may begin acquiring components for an object-counting skill piecemeal—before they have an intention to number collections. For example, they appear to master pointing to objects one at a time before they learn to coordinate this skill with saying the number sequence (Beckwith & Restle, 1966; Wagner & Walters, 1982). Moreover, children may initially tag objects with numbers without any effort to use one tag for each item or to summarize the count (Baroody, 1987b; Saxe, Guberman & Gearhart, 1987).

Wagner and Walters (1982) suggested that children construct a "stop rule": Stop the number-word sequence when the last item of a collection is tagged. They found that 2- and 3-year-olds tended to use a *list-exhaustion scheme*. That is, if a collection was smaller than a child's count list, he or she tended to exhaust the available terms: Given two objects, a child who knew "one, two, three, four" might label each item twice. Because a stop rule is an integral component of one-to-one counting, these researchers concluded that a one-to-one principle was a relatively late development. Baroody and Price (1983) did not find any evidence of a list exhaustion scheme with 3-year-olds, and Fuson (1988) also found little evidence of it among children this age. However, it is possible that these "older" children had already constructed a stop rule.

As with the stable-order principle, error-detection data regarding the one-to-one principle (Briars & Siegler, 1984; Frye et al., 1989; Gelman & Meck, 1983, 1986) is inconsistent and ambiguous (see Fuson, 1988; Wynn, 1990). For example, Gelman and Meck (1983) demonstrated that on an error-detection task, children as young as 3 years of age can identify correct and incorrect instances of one-to-one counting, even with collections they cannot themselves count. However, such evidence does not demonstrate that the one-to-one principle exists before any counting skill. In brief, it is not clear whether a one-to-one principle drives the acquisition of object-counting skill or whether such a skill is assembled gradually, at least partly through imitation.

The Cardinality Principle

Research indicates that after counting a collection, children can respond appropriately to the "how many?" question quite early (Fuson, 1988; Gelman & Gallistel, 1978; Schaeffer et al., 1974; Wagner & Walters, 1982). Gelman (e.g., Gelman & Meck, 1983) concluded that this implies knowledge of the cardinality principle.

Fuson (1988), however, argued that responding with the last word counted does not necessarily imply understanding that this term refers to the whole collection. Children may simply have discovered that repeating the last tag of a count satisfies others'—sometimes persistent—queries of "how many?" Fuson concluded that her research indicates that a last-word rule precedes an understanding of the cardinality principle.

Although the last-word rule is powerful, in the sense that it generalizes across set size (Fuson, 1988), there are several reasons why it might be appropriately described as a weak schema. One is that it represents an incomplete understanding of the cardinality principle. A second is that it represents relatively mechanical knowledge: procedural knowledge that is somewhat tenuously connected to the rest of children's counting knowledge. Frye et al. (1989) reasoned that if children learn a last-word rule as a way of dispatching with others' "how many?" questions, they might not understand related but different questions and, thus, may respond incorrectly to them. In fact, they found that the "how many?" task was easier than an "are there x objects here?" task, which, in turn, was easier than a "Give me x objects" task. These results are consistent with Fuson's framework of an evolving cardinality concept in that the three tasks require a count-cardinal concept, a cardinal count-cardinal comparison, and a cardinal-count concept, respectively.[10]

To counter the evidence that suggests young children do not have a principled understanding of cardinality (e.g., Wynn, 1990), Gelman and Meck (this volume) reconsidered Bullock and Gelman's (1977) magic-task data. The original study found that under optimal conditions (the Control Condition), a reliable number of 29- to 38-month-olds correctly judged the ordering relationship between two numerosities. That is, young children, in the first phase of the task, learned to identify a set of two as the winner and a set of one as the loser (or vice versa) and, in the second phase of the task, used this relationship to identify four as the winner and three as the loser (or vice versa).

However, how children in the Control Condition arrived at their answers is unclear. Consider the protocol of Subject #3 reported in Gelman and Meck (this

---

[10]The results of another experiment reported by Frye et al. (1989) also appear to support the view that the last-word rule precedes a cardinality principle. Using an error-detection task, Gelman, Meck, and Merkin (1986) had previously found that young children rejected an incorrect cardinality response after witnessing a correct count. Subjects also rejected the last word as the cardinal value of a set after an incorrect count. Using a trick task, Gelman and her colleagues found that young children rejected a different outcome when a surreptitious error was made re-counting a set in a different direction. However, Frye et al. argued that these data are ambiguous evidence for a cardinality principle. On the error-detection task, subjects may have detected an incorrect cardinality response to correct counts simply by noting a discrepancy with their last-word rule. Responses to incorrectly counted trials may have been due to noting the incorrect counting procedure, not the incorrect cardinal designation of a set. The trick trial also does not clearly distinguish between responses to the (unseen) counting procedure and the change in the cardinal designation: For example, a young child might consider the absence of pointing incorrect.

Frye et al. (1989) used a refined error-detection task that entailed assessing counting and cardinality errors separately for the same situation. According to a some-principles-first view, children who successfully identify counting (stable-order or one-to-one) errors should correctly reject the last tag as a response to "how many?" questions. Frye et al. reasoned, though, that some children who correctly identify counting errors may, nevertheless, incorrectly accept an incorrect cardinal designation because of their last-word rule. They found that 3- and 4-year-olds were, in fact, significantly less successful in rejecting an incorrect cardinal designation than in detecting counting errors, and concluded that such children did not link a last-word response to the numerosity of a collection.

volume). This child was trained to identify two as the winner and one as the loser. In the second phase of the task, Subject #3 guessed, choosing one set then the other. Instructed to count, the child correctly counted the set of four but incorrectly identified the set of three as, "Five." The child then chose four as the winner and three as the loser and was scored as correct.[11] If the child was using the cardinality principle rather than subitizing, Subject #3 should have identified three items ("five") as the winner.

Gelman and Meck (this volume) reanalyzed Bullock and Gelman's (1977) data to see whether 2½- to 3½-year-olds (regardless of condition) both counted and gave the same cardinal answer on either the same trial or across trials. Of the three protocols they report, two describe a child (Subjects #9 and #11) using the cardinality principle on a single trial. Otherwise, there is no clear evidence that children counted rather than subitized and then used a counting-derived cardinal designation across trials. (The protocols do show, however, that children repeatedly counted a set or failed to answer "how many?" questions.) Even if there was clear evidence that children did engage in principled counting as early as 2½-years of age, it would not necessarily imply a skeletal knowledge of the cardinality principle. It would not be surprising that some children *learn* much about counting by the time they are 2½. In brief, there is no clear evidence that children have innate skeletal knowledge of the cardinality principle.

The Abstraction Principle

Research indicates that preschoolers willingly count collections composed of diverse items, and that their counting proficiency with such collections does not differ from that with arrays composed of identical items (Fuson, 1988; Gelman & Gallistel, 1978; Gelman & Tucker, 1975). Although the evidence is clear, what to make of it is less so. Gelman and Meck (1983) concluded that such evidence indicates preschoolers understand the abstraction principle. However, unlike the principles already discussed, the abstraction principle does not establish constraints for counting procedures. In a sense, it does the opposite: It gives children a free hand to define anything as an element of a collection.

Such an "understanding" may arise by default from a relatively weak schema. That is, nothing in children's previous experience specifies that they cannot treat diverse items as a collection and so they do. If, however, children were largely exposed to counting situations in which items consisted of like items—as occurs in many counting books for children—they may incorrectly conclude

---

[11]Like Subject #11, Subject #3 did not explain her revised (correct) answer. Repeated questioning or not terminating a task can signal to children they need to change their answer. Thus, an interactive interview without the safeguard of justified answers invites a Clever Hans effect and may overestimate a child's competence. If justifications are not required in an interactive interview, then questions should be repeated after children respond correctly as well as when they respond incorrectly.

from these precedents that counting must involve like elements. Most children, however, may have sufficiently diverse experiences that they do not induce such a well-specified constraint.

The Order-Irrelevance Principle

Different Views.   According to Gelman and Gallistel (1978), "the child who does appreciate the irrelevance of the order of enumeration [the order-irrelevance principle] can be said to know, consciously or unconsciously, the following facts: (1) that a counted item is a *thing* . . . (the abstraction principle); (2) that the verbal tags are arbitrarily and temporarily assigned to objects and do not adhere to those objects once the count is over; and *most importantly* [emphasis added], (3) that the same cardinal number results regardless of the order of enumeration" (p. 82). Some-principles-first proponents (e.g., Gelman & Meck, 1986) assume that all of this knowledge exists prior to different-order skills, that all three understandings are a necessary condition for these skills, and that the use of the skills implies knowledge of all three facts.

According to a mutual-development view, children may have early implicit or even explicit knowledge of Facts 1 and 2 just discussed, but not Fact 3. In this view, Fact 2 constitutes a different-order schema, a relatively weak schema that underlies different-order skills. Fact 3 constitutes the order-irrelevance principle, a relatively strong schema that develops after the different-order skills. Indeed, in this view, different-order skills are a necessary condition for inducing the order-irrelevance principle (Baroody & Ginsburg, 1986). Piaget (1964), for example, cited a case where a boy apparently discovered that differently ordered counts (and different arrangements) of a collection did not affect its cardinal designation.

Possible Difficulties with the Original Evidence for a Some-Principles-First View.   Gelman and Gallistel (1978) found that even preschoolers have different-order skills and inferred from this evidence that young children understand the order-irrelevance principle. One problem with this conclusion is that many of their subjects were not successful on all of the skills tasks. In fact, it was not until 5 years of age that a majority of the children in their study successfully completed the constrained-counting task. This different-order task requires a child to count a display of five items with the constraint, for instance, that the second item has to be labeled *one* on the first trial, *two* on the second trial, *three* on the third trial, and so forth. Successful completion of the task necessitates counting the display in a different order on each trial.

A second problem is that success on skills tasks does not necessarily mean that young children understand Fact 3. That is, even if preschoolers were invariably successful on different-order tasks like the constrained-counting task, it would not necessarily mean they understand that different count orders yield the *same* cardinal designation. I have argued (Baroody, 1984) that more direct means than different-order tasks were needed to assess knowledge of Fact 3 and proposed a prediction task. This task requires a priori (principled) reasoning, in that children must specify the outcome of differently ordered counts before they actually re-count a collection. Like Ginsburg and Russell (1981) and Saxe et al. (1987), I found that young children did display different-order skills, but some could not correctly predict the outcome of differently ordered counts with the same display. These results suggested that some 4- and 5-year-olds do not yet understand Fact 3.

Gelman et al. (1986) noted that the two problems just discussed could be explained by invoking the constructs of utilization and procedural competence. That is, young children's lack of success on the constrained-counting and prediction tasks does not necessarily mean they did not understand the order-irrelevance principle.

New Data on the Constrained-Counting Task. Gelman et al. (1986) argued that children might fail the constrained-counting task because of its novelty and heavy strategic demands. To test this hypothesis, they varied the demands of the task. In an easy condition, children were introduced to the task with 3- and 4-item displays before they worked with a 5-item display. In a repeat condition, all three trials involved 5 items; in a count-control condition, children practiced object counting before they were introduced to the constrained-counting task with 5 items. Although Gelman et al. (1986) found clear evidence for a predicted size effect, they did not find unequivocal evidence for predicted practice or transfer effects (see Table 5.1).

In addition, a strategy analysis yielded a curious finding. Gelman et al. argued that an analysis of incorrect trials indicated that as a result of their preliminary counting task, children in the count-control condition had developed a mental set for left-to-right (or right-to-left) counting. They noted that seven of the ten 3-year-olds in this condition counted from one end or another and made a counting error to take into account the restraint imposed by the tester. For example, to make the second item *three,* a child might count "one, *three,* two, four, five" (rearrange the count words); "one, three, four, five, six" (skip a count word); or "one, *two-three,* four, five, six" (assign two count words to an item). Gelman et al. noted that only three same-age children (15%) made such errors in the other two conditions. Moreover, among 4-year-olds, only one (10%) in each of the three conditions made such errors. They concluded that these results suggest conceptual competence was masked by a failure of utilization or procedural competence.

Such errors, however, are not simply the failure to apply the order-irrelevance principle to an appropriate situation; they *violate* this or other counting principles. Rearranging count words or skipping a count word negates the stable-order principle; double-labeling an item contravenes the one-to-one principle. Moreover, recounting a display of five and labeling the last item as something other than *five*—as in the case of skipping a count word or double-labeling— contradicts the order-irrelevance principle.

TABLE 5.1

Gelman et al.'s (1986) Predictions and Results Regarding the Constrained-Counting Task

Effect	Expected Pattern	Result
Size Effect	Young children should do significantly better on the 3-item display than on the 5-item display.	Confirmed
Transfer Effects	1. Children in the easy condition should do significantly better on their 5-item (transfer) display than	Not confirmed
	(a) children in the repeat condition on their initial 5-item try; or	Confirmed[a]
	(b) those in the count-control condition on their single 5-item display	Ambiguous[a]
	2. Performance in the repeat condition should improve on successive trials with the 5-item display	

[a]For the 3-year-olds at least, this result is suspect because the difference between the two groups may have been due to the curiously poor performance of the children in the count-control condition rather than to transfer by children in the easy condition. In theory, children in the count-control condition should have performed as well on their single 5-item display as the children in the repeat condition did on their initial 5-item display. In fact, among 3-year-olds, 0% in the count-control condition were correct on initial responses, whereas 30% in the repeat conditon were correct. (The children in the easy condition also had 30% correct.) Using second-try data, the evidence for transfer is stronger but still not clear-cut. The percent correct in the count-control, repeat, and easy conditions were 10, 30, and 50.

[b]Using immediate responses, both the 3- and 4-year-olds improved 10% on the second trial. Using best (second) responses, both the 3- and 4-year-olds improved 20% on the second trial. Statistics were not reported, so it is unclear whether any of the gains on the second trial were significant. The unexpected drop-off in performance on the third trial was attributed to boredom.

It is not clear what to make of these results. On the one hand, it is possible that children with a principled understanding of counting would overlook this knowledge because they were misled, were not thoughtful, or were unable to devise another (legal) means to please the tester (Fuson, 1988). On the other hand, it is also possible that young children's counting knowledge is not as well-developed as some-principles-first proponents suggest. In the count-control condition, it would be relatively easy to create a left-to-right (or right-to-left) mindset if one's comprehension were precedent-driven rather than principle-driven. Labeling the last item of a display differently on successive counts is the kind of inconsistent performance characteristic of a relatively weak schema. (Note that such errors were not restricted to children in the count-control condition.) Further research is needed to determine the reasons for such errors; that is, follow-up testing should determine whether children understand the basic principles but violate them for the sake of convenience or whether they lack principled knowledge.

The meaning of another result of the constrained-counting task is equally unclear. When children were given a second try, Gelman et al. found that best-response scores were higher than immediate-response scores and ascribed this difference to difficulties with utilization and procedural competence. Dismissing a child's first incorrect answer and using his or her second answer, however, may overestimate prior knowledge of counting principles: Children may use selective feedback to construct a strategy for producing correct responses, with or without realizing that the outcomes of differently ordered counts of a collection are the same.[12]

Gelman (personal communication, October 1, 1990) suggested that the results of Gelman and Cohen (1988) mitigate my argument that Gelman et al. overestimated children's competence by letting them try again. Gelman and Cohen found that normal 4- and 5-year-old "preschool children . . . improved much more than did the DS" (Down's Syndrome) children, when given a second chance on the constrained-counting task (p. 75).[13] They surmised that these

---

[12]The results of an error-detection task used by Gelman and Meck (1983) and Gelman et al. (1986) are ambiguous for the same reason. They found that children would judge noncanonical counts (e.g., counts starting with the middle item) as correct when best answers were used. These results differ from those of Briars and Siegler (1984) and Frye et al. (1989), who did not use an interactive interview.

[13]In fact, the results of Gelman and Cohen (1988) did *not* clearly show that the DS children and the normal preschoolers responded to the novel constrained-counting task in a qualitatively different fashion. Although many DS children responded in a relatively mechanical or ineffective manner, 2 of these 10 subjects solved the next task on the first try. Additionally, because of the small samples, it is not clear that the difference between the gain of either the 4-year-olds or the 5-year-olds and that of the DS children was significant: It appears that the percent correct on the second try rose by 35% for the normal 4-year-olds ($n = 16$), 25% for the normal 5-year-olds ($n = 16$), and 20% for the remaining DS children. Moreover, any comparison between the preschoolers and the DS children is complicated by the fact they were not tested with the same tasks. For half the normal preschoolers, the target item was always the second item from the left, and only its label was varied ("Make this one, two, three, four, or five"). For the DS children, both the position of the target item and its label were varied. This may have made it more difficult for the DS children to benefit from previous trials.

results "support the conclusion that normal individuals benefit from the avail-ability of counting principles from the outset, ones that support the acquisition of counting knowledge and the generation of novel solutions" (pp. 93–94). How-ever, Gelman and Cohen's results do not clearly demonstrate the existence of innate skeletal counting principles, nor do they counter my point that allowing children to try again may overestimate their competence. Readiness to benefit from a second try might have been due largely or entirely to prior learning: understanding constructed from counting experiences. Moreover, Gelman and Cohen's results do not address the issue of whether subjects who are successful on the constrained-counting task also comprehend Fact 3.

The results of a trick trial administered by Gelman et al. (1986) do not unequivocally support a some-principles-first position either. On the last trial of the constrained-counting task, subjects were asked to make, for example, the second item of a set of 5 *six*. Children who comprehend Fact 3 should immedi-ately reject this as impossible. Gelman et al. reasoned, though, that task diffi-culty (condition) should again affect the performance of 3-year-olds, but not of 4-year-olds. Although consistent with the view that utilization and procedural competence should disguise younger children's understanding of the order-irrele-vance principle (see Table 5.2), their results may also have overestimated initial competence. Unlike children in the hard or count-control condition, children in the easy or the repeat condition had multiple exposures to the trick trial and, thus, greater opportunity to *construct* a principled understanding or to respond cor-rectly in a nonprincipled manner.[14] Furthermore, from Table 5.2, it is evident that at least 40% of the 3-year-olds and at least 20% of the 4-year-olds were not successful even in the easy and repeat conditions, in the conditions that did not tax utilization or procedural competence. The fact that a substantial portion of 3- and 4-year-olds were not successful on a relatively direct and nontaxing measure of the principle is consistent with the view that they had not constructed either the order-irrelevance principle specifically, or a systematic and logical understanding of counting generally.

New Evidence on the Prediction Task.   Gelman et al. (1988) theorized that children might fail the prediction task because of task demands, not a lack of principled understanding. In the original prediction task (Baroody, 1984), chil-dren were required to count a set one way and were then asked, "We got x [where x was the result of a child's initial count] by counting this way. What do you think we would get counting the other way?" Restating x was intended as a reminder to

---

[14]Gelman et al. (1986) scored a trick trial correct if, on at least one of the three trials, a child (a) refused to carry out its instructions, (b) said he or she could not do so, or (c) asked for an additional item. The first two responses might *not* indicate principled understanding if the child responded in a similar manner to non-trick trials or if the response was due to fatigue. The third criterion might *not* indicate principled understanding if the child subitized. This most likely would have occurred in the easy condition where one of the trials involved three items.

TABLE 5.2
Percent Successful on the Trick Trial of the Constrained-Counting Task
by Condition for Two Studies Conducted by Gelman et al. (1986)

Age	Preliminary Study Conditions		Follow-Up Study Conditions		
	Easy	Hard	Easy	Repeat	Count-Control
3-years	50%	0%	60%	60%	10%
4-years	75%	70%	80%	80%	80%

Note: A child in the easy and repeat conditions was scored as successful if he or she responded correctly on at least one of three trials. Children in the hard and count-control conditions were administered only one trick trial.

forestall a performance failure due to forgetting the result of the original count, but Gelman and her colleagues reasoned that some children may have interpreted the reminder as a challenge to their initial count and, thus, picked a new number for their prediction.

To test their hypothesis, Gelman et al. (1986) compared the effects of the original prediction task with a count-three-times task and an altered-question (a revised prediction) task. The second task gave children three opportunities to count an array before the reverse-count prediction, a procedure which presumably helped them feel more confident about their judgment about the array's cardinal value. The third task was reworded to avoid challenging the children's initial count. Specifically, it omitted any reference to the initial count: "How many will be there?" or "What will you get?" Although 4-year-olds performed poorly on the original prediction task, they did well on the count-three-times task and the revised prediction task (see Fig. 5.1). These results suggest that the original prediction task can underestimate knowledge of Fact 3.[15]

_____

[15]The results are not entirely unambiguous, because the count-three-times and the revised prediction tasks may have overestimated competence. The repeat-three-times task may have fostered a response bias. A child required to count the same array three times might become bored and inattentive. (Recall that children did not continually improve in the repeat condition of the constrained-counting task as predicted by Gelman et al., and this was attributed to boredom.) After the first two or three counts, a child might—without reflection—simply repeat the answer that satisfied the adult interviewer earlier. Even an explanation that involved a reference to previous counts might simply be the effort of an impatient child to satisfy the interviewer.

On both the count-three-times and the revised prediction task, a response bias might arise for another reason. Uncertain about the outcome of the reverse count, some children—operating on the philosophy that some answer is better than no answer—might simply respond with their previous answer. Without a lucid explanation, it is unclear whether a correct prediction indicates competence or not. According to Gelman and Meck (1986), most but not all correct answers on the revised prediction task were justified. The response bias just discussed would have been countered by the misleading wording of the original task.

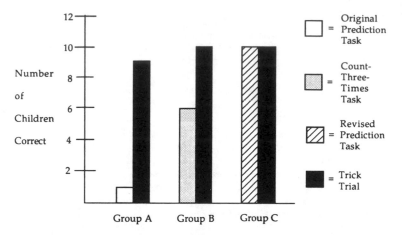

FIG. 5.1.   Four-year-olds' performance on three different prediction tasks and a trick trial (Gelman et al., 1986).

The results of a follow-up study with 3-year-olds were less conclusive. In this study, performance on the original prediction task was compared to performance on a task that combined the features of the count-three-times task and the revised prediction task. Despite the fact that success on the latter task may have been inflated (see footnote 15), a Fisher test indicates that the difference between the two groups was nonsignificant, not significant as reported by Gelman et al.

Moreover, the revised-prediction data collected by Gelman and colleagues seem inconsistent with the some-principles-first position in one key respect. If principled knowledge (Fact 3) were a prerequisite or necessary condition for the development of counting skills, then theoretically no child who failed the revised prediction task should be successful on the different-order tasks. However, a post-hoc analysis revealed that of their 22 3- and 4-year-old subjects, 18 were successful on both tasks, 3 were successful on the different-order task but not on the revised prediction task, and 1 was unsuccessful on both tasks (R. Gelman, personal communication, July 9, 1985). These data suggest that different-order skills evolve before an understanding of Fact 3, the order-irrelevance principle. Although statistically significant ($\chi^2 = 3.0$, $p < .05$, one-tailed McNemar chi-square test for non-independent data), Gelman and Meck (1986) noted the small number of subjects who failed the revised prediction tasks and justifiably dismissed these results as an anomaly due to measurement error.

To re-evaluate the developmental relationship between different-order skills and knowledge of Fact 3, I undertook a partial replication of the Gelman et al. study with a somewhat larger sample. Twenty-nine 4-year-olds were tested on different-order skills tasks (see Baroody, 1984) and the revised prediction task. To check for an attention or a memory confound (that a child simply forgot the

TABLE 5.3
Performance on the Different-Order Task
and the Revised Prediction Task

Different	Revised Prediction Task	
	Unsuccessful	Successful
Successful	6 (6)	16
Unsuccessful	0 (1)	0

Note: The numbers in parenthesis indicate children who were incorrect on two or three prediction trials, but who had trials discounted because they failed the memory probe.

result of the original count), a probe was administered *after* a child failed to predict the outcome of a reverse count: "How many did you get when you counted?" If children could remember the original count, the prediction trial was scored as incorrect. If they could not remember the original count, the trial was discounted. Three trials were presented for each task. Children were scored as successful on the different-order task or the revised prediction task if they were correct on at least two of the task trials.

Performance on the different-order skills and the revised prediction tasks are summarized in Table 5.3. Consistent with other evidence (e.g., Briars & Siegler, 1984; Gelman & Gallistel, 1978), the children had little difficulty with the different-order task gauging knowledge of Fact 2: reassigning verbal tags to objects. A reliable number, however, were not successful on the revised prediction task, which gauged knowledge of Fact 3. Even when subjects who failed the memory probe are excluded, the different-order task was significantly easier than the revised prediction task (McNemar χ^2 for non-independent samples = 6.0, $p < .05$, one-tailed).[16] Like my earlier study with the original prediction task (Baroody, 1984), these results suggest that different-order skill cannot be equated with knowledge of Fact 3; unlike my earlier study, these results cannot be attributed to a language problem.

Other New Evidence.   To check the results of the prediction tasks, Gelman et al. (1986) also administered a trick trial. This required children to evaluate a

[16]Because Gelman et al. (1986) administered a single revised prediction trial, and because of possible learning effects, the data were reanalyzed using the first trial on each task. Note that the memory probe could not have affected a child's first response to the revised prediction task. Although children were somewhat less successful on the first trial of both tasks in the replication study, the pattern of results was essentially the same as that reported: Four children were successful on the skills task but not the revised prediction task (five more fit this category but could not recall their original count); one was successful on the revised prediction task but not the skills task.

puppet's correct response to the "how many?" question after an initial count in one direction and an incorrect (changed) response after a surreptitious count in the opposite direction. Such a discrepancy should bother children "only if they believed the two counts should yield the same result" (Gelman et al., 1986, p. 12). Unlike the results of the prediction tasks, children in all three conditions registered a high level of success (see Fig. 5.1). Similar results were obtained with a second check task, an error-detection task. Gelman et al. concluded that the discrepancy between results of the check tasks and those of the original prediction task further confirmed that the latter task underestimated understanding of the principle.

Again, unfortunately, the check tasks may have overestimated children's initial understanding of Fact 3. Gelman and Meck (1986) reported that the trick trial and error-detection task were administered two to three months after the prediction task. It is quite possible, then, that the discrepancy data of Gelman et al. were confounded by learning: history and/or testing effects. It is well documented that children's performance on counting tasks improves with age. This was especially likely on the trick trial, where previous exposure to the related prediction task may have prompted reflection and learning. (The check tasks should have been administered before the prediction task so that these order effects worked against Gelman et alia's discrepancy hypothesis rather than in favor of it.) Moreover, 7 of the 29 who were scored as correct on the magic task did not justify their answer, and so the basis of their response was unclear. In regard to the error-detection task, the trials involved correct counts, one-to-one counting errors, and cardinality errors but not order-irrelevance errors. Although Gelman and Gallistel (1978) assumed that an understanding of Fact 3 is a consequence of an understanding of the stable-order, one-to-one, and cardinality principles, this is not necessarily the case. That is, successful performance on the error-detection task used by Gelman et al. did not necessarily imply an understanding of Fact 3.[17]

What to Make of the Data?   In summary, there is no evidence that children understand Fact 3 before they can use different-order skills. On the other hand, there is evidence that children do not realize that differently ordered counts yield the same cardinal designation, even when they exhibit different-order skills. This discrepancy is evident even with the revised-prediction task, which does not involve the challenging and misleading instructions of the original task.

---

[17]Furthermore, as with the prediction tasks, not all subjects were successful on the check tasks. For example, seven of ten 3-year-olds and ten of twelve 4-year-olds in the revised-prediction condition were successful on the trick trial. (The failure rate in the other conditions was the same or slightly higher.) Whether or not the 23% who failed the trick trial included those who failed the revised-prediction task is not clear. Although not conclusive, consistent failure on tasks gauging a principle would make it more difficult to argue that children understand the principle but performed poorly because of inadequate utilization or procedural competence.

Although language difficulties may not be a factor with the revised prediction task, some-principle-first proponents could argue that tasks gauging knowledge of Fact 3 are relatively difficult for other reasons. Gelman (personal communication, October 11, 1990) noted that order-irrelevance tasks (tasks gauging knowledge of Facts 2 and 3) are complex and make demands on attention, motor skill, planning skill, and so forth. This would help to explain why young children are not successful on the constrained-counting task or other order-indifferent tasks that gauge an understanding of Fact 2. It is more difficult to see how such factors affect relatively direct measures of Fact 3 knowledge such as the revised prediction task. Recall that in my replication study, only the data of children who could recall the original count were analyzed. It is not likely that such children failed to make a correct prediction because of inattentiveness. Furthermore, the revised-prediction task does not put demands on motor skills, and it is not clear how planning skills could prevent a child who understands Fact 3 from making a correct prediction.

Gelman and Meck (1986) do advance an argument that might account for why children in my replication study had more difficulty with the revised prediction task than they had with different-order tasks. They suggest that children have difficulty making the reverse-count prediction because it requires an analytic mode of thought. Children who can successfully engage in the a priori reasoning required by the prediction task "can be said to have accessed implicit knowledge about counting. In other words, they may have demonstrated a beginning *explicit* understanding of the order-irrelevance principle" (p. 49). Children who cannot predict correctly have simply failed to tap their implicit knowledge of the counting principle.

This explanation is possible, but it does raise several questions. Why would skeletal knowledge that supposedly directs attention and guides the generation of novel solutions (Gelman & Cohen, 1988) not be accessed when a child is confronted by a task directly related to this knowledge? Is it meaningful to speak of principled understanding when many children, asked to make a prediction based squarely on the order-irrelevance principle, fail to access the principle? What knowledge is accessed to make incorrect predictions?

To address questions such as those just mentioned, Gelman and Greeno (1989) noted that *interpretative competence*, which includes understanding the rules of conversation for different social contexts, is essential for interpreting an experimenter's questions. They noted that the prediction task violates a rule of everyday conversation: "Do not repeat what is already known by the listener" (p. 146). To make matters worse, children are asked to state the same obvious answer twice (once for the initial count and again for the prediction). Because children do not realize that experimental settings have a special set of social conventions, they avoid a social gaffe by remaining quiet or by changing their answer. Gelman and Greeno also suggested that children sometimes try to please the experimenter rather than tell what they know.

As applied to the prediction task, the interpretative-competence argument raises a number of questions. If children believe that the outcome of a reverse count is obvious, why did one girl in my replication study preface her prediction with "may be," and why did two other children respond to the prediction question with "I don't know"? If children in the Gelman et al. (1986) study were concerned about repeating what was evident to a listener, why did they answer the initial cardinality question correctly? As Gelman and Meck (this volume) point out, answering the "how many?" question after counting a collection is redundant: It is clear to everyone present how many items are in the collection. In my replication study, two children did not respond correctly to cardinality or prediction questions. However, why is it more plausible to attribute this to a difficulty with interpretative competence rather than a difficulty with conceptual competence?

Moreover, how does interpretative competence explain observations of children who appear interested in what happens when a set is counted in different orders and, through spontaneous experimentation, discover the outcome is the same (see Baroody & Mason, 1985; Piaget, 1964)? If children believe that the outcome is obvious and do not wish to repeat what is known, why do some try to re-count a set before making a prediction?

Even if children thought it was unnecessary to repeat what was obvious, why would they contravene an arguably more important social norm (It is important to tell the truth) and respond with a prediction that is obviously wrong? Is it likely that children would prefer experimenters to view them as untruthful or willful, rather than modestly impolite? Moreover, would a child—for the sake of politeness—respond with an obviously incorrect prediction and risk being considered ignorant or bizarre? Why would a child believe that an incorrect prediction would please an experimenter? Would they not expect that an obviously wrong answer would bring social disapproval?

Undoubtedly, interpretative competence plays a role in any experimental setting. It is not clear, though, that this construct is a plausible explanation for why a reliable number of children failed the revised prediction task in Gelman et al.'s (1986) study or in my replication study.

CONCLUSIONS

Ambiguous Evidence

Existing research does not settle the debate about the developmental *relationship* between counting principles and counting skills. The available evidence does suggest that children typically do understand the principles adduced by Gelman and Gallistel (1978) some time before they begin school, but it does not show that such understanding exists prior to the development of any counting skill. It is not clear that children have an innate nonverbal counting mechanism rather than an innate subitizing mechanism, that an innate counting mechanism would require all five counting principles, or that such principles actually guide the initial development of number-word counting skills.

Moreover, all the evidence adduced to support the some-principles-first view can be explained in other ways.[18] Gelman et al. (1986) noted that variable performance due to task difficulty, children's ability to detect counting errors, and their ability to deal with novel tasks are all consistent with the some-principles-first model. Although not all of this evidence can be easily explained by an association-based, skills-first view, this does not mean that all plausible alternative explanations to the some-principles-first view have been eliminated. The evidence cited by Gelman et al. is also consistent with a schema-based, mutual-development view.

Three lines of evidence would strengthen the case of the some-principles-first model. One is that newborns use a counting mechanism rather than a subitizing mechanism. To establish that all five of Gelman and Gallistel's counting principles are involved, the evidence would have to show that infants use a quantitative rather than a qualitative process: view the last tag as representing the whole collection rather than the last item or end state. A second is that innate principles govern and inform children's earliest efforts to construct number-word counting skills: that connections to the innate principles are established from the onset of number-word counting development. A third would entail discounting plausible alternative explanations, not just the association-based, skill-first model. Whether or not it will be possible to adduce such evidence, only time will tell. In the meanwhile, whether one agrees or disagrees with the some-principles-first-model reduces to how much understanding and influence you wish to attribute to children's innate knowledge.

The Meaning of "Principled Counting"

I am inclined to agree with Fuson (1988) that Gelman and Gallistel's (1978) use of the term "counting principles" is somewhat misleading. She concluded that the five principles described by Gelman and Gallistel (1978) "involve quite different kinds of conceptual understanding and relate to procedural competence in different ways [and] thus vary in the extent to which the term principle seems

---

[18]Consider the evidence of numerical competence in animals. Gallistel and Gelman (1992) suggested that such evidence implies that some animal species have innate counting principles and that, from an evolutionary perspective, it makes sense to grant humans this competence also. However, animal studies may suffer from the same problem that plague studies with young children: Competence may reflect learning rather than innate knowledge. After all, it is now widely recognized that learning plays an important part in many animal behaviors that were once thought to be innate (e.g., the songs of birds, the hunting strategies of cats, and the mothering actions of primates).

appropriate" (p. 372). She recommended abandoning the term *counting principle* and using the term *conceptual, procedural,* and *utilization competence.*

I would argue that it is useful to characterize conceptual competence in terms of weak versus strong schemata and to reserve the term principles for describing the latter type of knowledge. It seems inappropriate to describe disconnected, task-specific knowledge that does not allow a priori predictions as principled knowledge. Consider, for instance, the inability to reason a priori in the straightforward, revised prediction task. Such behavior suggests only a weak schema: a fundamental gap in a child's understanding of number-word counting. In contrast, it seems appropriate to describe well-connected, general knowledge that permits a priori predictions as principled knowledge.

Clearly, the development of strong schemata for number-word counting takes considerable time and learning. How much and when the relatively weak schemata that constitutes children's innate endowment play in this development remains a question.

6

Relationships Between Counting and Cardinality From Age 2 to Age 8

Karen C. Fuson
Northwestern University

Young children begin to understand and to use number words in seven different kinds of contexts (see Fig. 6.1). Three of these contexts are mathematical ones: a cardinal context, in which the number word refers to a whole set of entities (a discrete quantity) and describes the manyness of the set ("I want two cookies"); an ordinal context, in which the number word refers to one entity within an ordered set of entities and describes the relative position of that entity ("I was second"); and a measure context, in which the number word refers to a continuous quantity and describes the manyness of the units that cover (or fill) the quantity ("I am two years old," perhaps with two fingers showing, making it also a cardinal context). Two other contexts, sequence and counting, provide cultural tools for ascertaining the correct number word to be used in cardinal, ordinal, or measure contexts. The sequence context is a recitation context in which number words are said in their correct order but no entities are present, and the number words refer to nothing; this context is originally like reciting the alphabet or the days of the week. In the counting context, number words are put into a one-to-one correspondence with entities; each number word refers to a single entity but describes nothing about it (it is just a count label, or tag, for the entity). Number words are also used to say written numerals. This symbolic context (or perhaps better, a numeral context) originally elicits a number word with no accompanying meaning and no reference beyond the numeral itself ("That's a six" upon seeing 6). Later on, written numerals themselves can take on cardinal, ordinal, measure, counting, or sequence meanings. Finally, number words are also used in non-numerical (or at least quasi-numerical) contexts, such as telephone numbers, television channels, zip codes, house addresses, and bus numbers.

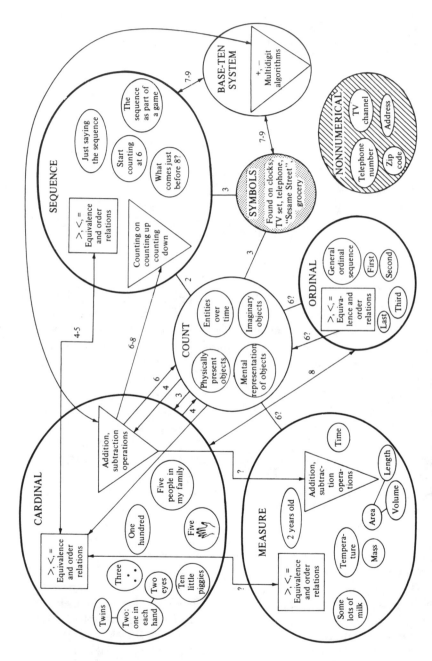

FIG. 6.1. Relationship among cardinal, ordinal, measure, sequence, count, symbol, and nonnumerical contexts (numbers on connecting lines are approximate ages).

Young children hear number words being used in these seven different contexts and begin to use number words themselves in these various different contexts. These meanings are originally separate meanings for children. Gradually a child begins to make connections among these various meanings and a single spoken number word then may take on more than one meaning simultaneously. Learning all of these relationships takes a long time, from age 2 to about age 8 for most children. This chapter summarizes the developmental relationships that children construct among these various meanings. This construction culminates, finally, in a seriated, embedded, unitized, cardinalized sequence of number words, a postconservation construction related to what Piaget called "truly numerical counting." The evidence supporting the developmental paths to be described here is discussed in my book, *Children's Counting and Concepts of Number* (Fuson, 1988), where work of other researchers working with children from the United States and England is also discussed; parts of this chapter reflect thinking that has progressed since the book was completed. Major elements of the construction of relationships among all of these different meanings of number words seem to be shared by children in most cultures. For example, the main developmental path to the understanding of addition and subtraction followed by most children in the United States is shared by children in the Soviet Union (Davydov & Andronov, 1981) and Oksapmin children in New Guinea (Saxe, 1982). There also seems to be another related path taken by some children in Sweden and by children in Asian countries; this alternative path and differences between that path and the path described here are discussed by Fuson and Kwon (this volume, chap. 15). The path to be described here is not supported by teachers in classrooms in the United States—in fact, many teachers have traditionally tried to suppress this path while offering nothing but memorizing facts to replace it—but the evidence is quite robust that many children in the United States independently construct this path for themselves as a way to give meaning to numerical situations.

This book is a celebration of Piaget's book on children's construction of number. This chapter and the work it summarizes are framed within that Piagetian work on number. It assumes that each child must construct his or her own path through increasingly complex number concepts, and the Piagetian stages of conservation of numerical equivalence describe some of these increasing complexities. My own work has concentrated on understanding how children come to understand numerical situations with numbers that are too large to process perceptually, that is, numbers greater than six. This has led to a concentration on the cultural tool of counting because counting is used by children in constructing cardinal, ordinal, and measure number concepts for all but very small and very large sets. Thus, much of my work has focused on contexts of specified numerosities rather than the contexts of unspecified numerosities studied by Piaget. My work, and the related work of others, has attempted to fill gaps in the Piagetian logical account of the construction of number. It has pointed out various critical roles that counting plays in children's developing understanding of number, and shown that the Piagetian framework underestimated the importance of these roles of counting. Piaget's account also underestimated the role that the empirical strategy of matching can play, in spite of Piaget's emphasis on one-to-one correspondence, but relatively little research has been done on matching as opposed to counting. However, my work and that of others does support the general Piagetian position that counting alone is not sufficient for an adequate understanding of number and that, in transformed situations, operational thinking moves beyond counting and matching. Thus, we now have a richer and more complete view of the complementary roles of the cultural tools of counting and matching and of general operational, quantitative thinking.

In order to understand young children's thinking about numerical situations, it is important to clarify some common errors in the use of the word *ordinal*. This word is used to refer to three different meanings of number words: sequence meanings, count meanings, and ordinal number meanings. An *ordinal number* refers to a context in which the entities are ordered (such as in a queue), and the number refers to the relative position of that entity. Many languages signify this special numerical context by using entirely different number words or by adding special letters to the usual counting words (in English the counting words are *one, two, three, four, five, . . . ,* whereas the ordinal words are *first, second, third, fourth, fifth, . . . ,* with most later ordinal words made from counting words by adding *th*). The very fact that two different lists of words are used clearly indicates that the culture differentiates between counting contexts (in which counting words are used) and ordinal contexts (in which ordinal words are used). Another difference between count and ordinal contexts is that an ordinal context has one given, unchangeable order. In counting contexts, one must impose an order on the entities to count them, but one can make many different orders on those entities and count a set in many different ways. Thus, in a counting context, an entity can take any given count word, whereas in an ordinal context a given entity can take only its single correct ordinal word, according to the given ordering. A *sequence context*—saying the number words in their standard order—is also sometimes called an ordinal context because number words in every language have a single correct order. This order does create sequence meanings for number words, and certain relationships derive from this single correct order, but these sequence meanings are like the meanings that accrue to any ordered list—the alphabet or the months of the year—and are not originally quantitative. The word *ordinal* is also used erroneously to refer to order relations (greater than, less than) on cardinal numbers (seven is more than four). Order relations ($>$, $<$) can be established on cardinal, ordinal, or measure numbers or number situations and on sequence words (seven comes after four). It is considerably easier to understand and describe the task of the child in constructing a developmental path of numerical concepts if these three meanings—ordinal, count, and sequence—are differentiated clearly and used accurately and if order relations are labelled as such and the type of number word meaning used in the order relation is specified.

There is relatively little work on measure and ordinal number contexts. Walter Secada and I did some unreported work on conservation of ordinal number in which toy animals were lined up in a queue to go into cages and one queue was then transformed to be longer or shorter than the other. We found that children who were at Stage 2 of conservation of cardinal number (the traditional Piagetian conservation of numerical equivalence task) had great difficulty with this ordinal task, partly because they did not know the ordinal words, but many also had difficulty when ordinal words were not used. In children in the United States knowledge of the ordinal words lags behind knowledge of the counting words by years (Beilin, 1975), so much ordinal number knowledge seems to lag behind cardinal knowledge. Understanding of measure contexts also lags considerably behind knowledge of cardinal contexts because measure contexts require understanding the unit of measure (and the inverse relationship between the size of the unit and the measure number of the quantity), whereas much understanding of cardinal contexts can be accomplished by a child who uses only perceptual unit items in which each entity in the cardinal context is taken as an equal, single entity (see Steffe et al., 1983). Because most cardinal relationships are constructed before ordinal and measure relationships are constructed, I concentrate in this chapter on the relationships constructed by children among sequence, counting, and cardinal meanings of number words.

EARLY CONSTRUCTIONS: PATTERN NUMBER WORDS AND COUNTED NUMBER WORDS

Young children's first cardinal uses of number words refer to small numbers of entities and seem to rest on *subitizing,* the immediate apprehension of small numerosities. There is controversy concerning the basis for subitizing; the ages at which children can subitize two, three, and four entities; and the developmental relationship between subitizing and counting. What is clear is that young children do learn to subitize at least two entities and that many children learn to label particular patterns or situations with a cardinal label (e.g., "There are five people in my family."). Children continue to use this pattern-based approach of seeing certain situations as patterned sums of small numbers of entities (e.g., After I cut a peanut butter sandwich in half, and in half again, to make four small squares, my daughter aged 2 years, 10 months said, "Two and two make four."). These special pattern-based small numerosities continue for several years to play important roles in some equivalence, addition, and subtraction situations.

Before children can count entities, they must learn the correct sequence of number words. Errors made in learning this sequence seem to depend on the structure of the sequence. In English the irregularities in the number words after *ten—eleven, twelve, thirteen, fourteen, fifteen, sixteen, seventeen, eighteen, nineteen, twenty*—seem to hide even the irregular relationship of the *-teen* words to the words before *ten;* thus, most children learn the sequence of words to *twenty* as a rote list of meaningless words, much like the alphabet. The incorrect sequences produced by 3- and 4-year-olds in the United States possess a typical structure (see Fuson et al., 1982): They consist of a first portion of number words in their correct order, followed by a stable portion that is not correct, followed by an unstable portion that varies each time number words are said. The stable incorrect portion usually consists of words in the correct sequence but with some omitted (e.g., "11, 12, 13, 16" or "13, 14, 16, 18"); reversals of word order are uncommon. These incorrect stable portions may be said by a given child for several months or even longer.

Most middle-class children in the United States below the age of 3½ are just learning the sequence to 10, those between 3½ and 4½ have correct sequences to 10 but have incorrect portions somewhere between ten and twenty, and many between 4½ and 6 are working on the decade structure between twenty and one hundred, although a substantial proportion of children in this age range may still have incorrect portions in the upper teens (see Fuson, Richards, & Briars, 1982). As soon as children's accurate portions reach into the 20s, their sequences show evidence of understanding of the decade structure of the English words (the *x-ty, x-ty–one, x-ty–two, . . . , x-ty–nine* pattern), but it takes them a very long time to learn the decade words themselves (*twenty, thirty, forty, . . . , ninety*) in their correct order. They produce a series of *x-ty* to *x-ty–nine* chunks that may be out of order, and may even repeat chunks for as long as a year and a half.

Two-year-olds often begin to count objects. They typically point to objects and say number words. Counting entities distributed in space (as opposed to counting entities occurring over time, such as clock chimes) requires an indicating act, such as pointing, to connect the words said over time to the entities distributed in space. Pointing (and other indicating acts, such as moving objects into a counted pile or eye fixation on particular entities) isolates a particular spatial location at a particular moment of time. It thus creates spatial–time units that enable a one-to-one correspondence in time to be made between the points and the spoken number words, and a one-to-one correspondence in space to be made between the point locations and the entities. If each of these correspondences is correct, the counting is accurate. Preschool children make errors that violate each of these correspondences in both possible ways: They make a point without saying a word and say a word without making a point; they give extra points to an object and leave some objects without any points. They also occasionally produce complex combinations that violate both correspondences (e.g., give an object three words and two points) and produce degenerative pointing (a skimming across the objects with the finger while saying words at random).

The rates at which 3-, 4-, and 5-year-olds make these errors, and how object characteristics of number, color, homogeneity, and arrangement affect error rates is discussed in several chapters in Fuson (1988). Preschoolers show surprising competence in creating correct correspondences in counting objects arranged in rows, with children aged 3 to 3½, 3½ to 4, and 4 to 4½ making correct correspondences on 84%, 94%, and 97% of the objects, respectively, in rows of 4 to 14 objects. The error rate increases with longer rows, falling to 56%, 64%, and 71% of the objects correct, respectively, in rows up to 32 objects. Counting accuracy also varies considerably with how hard the child is trying to count accurately (i.e., with effort). When objects are maximally disorganized, children not only have to carry out the local time–space number word–point–object correspondences, but must also create a global correspondence over all the objects, so that each object is counted and no object is re-counted. This requires the child to use either a remembering strategy, to keep track of which objects have been counted, or a physical strategy, such as moving objects into an already counted pile, so that remembering is not necessary. Young children are much less successful at creating such a global correspondence than they are at carrying out the local correspondences in a linear set of objects, and 5-year-olds still make many re-count or uncounted-object errors on large, disorganized arrangements having 10 to 30 objects.

When young children first begin counting, the counting does not have a cardinal result. They count only to imitate the social-cultural counting activity. If asked how many there are after counting, children re-count (and continue to re-count each time they are asked "how many?"), they say a number word that is not their last counting word, or they say a sequence of number words (often different from the words they said in counting). It is not clear how children first learn the relationship between counting and cardinality and about how much understanding of cardinality is indicated even when children answer a "how many?" question with the last word they said in counting. My own work (summarized in Fuson, 1988, chap. 7) indicates that different children may use different ways to make the connection between their last counted word and that word as indicating how many objects there are. In most cases children then generalize this relationship fairly rapidly and use this relationship across sets of different sizes. Some children may count a very small set and also subitize that set, and then notice that the last word said in counting is the same as the subitized numerosity. Something may make the last counted word particularly salient to the child, and that child may then answer a "how many?" question with that word. Children may be told by a parent or sibling that their last counted word tells how many objects there are, and this may be sufficient for them to start responding correctly. Young children's recency bias (their tendency to answer a multiple-choice question with the last listed answer) may also contribute to their answering a "how many?" question with the last word they say. Failing to remember their last counted word does not seem to be a major reason children fail to answer a "how many?" question with their last counted word: Most 2- and 3-year-old children who do not answer the "how many?" question correctly *do* remember the word they said for the last object in a row.

Many children who do answer a "how many?" question with the last counted word seem to have constructed only a last-word rule, in which that last word does not refer to the whole set and does not refer to the numerosity of that set. Children give the last counted word even when their counting is very inaccurate and yields a last-word response that is considerably discrepant from the cardinal meaning of that response: for example, counting a set of 26 objects: "1, 2, 3, 6, 7, 8, 9, 1, 2." "How many are there?" "Two," or counting a set of two objects: "1, 2, 3. There are 3."; or repeating a given number several times in counting, but still giving it as the last-word response: counting a set of 23: "1, 2, 3, 4, 5, 6, 7, 8, 9, 10, 11, 12, 16, 14, 15, 16, 14, 16, 15, 15, 16, 11-teen, 15." "How many are there?" "15." Many 3-year-olds giving last-word responses nevertheless show confusion between counting and cardinality meanings, and they use cardinal plural forms to refer to the last object, that is, as a count reference, rather than as a cardinal reference to all the objects. Three examples reported in Fuson (1988) are "Those are the five soldiers" as the child points to the last soldier; "This one's the five chips" as the child points to the last chip; and "This is the four chips" as the child points to the last chip. Other recent evidence, using a trick game methodology to decrease overestimates and underestimates of children's knowledge (Frye et al., 1989), also indicated that some 3- and 4-year-olds use a last-word rule rather than connecting counting to cardinality, because they answered assertions of the interviewer, "I think there are *x*," by agreeing only with last-word responses even when the interviewer made a counting error and the child noticed and identified the counting as incorrect.

Some children may immediately relate the counting meaning to a cardinality meaning, and many 4-year-olds come to make such a count-to-cardinal transition in word meaning, in which the word shifts from the count reference (a reference to the last counted object) to a cardinality reference (a reference to the numerosity of all of the counted objects). Such a transition requires the child to gather conceptually all the counted entities so that the cardinality reference can be to all of these entities. This conceptual gathering together is called *cardinal integration,* following a related use of *integration* by Steffe et al. (1983). This count-to-cardinal transition allows children to begin to understand numerical equivalence, and to add and subtract in certain situations. (These are discussed in the following sections.) The reverse cardinal-to-count transition in word meaning is required in order for a child to be able to count out a given number of objects. When instructed, "Get five cars," or "Give me five dolls," the child must shift from the cardinal meaning of the *five* to a counting meaning of *five* and know that when counting, the counting must stop when *five* is said. The child must also be able to remember the goal of counting (*five*) while carrying out the counting and to monitor the counting in order to stop at the required word. It may take some time for children to be able to present their counting activity to themselves sufficiently to anticipate this cardinal-to-count transition. Of 28 children, 2 and 3 years old who were last-word responders (children who gave the last counted word in response to a how-many question), 22 did not show any cardinal-to-count transitional ability on any trial. After being told that a row of objects had x of those objects, they were not able to predict what number they would say when they counted the last object in the row. These children did not even guess x; most of them tried to count to find out what they would say last.

There is still controversy concerning the relationship between children's counting behavior and their understandings of counting. I have argued that this relationship is more complex than a simple "skills-first" or "understanding-first" approach (Fuson, 1988, Chapter 10) and discuss evidence concerning the developmental relationships among the Gelman and Gallistel (1978) how-to-count principles. There are many aspects of accurate counting, and children may understand that some of these are required for correct counting before they are able consistently to meet these requirements; they also may carry out accurately certain aspects of counting before they understand that these are required for the counting to be correct. Relationships among a child's saying an accurate sequence of number words, carrying out correct correspondences between number words and objects, and knowing at least a last-word rule vary with the number of objects. For small sets, most children do the first two before the third. For sets between about 4 and 7, children produce correct sequences but may produce correct correspondences and no last-word rule, or may use a last-word rule but make incorrect correspondences. For sets between about 7 and 16, these aspects are ordered: sequence, last-word rule, then correct correspondences. For even larger sets, children may use a last-word rule while producing neither correct sequences nor correct correspondences. With respect to developing understandings of relationships between counting and cardinality, certain aspects of these relationships may be understood earlier for small sets than for large ones.

EQUIVALENCE AND ORDER RELATIONS ON SPECIFIED AND UNSPECIFIED NUMEROSITIES

Between any two sets of entities (two unspecified numerosities) or between any two specified numerosities, A and B, one of three possible cardinal relations will be true: The sets or numerosities will be equivalent, A will be greater than B, or A will be less than B. Table 6.1 outlines different relational situations that have been studied. Piaget's conservation of numerical equivalence situation stimulated many studies of the second and especially of the third type of situation: understanding the effect of a transformation on the relationship between two sets of entities. Various strategies for determining the relation between two unspecified numerosities or two specified numerosities are outlined in the right-hand column

TABLE 6.1
Equivalence and Order Relations on Specified and Unspecified Numerosities

<table>
<tr><th>Situations</th><th>Strategies</th></tr>
<tr><td>
Comparing two static sets

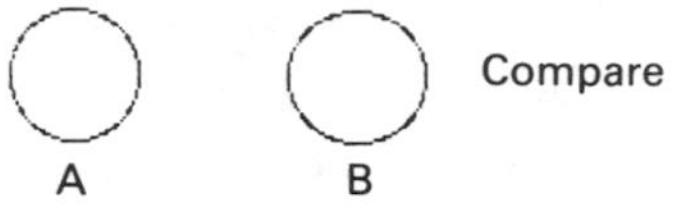

$A \cong B$ or $A > B$ or $A < B$?
</td><td>
Unspecified numerosity strategies
General perceptual
Length
Density
Matching: move objects
Matching: not move objects
If there is no extra, $A \cong B$
If there is extra, $A \neq B$
If extra is in A, $A > B$
If extra is in B, $B > A$

Specified numerosity strategies
Subitize
Subitize sums
Count
If $N_A = N_B$, then $A \cong B$
If $N_A \neq N_B$, then $A \neq B$
If $N_A < N_B$, then $A < B$
If $N_A > N_B$, then $A > B$
</td></tr>
<tr><td>
Comparing the pretransformation state to the postransformation state of a single set

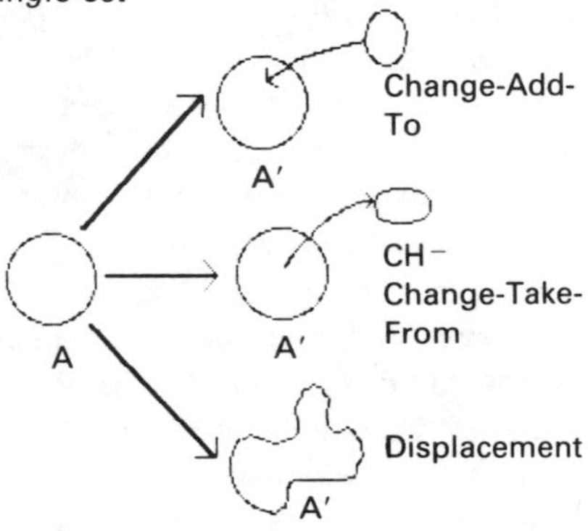

$A \cong A'$ or $A > A'$ or $A < A'$
</td><td>
Nature of the transformation
If Change-Add-To, then $A' > A$
If Change-Take-From, then $A' < A$
If Displacement, then $A' \cong A$
</td></tr>
<tr><td>
Comparing the postransformation state of one set to an untransformed set whose relation to the pretransformation state of the first set is known

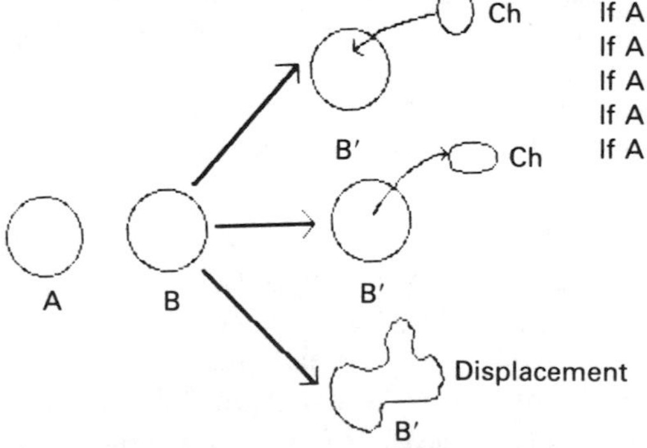

$A \cong B'$ or $A > B'$ or $A < B'$ depends on the transformation and on the relation of A to B
</td><td>
Nature of the transformation and the original relation
If $A \cong B$, then the relationship of A to B depends on the transformation as above
If $A > B$ and Ch^+, then A ? B′
If $A > B$ and Ch^-, then $A > B'$
If $A > B$ and Displ, then $A > B'$
If $A < B$ and Ch^+, then $A < B'$
If $A < B$ and Ch^-, then A ? B′
If $A < B$ and Displ, then $A < B'$
</td></tr>
</table>

of Table 6.1. Both the unspecified numerosity strategies and the specified numerosity strategies can be used whenever objects are present, whether or not the numerosities of those sets are initially specified. The basis for making the relational judgment is similar for all unspecified numerosity strategies: They depend on identifying and locating any extra objects. The basis for making the relational judgment for the specified numerosity strategies is also similar: Knowledge about the relations on the obtained specific number words is required to determine the relation on the objects. The transformational strategies are only used in situations where a transformation is made; in such situations, the unspecified and specified numerosity strategies can also be used. Empirical strategies (matching and counting) are, however, the only reliable strategies to use in the static comparing situations, and in the Change-Add-To and Change-Take-From situations resulting in A? B' in the table.

Young children learn important aspects of these comparison strategies before they start school, and learning about these strategies continues in the early years of school. There is a huge literature on children's learning in this area, much of it a reaction to Piaget's original book on number (Piaget & Szeminska, 1941). In spite of the many studies, however, our picture of how children's understanding develops in these different comparison situations is still unclear in several places. A summary outline of this development is presented in Table 6.2. This summary and the brief discussion that is possible here of course ignore many subtleties in this learning. A much fuller discussion is available in Fuson (1988, chap. 8).

At least by age 3, children can use perceptual strategies for comparing two sets, and they understand that adding things to a set means that the set has more and that taking some away means that the set has less. The perceptual strategies, including the use of length or density when objects are arranged in rows, continue to be very powerful during much of the preschool years. During this time children will attend to a transformation on a set and ignore the relation that existed on that and another set originally, but as children learn the cultural tools of counting and matching, these tools become strategies that are increasingly trusted and used in comparison situations. When children learn these tools, of course, depends upon their own culture, so the age may vary widely. The ages given in Table 6.2 primarily reflect research done with English-speaking children in the United States and England.

Children can correctly carry out counting or matching and know how to use the counting or matching information to make an equivalence judgment before they will choose to carry out these strategies voluntarily. If asked to count or match, although they can do so, they will choose to use perceptual strategies instead. In situations in which information obtained from perceptual strategies conflicts with that obtained from the quantitative strategies of counting or matching, children initially will use the information from perceptual strategies. In these cases they may say things like, "This seven has more than that seven does," thus saying the specific numerosities obtained by counting but choosing to use the

TABLE 6.2

Development of Strategies for Establishing Equivalence and Order Relations on Specified and Unspecified Numerosities

Age	Perceptual	Quantitative	Transformation and Original Relation	Transformation Alone
3	General perceptual Length + density Choose L more than D			Ch+ means changed set has more Ch− means changed set has less Displacement changes the quantity only if it looks like there are more after the transformation
4	General perceptual L + D, L, D Ch Ul	Count, Match	Like transformation alone, cannot use both transformation information and information about the original relation	
4½	General perceptual L + D, L, D Ch	Ul Count, Match		
5½	General perceptual L + D, L, D Ch	Ch, Count, Match Ul		
6		Ch, Count, Match Ul ↑ ↑	For Ch+ and Ch− begin to consider transformation and original relation and compare size of the difference in each case using count or match For Displacement, relate count and match results to the Displacement transformation Inductive generalization that Displacements do not affect the equivalence relation	Deduction of invariance of displacements even with perceptually misleading information (identity conservation plus transitivity) Immediate equivalence judgment with justification Irrelevance of transformation No addition or subtraction
7			Deduce conservation from reversible counting and matching: reversibility or from simultaneous length and density: compensation	
7½	Estimation L × D (development continues)	Cardinal Number: Seriated, embedded number-word sequence		

... e of that strategy. Ul is being able to use information if it is provided or if the experimenter suggests that the child obtain it.

perceptual information of "more" (i.e., extra) in one row rather than using the numerosity information that the last words are the same. Eventually, if children are asked to count or match, they *will* use this counting or matching information to make the equivalence judgment even though it contradicts the perceptual information. They may do this first for equivalent sets and then later for unequal sets, where they have to use an order relation on the cardinal numbers to decide which has more. Finally, they will carry out counting or matching voluntarily and will use this information rather than the misleading perceptual information. There are wide individual differences in when these changes are made, with a few 3-year-olds and more 4-year-olds voluntarily counting or matching, and some 5-year-olds still not accepting count or match information over perceptual information when these conflict.

This conflict between perceptual and quantitative strategies occurs in all of the comparing situations outlined in Table 6.1, and the same developmental path through this conflict seems to occur in static and transformation situations. The urge toward counting is so strong in many 5- and 6-year-olds that they try to count even when objects are hidden. I once did a Bruner version of the Piagetian conservation of numerical equivalence task in which one set was hidden while the transformation was made and the set was kept hidden afterwards, but many children still tried to count the hidden objects. The eventual strength of the counting strategy, especially, has been partially obscured by the many Piagetian conservation studies in the United States in which children have been prevented from counting. Sufficient evidence has accumulated concerning counting, and also concerning young children's competence in matching (see Fuson, 1988; Kwon, 1989), to indicate that the developmental sequence of conflict between perceptual and quantitative strategies summarized in Table 6.2 is fairly robust.

The original Piagetian account of transformation situations, although under-emphasizing the roles of counting—and perhaps matching—in dethroning the perceptual strategies, is accurate, in that children do not stop their thinking about these situations even when they can carry out counting or matching accurately. Something seems to impel them on to understand the nature of the transformation itself. Thus, initially children may have to count or match when faced with a transformed situation (and may even use perceptual strategies if prevented from counting or matching); because they must obtain the equivalence information empirically by counting or matching, they are, of course, not conservers. Eventually these children do not count or match when faced with a displaced set: They know that displacement does not affect the original quantity and thus does not affect the original equivalence or nonequivalence relation. This knowledge may be constructed by making an inductive inference from past experiences of counting or matching sets (and be justified by statements that the transformation does not change the quantity or that nothing was added or subtracted); or it may be a deductive inference based either on conceptual knowledge that enables the objects to be transferred mentally to the pre-transformation state and tracked during this reversal (and justified by statements about reversibility) or on knowledge that enables the child to consider length and density simultaneously (and justified by statements about compensation of length and density). Counting or matching may play a role in these inductive or deductive inferences. In Fuson, Secada, and Hall (1983) children spontaneously counted or matched and also gave one of the Piagetian justifications on the very same trial. Sometimes the counting or matching occurred first and the justification seemed to be an attempt to explain the empirical result, and sometimes the justification was given first and then the child counted or matched as if not certain that the explanation was really correct. At present adequate data do not really exist to address the hypothesized developments at ages 6 and 7 that are given in the transformation columns in Table 6.2. We need research in which children are allowed to count or match if they want but are also asked to explain their answer. Studies also need to report the different justifications separately to ascertain if there is any developmental order in them, and children's understanding of all of the justifications needs to be ascertained rather than having questioning stop with the child's first choice of a justification.

ADDITION AND SUBTRACTION

We know at this time very little about relationships between the conceptual structures children construct and use for addition and subtraction and those they construct for equivalence and order relations, but addition and subtraction and equivalence and order relational situations are clearly related. The Change-Add-To and Change-Take-From transformations of a single set are two very fundamental addition and subtraction situations. When these transformations are carried out on one set in an original relation to another set, a Compare situation (a standard subtraction situation) is related to a second Compare situation; such situations are integer addition and subtraction situations (see, for example, Vergnaud, 1982). Thus, the mathematical situations first studied by Piaget form a rich complex of mathematical situations whose comprehension by children we still only partially understand.

The initial relationships children construct among sequence, counting, and cardinal meanings of number words have already been discussed. Children continue to construct increasingly complex relationships among these meanings that enable them to solve addition and subtraction situations in increasingly sophisticated and efficient ways. In the United States children move through a developmental sequence of such constructions that in most cases are little affected by classroom instruction and frequently are even carried out in the face of active opposition by teachers who may forbid counting or the use of fingers in the classroom. The relationships that are established change the very nature of the sequence of number words: The sequence moves from being a rote, meaningless series of utterances to being constituted by number words that come to stand for objects in the counting procedure and that can take on cardinal meaning as the sum of the words earlier in the sequence. Various levels of meaning that the number word sequence goes through are outlined in Table 6.3. The first four lines in the table (through the Unbreakable List level) have already been discussed. Different parts of the sequence may be developing at different levels

TABLE 6.3
Developmental levels within the number-word sequence

Sequence Level	Meanings Related	Conceptual Structure Within the Sequence and Relationships Among Different Number-Word Meanings	
String	Sequence	onetwothreefourfivesixseven	Words may not be differentiated.
Unbreakable List	Sequence	one-two-three-four-five-six-seven	Words are differentiated.
	Sequence-Count	one-two-three-four-five-six-seven ● ● ● ● ● ● ●	Words are paired with objects.
	Sequence-Count-Cardinal	one-two-three-four-five-six-seven →[seven] ● ● ● ● ● ● ●	Counting objects has a cardinal result.
Breakable Chain	[Sequence-Count-Cardinal]	[four] → four-five-six-seven → [seven]	The addends are embedded within the sum count; the embedded first addend count is abbreviated via a cardinal-to-count transition in word meaning.
Numerable Chain	[Sequence-Count-Cardinal]		The sequence words become cardinal entities; a correspondence is made between the embedded second addend and some other presentation of the second addend.
Bidirectional Chain/Truly Numerical Counting	[Sequence-Count-Cardinal] ↕ [Sequence-Count-Cardinal]		The sequence becomes a unitized seriated embedded numerical sequence; both addends exist outside of and equivalent to the sum; relationships between two different addend/addend/sum structures can be established; addends can be partioned.

Note: A rectangle drawn around related meanings indicates meanings that have become integrated. A number word alone has a sequence or count meaning; a number word enclosed by a bracket has a cardinal meaning.

simultaneously: A child may start counting from given words less than ten while still learning words just before twenty.

At the Breakable Chain level children become able to begin counting at any point in the sequence. The sequence and counting meanings become merged (signified by the rectangle around these meanings at this level), children become able to consider objects that present an addend as also at the same time presenting the sum (one addend becomes embedded within the sum count), and they can move from the cardinal meaning of a given addend ("There are three cats") to the sequence/counting meaning of that addend as the last word said in counting the objects for that addend without needing actually to count the objects or even needing the objects to be visible. They then continue the count of the second addend objects as at the earlier level and make a final count-to-cardinal transition to find the total number of objects. The second addend objects must also be able to be embedded within the sum objects if such children are to continue the count from the first addend. In Secada, Fuson, and Hall (1983) we found many first graders who initially did not embed the second addend within the sum and answered that when counting all the objects they would count the first object in the second addend as *one* or as *five* (or whatever the second addend actually was).

At the next Numerable Chain level all three meanings—sequence, count, and cardinal—are merged, and the sequence words themselves become the objects that present the addends and the sum in addition and subtraction situations. No objects are used to present either addend; the number words are said beginning with the first addend word (or the addend taken by the child to be the first addend) and as many words are then said as are in the second addend (for 6 + 8, start with *eight* and say six more words: *nine, ten, eleven, twelve, thirteen, fourteen*). When the second addend is very large, it is necessary to use some method of keeping track of how many more words are said. Children do this by matching the words said to some known set of entities (e.g., a pattern of six fingers that are extended successively as each word is said or an auditory pattern of speaking three words and then three more words) or by counting the words said (*nine* is one, *ten* is two, *eleven* is three, . . . , *fourteen* is six").

Finally, at the highest level the sequence is a unitized, seriated, embedded, bidirectional, cardinalized sequence. There has been much less research about this level than about the lower levels, and the several conceptual structures portrayed at this level in Table 6.3 may, in fact, occur at different times; that is, this level may eventually be differentiated into different levels. At this level children can construct relationships between two different addend-addend-sum situations and can chunk addends into parts for more convenient adding or subtracting. These various addition and subtraction strategies have been called *derived fact* or *thinking strategies* in the research literature. They usually have not been differentiated, and deciding their developmental sequence is complicated (as is the research on the other sequence levels) by the fact that children can use pattern presentations of numbers to solve problems with small numbers before they can do so in general (e.g., they can count on 1 or 2 before counting on in general and may be able to move one object from addend to addend before moving two objects).

The actual counting that children do in addition and subtraction situations at each level is pictured in Table 6.4. The first two columns show forward counting procedures (one to find a sum and one to find a missing addend), and the second two columns show backward counting procedures. The first and third column procedures reverse each other, and the second and fourth column procedures reverse each other. At the second and third levels, the counting for the first and third columns is governed by the objects for the second addend (one counts forward or backward the number of objects in the second addend), whereas the counting for the second and fourth columns is governed by the auditory count (up to the sum word for the second column and down to the known addend word for the fourth column) and the number of words counted is then found. For most children, counting down is considerably more difficult than counting forward, so there are more errors in the backward counting procedures. The sequence–counting–cardinal relationships are also somewhat more difficult to establish in the backward procedures, introducing other kinds of errors. There are two different backward procedures, and children sometimes confuse them, ending with one object too many or one object too few. The second counting down procedure shown in Table 6.4 may be conceptually based (saying *eight* may mean "eight and one taken away"), or it may be only a procedure not related to the underlying addend structure ("I say four words backwards, and the last word I say is the answer"). There is also a discontinuity between the object counting procedures at Level 1 for the backward procedures but not for the forward procedures, because all of the object counting at Level 1 is forward counting.

The drawings in Table 6.4 show situations in which a problem is given in number words or in written numerals and children then have to count out objects to make the two known quantities. In textbooks and in research studies addition and subtraction situations are also given with objects already presenting the quantities; in such cases the earlier steps would be omitted. Objects are shown for Level 1, but children frequently count out fingers as objects also. At Level 2, children may initially count out objects for the second addend or they may use fingers; this finger use may involve a known pattern of fingers that is made or recognized rather than counted. At Level 3, fingers are not sets of objects that are counted on or counted back as part of the sum, but instead constitute a keeping-track procedure matched to the number words used to count on or count back the sum. The number words themselves present the addends embedded within the sum (i.e., they present the quantities of the addends and the sum), while the fingers (or other keeping-track procedures) just match the number words and then either stop the counting when the correct second addend finger pattern has been produced (in the first and third columns) or present the second addend for

TABLE 6.4

Developmental levels of addition and subtraction solution procedures

Level	Addend + Addend = [Sum]	Addend + [Addend] = Sum	Sum – Addend = [Addend]	Sum – [Addend] = Addend

LI

Addend + Addend = [Sum]:
count all
(4) (3) ... $\rightarrow$ 7

4 + 3 $\rightarrow$ 7

Addend + [Addend] = Sum:
add on up to sum
(4) (7) ... 3

4 + ? = 7 ?=3

Sum – Addend = [Addend]:
take away known addend
(7) (3)

7 – 3 = 4

Sum – [Addend] = Addend:
take away to known addend
(7) (4)

7 – ? = 4 → ? = 3

LII Fst Add Abb

object count on
4 ... 567 → 7

4 + 3 $\rightarrow$ 7

object count up to sum
4 ... 123 3

4 + ? = 7 ? = 3

object count down known addend
7 ... start

7 – 3 = 4

object count down to known addend
7 ...

7 – ? = 4 → ? = 3

LII Sec Add KT

sequence count all
①②③④ ⑤⑥⑦ → 7
hear 3 words (3)

4 + 3 → 7

sequence count all up to sum
①②③④ ⑤⑥⑦ stop 1 (7)
3 hear 3 words

4 + ? = 7 → ? = 3

sequence count down known addend and then down to one
⑦⑥⑤ ④③②① hear 3 words (3) 4

7 – 3 = 4

sequence count down to known addend and then down to one
⑦⑥⑤ ④③②①
hear 3 words before hear ④ (4)

7 – ? = 4 → ? = 3

144

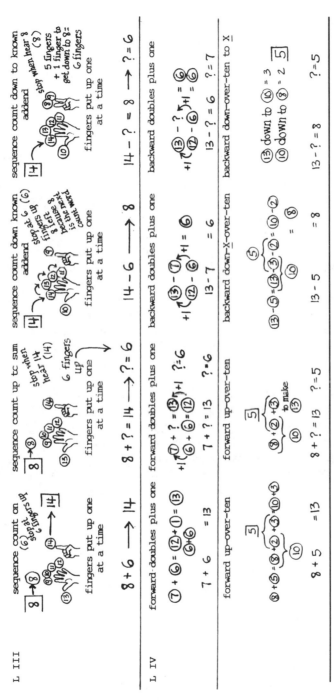

Note: A number in a right-hand bracket, 4], means a cardinal number (a number that tells how many); a circled number is a sequence number (a number within the counting sequence); and a number in parentheses, (4), means that this number is monitored in a keeping-track process so that some count can end at that number or after that many numbers have been said.

the answer after the counting stops at the sum or the known first addend word (the second and fourth columns). Finally, at Level 4, derived fact strategies are carried out either by operating on the cardinalized sequence and moving through the sequence in chunks or by moving unitized number words from addend to addend within the sequence.

Between Levels 1 and 3, children make major advances with respect to both addends. The counting of the first addend becomes abbreviated as children embed the first addend within the sum and move from counting all to counting on. Some kind of keeping-track process for the second addend enables children to use sequence solution procedures instead of just counting objects. Because different researchers using different tasks have reported on each of these kinds of advances, we do not yet have definitive evidence concerning the developmental relationships between these two advances. Therefore, Level 2 could be considered to have two sublevels, each reflecting an advance for one addend (see Fuson, in press-a). Or both such sublevels could be viewed as transitional, and only three major levels could be identified (Fuson, in press-b). The developmental progression outlined in Table 6.4 also is not the only possible progression. The structure of the number–word sequence and the way in which fingers present addition and subtraction both seem to affect the developmental sequence of solution procedures used by children in a given culture. Other developmental paths are discussed in Fuson and Kwon (this volume, chapter 15).

The addition and subtraction strategies described in Table 6.4 are not rote procedures. They all require a considerable amount of conceptual understanding (see Fuson, 1988, Chapter 8, for a discussion of the conceptual structures involved). Counting at each level requires a conceptual operation of constructing unit items for that level, moving from perceptual unit items at Level 1, in which each object is taken as an identical countable object, to Level 2, where unit items are simultaneously in an addend and in a sum, to Level 3, where the words are considered by a child as the unit items, to Level 4, where the unit items are even more abstract and are able to be separated and combined outside of their addend structure while also staying within it (see Steffe & Cobb, 1988, and Steffe et al., 1983, for more discussion of various unit items children use in addition and subtraction situations). Conceptual uniting operations, *cardinal integrations,* are also required at each level in order to form the unit items into addends and into the sum; the results of these cardinal integrations provide the reference for the cardinal meaning of a number word.

There is a considerable literature in English concerning a range of addition and subtraction situations, particularly addition and subtraction word problems. The main categories of such word problems (these are actually possible real-world addition and subtraction situations) are shown in Fig. 6.2. Each situation involves three quantities, any one of which can be unknown, yielding a large number of kinds of addition and subtraction problems. The performance of children in the United States on a range of these problems has been summarized

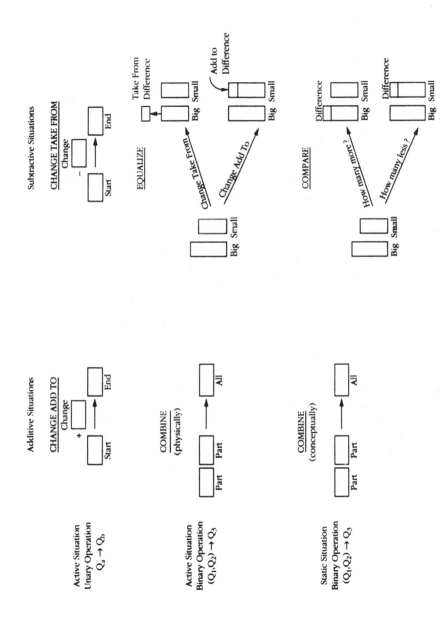

FIG. 6.2. Real world addition and subtraction situations.

147

in several papers (e.g., Carpenter & Moser, 1983; Fuson, 1988, chapter 8; in press-a, in press-b; Riley, Greeno, & Heller, 1983). Initially children directly model the actions in the addition or subtraction situation, using the strategies described in Table 6.4 that reflect the problem situation. For example, they add on or count up for a Change-Add-To problem in which the change is unknown, but they take away or count down for a Change-Take-From problem in which the end quantity is unknown. At this direct modeling level some types of problems cannot be solved by many children. Later, solution procedures may be more freed from the given situation and are no longer direct models of the problem situation. For example, some children choose to solve all subtraction problems by counting up even for situations that fit the third or fourth columns in Table 6.4.

The present mathematics curriculum in the United States (manifested chiefly through textbooks, because there is no national curriculum) mostly ignores how children think about numerical situations (see Fuson, in press-b, for a review). Children in the United States are provided with a very restricted sample of addition and subtraction situations (Stigler, Fuson, Ham, & Kim, 1986) compared to children in the Soviet Union, who solve problems from the whole range of possibilities. The problems used in the United States are generally only the simplest kinds of problems, which many children can already solve when they begin kindergarten. Textbooks in the United States initially present pictures of objects to count for addition and subtraction problems, but suddenly expect children to solve numeral problems without objects. Flashcards and drills are used to help children memorize the facts, and counting may even be forbidden, being viewed as immature and as interfering with later competence. In fact, we found that when children were given opportunities in the classroom to move through the usual developmental sequence in Table 6.4 up to Level 3, counting on for addition and counting up for subtraction, these counting procedures were efficient and comprehensible enough to be used in multidigit addition and subtraction of up to 10 places if the children used one-handed finger patterns to keep track with their nonwriting hand (Fuson, 1986a, 1986b; Fuson & Briars, 1990; Fuson & Secada, 1986; Fuson & Willis, 1988). Learning to subtract by counting up did not interfere with children's understanding of Change-Take-From situations and made subtraction as easy as addition, because the keeping-track process used the sum rather than a known finger pattern to tell a child when to stop counting. First graders of all ability levels learned these Level 3 procedures for all sums and differences to 18 (i.e., through $9 + 9 = 18$ and $18 - 9 = 9$), a considerable acceleration of the usual expectations for children in the United States, who may not even be given the opportunity to add and subtract all sums to 18 in the first grade (Fuson et al., 1988). Children were quite accurate and fast at such counting and easily used counting on and counting up to find addition and subtraction combinations they did not know when adding and subtracting multidigit numbers in second grade.

There are a number of factors that complicate the effort to understand the conceptual structures for addition and subtraction that are possessed by a given child. Children solve a particular problem in a range of ways and may not use their most advanced solution procedure. Subitizing or subitizing plus adding enable children to carry out procedures with certain small numbers before they can do so in general. Memorized facts enable certain problem types to be solved that cannot be solved for unknown facts. Conceptual structures can be affected by instruction and previous experiences. However, it is clear that children can construct conceptual structures that enable them to understand and solve many different kinds of addition and subtraction problems and that mathematics curricula in the United States considerably underestimate the kinds of problems children can successfully engage.

In first or second grade, children begin to construct multiunit conceptual structures for multidigit numbers. In all of the conceptual structures and solution procedures discussed so far, each number is a unitary collection of single unit items. Larger numbers require children to construct multiunits of ten, hundred, and thousand, from which these larger numbers are composed. These multiunits enable children to understand and use English number words and the standard base-ten written marks for four-digit numbers. Research concerning children's understanding of these larger numbers and of multidigit addition and subtraction is summarized in Fuson (1990), and multiunit conceptual structures are discussed there. Instructional issues concerning multiunit numbers are discussed in Fuson (in press-b), and disadvantages of English words for multiunit numbers are described in Fuson and Kwon (this volume, Chapter 15).

CONCLUSION

For several years young children need to present numerical situations to themselves in some concrete way using objects and, later, number words as objects. The originally separate sequence, counting, and cardinal meanings of number words become related and finally integrated over this period so that the number-word sequence itself becomes the primary conceptual tool for solving addition and subtraction situations. This sequence eventually becomes an embedded, seriated, cardinalized, unitized, numerical sequence.

II STRUCTURE OF THE NUMERICAL DOMAIN

7 Number Conservation: Distinguishing Quantifier From Operator Solutions

Linda Tollefsrud-Anderson
University of Wisconsin Barron County Center

Robert L. Campbell
IBM T. J. Watson Research Center

Prentice Starkey
University of California at Berkeley

Robert G. Cooper, Jr.
San Jose State University

Ever since its introduction by Piaget and Szeminska (1941), conservation of number has been one of the most widely researched topics in cognitive development, yet debate continues about this developmental issue. Conflicting definitions of conservation have led to conflicting ways of assessing it. Conflicts about how to assess conservation have led, in turn, to theoretical disputes like the question of small number conservation. We reconsider here the nature of number conservation and the appropriate methods for assessing it. We present refinements in method that make it easier to determine how children are solving conservation tasks. Specifically, we recommend ways to distinguish solutions based on reasoning about the transformation from solutions based on counting or matching. Being able to make these distinctions should help us to understand the developmental transition from nonconserver to conserver.

WHAT CONSERVATION IS AND IS NOT

We define conservation as the ability to know what does and does not change a given quantity. Conservation of number involves the application of a number reasoning principle or *operator* (Gelman, 1972) to the task: specifically, the principle that number does not change when nothing is added or subtracted. In its insistence on transformations and reasoning about them, our definition agrees

151

with those of Piaget and Szeminska (1941) and other Piagetians (e.g., Peill, 1975).

Our definition has a number of implications regarding what conservation is not. It is not the same as recognizing that the configuration of two static arrays is irrelevant to number (as in Siegel, 1978); conservation involves reasoning about transformations. Conservation should not be confused with a response bias either. Some children tend to answer *same* regardless of the nature of the task. If researchers look only at children's judgments and administer only standard conservation trials (on which the correct answer is always *same*), these children may be classified incorrectly as conservers.

Also, our definition of conservation excludes solutions to the conservation task by means of *quantification* procedures. These potentially accurate procedures for determining the numerosity of a set include subitizing, counting, and matching for one-to-one correspondence (Cooper, 1984; Klahr, 1984b). Number conservation tasks can always be solved by quantifying the arrays after the rearrangement transformation. If quantification is *necessary* to arrive at a solution, there is no evidence that the child is using an operator. Of course, quantification procedures may be important in acquiring conservation, and may be used in addition to the child's conservation operator.

Similarly, our definition implies that using quantifiers to establish the equality of the arrays before the transformation is not the crucial issue in number conservation. Gelman (1982a) has suggested that the main obstacle to solving number conservation tasks is the need to use matching for one-to-one correspondence to establish the equality of the initial arrays. However, 2- and 3-year-olds can already use one-to-one correspondence information to solve *primitive* addition and subtraction problems. Given two arrays whose equality was established by one-to-one correspondence, they know that adding to one of the arrays will make it have more than the other array, and that subtracting from it will make it have less (Cooper, Campbell, & Blevins, 1983).

WHAT TYPES OF SOLUTIONS ARE POSSIBLE?

First, quantifier solutions always need to be considered. Children may give a correct answer by counting or matching the arrays after the transformation. This may be done overtly by pointing, counting aloud, drawing lines of correspondence, lip movements or head nodding in correspondence with the items in the arrays, or the quantification may be covert: Children may count or match without clear external signs of doing so. Finally, with small numerosities, *subitizing*, using a rapid perceptual enumeration process, a covert form of quantification, is possible. It has been reported in infants for two- and three-object arrays, and in older children and adults for numerosities up to four (Campbell, Cooper, & Blevins-Knabe, 1988; Chi & Klahr, 1975; Starkey & Cooper, 1980).

Second, operator solutions are of concern. In this case, children base their judgments on an understanding of the rules that apply to the situation, that is, a knowledge of which transformations do and do not change number. Children in this group have traditionally been identified by their ability to explain number conservation (Piaget & Szeminska 1941), but it is also possible for children to use an operator and fail to verbalize about it. In addition, even when the judgment is based on an operator, children may also choose to quantify the arrays.

Third, other types of solutions, neither quantifier- nor operator-based, are possible. Children may respond according to the relative length—or, less frequently, density—of the arrays, may use response perseveration (typically the *same* response), position bias, guessing, and so forth.

All of the aforementioned types of solutions need to be considered in the design of conservation studies. Without checks on each type of response, subjects may be misclassified, making results difficult to interpret. Because of lack of concern about the different possible types of solutions, the literature on number conservation has become muddied by poorly designed investigations. A method for clarifying these issues is introduced here.

Criteria for Conservation: Theoretical Implications

Is There Small-Number Conservation? Piaget and Szeminska (1941) spoke of number conservation abilities as all-or-none. Small numbers were not presented on the grounds that they were intuitive. Since that time, many researchers have found that children are more likely to be correct on conservation problems with small numbers (up to four or five) than on problems with large numbers, and some have interpreted such results as evidence for small-number conservation (e.g., Bever, Mehler, & Epstein, 1968; Siegler, 1981). Others have failed to find an advantage for small numbers (e.g., Cuneo, 1982), or have considered quantifier solutions as a basis for some (but not all) small-number conservation success (e.g., Moore & Frye, 1986). It has been generally assumed, however, that young children can have a conservation operator that is restricted in scope to small numbers.

Strikingly, none of the advocates of small-number conservation have suggested that young children can give explanations for small-number, but not large-number tasks; their arguments are invariably based on correct judgments alone. Therefore, there are reasons for suspecting that success on small-number conservation problems is due to quantification strategies and not to a conservation operator.

One *covert* quantification strategy specific to small numbers would be to subitize the arrays on the conservation task after the transformation. Children could notice, for instance, that both arrays have two items and conclude that they are still equal. Subitizing is difficult to observe without controlling exposure durations and measuring response latencies, but it must be considered as a possible strategy. If only correct judgments are required on the conservation task, children who solve problems by subitizing may get small-number problems correct, but not large-number problems. They may then be classified as small-number conservers, even if they lack a conservation operator.

Moreover, most studies of number conservation have not even monitored solutions by *overt* quantification. Children may be able to count the arrays, or match them for one-to-one correspondence, and do this accurately for smaller but not larger numerosities. Again, if only correct *judgments* are required, such children may be classified as conservers of small number only, when in fact they are not applying a conservation operator at all. Overt quantification procedures, unlike covert ones, are easy to observe when considered worth noting.

Of course, children may use subitizing, or other overt or covert means of quantifying, yet still possess a conservation operator. How can the experimenter know which children use an operator and which do not? One answer is that requiring explanations makes it clear which children understand the conservation principle.

Should Explanations be Required?   Piaget and Szeminska (1941) required, in addition to correct judgments, that children give some verbal account of the number conservation principle before classifying them as conservers. In more recent work, this requirement has often been rejected. Of Brainerd's (1973) arguments in favor of correct judgments as a sufficient criterion, the strongest is that some children may be able to apply a number conservation operator to solve conservation problems, yet fail to express that understanding verbally. If that were true, requiring explanations would lead to some conservers being mis-classified as nonconservers, a case of false negatives. Even Piaget (1974) de-scribed tasks that children could solve without being able to explain how they did so.

Explanations, however, provide useful information about children's reasoning processes that should not be disregarded. Requiring explanations might help to distinguish quantifier solutions from operator solutions, and, additionally, might resolve the status of small-number conservation. A child who can explain a conservation judgment in terms of the nature of the transformation clearly has a conservation operator, regardless of varying overt strategies that might be em-ployed, and regardless of the speed of response.

When the explanation requirement is dropped, there is an increased risk of false positives. The possibility that children are relying on various quantification procedures is difficult to rule out unless explanations are required. For small numerosities, how can one tell whether the child is using a conservation operator, subitizing, or covertly counting? For larger numerosities, what if counting or matching is being used? If the child is obviously counting or matching, he or she could be labeled a nonconserver. This seems inadequate, however, because some children who count or match might also be able to give adequate explanations, which suggests that they are not *relying* on quantification to solve the problems. And what of children who count or match the arrays, but do so covertly rather than overtly? The most obvious way for the experimenter to know whether these children understand conservation or not is to elicit explanations.

What is the Relation of Conservation to Other Number Tasks?   First, it is necessary to consider the relation of conservation abilities (recognizing sameness) to addition or subtraction abilities (recognizing a change in number). In our studies, we include addition and subtraction trials (starting with equal arrays, and then going to unequal arrays) at each numerosity. Including these trials helps us to identify children with a *same* response bias; children must vary their response in accordance with the type of trial presented to be consistently correct. These trials are also important because they assess children's understanding of what does change number, as well as what does not. Both conservers and nonconservers (when not engaging in biased responding) should do well on addition and subtraction trials of this type, because they require only primitive addition and subtraction (Cooper et al., 1983).

Second, what is the relation of conservation tasks (where there is a transformation) to nontransformational (static) tasks? Static trials allow us to see how children solve the task when the conservation operator is useless. Including static tasks is a way of finding out what variety of strategies the children have available, and to what extent they can choose a strategy appropriate to the task. More advanced children might be expected to use the conservation operator on a transformation task, and to use quantification strategies to make relative numerosity judgments when there is no transformation.

EXPERIMENT 1

Issues Addressed

In Experiment 1, we explored the issue of small number conservation by comparing performance on smaller numerosity ($N = 2$ and 4) and larger numerosity ($N = 8$ and 20) trials. Addition and subtraction trials were included at each numerosity to check for response bias. Static trials were presented to more generally assess strategies across tasks. Finally, to address the issue of solving the conservation task by overt quantification, we noted whether children overtly counted or matched the arrays after the transformation.

Method

After 3 children were dropped for various reasons, 32 children (sixteen 4-year-olds and sixteen 5-year-olds) enrolled in private preschools served as subjects.

Materials and Tasks.   The materials for the tasks were linear arrays of 2 × 2 cm black cardboard squares. The experimenter put two arrays of squares on a large sheet of white paper placed on a table in front of the child. One of the two arrays in a pair always contained 2, 4, 8, or 20 squares. On a given trial, the arrays were either equal in numerosity or differed by one square.

On the conservation trials, the experimenter moved the squares in one array in different directions to break up the spatial one-to-one correspondence, and lengthened or shortened the array. On the addition and subtraction trials, the one-to-one correspondence was disrupted by moving squares in different directions, and one square was added to or taken from a predetermined location in the array, without changing the array's overall length. For each absolute numerosity, there were four different transformations. The length of the arrays was misleading on both the conservation and the addition/subtraction trials. In the static task, the arrays were made directly analogous to the post-transformation arrays in the transformation tasks. Thus, there were four static array pairs for each absolute numerosity.

Procedure.   The children were tested individually in two 20-minute sessions. On each transformation trial, the experimenter constructed the arrays as the child watched, using one-to-one correspondence information to draw attention to the equality of the arrays. The array closer to the child was designated as the child's array, and the other as the experimenter's. The experimenter then asked, "Do you have the most squares, do I have the most squares, or do we both have the same number of squares?," varying the order of clauses in this question from trial to trial.

Once the child affirmed the initial equality of the arrays, the experimenter transformed one of them as the child observed. The array that was transformed was counterbalanced over trials. The experimenter then asked the child to judge the relative numerosity of the arrays. On the static trials, the experimenter laid preconstructed arrays on the presentation sheet, then asked the child to judge the relative numerosity of the arrays. On each trial the experimenter recorded overt qualification behavior (counting or matching). On the conservation and the addition/subtraction numerosity trials with four-item arrays, explanations were elicited.

Results and Discussion: Experiment 1

Criteria for Conservation.   In order to classify children as conservers or nonconservers, we examined the explanations of all of the children who succeeded on at least one small-number ($N = 2$ or 4) conservation problem. Typical adequate explanations asserted that length transformations could not change numerosity (e.g., "You just moved them; moving doesn't make it have more") or that addition or subtraction was necessary to change numerosity (e.g.,

"They're the same 'cause you didn't put another one on"). Explanations were considered inadequate if they referred only to the absolute numerosity of the final arrays (e.g., "We've both got the same 'cause you got four and I got four") or were irrelevant (" 'Cause I can see them").

Of the 23 children who made at least one correct small-number conservation judgment, 14 gave adequate explanations and never overtly quantified, 7 overtly quantified and never gave an adequate explanation, 1 gave an adequate explanation and overtly quantified, and 1 neither overtly quantified nor gave an adequate explanation, $p < .001$ (χ^2 test of independence). We also observed 9 classic nonconservers who gave no correct judgments, and presumably used the length of the post-transformation arrays as a criterion, and 1 child was correct and did not overtly quantify but could not explain either. By our criterion of at least one adequate explanation, there were 15 conservers and 17 nonconservers in our sample.

Overall Performance of Conservers and Nonconservers. The mean proportions of correct judgments on transformation and static tasks, of equal and unequal relative numerosity, for conservers and nonconservers, are shown in Table 7.1.

There were four significant main effects ($p < .001$). Conservers performed better than nonconservers overall; performance was better on the transformation tasks than the static tasks; performance was better on unequal than equal numerosity problems; and there were fewer errors on small-number than on large-number problems. The pattern of results can be explained in terms of ceiling performance on addition/subtraction trials, differences between small- and large-number conservation performance, and the effect of numerosity on static task performance.

Addition and Subtraction Performance. Both conservers and nonconservers averaged over 90% correct on addition and subtraction problems, regardless of numerosity and despite misleading length information (see Table 7.1). Every child performed at least as well on the addition and subtraction problems as on the conservation problems, and usually better. Also, each child performed as well on the addition and subtraction trials as on the corresponding unequal-numerosity static trials, and usually better. No child ever overtly quantified the post-transformation arrays on the addition and subtraction problems. Other studies have previously shown that primitive addition and subtraction are much easier than conservation (Cooper et al., 1983; Silverman & Briga, 1981; Starkey & Gelman, 1982).

Conservation Performance: Small Versus Large Numbers. Although our conservers qualified as such on the basis of one adequate explanation on a small-number trial, in fact their performance was uniformly high (over 90% correct) on

TABLE 7.1

Proportion of Correct Judgments for Conservers and Nonconservers
on Transformation and Static Tasks in Experiment 1

	Transformation Task				Static Task			
	$N = 2$	$N = 4$	$N = 8$	$N = 20$	$N = 2$	$N = 4$	$N = 8$	$N = 20$
Conservers								
TS order[a] (n = 6)								
Equal-numerosity	.92	.92	1.00	1.00	1.00	1.00	.83	.75
Unequal-numerosity	1.00	1.00	1.00	1.00	1.00	.92	.50	.25
ST order[a] (n = 9)								
Equal-numerosity	1.00	1.00	1.00	1.00	.94	.94	.61	.44
Unequal-numerosity	1.00	1.00	1.00	1.00	1.00	1.00	.61	.44
Nonconservers								
TS order (n = 10)								
Equal-numerosity	.15	.00	.05	.10	.35	.30	.05	.15
Unequal-numerosity	1.00	1.00	.85	.85	.85	.70	.55	.35
ST order (n = 7)								
Equal-numerosity	.43	.43	.21	.14	.79	.50	.36	.36
Unequal-numerosity	1.00	1.00	.93	1.00	1.00	.86	.36	.43

[a] TS order is transformation task before static, and ST order is static before transformation.

large and small numerosities. In addition, the conservers' performance did not vary with order of task presentation (transformation first or static first). The conservers were significantly better than the nonconservers on conservation (equal-numerosity transformation) problems at all levels of absolute numerosity and for both task orders. The conservers' pattern of performance was what we would expect if they were consistently using an operator to solve the conservation problems.

The nonconservers, by contrast, performed differently on conservation problems depending on task order. Those who received the static tasks first averaged 30% correct on conservation trials, and their performance declined with increasing numerosity. Those who received the transformation tasks first averaged 8% correct and performed poorly across all numerosities. Giving the static tasks first apparently encouraged nonconservers to attempt quantifier solutions, leading them to succeed on small-number problems, but leaving them vulnerable to counting errors on large-number problems. Giving the transformation tasks first discouraged quantifier solutions in favor of length responses, leading to failure on both small- and large-number conservation problems.

Conservers can be distinguished from nonconservers in a number of ways. The conservers in this study performed equally well on small- and large-number conservation problems, did not solve conservation problems by overt quantification, and were not affected by task order. Those nonconservers who were able to solve small-number but not large-number conservation problems were using overt quantification of the final arrays. There was, therefore, no small-number conservation, just quantifier solutions to small-number conservation problems.

Static Task Performance: Use of Appropriate Quantifiers.   Children needed to count or match to be correct on the static trials, at least for numerosities beyond the subitizing range. However, young children are prone to errors in quantification, so the proportion of correct judgments underestimates how often children quantified the arrays. A child was said to be using appropriate quantifiers if he or she made a correct judgment, or made an incorrect judgment that resulted from an error in overt quantification. The proportion of trials on which conservers and nonconservers used appropriate quantifiers on the equal-numerosity trials of the static task is shown in Table 7.2.

Conservers made significantly more correct judgments (at the .05 level) than nonconservers, and used appropriate quantifiers more often, in both task orders. This is not to say that the nonconservers lacked overt counting or matching skills, just that they were less likely to use them.

Conclusions.   We conclude that children cannot conserve small numbers before they can conserve large numbers. Better performance on small-number conservation tasks is better attributed to quantification skills than to a conservation operator specific to small numbers. This conclusion is based on three facts:

TABLE 7.2
Proportion of Use of Appropriate Quantifiers on the Static Task
for Conservers and Nonconservers in Experiment 1

	$N = 2$	$N = 4$	$N = 8$	$N = 20$
Conservers				
TS order ($n = 6$)	1.00	1.00	.92	.83
ST order ($n = 9$)	.94	.94	.83	.78
Nonconservers				
TS order ($n = 10$)	.35	.30	.15	.25
ST order ($n = 7$)	.79	.57	.64	.57

(a) Young children can quantify small-number arrays more accurately than large-number arrays; (b) some young children use quantification skills like counting to solve number conservation problems; and (c) these children cannot adequately explain their solutions.

The quantification strategies of conservers and nonconservers were clearly different, with the conservers spontaneously using appropriate quantifiers on the static task more often than the nonconservers did. However, our results do not establish a sequential relation between situationally appropriate quantification and number conservation. Finally, we found an important relation between explanations and overt quantification. We have contended that children who can explain their answers solve conservation problems by applying a conservation operator, and therefore do not need to quantify the post-transformation arrays. To be sure of this, however, we need to establish that children who explain their answers are not quantifying *covertly*.

EXPERIMENTS 2 AND 3

The purpose of Experiments 2 and 3 was to detect or control children's use of covert counting or matching for one-to-one correspondence. In order to do this, we measured response latencies in both studies. Covert quantification should result in longer response latencies, whereas solutions from applying a rule, whether correct like the conservation operator, or erroneous like length, should result in shorter latencies. In Experiment 3, we also introduced a bunching transformation (in place of the usual linear expansion and contraction) that made accurate quantification difficult, and that was intended to force children's attempts at covert quantification out into the open.

Covert Quantification.   We have assumed that the presence of overt quantification without explanations indicates conservation judgments based on quantification. Its absence, however, does not necessarily indicate judgments based on a conservation operator. There are three covert quantifiers on which preschoolers might base their judgments: subitizing, covert counting, and covert matching.

Subitizing is the only covert quantifier known to be generally available to preschoolers. It can certainly be used to solve conservation problems for small numerosities. Subitizing is fast (Chi & Klahr, 1975), so response latencies cannot discriminate it from quick reasoning processes. However, subitizing is tightly limited in range ($N = 1$ to 3, or perhaps 4), so it can be ruled out by using numerosities of 4 or larger. Hence, the $N = 2$ trials of Experiment 1 were dropped in Experiments 2 and 3.

Covert counting, mental counting without external signs like lip or finger movements, may be available to preschoolers, but there is little evidence for it. There is no evidence at present that preschoolers can count more than five items covertly (Cowan, 1979); claims to this effect by Gelman and Tucker (1975) and by Ginsburg and Russell (1981) are not backed by latency data. By contrast, covert counting is known to be available and widely used in the early school years (Siegler & Shrager, 1984; Campbell et al., 1988). Covert counting is slow. Chi and Klahr (1975) found that, outside the subitizing range, 5-year-olds' (overt) counting times showed an average increment of 1.05 sec/item. Overt and covert counting have similar time courses. For a solution to our $N = 8$ conservation problems, Chi and Klahr's functions predict a latency of at least 14 sec. For an $N - 20$ problem, the predicted latency is 38 sec. By contrast, operator-based solutions should be rapid and should not vary with numerosity.

Given the sensitivity of young children's counting to spatial arrangement, and their reliance on pointing to keep track of objects (Shannon, 1978), bunching or piling up objects from one of the arrays should seriously impede covert counting. Children would be forced to count or match overtly to have any chance of being accurate. Bunching was employed for this purpose in Experiment 3.

Covert matching, visually pairing objects in adjacent arrays for one-to-one correspondence, is a poorly understood process. Fuson et al. (1983) claimed that 5-year-olds were using covert matching on a conservation task, although the children did not mention it in their explanations. This seems unlikely because young children find even *overt* matching very difficult when the arrays are not in spatial one-to-one correspondence, for example, in the post-transformation arrays of a number conservation task (Piaget & Inhelder, 1966a). It should be noted that Fuson et al. (1983) did not record response latencies, and hence could not distinguish covert matching from operator solutions.

Although response latency data are not available for overt or covert matching, the process must be incremental. Matching items from two N-item arrays should take about as long as counting N items. Moreover, our bunching transformation should destroy spatial one-to-one correspondence information, making accurate covert matching impossible.

EXPERIMENT 2

Method

Complete and usable data were collected for 21 children (aged 4 years, 3 months to 6 years, 1 month) enrolled in private preschools. Thirteen children were dropped from the study for various reasons: Three, for example, had to be excluded because of a response bias to say *same* on the transformation tasks. (Response bias was presumed if a child gave the same relative numerosity judgment on all four equal and unequal-numerosity transformation trials for at least one absolute numerosity.)

Tasks and Materials. The materials were unequally spaced linear arrays of 2 × 2 cm black paper squares on a strip of white construction paper. The transformation task began with two arrays of equal numerosity which were placed in spatial one-to-one correspondence. The array to be transformed was movable; the other array was fixed. In the movable array, the squares at the ends were simply laid on the paper, whereas the squares in the middle were glued to a narrow white paper strip so that they could all be moved at the same time. In the fixed array, all of the squares were glued to the white paper strip. There were two conservation trials, one addition trial, and one subtraction trial for each absolute numerosity. In the static task, both arrays were identical to the post-transformation arrays on the corresponding transformation task.

Procedure. All children were tested individually, in two 15- to 20-minute sessions. The transformation and static trials were presented in a similar manner to those of Experiment 1. On each test trial, the experimenter measured the child's response latency. Explanations were elicited on the first addition/subtraction and the first conservation trials of each absolute numerosity block. Children who did not give an adequate explanation on the first conservation trial were given another chance on the second conservation trial of that block.

EXPERIMENT 3

Method

Complete and usable data were collected for 21 children, aged 4 years, 1 month to 6 years, enrolled in preschools. Ten children were dropped from the study for various reasons, including two who showed a response bias on the transformation trials.

Materials and Tasks. Arrays of 2 × 2 cm black paper squares were used; one of the arrays always had 4, 8, or 20 squares. In the transformation task, two unequally spaced linear arrays of equal numerosity were first presented in spatial one-to-one correspondence. The fixed array was glued to a white cloth. The array to be transformed was laid out on a long strip of white cloth with a red border that served to separate the two arrays. The experimenter transformed the movable arrays by lifting the ends of the red-bordered strip of cloth, causing the black squares to fall into a bunch (in which some of the squares were hidden from view). On the unequal-numerosity trials, one square was added to or taken from the bunched array after the bunching transformation.

In the static task, both arrays were glued to a single sheet of white paper. The static arrays corresponded to the post-transformation arrays in absolute numerosity, but not in spatial layout. Whereas one of the arrays was identical to the fixed array in the transformation task, the other array consisted of squares randomly scattered across two thirds of the width of the white paper strip. The arrays were separated by a red line. Although the static arrays were not bunched, the lack of one-to-one correspondence made matching difficult.

Procedure. All subjects were tested individually in two 10- to 20-minute sessions. The procedure was essentially that of Experiment 2, and the same dependent measures were taken.

Results and Discussion: Experiments 2 and 3

Quantification and Response Latency Measures. Overt quantification was less prevalent here than in Experiment 1. In Experiment 2 (linear arrays) only 3 out of 21 children were ever observed to quantify on the transformation trials, and only 10 out of 21 ever quantified on the static task. In Experiment 3 (bunched arrays), 5 out of 21 children quantified at least once on the transformation trials, and 14 out of 21 did so on the static task. A few of these children quantified consistently across trials, whereas others quantified only once or twice on the 12 trials of a given task.

We expected a strong positive relation between the presence of overt quantification and longer response latencies. A point-biserial correlation was calculated between the mean response latency over two trials (within absolute numerosity, experiment, and relative numerosity) and the presence versus absence of overt quantification. All correlations were significant at the .05 level (and many were at the .001 level). The expected high correlation between response latency and overt quantification was obtained despite sporadic overt quantification, highly variable response latencies, and the small number of trials. The pattern of results for the transformation tasks were similar, although overt quantification was too infrequent to make statistical tests appropriate.

We also examined the distributions of response latencies. These were bimodal for $N = 8$ and $N = 20$ on the static task. The bimodality appeared to reflect the difference in response latencies between the quantifiers (those who counted or matched at least once on the four trials at each absolute numerosity) and the nonquantifiers (those who never quantified for that numerosity).

To classify the children as having generally long or generally short response latencies, the response latency measure was dichotomized. The median response latencies associated with overt quantification and nonquantification were determined for each numerosity in the static task, and the mean of the two medians became the cut off value for long versus short latencies. For instance, for $N = 8$ in Experiment 2, the median response latency for overt quantification was 12.68 sec, and the median latency for nonquantification was 3.74 sec; hence the cutoff value was 8.21 sec. In contrast to the consistently short medians for trials without quantification, the medians for trials where overt quantification was observed varied linearly with numerosity.

Criteria for Conservation: Quantification and Explanation.   Because the frequency distributions for overt quantification indicated that the children were basically of two types, they were divided into two groups: those who seldom or never overtly quantified and those who did so frequently. A child was classified as a quantifier if overt quantification was evident on three out of the eight larger numerosity trials, but only if he or she quantified at least once at each of these numerosities (8 and 20), to ensure that the quantification strategy was a consistent one. Other children were classified as nonquantifiers.

An analogous criterion was adopted for the response latency measure. To classify a child as a long-latency responder, three out of eight long latencies on the larger numerosity trials were required. Children were classified as quantifiers or nonquantifiers, and as long- or short-latency responders on the static task, and separately on the transformation task.

The classification of children's quantification and latencies across numerosities permits us to address the issue of *covert quantification*. A *covert quantifier* would be a child who showed consistently long response latencies (not just occasional hesitations) without any overt quantification. One child in Experiment 3 had long latencies but did not overtly quantify. This is the only possible case of covert quantification in either study; moreover, this child showed the covert quantification response pattern only on the static task (correct on two-thirds of the trials and long latencies on seven out of eight). By contrast, this child was 100% correct and gave adequate explanations on the conservation task, accompanied by short response latencies on every trial. One child in Experiment 2 quantified overtly but did not have long latencies. This child would start to count and give up early. All other children either quantified overtly on a consistent basis and had consistently long latencies, or did not quantify consistently and had short latencies.

Children were also classified according to their conservation explanations. There were 8 conservers and 13 nonconservers in Experiment 2, and 10 conservers and 11 nonconservers in Experiment 3. In Experiment 2, there were no children who consistently quantified on the transformation task; in Experiment 3, two children quantified consistently, and neither of them ever gave an adequate conservation explanation. Consistent quantification was much less common in Experiments 2 and 3 than in Experiment 1, perhaps because the children in Experiment 1 were encouraged to count in their nursery school. The timing procedure and the bunching transformation may also have inhibited counting in Experiments 2 and 3.

Overall Performance of Conservers and Nonconservers.   Children's performance on the transformation and static tasks can be seen in Table 7.3. Unlike Experiment 1, there was no effect of the order in which tasks were presented. Conservers performed better than nonconservers, and transformation performance was better than static performance overall. More errors were made with larger numerosities on the static task.

Addition and Subtraction.   The advantage for transformation over static performance was partly due to good performance on the addition and subtraction trials by both conservers and nonconservers. Although such trials were easy, without them five children with a bias to say *same* would have been retained in our samples. Addition and subtraction performance was nearly perfect for nonconservers in Experiment 2 (linear arrays), but was worse than expected in Experiment 3 (bunched arrays). The bunching transformation used in Experiment

TABLE 7.3
Proportion Correct Judgments for Conservers and Nonconservers
on Transformation and Static Tasks in Experiments 2 and 3

	Transformation Task			Static Task		
	N = 4	N = 8	N = 20	N = 4	N = 8	N = 20
Experiment 2						
Conservers (n = 8)						
Equal-numerosity	1.00	1.00	1.00	.88	.81	.69
Unequal-numerosity	1.00	.88	.75	.95	.56	.44
Nonconservers (n = 13)						
Equal-numerosity	.35	.38	.38	.46	.38	.31
Unequal numerosity	.96	.96	.92	.85	.19	.19
Experiment 3						
Conservers (n = 10)						
Equal-numerosity	1.00	1.00	.95	.90	.85	.70
Unequal-numerosity	1.00	1.00	1.00	.90	.60	.55
Nonconservers (n = 11)						
Equal-numerosity	.68	.59	.55	.77	.77	.36
Unequal-numerosity	.82	.77	.73	.64	.64	.27

3 produced a great disparity in length between the post-transformation arrays, which may have encouraged reliance on length information. In fact, all of the addition and subtraction errors in Experiment 3 were made by four nonconservers.

Transitional Conservers.   We discovered that some children who did not give adequate explanations were consistently correct (on at least five out of six conservation trials) across numerosities, yet had short response latencies. Nine children (21% of the total) from Experiments 2 and 3 fit into this category. Because our method rules out consistently correct answers due to response bias, positional responding, or quantification of any kind, we concluded that we had evidence for the existence of *transitional conservers,* children who apply the conservation operator, but cannot yet explain it.

Static Task Performance: Use of Quantifiers.   In Experiment 1 it appeared that conservers would use appropriate quantifiers when the problem called for them. However, 5 out of 8 conservers in Experiment 2, and 3 out of 10 conservers in Experiment 3 failed to quantify consistently on the static task. The relationship between possessing a conservation operator and using appropriate quantifiers appears more complicated following Experiments 2 and 3 than it did in Experiment 1. The presence of transitional conservers complicates it further.

We cross-classified children according to their conservation explanations and their response latencies on the transformation and static tasks. Five groups resulted from this cross-classification (see Fig. 7.1), each with a specific profile of conservation and static task performance.

The NSL group's performance is difficult to interpret. Some of the NSL children resembled the CSL group, except for their lack of conservation explanations. Others performed poorly on the conservation trials, but quantified on the static task. The reason for these differences is that four of the children (two in each experiment) were transitional conservers; the three remaining children (all in Experiment 3) were nonconservers. In addition, three NSS children in Experiment 2 and one in Experiment 3 were transitional conservers.

Conclusions.   Experiments 2 and 3 show a clear relation between overt quantification and longer response latencies. Children who were clearly quantifying took about .75 sec per item in the arrays to arrive at a judgment. Children who were not observed to quantify decided, on the average, in under 4 sec, regardless of the numerosity of the arrays. No child was found covertly quantifying on the transformation task (one child in Experiment 3 may have been using such a strategy, but on the static task only).

When overt quantification was observed, it was usually counting. Only two children in Experiment 2 ever used overt matching to solve the problems, and none in Experiment 3 did so. (Two children in Experiment 3 did, however, point

- Conservers, Short on Transformation, Long on Static (CSL). Ten children, mean age 5 years, 4 months. The most advanced children. They gave correct judgments without quantifying on the transformation task, and they adequately explained their conservation judgments. On the static task, this group used overt quantification; their performance declined with absolute numerosity on the static task because of counting errors.

- Conservers, Short on Transformation, Short on Static (CSS). Eight children, mean age 5 years, 1 month. These children had a conservation operator, but they chose not to quantify on the static task. Performance on transformation trials was virtually perfect, but on the static task, they performed much more poorly than the CSL group.

- Nonconservers, Short on Transformation, Short on Static (NSS). Fifteen children, mean age 4 years, 10 months. Mostly classic nonconservers. Performed poorly on the conservation trials, much better on the addition and subtraction trials. On the static task, some showed a *same* response bias, whereas others were length responders.

- Nonconservers, Long on Transformation, Long on Static (NLL). Two children in Experiment 3, mean age 4 years, 5 months. Nonconservers who counted on both transformation and static tasks. Their performance declined with increasing numerosity on both tasks, and there was no clear advantage for transformation over static performance.

- Nonconservers, Short on Transformation, Long on Static (NSL). Seven children without a consistent performance profile. Three were real nonconservers and four were transitional conservers.

FIG. 7.1.   Performance profiles for children classified by conservation explanations and response latencies on transformation and static tasks in Experiments 2 and 3.

out the one-to-one correspondence of the arrays when asked to explain their judgments.) Counting was less frequent here than in Experiment 1, and the simple dichotomy between conservers, who counted on the static task, and nonconservers, who tended not to count on the static task, was not found. The relation between counting and conservation is clearly more complex than Experiment 1 suggested; as Meljac (1979) has shown, children's counting is highly situation-dependent.

Our response latency data cast new light on number conservation as well as on the prevalence of covert quantification. They indicate that an adequate explanation criterion for conservation is too conservative. Nine children (21% of the total) in Experiments 2 and 3 seemed to possess the conservation operator, but did not give adequate explanations. These transitionals were included in the nonconserver group for the analyses reported here, but such children merit investigation as a separate group in the future.

On the other hand, a correct judgment criterion for conservation is not sufficient. Although solutions by covert quantification seem negligible, at least for 4- and 5-year-olds working with larger numerosities, solutions by overt quantification do occur and must be monitored. With older age groups, response latencies should also be measured to check for covert quantification. In consequence, we recommend the following minimum criteria for an operator-based understanding of number conservation: consistently correct judgments, lack of response bias, and consistently short response latencies or lack of overt quantification.

GENERAL DISCUSSION

Our findings have a number of implications for the assessment of number conservation and for the interpretation of success on number conservation problems. A distinction between small and large numerosities should be made in research on number problems, and the use of quantification on number problems should be monitored consistently. The existence of a group of children who solve conservation problems by quantifying must be acknowledged. Being alert for these children, and for transitional conservers, complicates the assessment of number conservation, but it also makes us sensitive to details that may help us to understand how conservation develops.

Small-Number Conservation.   Young children perform better with small numbers than large on varied kinds of number reasoning problems (Cooper, 1984; Cooper et al., 1983), not just conservation. However, children who solve small-number conservation problems, but not large-number problems, do not have a special conservation operator for small numerosities ($N = 1$ to 4). They solve conservation problems by simply quantifying the arrays after the transformation. We summarize our reasons as follows: (a) Children can always quantify the final arrays on a small-number conservation problem by subitizing or counting them; (b) performance on small-number conservation problems is as good as, or worse than, performance on the corresponding static comparison problems, but never better (e.g., Beilin, 1968; Cowan, 1979; LaPointe & O'Donnell, 1974); (c) children do not give adequate explanations for small-number conservation problems without also giving them for large-number problems.

Children who have a small-number conservation operator may exist, despite out failure to find them but demonstrating that would require clear and reliable counterexamples to points (b) or (c). In the absence of such counterexamples, quantification is the best explanation of success on small-number conservation problems.

Monitoring Quantification.   We recommend that an index of quantification be included in all studies of number conservation and related number operator problems. Children who rely on quantifier solutions are not using a conservation operator. Checking for quantifier solutions is also necessary to detect transitional conservers. Identifying children who solve by quantifying and children who are transitional is essential for accurate assessment of conservation performance, especially when conservation is being related to other task accomplishments or when the effectiveness of training is being assessed. Normally, looking for overt counting and matching should suffice. Covert quantification is rare at the age that most children come to understand number conservation (see Tollefsrud, 1981). When covert counting or matching is suspected, however, response latencies must be measured.

Quantifier Solutions as an Intermediate Level.   Attending to children's use of quantification on number conservation tasks might help us to understand the origins of number conservation. Quantifier solutions to large-number conservation problems have often been reported (Gréco, 1962; Meljac, 1979; Saxe, 1979; Siegler, 1981) but have never been studied systematically. A child who relies on quantification to solve conservation problems is clearly more advanced than a nonconserver who still relies on length and less advanced than a conserver who applies an operator and can explain his or her answer.

It should be emphasized that this intermediate level involves *reliance* on quantifiers to *solve* conservation problems. Children can also quantify in order to *verify* answers that they arrived at in other ways. Some conservers or transitionals in our studies (three in Experiment 2 and seven in Experiment 3) counted or matched the arrays when asked for an explanation, although they had not quantified to solve the problem. Children may quantify the arrays in a conservation task even though they could solve the problem without counting. Fuson et al. (1983), for instance, found a number of 5-year-olds who counted the arrays on conservation problems, but were able to give adequate explanations. Monitoring quantification and eliciting explanations makes it possible to judge whether or not children are relying on quantification to solve conservation problems.

In any case, it is not known how widespread quantifier solutions really are. Is there a substage at which all children solve large-number conservation problems by quantification, or are there branching developmental pathways, with or without quantifier solutions as an intermediate step? Piaget and Szeminska (1941) rejected any constructive role for counting in the development of conservation. Other approaches acknowledge a role for counting, but point out that conservation takes more than an empirical determination of the relative numerosity of the post-transformation arrays. Conservation also requires knowledge of addition and subtraction, and knowledge of the reliability of length strategies (Cooper, 1984; Klahr, 1984b). More research is needed on quantifier solutions and their place on the paths that lead to number conservation.

The Developmental Status of Number Conservation. There have been numerous attempts (e.g., Bryant, 1974; Gelman, 1982a; McGarrigle & Donaldson, 1975) to refute Piaget by showing that children have a basic understanding of number conservation, or an *invariance principle,* much earlier than he thought. The claim that children have a conservation operator for small numbers before they have one for large numbers is one type of early conservation claim. To contend with such claims, we need to ask where number conservation is located in the overall course of number development. We cannot maintain, as Piaget and Szeminska (1941) did, that conservation is the single true mark of having a "number concept." Children's quantifiers and operators develop considerably before conservation normally emerges. By the same token, we do not need to claim that they understand conservation from the start in order to validate young children's knowledge of number. We need to ask what problems a conservation operator would solve for the young child, and indeed how conservation gets identified as a problem in the first place. Perhaps children have to represent addition and subtraction transformations for large and small numbers before they seek a rule for what happens when nothing is added or subtracted (Cooper, 1984). To explain the development of number conservation, we need to place it in a complex developmental sequence.

On the evidence we have presented here, number conservation is complicated. It is not enough to collect judgments on conservation tasks and make a binary classification of conservers and nonconservers. Children's performance on related problems needs to be assessed, and multiple measures of performance (explanations, overt quantification, and response latencies) are needed. The classification system needs to be expanded to four categories: length responders (the classic nonconservers), quantifiers, transitional conservers, and conservers who can explain their judgments. Through such efforts, we should be rewarded with richer information about the relationships between number conservation and the quantifiers and operators that are its prerequisites.

ACKNOWLEDGMENTS

We wish to express our thanks to the staff and students of All Saints' Episcopal Day School, First Baptist Church Kindergarten Day Nursery, Teri Road Baptist Child Care Center, University Child and Family Laboratory, and Faith Presbyterian Church School in Austin, TX. We would like to thank Kevin Miller for his comments and Jean-Paul Fischer for his extensive editorial suggestions. An earlier version was presented at the Midwestern Psychological Association meeting, Chicago, May 8, 1986. A full report of the experiments is available in Tollefsrud-Anderson, Campbell, Starkey, and Cooper (1986).

8 Early Principles Aid Initial but Not Later Conceptions of Number

Rochel Gelman
Betty Meck
University of California, Los Angeles

Our account of number concepts shares with Piaget and Szeminska's (1941) the assumption that infants and children are actively involved in the construction of their knowledge. Unlike Piaget and Szeminska, we grant infants some skeletal domain-relevant structures, ones that help them search and use environments, assimilate and accommodate. We do not assume that such implicit knowledge is well-articulated. Early principles help children find and attend to what is relevant and therefore start them down the right developmental path. Although these structures are outline in form, they help keep together domain-relevant bits of material before their relationships to each other are understood.

By adopting a rational-constructivist view of cognitive development we do not expect immediate skill and perfection when children perform. Young children have a great deal to learn and their performance will vary as a function of experience, age, and setting. A key feature of our account of learning and development is that both mental representations *and* their class of potentially relevant inputs are defined with reference to abstract relations. We also offer an account of children's domain-specific errors that expands the list of error sources. In addition to the traditional ones—a lack of conceptual competence or random noise—errors can be attributed to limits on the ability to generate competent plans of action and/or to interpret correctly the question-answering routines used in a wide range of cognitive developmental assessments.

Although we presume there are some universal sets of skeletal principles underlying some early domains of knowledge acquisition, we do not believe that such principles are operative in all domains. Like Brown and Kane (1988), we maintain that our young have an advantage in their early learning if they already have some skeletal organizations with which to organize their memories of the inputs they are offered or find. Otherwise they have to acquire from scratch both the structure and knowledge of the data that is organized by the structure. We develop in this chapter this distinction between privileged and non-privileged acquisitions by comparing initial conceptions of number, ones that are rooted in counting and knowledge of specific numerical values, with ones that follow. For example, the idea that fractions are numbers is not consistent with the assumption that numbers are what one gets when one counts.

A BRIEF REVIEW OF OUR EARLY WORK

Gelman and Gallistel (1978) argued that investigations of the nature and acquisition of number concepts should take into account two kinds of related abilities: those that are used to generate representations of numerosities and those that are used to reason about numerosities. The achievement of mathematically meaningful representations of numerosity involves the ability to relate number-abstractors to number operations and relations (e.g., $<$, $>$, $=$, $+$, $-$).

The distinction between number-abstraction and number-reasoning abilities was first introduced in the context of an evaluation of Piaget's treatment of early numerical abilities. Gelman (1972) noted that young children's use of number operators is related to whether or not they achieve reliable and/or confident representations of the numerical values of the test displays. This led to the suggestion that Piaget and Szeminska (1941) were too quick to dismiss young children's counting as "rote" or non-meaningful, that is, not related to mathematical relations and operations. The idea was that studies of the relationship between numerical abstraction and numerical reasoning abilities might reveal the early presence of numerical concepts, ones that precede understanding of the mathematical operation of one-to-one correspondence.

The last twenty years has witnessed a veritable explosion of research on the ability of young children, including infants, to respond to numerically relevant inputs. Studies of numerical reasoning abilities have not been as ubiquitous. This turns out to be crucial to investigators' conclusions: (a) that infants' and very young children's responses to number are based on "subitizing," as opposed to counting; and (b) that early counting is not principled. We argue that both conclusions are premature. First, they typically are reached in the absence of a consideration of what is known or needs to be learned about these same children's knowledge of numerical operators and relations. Additionally, the source of performance variability is taken to follow from random noise or a lack of conceptual competence when there are reasons to assume other systematic factors are involved.

SUBITIZING OR COUNTING?

Some Reasons for Choosing 'Subitizing' as the Answer

Several recent papers have concluded that very young children do not use counting in a principled way to abstract a numerical representation of a collection (Fuson, 1988; Shipley & Shepperson, 1990a, 1990b; Siegler, in press; Wynn, 1990). Three kinds of reasons are given. First, the early numerical abstraction abilities of infants and toddlers is limited to small set sizes. For example, infants discriminate between the class of two and the class of three items: Their interest in looking at sets of three stimuli habituates and only recurs when the value of the set is changed to two, and sometimes, to four different kinds of items (Cooper, 1984; Starkey, Spelke & Gelman 1983, 1990; M. S. Strauss & Curtis, 1981). However, they do not discriminate reliably between sets representing larger values. Similarly, toddlers may answer "how many?" questions for sets of one, two, or three items with the correct cardinal term. Still they will fail to repeat the last tag they use when "counting" sets of this same size, and instead re-count when asked, "how many?," after they have already counted (Schaeffer et al., 1974; Wynn, 1990). Second, even older children who use count words to tag items in rather largish sets fail to distinguish between correct and incorrect counts and therefore, when asked, "how many?," after they count, will repeat the last tag whether or not it is the right answer (Fuson, Pergament, Lyon, & Hall, 1985). Third, the counting abilities revealed during the preschool years are variable and do not always generalize to novel settings (Baroody, 1984; Briars & Siegler, 1984; Wynn, 1990).

Ignoring for the moment that there are data that contradict or limit this pattern of findings (e.g., Gelman & Meck, 1986; K. F. Miller, Paredes, & Madole, 1989), we turn instead to the conclusions authors have reached about such patterns. First, very young children are said to respond to numerical displays by 'subitizing,' by reciting a number word they have learned to associate with a given visual pattern, much as they learn to associate common nouns with common objects. Second, the set size limit is taken as evidence that young children and infants do not count because they need not count: They can 'subitize' or 'perceive' number instead. Finally, the acquisition of a principled understanding of number is said to depend on learning—by imitation and association—bits and pieces of routines, procedures, habits, and so on, that look like components of counting. Only when children have acquired a sufficient amount of such knowledge, can they induce the principles of counting. A related assumption is that children's responses in experiments mimic the ways they learn to respond to environmental inputs in their everyday life. For example, it is assumed that children learn to repeat the last tag in a count sequence by rote because they see adults doing this and not because they realize that the last tag represents the cardinal value of the set (e.g., Fuson, 1988; Wynn, 1990).

Some Reasons for Rejecting 'Subitizing' as the Answer

It would be easier to evaluate the conclusion that very young children do not count and instead 'subitize' if there were a model of how the subitizing process maps a given numerosity into a unique symbol or state of the system that is estimating numerosity. Without this account, we have to assume that the idea is that "oneness" and "twoness" is processed much as is "cowness" and "tree-ness." Although we lack an account for the latter perceptual classification ability, there are some things that are surely true about it. Whatever the process, its description does not include an ordering principle such that cowness is always mastered before treeness, or such that the time needed to process *cow* will always be longer than the time needed to process *tree,* and so on. Therefore, the idea that the 'subitizing' process is like the processes that underlie object perception runs into difficulty explaining why oneness is always learned before twoness, twoness before threeness, and so on (Siegler, in press). Further, there is no account of why reaction times and error rates increase as a function of increases in set size, for both children (Chi & Klahr, 1975; K. F. Miller et al., 1989) and adults (Mandler & Shebo, 1982), no matter how small nor how much they are prac-ticed. There are no comparable constraints on object pattern recognition. Addi-tionally, there is no pattern perception model that is indifferent to all charac-teristics of the input it recognizes as exemplars of a kind. In order to recognize a cow, one must encounter cow-like stimuli, ones that look like cows, have cow parts, sound like cows, move like cows, and so forth. To some extent the size, color, age, posture, and so on can vary, but overall shape and kinds of parts cannot. In contrast, whatever the subitizing mechanism, there are no restrictions on the degree to which inputs can vary in terms of size, color, shape, or orienta-tion. For geometric reasons there are some limits on the shapes that can be represented with a small number of distinct items but nevertheless there is always more than one way to arrange sets of at least two items. Likewise, there are many common arrangements that can be imposed on larger sized sets. Finally, if subitizing is a general perceptual process, why should judgments of numerosity, no matter how small the set, serve as inputs for numerical reasoning processes? What is there about the perception of cowness or treeness that would lead one to ponder the effect of adding or subtracting items or whether one display has more (or less) items in it? Yet, we know that babies as young as 12 months order different set sizes (Cooper, 1984) and take into account surreptitious changes in the number in an expected set (Sophian & Adams, 1987; Starkey, 1987).

Logic and Data May Not Be Enough to Change Theorists' Minds.   In sum, neither logical considerations nor research findings support the conclusion that infants and very young children first use a standard pattern perception mechanism to discriminate between different numerosities. Even though there is much evidence against the belief that numerosity is simply perceived (K. F. Miller et al., 1989), the evidence does not seem to have much effect on adherents of the 'subitizing'-first hypothesis. Belief in the hypothesis does not even seem to be influenced by the ever-increasing body of research that shows that animals (another group of nonverbal subjects) are able to work with numerosities well beyond the presumed subitizing range (see Gallistel, 1989). Why is this?

We suspect that the persistent appeal to 'subitizing' as an account of early numerical discriminations follows from individual theorists' commitment to an empiricist account of learning. Within this frame of reference, primitive (i.e., initial) inputs are characterized in terms of sensory details (see Gelman, 1990, in press, for more on this point). To grant infants the ability to respond to the number of items on the basis of a skeletal set of counting principles (or some other number-based set of organizing principles) is to adopt a theory of the environment that is decidedly *not* empiricist in kind. However, this move does not, on its own, generate the corollary that infants come into the world with a full-blown, fully articulated, principled understanding of counting and number. What it does generate is an alternative way to construe the nature of learning and the definition of foundational inputs. Instead, relevant inputs for learning are defined with reference to structural considerations. This is a move that is not unique. It is quite common in accounts of perception (e.g., Marr, 1982) and fits well with the fact that children (young or not) contribute actively to their own cognitive development. Inputs that have potential to nourish children's nascent, skeletal knowledge are those that meet the structural definitions given by the domain (Gelman, 1990, 1991).

Some Reasons for Choosing Counting as the Answer

"A counting process is a process that maps from the numerosities of sets to symbols or states of the representing system" (Gallistel, 1990, p. 338). Such a mapping repeatedly assigns to a set of a given numerosity a unique symbol or state of the system that is an estimate of numerosity. Gelman and Gallistel (1978) coined the term *numeron* to refer to these representatives of numerosity in order to distinguish between what is being represented (numerosities) and what represents it (numerons). Numerons refer to the "inner marks" and support thinking about what Koehler (1950) referred to as "unnamed numbers." Gelman and Gallistel also provided an analysis of counting, by characterizing the formal properties of any process that we would want to call a counting process, conditions that have to be met by any competent plan for counting (Gelman & Greeno, 1989). The formal characteristics of counting processes are captured by three principles: the *one-to-one principle:* Each and every item in a set must be tagged with one and only one tag or numeron; the *stable-ordering principle:* Whatever the tags or numerons, they must be used in a repeatable ordered way; and the *cardinal principle:* The last numeron or tag used has the special status of representing the cardinal value of the set.

Notice that the one-to-one principle does not require that the items being counted be tagged in any particular order. It only requires that each item be assigned one and only one numeron. The absence of any such order requirement in the principles that define counting processes means that counting processes conform to what Gelman and Gallistel (1978) called the *order-irrelevance principle.* Notice also, that the three principles that define counting processes do not specify anything about the items in the set that is to be counted. They do not require that these items have any particular sensory characteristics, nor that they all have the same sensory characteristics, and so on. The absence of any such specification in the principles that define counting processes means that counting processes conform to what Gelman and Gallistel called the *abstraction principle,* which is that counting processes abstract from the items being counted only their distinguishability as distinct entities (Shipley & Shepperson, 1990a). It was perhaps an error to use the word *abstraction* here, for we did not mean to suggest that anything like a complex classification process is necessarily involved. Indeed, we noted that this condition of counting can be satisfied for objects if one merely has the ability to keep figure separate from ground.

We have already cited some of the findings that challenge our conclusion that skeletal sets of counting principles are available to help children attend to and learn about counting-relevant inputs. One especially problematic line of evidence is presented in Wynn (1990). In one of her tasks she asked 2- to 4-year-old children to count so as to indicate how many items were in a given display. Children younger than 3½ tended to simply recite as many count words as there were items and then to stop without repeating the last tag, the cardinal value of the set. When asked again "how many?," the young children re-counted. Fuson, Pergament, and Lyons (1985) reported a different problem in older preschoolers, sometimes as old as 5 years of age: They will repeat the last tag after both correct and incorrect counts.

Wynn also reported that her younger subjects (especially between 2 and 3½) solved her give-X task by grabbing two or three items no matter what the set size (other than one). Only "non-grabbers" counted out the number of items they were asked to give to a puppet. Wynn concluded that "grabbers" are especially disinclined to repeat the last tag after they count in response to a "how many?" question, doing so on only 26% of their correct count trials. In contrast, the group she called "counters" gave the cardinal value after 78% of their correct count trials. Because the tendency for children to give the cardinal answer after their count shifts abruptly at 3½ years—the same age that separates grabbers from counters—Wynn concluded that the younger children did not have a principled understanding of counting, that they do not understand that counting is related in a principled way to the cardinal value of the set.

THERE IS MORE THAN ONE SYSTEMATIC SOURCE OF ERROR

Granted, our theoretical life certainly would be simpler without findings like those just reviewed. But it is one thing to say these results deserve our attention and another to say our position has been dealt a mortal blow. First, those who reject our account have not dealt with the full range of the evidence we have developed. For example, neither Siegler (in press) nor Wynn (1990) considered Gelman and Cohen's (1988) finding that Down Syndrome children approach a novel counting task in qualitatively different ways than do normal preschool children. Similarly, our data from reasoning tasks (e.g., Gelman, 1977; Starkey & Gelman, 1982) are seldom mentioned. Finally, our efforts to explain failures in terms of systematic non-arithmetic sources of error are either ignored or treated as a claim on our part that young children do not have the vocabulary in question. Our position regarding the kinds of non-numerical knowledge needed in particular task settings goes well beyond this.

Siegler (in press) is correct in his observation that investigators would do well to replicate their critics' results and then go on to variations of the original design. Although Gelman et al. (1986) did not do this in their response to Briars and Siegler (1984), they did in their response to Baroody (1984). Furthermore, in ongoing research we also follow the strategy of replicating problematic results before systematically manipulating potential sources of variation other than a lack of the domain-specific *conceptual competence,* the implicit knowledge of the counting principles. Other sources include (a) inadequate *procedural competence,* which supports the generation of plans of action; and (b) limited *interpretative competence,* that constellation of abilities that allows one to understand how to deal with tests, to take settings into account, and so on.

Analyses like those in Gelman and Meck (1986), Gelman and Greeno (1989), and Greeno et al. (1984) led us to ask both whether we could adduce evidence of conceptual competence in children younger than 3 years and show that limits on interpretative or procedural competence interfere with young children's ability to reveal such early conceptual competence. It is reasonable to suppose that children under 3 are still developing skill at inhibiting prepotent response tendencies and matching the correct response class to a task's requirements—the kinds of skills that contribute to procedural competence. Our studies of the potential role of procedural competence in the "make *x*" (or "get *x*") task are not far enough along to merit discussion here. Similarly, because interpretative competence is underdeveloped at this age (Shatz, 1983; Siegal,   1991), it, too, could have affected the performances already summarized. We turn now to this possibility.

New Findings with Adult Counters: The Gelman, Kremer, and Macario Studies

The more we thought about the matter, the more we wondered why anyone would repeat the last tag after counting a single array in response to a "how many?" question. So, with Kathleen Kremer and Jason Macario, we asked adults (UCLA undergraduates enrolled in an introductory psychology course) to answer this question. In our first study, we told each student that we wanted to see how adults do on tasks that we have used with children. As we dropped 18 blocks in front of them (resulting in haphazardly arranged displays), we asked, "How many blocks are here?" We told them to think out loud while figuring out how many there were, but we did not tell them to count. All 13 subjects counted— sometimes using grouping strategies, such as counting by twos. Only one repeated the last tag spontaneously, and this was the only individual who made a counting mistake.

Our subjects' failure to tell us the cardinal value after they counted led to a second version of the procedure. Now, we repeated the "how many?" question if subjects did not repeat their last counting tag after they counted. The follow-up question was presented with a flat to falling pitch contour, so as to avoid a challenging tone. Of the 10 students in this variant of the task, 4 simply repeated their last count tag when asked, "how many?" again. The remaining 6 behaved as though they thought the question was odd. One person said, "Huh?," another laughed nervously, another thought we meant that she got the wrong answer and therefore re-counted, and still another said, "Eighteen, I hope." The remaining 2 subjects registered surprise and/or raised their voices.

Might adults treat "how many?" questions differently when they are with young children? Cohen's (1987) observations of adult-child pairs who visited the "How many?" Box at the Please Touch Museum in Philadelphia suggest they do not. First, only one third of adults actually read the "How many?" sign to their charges who were all too young to read by themselves. Second, those who did almost always accepted counting strings as answers. They neither offered the cardinal value themselves nor asked questions like, "And how many is that?" Gelman and Massey (1988) presented a related report.

Recall the associationist assumption that children learn to repeat the last tag because they are reinforced for imitating the input they are offered. The preceding results open the possibility that children do not encounter the assumed input. Instead, adults seem to assume that they should *not* repeat the last tag when they are shown a set and asked, "How many?" If number is taken as the shared topic of conversation, there is no need to repeat what is obvious to both speaker and listener, that is, that the last tag answers the "how many?" question. Repeating the target question violates Grice's conversational maxim of quantity: Do not say more than necessary.

Given the foregoing, we conclude that the seemingly straightforward "how many?" task affords a potential confound of preschoolers' ability to repair violations of conversational rules with assessments of their cognitive abilities (Donaldson, 1978; Siegal, 1991). This is especially so if a child responds to a "how many?" question by counting and is then asked this question again. Children learn relatively late that it is permissible to repeat or tell what is already known by the speaker in test settings (Heath, 1983). Therefore, data from the "how many?" task are as consistent with a developmental account that emphasizes acquisition of the knowledge that violations in conversational rules are allowed in test settings as is an account that denies young children counting competence. If so, we need to find settings where repeated requests to count and answer "how many?" questions are less likely to be conversationally anomalous before making a choice between these alternative accounts. The "Magic" paradigm turns out to offer such a setting.

Bullock and Gelman (1977) Reconsidered

Bullock and Gelman (1977) used the Magic paradigm, a two-phase game, to determine whether 2½-, 3-, 4-, and 5-year-olds could reason with and about numerical relations. The children were tested individually. In Phase 1 the experimenter hid one item on a plate under one can, and two items on another plate under a second can. *Without mentioning the numerical values,* the experimenter proclaimed one display the *winner*. Half the children saw the experimenter point to the 1-plate and call it the the *winner* (the less condition); half were told the 2-plate was the *winner* (the more condition). The displays were then covered and shuffled. The child had to guess which one had the winner, look under the chosen can, and then decide whether they were correct. If the child chose the "wrong" plate but correctly labeled it the *loser,* she was allowed to find the winner under the other can. Errors of identification led to the start of a new trial. Phase 1 continued for 10 or 11 trials, or until a child reached criterion. Phase 2 started when the experimenter surreptitiously added two items to each display (something that was easy to do with young children because they liked looking at the prizes they collected for correct Phase 1 identifications). During Phase 2, the children had to decide which of the uncovered new values (3 or 4) was a *winner*. Those who were initially rewarded for finding 1 now had to designate 3 the *winner;* those initially rewarded for 2 had to choose 4 to be scored as correct.

In Bullock and Gelman's first experiment, 3-, 4-, and 5-year-olds succeeded in what we henceforth call the *regular condition*. In contrast, the 2½-year-olds in the same condition did not choose correctly on the basis of a common numerical relationship between Phase 1 and Phase 2.

Bullock and Gelman conducted a second experiment, henceforth called the *control condition,* to test the hypothesis that the youngest children in the regular condition simply did not think to transfer the knowledge they acquired in Phase 1 to deal with Phase 2. Two variants of the follow-up experiment provided hints to do this. In one, the initial displays were left in place with their covers on; in the other, the initial displays were left in place uncovered. Then, in Phase 2 of the control condition, the experimenter introduced a new game "like the one we just played" and put two new covered displays on the table. Whether the Phase 1 displays were left covered or uncovered had no effect. In both variants of the control condition, a reliable number of 2½-year-olds chose relationally, selecting in Phase 2 either the 4-item (more) or 3-item (less) as a function of their Phase 1 reinforcement.

In the Magic paradigm we sporadically asked the children why a given display won or lost during Phase 1. After the children answered the Phase 2 questions for the altered display(s), we interviewed them to determine whether they knew how many items were present during both Phase 1 and 2, how many were added or removed, and so on. Because these questions were asked for different values that were either physically present or to-be-remembered, this is a setting where they should have found it acceptable for us to repeat "how many?" questions. Because the children could compare different set sizes, they had reason to count more than once. Further, by asking how Phase 1 and Phase 2 displays differed, we also gave them opportunities to reason about the numerosities represented. Given these considerations we returned to the Bullock and Gelman transcripts to see if they contained evidence that bears on the present discussion.

A Reanalysis of Bullock and Gelman's (1977) Youngest Subjects.   The data under consideration here come from the transcripts of the twelve 2-year-olds in each of the control and regular conditions as well as the 12 (of 24) youngest children (those less than 42 mos) in the 3-year-old regular condition. We included the latter children because they, too, are within the age range in which, according to others, children lack the verbal cardinal principle. Bullock and Gelman focused on: (a) children's answers to the beginning Phase 2 "Which is the winner?" question; (b) whether the children knew how many items had been and were present on the displays; and (c) how much the children knew about the relevant transformations. Although Bullock and Gelman presented some data on children's tendencies to talk about number, they did not determine whether the children applied the verbal cardinal principle. To do this, we considered all Phase 2 talk about number that occurred following the surprise trial, keeping track of whether it was spontaneous or elicited, and what the experimenter said before and after each utterance that included number talk.

Wynn's (1990) findings and conclusions led us to focus on whether children's use of number in Bullock and Gelman's study reflected an ability to count and say the cardinal value for set sizes of 3 or smaller. Wynn acknowledged that young children will count small sets when asked to do so; her claim was that they will not count and offer the cardinal value of such sets when asked about cardinal number, as is the case for the "how many?" question. Therefore, we analyzed the children's talk about number in two ways. The first made use of all number talk, including any that occurred in response to the experimenter's request to count. For the second, all number talk that followed a request to count was excluded. The different data bases are clarified by a consideration of samples of the Bullock and Gelman transcripts given further on. Subject #3, for instance, was asked to count about halfway through the excerpt, and Subject #9 was asked to count near the end of her interview. Their subsequent answers formed part of the data for our first analysis of whether the young children in Bullock and Gelman's study applied the cardinal principle. Such answers were excluded from the data base used for the second analysis. Therefore, for our first analysis, we scored a child as having given both a cardinal and counting response who (a) did so spontaneously, (b) offered two kinds of answers to the same questions (be it "How many?" or "Can you count . . . ?"), or (c) when asked to both count and answer the "how many?" question for the set size, gave both a counting and a cardinal response. When we redid the analyses, such count or cardinal answers to our request that a child count were ignored.

Wynn concluded that children do not mix 'subitizing' and counting strategies once they apply the verbal cardinal principle, that is, once they show evidence of understanding that counting generates the cardinal value of a set. For us, this meant that we could conclude that the young children in the Magic experiment revealed a principled understanding of the verbal cardinal principle only if they both counted *and* gave cardinal values for small sets. Children who simply counted, simply stated a numerical value, or failed both to count and to state a cardinal value for small sets, provided negative or ambiguous evidence for our position. Finally, Wynn reported that there were 4 (of 22) children who counted and applied the cardinal principle in her main study. Therefore, in order to affirm our hypothesis, the proportion of children in Bullock and Gelman's data scored as having counted and applied the verbal cardinal principle had to be reliably larger than this.

Bullock and Gelman reported that their youngest subjects were disinclined to talk about number during Phase 1. The transcripts showed that they were nowhere near as reticent in Phase 2, especially in the control condition. The youngest children in the regular condition made more number-use errors; they also seemed more tongue-tied at the start of Phase 2, possibly due to the surprise generated by the violation of expectancies. Still, by the end of the interview, every child, whether in the regular or control condition, used some number words correctly, even though they were never explicitly corrected for earlier errors. (This tendency to improve without explicit feedback fits our model. Skeletal principles give young children a way to first identify potential number-relevant environments and then engage in on-line, but not conscious, monitoring and self-corrections. See Gelman & Cohen, 1988.) The kind of conversation that occurred in this setting is illustrated in the following sample of protocols. (Subjects' comments are in italics. Their spontaneous Table 1 count code ends a protocol.)

S#9 (34 months). [Regular-2s Condition. Reinforced in Phase 1 for 1 (less). S never said why correctly identified displays were winners or losers.]

Phase 2, Trial 1: S selected and uncovered the 4-item display. "Well, is that the winner?" *Why did you put three in there?* "How many are on there?" *1-2-3-4-5* (5 emphasized). While E goes on talking, S continues: *I, it should be . . . ; three. Oh, 1-2-3-4, that's four.* (E continues to ask which wins, which is the best winner, and so on. S does not use numbers throughout the next quarter of the interview.) When S designates the 3-plate the winner and says: *Best,* the experimenter asks, "Why?" *Three?* "Huh?" *This be two, or one (4-plate). Two, two (3-plate).* (S possibly wants to pretend that the new displays are the old 1-item and 2-item displays). "How many are on this (4) plate?" *1-2-3-4.* "How many are on this (3) plate? Can you count them?" *1-2-3.* "So which one is the winner?" *This one?* (pointing to the 3-plate again). "Why?" S leaves the table to play with prizes. . . . S returns and resumes counting correctly. S also counts a 2-item display, *1-2* in response to, "How many?" [Card +, Count +]

S#3 (34 months). [Control-2s Condition. Reinforced in Phase 1 for 2 (more). Phase 1 plates left covered on the table when 3- and 4-item displays (with covers) are put on the table to start Phase 2.]

Phase 1, Trial 4: S chooses a covered plate and correctly identifies it once uncovered. "Why is that the winner?" No answer. Trial 5: Wrong guess of which can, but correct at saying it is not the winner once can is lifted. "Why is that the loser?" *I don't know.* (Pattern repeats for Trials 6 and 8, the other Phase 1 probe trials.)

Phase 2: "I've got another game in my bag; want to see it? *Yes.* "It's kind of like another game. What do you think, J, which one's the winner?" J guesses, picking one and then the other . . . "How many are on this plate. Can you count them?" *Oh.* "Can you count them? How many are here? (4)?" *Four.* "How many ducks are here (3-plate)?" *Five.* "Can you count these (4-plate) with your fingers?" *1-2-3-4.* "That's terrific, J . . . Do you remember how many used to be the winner?" *This.* (Points to a Phase 2 plate). "Before, how many used to be the winner?" *1-2-3-4-5.* . . . "Let's look at these plates. Which one is the winner?" *Two.* "How many on here?" *One.* "Now which is the winner over here" (Phase 2 plates). *This is the - that's the loser (3-plate) and this is the winner* (4-plate). "Why is that the winner?" *You win.* (J starts reciting count string.) [Card +, Count −]

S#11(35 months). [Regular-3s Condition. Reinforced in Phase 1 for 2 (more).]

Phase 1, Trial 4: S correctly selects and identifies the winner. "Why is that the winner?" *Cause it has a bird.* Trial 5: S selects the winner, correctly identifies it, and says: *The bird, the bird and then there was a bird.* "Why is that the winner?" *Cause it has two birds.* Trial 6: S uncovers the loser and says so. "Why is that the loser?" *Cause it is.* Trial 7: Correct guess and identification. "Why is that the winner?" *The winner 'cause it has two birds.* Trial 8: "Why is that the loser?" *'Cause it has one bird.*

Phase 2, Trial 1: S uncovers a 3-plate. "Is that the winner?" *Yes.* "How many are on there?" *1-2-3.* "What's under this can?" *1 bird, 2 birds, 3 birds, 4 birds.* "Well, which one is the winner?" *This one's the winner; it has 1-2-3; there's three birds.* S continues, making both new plates into 2-item plates by removing the right number of items. Finally, she returns to making a 3-plate and 4-plate and shows the latter while saying it wins. E continues, "How many does the winner have?" *1-2-3-4.* Again, S makes two 2-plates. E asks, "How many does the winner have?" *1-2.* [Card +, Count +]

Table 8.1 summarizes, subject by subject, the outcome of our analyses of both probed and spontaneous number use. For each child the table includes his or her age (in mos) and comments about the kinds and/or locus of the errors made and whether there were enough trials to warrant an attribution of competence. We use the term *Card* (cardinalize) where others would use *Subitize*, that is, when the child used a single count word to refer—either in response to a question or spontaneously—to the numerosity of a set. The terms Card and Count are modified + or − to indicate if a child did or did not Card or Count.

Regardless of whether we included answers following requests to count, the majority of children were scored as Card+, Count+, having given evidence of using the verbal cardinal principle. The number of observed Card+, Count+ children is greater than expected, whichever analysis is considered. Using Wynn's data as a baseline, we compared our data with hers and obtained ($X_1^2 = 7.09$ and $5.66, p < .02$). Inspection of Table 8.1 makes clear that the tendency to simply state the cardinal value without counting, was not a function of age. If anything, it was differences between the conditions that determined the level of numerical talk during Phase 2.

In sum, our reanalysis of the Bullock and Gelman data provides further evidence that even young children try to relate their efforts to learn to count to their implicit understanding of counting principles. There is no question that early knowledge about the conventions of counting is fragile. It would be surprising if this were not so. Count lists vary across language groups and some are easier to master than others (K. F. Miller & Stigler, 1987). Even within the United States different cultural groups have different ways of interpreting conversational postulates and their violations (Heath, 1983). Such matters of convention for a given culture are exactly the sorts of things children have to learn (Gelman & Greeno, 1989). By granting to our young skeletal knowledge—

TABLE 8.1

Reanalyses of the Transcripts from the Bullock and Gelman (1980) Magic Experiments to Assess Whether Children Younger than 3½ Applied the Cardinal Principle

Condition & Age of Each S	Relevant Features of Number Use In Phase 2*	Attribution of Cardinal Principle			
		Including Data from Requests to Count		Excluding Data from Requests to Count	
		Summary of Counting Ability	Grant Cardinal Principle?	Summary of Counting Ability	Grant Cardinal Principle?
Control Condition, 2-year-olds					
29 mos	Many count errors on large numbers of prizes; hard to code	Card+, Count-**	No	Card+, Count+	No
30 mos	—	Card+, Count+	Yes	Card+, Count-	No
32 mos	No card responses; counts correct only on x < 4	Card-, Count+	No	Card-, Count+	No
34 mos	One card error; easy to code	Card+, Count+	Yes	Card+, Count-	No
34 mos	Card values wrong; used like adjective slot fillers	Card?, Count-	No	Card?, Count-	No
34 mos	Both Card and Count correct on 1-3; count errors on 4	Card+, Count+	Yes	Card+, Count+	Yes
35 mos	Perfect counts on last half trials; errors to start	Card+, Count+	Yes	Card+, Count+	Yes
35 mos	—	Card+, Count+	Yes	Card+, Count+	Yes
35 mos	Never Cards	Card-, Count+	No	Card-, Count+	No
35 mos	—	Card+, Count+	Yes	Card+, Count+	Yes
35 mos	Never Cards; not clear can Count	Card-, Count-	No	Card-, Count-	No
35 mos	—	Card+, Count+	Yes	Card+, Count+	Yes

Age	Description *	Card/Count **		Card/Count **	
Regular Condition, 2-year-olds					
29 mos	One early counting error	Card+, Count+	Yes	Card+, Count+	Yes
30 mos	—	Card+, Count+	Yes	Card+, Count+	Yes
30 mos	One count error (of 3) on 4	Card+, Count+	Yes	Card+, Count+	Yes
32 mos	Not enough relevant data	Card−, Count−	No	Card+, Count+	Yes
33 mos	Only 1 count error on 4	Card+, Count+	Yes	Card+, Count−	No
33 mos	Errors; best guess is Card only	Card+, Count−	No	Card+, Count−	No
33 mos	One count error (of 4) on 4	Card+, Count+	Yes	Card+, Count+	Yes
34 mos	Wrong Card value; count errors on large xs	Card−, Count−	No	Card?, Count+	No
34 mos	Count errors in first half	Card+, Count+	Yes	Card+, Count+	Yes
34 mos	Card only	Card+, Count?	No	Card+, Count+	Yes
35 mos	—	Card+, Count+	Yes	Card+, Count+	Yes
35 mos	Not enough counting data	Card+, Count?	No	Card+, Count?	No
Regular Condition, 3-year-olds					
36 mos	Errorful counts; Cards "2" for 4	Card−, Count−	No	Card−, Count−	No
38 mos	Errors on 5; fine for x < 5	Card+, Count+	Yes	Card+, Count+	Yes
38 mos	Count errors on 3	Card+, Count+	Yes	Card+, Count+	Yes
38 mos	—	Card+, Count+	Yes	Card+, Count+	Yes
38 mos	Card values used like adjectives; not enough counting	Card−, Count−	No	Card−, Count−	No
39 mos	Not enough counting	Card+, Count−	No	Card+, Count−	No
39 mos	—	Card+, Count+	Yes	Card+, Count+	No
39 mos	Early count error of 5 prizes	Card+, Count+	Yes	Card+, Count+	Yes
39 mos	Easy to code; count errors on large x	Card+, Count−	No	Card+, Count+	Yes
40 mos	—	Card+, Count+	Yes	Card+, Count+	Yes
40 mos	—	Card+, Count+	Yes	Card+, Count+	Yes
40 mos	Count error on 5	Card+, Count+	Yes	Card+, Count+	Yes

*If coding was straightforward, this column was left blank. Code based on post-surprise, Phase 2 talk.

**Card+/− = Applies/Does not apply cardinal principle; Count+/− = Knows how/does not know how to count in range tested; Count− = Does not know how to count in range tested. See text for further details.

some principles of counting and arithmetic reasoning—we do not take away their need to learn. Rather, we give them a way to help themselves find what their culture offers their active tendency to use the knowledge they have, to assimilate and then to accommodate.

INITIAL PRINCIPLES OF COUNTING AND REASONING CAN INTERFERE WITH, AS WELL AS ENCOURAGE, LEARNING ABOUT NUMBER

So far we have focused on the idea that the acquisition of number concepts benefits from skeletal counting and reasoning principles. Like all constructivist theorists of knowledge acquisition, we assume that children will sometimes achieve the "wrong" interpretation of the data we offer them because they apply different knowledge structures than we do. The case of fractions serves to make this point, while showing in another way that young children have a potent tendency to apply their counting principles.

Do Young Children Know That Counting Numbers are not the Only Kind of Numbers?

It is not just young children who use counting algorithms to solve arithmetic problems; so do unschooled adults. Schooled or not, individuals have strong tendencies to decompose natural numbers into manageable or known components, to count when adding or subtracting, and to use repeated addition (or subtraction) to solve multiplication (or division) problems. Children use these proto-multiplication and -division solutions before and after they learn more standard multiplication and division algorithms in school; so do unschooled adults and children in a variety of settings and cultures (T. N. Carraher, D. W. Carraher, & Schliemann, 1985; Saxe, 1988; Starkey & Gelman, 1982).

Some of the algorithms invented by older children and unschooled adults are more complex than those used by preschoolers. Still, as Resnick (1986) noted in her analysis of these, all use principles of counting and addition (or subtraction) with the positive integers. Her subject, Pitt (7 years, 7 months) illustrates the point, solving 2×3 "*Two threes . . . one three is three, one more equals six.*" Similarly, schooled or not, individuals in Africa and Latin America use a combination of number decomposition moves and repeated additions (or subtractions) to solve investigators' multiplication problems. Young children are less able to work with large numbers than older children or adults, but beyond this it is hard to distinguish their invented, out-of-school, solutions from older children's and adults' (T. N. Carraher et al., 1985; Saxe, 1988).

We believe that the widespread invention of algorithms that are based on counting and/or repeated addition (subtraction) algorithms provides further support for our conclusion that a universal set of implicit principles governs the acquisition of initial mathematical concepts (Gelman, 1982b). Still, over the centuries, there have been changes in the definition of what is or is not a number, changes that are well-described in the history of mathematics. Much of mathematics involves operations and entities other than counting and the addition and subtraction of the counting numbers (or the positive integers). Might it be that when it comes time to transcend the early knowledge built on the counting principles these principles will hinder progress almost as much as they first promoted it?

We take the data on unschooled mathematical abilities as evidence that numbers are first thought to be "what one gets when one counts things." If so, common classroom inputs for lessons about fractions may be misinterpreted by young pupils. One cannot count things to get the answer to, "Which is more, ½ or ¼? 1.5 or 1.0?" Number lines are not simple representations of whole numbers, yet young children might think they are. Similarly, young children might know that one can take apart a circle and a rectangle and get two "halves" on both occasions and still not appreciate why each of these halves can be represented with the written expression ½. The interpretation of the latter might be assimilated to the idea that such marks on paper must be about whole numbers.

In the absence of implicit principles for dealing with fractions, young learners might overgeneralize their counting principles and produce a distorted assimilation of the instructional data on fractions. For example, if they do assimilate their understanding of the language of fractions to the implicit system of mathematical principles available to them, they might "read" fractions, or non-integer numerals, as if these, too, were representations for the counting numbers. For example, they might choose ¼ as more than ½; or, when asked to place 1½ circles on a number line, they might decide they have two things and place the stimuli at the position for 2 on the line. Such speculations have proven to be right.

Gelman, Cohen and Hartnett (1989) found that children in kindergarten, and first, and second grades repeatedly treated fraction tasks as if they were new occasions for counting. For example, 85% of 40 children misread the written expressions ½ and ¼. Many read the fractions as two integers, "1, 2"; "1 and 2". Others read the division symbol as *and, plus,* or *line.* Finally, some children behaved as if they had been given an addition problem; when asked to read ½ and ¼, they answered, "three" and "five," or even "1 plus 2, 3, 5, and 1 plus 4"! Additionally, the children in the study had a reliable bias to select the reciprocals with the larger denominators as "more" when they were shown ¼ versus ½ and ¹⁄₅₆ versus ¹⁄₇₆.

These and other results in the study make it clear that most of the children treated the test materials as novel occasions for counting and reasoning about whole numbers. Our inputs about fractions offered them further cases to which to assimilate their view that numbers are what one gets when one counts and adds counting numbers. Does this mean that learning about fractions as numbers will be difficult? There is reason to conclude just this.

Formally, fractions are numbers generated by the division of two numerosities, not by counting the number of things or parts of things. The formal principles for counting and addition do not include those that define the relations between multiplication and division: The distributive law is not a law of addition but a higher-order one. Therefore it is not clear how mathematically meaningful learning about fractions could be built from what is already known by young children. In other words, learning about fractions *should* be difficult. More generally, learning about fractions seems to depend on being able to use, in mathematically meaningful ways, conventional mathematical terms, tools, numerical symbols, and the notational systems for writing fractions. Thus, the mastery of the idea that fractions are indeed numbers requires both the learning of principles that go beyond those implicit, foundational ones available to the young child just as correct mathematical language does. (See also Hiebert & Wearne, 1986.)

Gelman and Gallistel (1978) reminded their readers that the formal description of arithmetic is a product of late 19th- and early 20th-century mathematics. Its emergence was accompanied by a profound shift in mathematicians' views about the relation between the laws of arithmetic and the definition of what constitutes a number. Whereas the 19th-century mathematician Kronecker assumed that the natural numbers were given and all else derived, there is a sense in which almost the opposite is true now. No matter how bizarre it might seem from the psychological point of view, in modern mathematics, a number is any abstract entity that can be shown to behave in accordance with the laws of arithmetic. Whatever intellectual discomfort negative numbers generate—one cannot count $-x$ real-world things— they are an essential part of modern formal arithmetic. Similarly, no matter how articulately a child denies numberhood status to fractions, they are numbers in modern, formal arithmetic. The property of closure with respect to division would not apply otherwise: It will not do to discard the remainder in a division problem simply because it is not a whole number.

If learning to go beyond the initial conception of number requires mastering some of the language and syntax of mathematics, then we are faced with a special challenge. The idea that there are noncounting numbers for purely formal reasons is historically young. Therefore, it is most unlikely that learning about concepts of number that are so characterized benefits from existing skeletal structures. If this is, indeed, the case, children not only have to develop new mathematical structures, but must learn how their entities behave mathematically as well (Gelman & Greeno, 1989).

In our introductory remarks, we took care to state that we do not believe that all learning about mathematics benefits from or is based on early skeletal principles. It only makes sense to grant learners the ability to actively find and learn about relevant inputs on their own when they have available structures with which to do so. In the absence of structure relevant to the concept(s) in question, learning is known to be exceedingly hard, even with the aid of structured inputs. Because much of mathematics involves operations and corresponding entities other than those relating to counting and addition with the counting numbers, mastery of the domains of mathematics has to involve development of novel structures. It is even possible that when this happens initial conceptions of number change in a deep way. Future work on the development of number concepts must focus on these matters. Doing so would be very much in the tradition of Piaget.

ACKNOWLEDGMENTS

Preparation of this chapter was supported by NSF grants BNS 85-19575 and BNS-8916220 as well as the UCLA Dean's fund to Rochel Gelman. We thank C. R. Gallistel, Kathleen Kremer, and Jason Macario for their thoughtful insights about the nature of the issues discussed here. Special thanks are due Jason Macario for his careful comments at every stage of manuscript preparation. We are especially grateful to our editors and publishers for providing us the oppertunity to note some matters of fact that bear on some of the ways that the Baroody chapter has been updated from the French to include considerable commentary on our chapter.

9 Subitizing: The Discontinuity After Three

Jean-Paul Fischer
*Institut Universitaire de Formation des Maîtres de Lorraine:
Site de Montigny-lès-Metz*

Subitizing is virtually instantaneous apprehension of number. Although this definition has the merit of making no assumptions as to the nature (perceptual, etc.) of the process, it fails to be adequate on other counts. In particular, recent evidence of infants' numerical abilities (J.-P. Fischer, 1985) calls for a more accurate definition.

First, subitizing should always result in an absolute number judgment. This restriction on the general definition is in accordance with the position of Kaufman, Lord, Reese, and Volkmann (1949), who originally coined the term. It thus eliminates all studies dealing with relative number or numerosity judgments, that is, with a comparison of two explicitly and often simultaneously presented collections. By the same token, it not only disqualifies all studies on infants, but also disbars data like those on 2- to 5-year-olds reported in Klein and Starkey (1988, Table 1), who concluded that there is subitizing up to and including 4.

The second caveat, which also draws on Kaufman et al.'s definition and, more specifically, on what they term *the method of direct reporting,* is that there must be verbal labeling of number in standard conventional terms.[1] This is obviously

---

[1] The requirement for standard, usual number words in my definition of subitizing obviously does not exclude other forms of number apprehension that do not fulfill this requirement. Furthermore, the nature of these forms of number apprehension may also change after 3. Biemüller's (1932) ingenious experiment testifies to this. The experiment consisted of rolling sets of marbles simultaneously down inclined parallel grooves (one marble per groove). Rolling lasted 840 msec, and then the marbles dropped into holes and were no longer visible. The subjects were asked at this point to state which holes the marbles had dropped into. Subjects were not explicitly told to pay attention to number or to name. Biemüller simply tested whether subjects do, in fact, keep track of numerosities. The findings speak for themselves: For 3, 83% of the nursery school children were correct, whereas only 12% were for 4; elementary schoolers were right 90% of the time for 3, but only 25% for 4. These findings again illustrate the same striking drop in performance between 3 and 4.

crucial for studies on young children. My own data show that children's reactions can vary considerably. For example, when presented with a collection of four objects and asked the "how many?" question, some children held up four fingers and said, "There are that many," whereas others stated, "There are two, and two more."

Because subitizing is often approached in terms of its relationship to counting, it seems important to specify what is meant by *counting* as well. My definition is based almost entirely on Gelman and Gallistel's (1978) first three principles. That is, to count (correctly) children should exhibit consistent use of the one-to-one principle (every item in a collection is only tagged once with a unique number word), the stable-order principle, and the cardinal principle (the last number word represents the cardinal value of the whole collection). The second issue raised with respect subitizing, however, prompted me to modify Gelman and Gallistel's stable-order principle by requiring that the stable-order sequence must be the conventional order sequence, the only one that always furnishes the standard number words.

In this chapter I first present empirical evidence for the existence of a specific apprehension mechanism for the first three natural (non-zero) numbers. The discontinuity in difficulty between the apprehension of 3 and the apprehension of 4 (henceforth, called the *discontinuity after 3*) is a powerful argument against any model of number apprehension based exclusively on counting. This applies, in particular, to the well-known model of Gelman and Gallistel (1978), which is still upheld by both Gelman (1983) and Gallistel (1988). An exclusively counting-based model predicts that performance will drop as the number of entities increases. A model of this type fails, however, to account for the fact that the differences in difficulty of apprehension between 2 and 3, and between 4 and 5 are almost impossible to detect, whereas the difference between 3 and 4 is enormous.

What happens between 3 and 4? The next section of this chapter presents studies dealing with the apprehension of 3 and the apprehension of 4. When the data are restricted to tasks involving linear collections of regularly spaced dots, the difference is striking.

If the exclusively count-based model fails to account for observations, is another theoretical explanation more satisfactory? I have argued elsewhere (J.-P. Fischer & Meljac, 1987) that initial subitizing of small numbers, even when restricted to 2 or 3, could play an important role in concept development. The opportunity to realize that these small uncounted numbers correspond to the total obtained by counting could enable the child to discover, reinforce, or even grasp the cardinal principle. Furthermore, this initial, restricted subitizing allows the child a chance to arrive at the same result in two different ways. This latter feature could be a general and basic principle of all mathematical learning. J.-P. Fischer and Pluvinage (1988) showed how this principle operates in the memorization of simple numerical facts. It can also be seen in relearning, following cerebral insult. Spiers (1987), for example, reported on a patient with severe Wernicke's aphasia (a type of aphasia that generally results in comprehension impairment) who rediscovered the usual algorithm for multiplication. When the patient attempted to use the normal algorithm to calculate 35 × 5 using the standard technique, he insisted on checking the answer by a series of additions (e.g., 35 + 35 = 70, 70 + 70 = 140, and 140 + 35 = 175; see Spiers, 1987, p. 14).

In the same way that close examination of initial subitizing led to hypotheses on what could be a fundamental principle of all mathematical learning, the discontinuity after 3 may be a key to certain features of the general architecture of cognition, including its neural bases. There is certainly no reason to assume that the brain has developed totally novel and specific mechanisms to process the apprehension of collections of regularly spaced dots! The final part of this chapter, therefore, is devoted to a more general theoretical interpretation of the findings.

THE DISCONTINUITY AFTER 3

The best place to start is a fairly recent article by Wagner and Walters (1982). Wagner and Walters observed nine children at least twice a month over a 5-year period, from age 1 to 6. They obtained approximately 2,000 pages of audiotape transcripts and notes per child. Their analysis of the ways in which the words *two* and *three* were used in the year following their initial appearance in each child indicate that the use of *two* or *three* was accompanied by counting only 15% of the time. However, arrays of 4 or more were accompanied by counting 95% of the time.

This striking difference between numbers up to 3 and numbers above is not an empirical quirk of the Wagner and Walters study. A number of child diary studies published at the turn of the century also draw attention to this disparity.[2]

Anecdotal Reports

- Binet (1890) collected data on two sisters. The elder sister, at 4 years, 3 months, labeled numerosities correctly up to 3, but beyond that recited number words in an entirely random fashion. The younger sister, at the age of 2 years, 6 months, knew the number 3. Binet wrote: "She makes practically no mistakes on this number and her errors are totally insignificant,

---

[2]Quotations originally in languages other than English were translated by me.

but as soon as another element is added everything changes: The number of mistakes immediately becomes much higher" (pp. 80–81).

- Cramaussel (1908) described S. and J., two of the four children he observed, in the following way: "S. at 53 months, and J. at 32 months count up to *five* but only really see 3" (p. 47).

- E. Scupin and G. Scupin (1910) published a diary account of their son. They reported that at 4 years, 8 months his mother held up four fingers but the child did not know how many there were. When she separated one finger from the others, he knew immediately: "three and one more." Scupin and Scupin commented that "the number sequence has been mastered up to three, but despite untiring efforts and liberally administered counting of coins, beans, marbles and buttons, a doubt remains starting with four" (p. 142).

- Decroly and Degand (1912) pointed out that Suzanne (age 56 months) immediately identified a group of 3, but counted with her fingers for 4: Her father put three cherry pits together and asked, "How many, Suzanne?"— "3." He adds another pit. "And now how many?" Suzanne counts "1, 2, 3, 4 pits" (p. 113).

- Oehl (1935) described a boy in the first year of primary school (aged 6 years, 2 months), who could point to three lines but not four, and remarked, "Here is an example of the incredible difference between numbers from 1 to 3, which are based on impressions of simultaneously apprehended groups, and the other numbers" (p. 317).

Studies on Forced Numerosity Judgments

I now turn to more statistical evidence. Figure 9.1 presents data from five experiments on success on typical subitizing tasks as a function of number of items. Clearly, going beyond 3 appears to be a major obstacle.

These experiments are alike in that they used horizontal linear arrays of regular spaced dots and required children to say how many dots there were. All were designed to discourage children from counting one by one either by limiting exposure time (Cuneo, 1982; J.-P. Fischer, 1984; Gelman & Tucker 1975[3]) or by specific instructions (Douglass, 1925).

Reaction Time (RT) Studies

Three RT studies on young children (Chi & Klahr, 1975; Svenson & Sjöberg, 1978, 1983) all report RT curves (after linear adjustment) as a function of number of items that are similar to the one in Fig. 9.2.

---

[3]In the Gelman and Tucker (1975) experiment, I only present the findings for exposure time limited to 1 second.

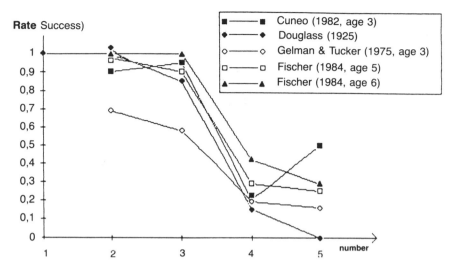

FIG. 9.1.   Success rate as a function of number.

The value for the s-threshold (see Fig. 9.2) is always located around 3 (closer to 2 for Chi & Klahr, nearer to 4 for Svenson & Sjöberg). In addition, the p_s (subitizing) and p_c (counting) slopes are in about a 1 to 10 ratio: in the Svenson and Sjöberg (1978) study, $p_s = 110$ msec and $p_c = 1030$ msec for 7- and 8-year-olds.

Chi and Klahr (1975) studied RT on tasks using collections of randomly

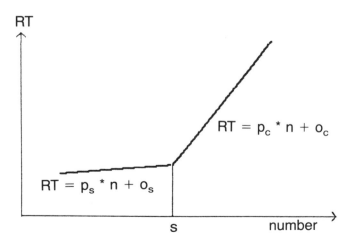

FIG. 9.2.   Theoretical curve for reaction time as a function of the number to be subitized.

spaced dots; Svenson and Sjöberg (1978, 1983) used linear collections. To my knowledge, there are no studies of RT in young children for canonical patterns of dots in geometric figures, such as 3 in an equilateral triangle (henceforth 3F), 4 in a square (4F) or 5 in a quincuncial pattern (5F; one item in each corner of a square plus one in the middle). However, several studies have dealt with these patterns in adults. These pattern recognition studies, involving both standard (Mandler & Shebo, 1982) and nonstandard subitizing tasks (Simons & Langheinrich, 1982; Wolters, van Kempen, & Wijlhuizen, 1987), have reported no increase in reaction times for familiar patterns with a greater number of items.

These RT studies illustrate another property of subitizing: Reports are confident. Confidence in responding is one of the hallmarks of subitizing. Kaufman et al. (1949) asked subjects to rate how confident they were about the number of items they had perceived on a 5-point scale. The functions for time and confidence are discontinuous in slope at nearly the same point.

Confidence in subitizing of numbers from 1 to 3 in young children is further confirmed by the percentage of errors in Chi and Klahr (1975). Their subjects (mean age 5 years, 8 months) had an error rate of 1.57% for items subitized in the 1 to 3 range, but 22.8% on collections in the 4 to 7 range.

Confidence in subitizing also suggests (but does not entail) that subitizing makes minimal demands on attentional or other resources. Hitch, Cundick, Haughey, Pugh, and Wright (1987) gave subjects (mean age 8.7) a subitizing task and a concurrent articulatory task. Their data show that subitizing up to 3 is not impaired by the concurrent task, a finding that clearly differentiates subitizing from counting.

Studies on Spontaneous Numerosity Judgments

In Fischer (1984), 96 four- and five-year-olds were asked to tell a story relating three pictures. The task involved implicit problem solving and was designed to elicit spontaneous use of number words to describe initial- and end-state numerosities.

In the problem shown in Fig. 9.3, the subjects were first shown the picture on the left of a girl holding five balloons, and a transformation picture showing two balloons floating away. The subjects were asked to finish the story by choosing one of the three response pictures, which show the same little girl with, respectively two, four, or three balloons. After the subjects chose the response card and placed it on the display rack to the right of the initial and transformation pictures, they were asked to tell the story in three steps following the sequence of three pictures. The children were not prompted in any way to use numbers (for the balloons) or, more generally, to tell a numerical story. All narratives were tape recorded.

The picture problems prompted spontaneous use of number words in a nar-

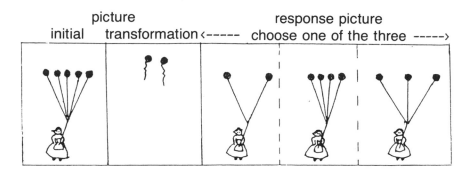

FIG. 9.3.   Example of a pictorial problem (J.-P. Fischer, 1984, p. 39).

rative context. In all 14 problems in the experiment, the object collections were always linear and horizontal and had regularly spaced objects, similar to the balloons in the example shown. Here is the narrative of Myr (aged almost 6 years), who chose the picture with four balloons as the response to the problem shown in Fig. 9.3, explaining, "The lady has (1.5 sec. pause) five balloons. Two fly away. She only has (1.5 sec) only has, has (3 sec) four left."

Table 9.1 presents the percentage of spontaneous numerosity errors on the initial picture as a function of item and age.

As is clear, the error rate rises sharply between 3 and 4, regardless of age group. For example, at 5 years, 9 months, spontaneous number labeling is nearly perfect for the first three numbers. In contrast, the error rate is 16 for 4. Obviously, the rate of error also rises between 2 and 3 for the age group 4 years, 3 months, and between 4 and 5 for the age group 5 years, 9 months. The increase between 2 and 3 can be accounted for, however, by the fact that subitizing is not necessarily the initial process.[4] In addition, the fact that some subjects in the 5 years, 9 months age group were able to implement an automatized procedure could explain the marked increase in error rate between 4 and 5 for the oldest group.

Conclusion.   The aggregate findings, regardless of theoretical framework or authorship, all confirm the discontinuity after 3, as concerns linear collections, at least. Furthermore, Descoeudres (1921/1946) who observed more than a hundred children noted that after 2 or 3, many children no longer know the number words and resort to the word *many*.

---

[4]The discontinuity after 3 may, at times, only become apparent at the age of 5 or 6. In other words, I am not taking a developmental position that 3 is subitized before it is counted. This is in line with Beckmann (1923), Gelman and Tucker (1975), and J.-P. Fischer (1981, 1984), all of whom report that 3 may be counted before it is subitized.

TABLE 9.1
Error Rate in Spontaneous Labeling as a Function of Number
and Age (Fischer, 1984, Table 1b)

M Age of Group	Number of Initial Items				
	1	2	3	4	5
4 years, 3 months	.02	.07	.36	.83	.80
4 years, 9 months	.00	.02	.11	.62	.65
5 years, 3 months	.00	.08	.08	.31	.26
5 years, 9 months	.00	.02	.01	.16	.44

THE APPREHENSION OF 3 AND
THE APPREHENSION OF 4

The discontinuity after 3 poses a twofold problem: Why is 3 so easy to apprehend and why, in contrast, is 4 (at least in a linear collection) so difficult? Before approaching these questions empirically, another difference between 3 and 4 should be pointed out. A study I conducted (Fischer, 1984) contained a standard subitizing task with linear collections and patterns, using 1 sec exposure time and no RT measures. Both 3 and 4 were presented linearly (L) and as geometrical figures (F); the resulting collections were labeled 3L, 3F, 4L, and 4F. Children aged 4 or 5 ($N = 144$) were administered four subitizing trials on each of the four collections. A correct score on a collection was earned for correct number labeling on three collections out of the four. The data matrix appears in Table 9.2.

As Table 9.2 shows, children did better on geometrical than linear collections. What is crucial, however, is that the difference in difficulty of apprehension is highly significant for 4, $\chi^2 (1, N = 144) = 18.69, p < 0.001$, but nonsignificant for 3, $\chi^2 (1, N = 144) = 1.00, p > .20$). The nonsignificant difference between 3L and 3F appears to undermine arguments for pattern recognition for 3 and, in contrast, is compatible with a counting hypothesis. I take a closer look at just this

TABLE 9.2
Comparison of Linear and Figural Collections (right-hand panel:
apprehension of 3; left-hand panel, apprehension of 4)

		3L: •••					4L: ••••	
		Success	Failure				Success	Failure
3F Success		92	10		4F Success		22	37
Failure		6	36		Failure		8	77

assumption—so as to be in a better position to refute it—in the discussion on Experiment 1, which follows.

Experiment 1: The Apprehension of 3

Hypotheses.   To apprehend 3, I will argue that children, at least 5- to 6-year-olds, have formed a perceptual-cognitive unit that enables them to know that there are "3" without counting or explicitly passing through pattern recognition (e.g., recognizing a triangle and then labeling it *three*). Because this unit forms a whole, an inseparable chunk, children should find it difficult to provide a clear explanation for their apprehension procedure. In fact, it is not even a procedure in the theoretical framework I presented further on.

Alternatively, children may use rapid and fully interiorized counting, and would be expected to exteriorize this counting procedure when their answer is challenged. This is an extension of Galperin's learning theory, as used in (formerly East) Germany (see J.-P. Fischer, 1986, for a brief description).

Method.   The alternative hypothesis was tested in a game situation. Thirty-five first graders (aged 6 or 7) took part in the experiment. All were first administered a conservation or a calculation test to encourage them to speak with the experimenter. This was followed by a standard subitizing task where the experimenter said, "You won" or "You lost," without explicitly presenting the rules.

The first collections of dots presented to the subjects were good gestalts (four in a square) or easy to apprehend. All the subjects (after some initial hesitation) were able to state the number correctly and "won" with these collections.

Subjects were then presented an array, such as 3L. All respond *three* and are told, "You won." This was immediately followed by 3F. Again, all respond *three* but the experimenter ironically said, "You lost"—placing card 3F on the table facing them—"because the *three* was this one"—placing card 3L approximately 10 cm from 3F. The subject could thus see cards 3L and 3F simultaneously and respond to the challenge regarding 3F. Approximately half of the subjects were given card 3L first and were tested on card 3F; the remainder were administered the cards in reverse order. The spontaneous reactions were the most interesting ones, and children who did not reply immediately, even after prompting, were quickly reassured that they were right. The standard subitizing procedure was used on other collections that were more difficult to apprehend. Testing on 4L and 5L showed that none of the children were disturbed by our particular technique for 3L/3F.

Results.   The results were somewhat disappointing in that 13 of the subjects did not react spontaneously (i.e., did not externalize). Nevertheless, reactions were obtained for 22 subjects.

Subjects were assigned to four categories on the basis of type of spontaneous reaction:

1. Those who restated their previous judgment, whether simply by stating it, as Rom (6 years, 4 months) did: "but there are three there, too" or by enumerating the "3s" like Yan (6 years, 3 months): "Oh! There are two 3s."
2. Subjects who did not immediately see what the problem was and got sidetracked, in particular by focusing on the sum of the two collections, like Lud (6 years, 6 months): "Oh yes; you have to say how many there are in all."
3. One subject (Kev, aged 6 years, 2 months) who referred to the difference in arrangement of dots on the cards: "Yes, it's not in the same order there."
4. One subject who counted to justify the answers: Vir (6 years, 2 months): "There are also three there, too (while pointing to the three gummed stickers one by one) one, two, three."

Subjects did not distribute evenly across the four categories: 16 reaffirmed their judgments; 4 got sidetracked, and Categories 3 and 4 contained 1 subject each.

Conclusion.   The fact that there was practically no counting in the spontaneous reactions is consistent with the assumption that 3 is a unit that does not need to be broken down for these children. This is further confirmed by the fact that some subjects counted sets of 3s, by stating, "There are two 3s." A few subjects, usually after experimenter prompting, also sidetracked toward a new, hierarchically superior unit including 3 as a subunit by stating "3 and 3 are 6" or considered the "3" to be a "4" with one missing.

If this method is, indeed, an appropriate empirical frame, the findings are extremely damaging for theories claiming that 6-year-olds apprehend 3 by rapid internalized counting, which is externalized when their answers are challenged. Even Vir, the only subject who spontaneously counted to prove that there were really three, does not confirm counting theory. Vir, in fact, had above-average mathematical knowledge and understood that counting could serve as a justification. Another part of her verbal report is illustrative of this:

E: Let's see if you know the number facts, too!
Vir: I know all of them.
E: All of them?
Vir: Even 2 times 7, 14.
E: Who taught you that?
Vir: I found out by myself.
E: Really?
Vir: Uh-huh. Because once I counted on my fingers, then I knew it. I'll always know it now.

E: Really! And can you count other ones?

Vir: 2 times 8 (1 sec pause) 16; 2 times 9 (1.5 sec) 18; 2 times 10 (instantaneous) 20.[5]

In contrast, the extremely low frequency of geometrical arguments is more difficult to interpret. The subjects who said there were two "3s" probably meant the "3s" were different in shape.

Experiment 2: The Apprehension of 4 (Linear Collection)

Working Hypothesis. In contrast to how they perceive 3, 6-year-olds do not have a perceptual-cognitive unit allowing them to subitize four dots in a row. When presented with a collection of this type, there is no immediate apprehension of 4. Rather, they need to implement a procedure to find the answer. When given enough time, young children will count one by one. Beckmann (1923) presents evidence for this (his Table 8, p. 28): 33% of his subjects aged 4 years, 9 months counted for 3. In contrast, 80% counted for 4, despite the fact that the collections were probably geometrical patterns. I obtained similar findings in one of my earliest experiments (Fischer, 1981) on young children. In the enumeration task, the subjects were allowed to count the collections, which were geometrical in shape. Analysis of overt counting showed that one third of the 4-year-olds explicitly counted for 3, but that twice this number counted for 4.

In contrast, when exposure time is limited or when children are discouraged from counting, they can only arrive at the correct answer of 4 by other means. One of the few efficient ones consists of breaking down the collection into "2 and 2," and obtaining 4 by relying on rote memorization of "2 plus 2 is 4." This process, when automatized, may be difficult to access by introspection. However, during that period of time when it is being automatized, the chances are better than it can be detected. This explains the choice of age range (6 or 7) and the time (second quarter of the first school year) for Experiment 2.

Method. Twenty-four first graders served as subjects. Each subject was administered a conservation test, a subitizing task, and a calculation test, in that order. The subitizing task dealt with collections 4F, 2L, 5F, 4L, 6F, 3L, 2F, 5L, and 3F, presented in that order first, and then in the reverse order. Exposure time was short (less than 1 sec) and reaction times were computed from tape recordings. (A more detailed description can be found in J.-P. Fischer, 1984.)

Results. Only the findings for 4L subitizing are presented here. Of the 24

---

[5]In France, addition is the only operation in the mathematics curriculum for first grade. Multiplication is generally taught in second grade.

subjects, 15 answered correctly at least once on 4L. Justifications subsequent to the first correct answer indicated that 10 (of the 15) broke down the 4L into 2 and 2. The transcripts for these 10 subjects are reproduced here. (Subjects' comments are italicized.)

> Mel (7 years, 1 month): *I saw that there were four.* "How did you see that?" *I saw two on each side.*
>
> Phi (6 years, 8 months): *Because there were two there* (points in one direction) *and two on the other side.*
>
> Mur (6 years, 4 months): *There were two and two; I know that two plus two is four.*
>
> Max (7 years, 2 months): *They were in a row.* "So how did you know there were four?" *Because there were two on each side.*
>
> Bar (6 years, 10 months): *Because I looked carefully.* "And what did you see?" *That there were four.* "But how did you see that?" *I saw right away.* "But did you count them?" *Um . . . yes.* "Yes or no?" *No.* "So what did you do?" *I just looked: I put two balls with two balls and then I saw that that made four.*
>
> Mic (6 years, 11 months): *Because I counted them.* "But how did you count?" *In a row.* "Really?" *Uh-huh.* "But you didn't have time to count!" *Because I saw the two over there* (points to one side) *and two there* (points to other side).
>
> Seb (6 years, 9 months): *Because there were two except that they were in a row.* "Yes! But there weren't two! There were . . ." *Four.* "Yes! But how did you see that there were four?" *There were two and then two more so I saw right away. I got it without thinking.*
>
> Cel (7 years, 2 months): *Because there are two, then there are two more.*
>
> Rem (6 years, 7 months): *Because there are two there and two there* (points to the table).
>
> Seb (6 years, 8 months): *Because I saw two on the top and two on the bottom, but before there was a square.* "Are you sure they were on the top and two on the bottom?" *Um, . . . they were on the same line the long way, I mean, the tall way.*

Three of the remaining five subjects counted one by one. This completes the demonstration that for 4L, at least, there is practically no perception of "4" as a unit. In contrast, as predicted, there was widespread use of an analytical procedure consisting of breaking down the set into 2 and 2, and obtaining the answer via the rote knowledge that "two plus two is four." Another verbal report (Ste, aged 6 years, 4 months) during a pilot experiment provides an even clearer account of the apprehension process: "I saw them all together in a row. Then I saw two on each side: so that makes four."

ISSUES AND INTERPRETATIONS

Why 3?

Evidence from hemispheric specialization as well as data from pathological studies, in particular on split-brain subjects, shed some light on this issue.

In lateralized tachistoscopy, sensory input is presented to either the left or the right visual fields. This technique can be used to impede certain highly automatized processes because information does not necessarily reach the hemisphere specialized for (initial) processing of this input. Charness and Shea (1981) reported that for numbers higher than 3, presentation to the left visual field—that is, to the right hemisphere, which it is directly connected to—yields better performance than presentation to the right visual field. Teng and Sperry (1974) reported that commissurotomized patients undercount sets of three or more units when using the left hemisphere (and this trend is accentuated as the sets become larger). Lecours and Lhermitte (1980) described a split-brain patient and reported that "the left hemisphere cannot handle more than 3 dots" (p. 628).

These data reinforce the assumption that an automatized procedure is implemented for numerosities above 3. This procedure may involve decomposition of the set into smaller, directly apprehendable units. This may be facilitated by (initial) holistic processing, which the right hemisphere (in right-handers) is known to be specialized for. When the neural mechanisms underpinning the automatized procedures are impaired by lateralized tachistoscopy or by lesions, the data suggest that the right hemisphere is needed for rapid apprehension of numerosities over 3; in addition that right hemisphere involvement is mandatory in the initial phases of processing.

The upper limit of perceptual attention is another famous number—seven—which is, itself, one of the major milestones in the literature on the apprehension of number.

A Revival of the Magic Number 7 ± 2?

Although it was G. A. Miller who popularized the "magic number seven" concept in his 1956 article, it was Taves who suggested in 1941 that 7 might be the cutoff point between two different forms of number apprehension. Taves claimed that arrays gave an overall impression or sensation of what he termed *numerousness,* which he measured by psychophysical methods. Close examination of Taves' instructions, however, shows that subjects were not explicitly warned against use of verbal numerical mediation (J.-P. Fischer, 1985). This considerably weakens Taves' argument for a single number impression discrimination mechanism for numbers below 7 that "apparently consists of rapid and direct recognition of number, without the use of counting" (Taves, 1941, p. 22).

Kaufman et al.'s (1949) subsequently reported that their subjects, all university students, responded rapidly and accurately for arrays under 5 or 6 but not for larger arrays. They thus confirmed the existence of a specific small-number apprehension mechanism that they dubbed *subitizing*.

G. A. Miller (1956) generally limited the amount of information people can input, process, and store in memory to seven chunks. This provided theoretical backing to Taves' (1941) cutoff point of 7 for number apprehension, and for the process Kaufman et al. (1949) had termed subitizing.

Theory, however, should be concordant with the facts. In J.-P. Fischer (1985, paragraph 4.1), I pointed out that there are two very different empirical definitions of subitizing. In some studies, subjects are said to have subitized if they produce the right answer at least 50% of the time. In other studies, proof for subitizing is derived from the discontinuity in the RT curve (see Fig. 9.2). These evaluations of subitizing lead to extremely different maximum array values. Studies using the 50% criterion generally set this value at about 7; studies using RT discontinuity points range downward as far as 3.

The 50% criterion was first used as a measure of attention span (Fernberger, 1921). This criterion is particularly lenient, however, and ill-suited to the assessment of accurate apprehension of number. Miller himself was quick to point to this problem; he and others underlined that the maximum number of digits the average individual can recall after one presentation is seven, but that "if we want to be sure that he will never fail, we must reduce the number to four or five" (G. A. Miller, Galanter, & Pribram, 1970, p. 131). Broadbent (1975), in an article titled "The Magic Number Seven After Fifteen Years," also stressed the disparities between the upper numerosity limit for a perfect score and the 50% correct criterion. He set the upper limit at 3 to 4, and cited many experiments placing this limit at 3.

Mandler and Shebo (1982) conveniently linked up the properties of 7 and 3. They suggested that subitizing can be divided into two component processes. The first, applying to arrays of 1 to 3, corresponds to the type of subitizing that has been described so far in this chapter. The second, which applies to brief presentations of arrays of 4 to 6, or a maximum of 7, is highly automatized in adults (students and psychology department staff who often serve as subjects) who are able to hold the arrays in consciousness (i.e., attention) long enough for mental counting.[6]

Which Cognitive Architecture?

Even though 3 and 7 are very specific numbers, there is no reason to assume that the number apprehension mechanism is equally specific or original. This leads

---

[6]The term *mental counting* in English covers more ground than the restricted meaning assigned to counting at the beginning of this chapter. Mental counting can also include partial counting, as in counting-on, or computation, such as the process described for the apprehension of 4 in the form of 2 + 2.

directly to the issue of the general cognitive architecture that can best account for this mechanism.

Basically, there are two types of architectures or unified theories of cognition. One makes a fundamental distinction between two types of knowledge, termed *procedural* and *declarative* (see J. R. Anderson's ACT* theory, 1983). The other posits a single form of knowledge, for example, procedural knowledge, which is often realized in the production systems (see Rosenbloom & Newell, 1987, on chunking theory).

Chunking, as developed by Rosenbloom and Newell, is like subitizing. For example, the Seibel (1963) 1023-alternative discrimination task, simulated by Newell and Rosenbloom, bears much in common with the Biemüller experiment (1932) discussed earlier. Seibel also designed a perceptuomotor task in which subjects were asked to reproduce arrays of (a maximum of 10) lights by pushing the buttons in one-to-one correspondence with them. (The name of the task reflects the number of alternatives—$1023 = 2^{10} - 1$—because Seibel excluded the case where no lights are lit.) Similarly in the Biemüller task, marbles simultaneously rolled down parallel grooves (a maximum of one marble per groove) and subjects were asked to state which of the 19 holes the marbles had dropped into.

Despite this analogy, a theory postulating two forms of knowledge accounts better for the initial independence of subitizing and counting that I believe takes place. A theory of this type forms a perfect conceptual frame to contrast two types of processing. A good example can be found in the notions of parallel and serial processing, which are subsumed in the more comprehensive Schneider and Shiffrin (1977; Shiffrin & Schneider, 1977) concept of *automatic* and *controlled processes*. Although Sagi and Julesz (1985) provided ingenious empirical evidence for parallel processing of numerosities in subitizing, the replication of this experiment by Folk, Egeth, and Kwak (1988) showed that subitizing nevertheless contains a serial component.

Furthermore, Richman and Simon (1989) presented cogent theoretical arguments against the parallel/serial dichotomy. In addition, in observational terms, it is problematic to differentiate a parallel process from an arbitrarily rapid serial one.

For all these reasons (and others, see J.-P. Fischer, 1991), I find it preferable to work with the distinction made by J. R. Anderson (1983) or Squire (1987) between procedural and declarative knowledge (or memory). Elementary arithmetic models (e.g., Ashcraft, 1982) were quick to integrate the procedural/declarative distinction but it has only recently been applied to subitizing (Wolters et al., 1987). A model of this type (see J.-P. Fischer, 1991) can account neatly for the data presented earlier. In the task dealing with the apprehension of 3, 5- and 6-year-olds know that there are three; that is, they have declarative knowledge of three. However, younger subjects many only know *how* to find the answer. For example, Nic (aged 3 years, 7 months) looked at 3F (3 tokens in a triangle) and then decided, "I'm going to count" (J.-P. Fischer, 1981, p. 292). In other words, children like Nic only have procedural knowledge of three.

In clinically normal individuals, in contrast to amnesics (Squire, 1987), these two types of knowledge are tightly interconnected. My hypothesis is that there is a unitization mechanism that makes it possible to transfer the end product of one procedure (for example counting) to declarative memory, where it then forms a fairly autonomous unit. Counting (in the Nic example) may be the basis for declarative knowledge of a numerosity. Further evidence for this process comes from Vir (cited in Experiment 1), who attributed her declarative knowledge that "2 times 7 is 14" to the fact that she once counted on her fingers. However, Vir is overly optimistic in stating that she will always know this: She is apparently unaware of the fact that declarative knowledge needs to be consolidated (Squire, 1987).

Conversely, a *proceduralization* mechanism makes it possible to incorporate certain types of declarative knowledge (for example "two and two are four") into procedures. The subjects in Experiment 2 who stated that they had apprehended the collection of four dots by breaking down the collection into 2 and 2 to count 4 were using a proceduralization mechanism. Note that this decomposition process itself integrates the perceptuocognitive unit 2 twice. Subjects then relied on another cognitive unit, "two and two are four," stored in declarative memory to arrive at the answer, "four."

CONCLUSIONS AND APPLICATIONS

The first section of this chapter provides abundant evidence for a discontinuity in the apprehension of 3 and the apprehension of 4 by 5- to 6-year-olds, at least for linear collections of regularly spaced dots. This discontinuity is entirely compatible with research data on neural mechanisms, and in particular, with hemispheric specialization data from the 1960s. This discontinuity cannot be explained by theories that assume that rapid and internalized counting is the sole number apprehension mechanism. Rather, it implies that arrays of 1 to 3 are apprehended in a way that differs from counting.

This apprehension mechanism can be termed *subitizing* provided that it is defined carefully. This is what I have attempted to do throughout this chapter. The definition of *subitizing* can be extended to include recognition of canonical geometric patterns such as 4 in a square or 5 in the die configuration.

The discontinuity after 3 has several direct applications for early number acquisition (see, e.g., the first grade counting exercise described in Fischer, 1984, pp. 116–124). It can also help pinpoint the easiest patterns to apprehend, which remains an area of investigation for educators today despite its long history. A finding in Maertens, Jones, and Waite (1977) has bearing here. Maertens et al. arbitrarily defined elemental groupings as groupings of 1, 2, 3, or 4 objects (p. 181). But the data show that, in most cases, regroupings occurring after three were more accurately perceived than regroupings after four (p. 191). In particular, nine in the form of three rows of three was better perceived than eight in the form of two rows of four each:

XXX		XXXX
XXX	vs.	XXXX
XXX		

After demonstrating the discontinuity after 3, I turned to apprehension processes for 3 and for 4 (in linear collections). In the theoretical terms defined in the latter part of this chapter (and more fully in J.-P. Fischer, 1991) the apprehension of 3 in 5- and 6-year-olds can be seen as declarative knowledge. This declarative knowledge may be a primitive or may be the result of counting through a unitization process. It should, however, be differentiated from counting as procedural knowledge, which younger children can use to find the answer, "three."

Unitization results in the creation of a new unit in declarative memory. This unit, which can be activated directly, is processed as a whole. It can be incorporated as a whole in a procedure by the proceduralization mechanism. It is only broken down when implemented in a procedure. Counting-on provides a good example. When asked to count five objects clearly arranged in two clusters of three and two, a 6-year-old may begin by announcing "three" and then label the first dot in the second cluster "four" and the second dot "five."

Children, in the case of nongeometric patterns larger than 3, probably initiate a procedural mechanism that implements procedural or strategic knowledge ("break down the collection") and that also includes declarative components (such as "two and two are four"). This type of procedure should emerge developmentally later than counting one by one.

This theoretical framework provides a good account of my own data. To be viable as a theory, however, it needs to account for other data as well. Some of the best known data deal with the magic number 7. This is not only a theoretical issue. Some instructors' manuals continue to stress the importance of the number 7. For example, Audigier, Clavier, Clavié, and Clesse (1985) referred to methods that do not take the special status of 7 into account as "nonsensical" (NONSENS, p. 3). Other works (e.g., Je. Jardy, Jy. Jardy, & Soumy, 1985) devalue 7 slightly by lowering the cutoff point to 6. I have argued that the number 7 is more likely to be the upper limit for holistic processing or attention span, in general, than for accurate apprehension or enumeration and thus is less critical pedagogically (see also J.-P. Fischer & Meljac, 1987).

The expression *perception as a whole* (perception globale) which is often employed by educators (see, e.g., Bringuier, Gorlier, Perrot, & Ragot, 1989, p.

75) is, in fact, only appropriate for the first three numbers and highly familiar patterns. The training they advise in perception as a whole may be an automatization of the procedural mechanism described at length for 4L, used for arrays over 3 and for nongeometrical patterns.

When a proceduralized mechanism is used, the expression *perception as a whole* is doubly inappropriate because the process is fundamentally cognitive and analytical. Further, pattern learning experiments suggest that beyond 3, only constant patterns can be apprehended by a declarative process. Vision research has shown that this is the case for arrangements of dice or dominoes. Kinesthetic and motor studies (Brissiaud, 1989) have shown that this type of learning is feasible and desirable for finger patterns.

Finally, in contrast to 4, an array of 3 is scarcely easier to identify when it is presented in a geometric pattern (a triangle) than when it is presented in a linear fashion. Phe (6 years, 9 months), one of the few children who was able to describe his geometric apprehension mechanism for 3, illustrated this, explaining, "Because that made a triangle and you can put them almost anywhere for three." The first part of his explanation suggests he used pattern recognition, but he corrects himself almost immediately and simultaneously by using the conjunction *and* to explain that the triangular pattern is not decisive! It is likely, in the end, that 3 was . . . subitized.

ACKNOWLEDGMENTS

I thank Jacqueline Bideaud, Rémi Brissiaud, and Claire Meljac for their helpful comments on earlier versions of this chapter.

10 From Number to Numbers in Use: Solving Arithmetic Problems

Michel Fayol
Université de Bourgogne

One type of classroom exercise that involves the use of numbers is the solving of arithmetic problems. Arithmetic problems are part of the stable school diet and students are known to encounter a whole host of difficulties with them. This chapter summarizes the state of the art in this area and attempts to form a coherent picture of the development of problem-solving strategies involving numerical operations. Given the data available at the current time, this overview will be restricted to additive problems: problems that can be solved by either addition or subtraction.

Research since the early 1980s has shown that two broad categories of factors affect the ease with which arithmetic problems are solved: conceptual and semantic factors, and linguistic and stylistic ones. First I examine these two categories. In later sections I show that a single interpretation can account for the obstacles created by both of these factors. The conclusion highlights unresolved issues.

EFFECTS OF CONCEPTUAL AND SEMANTIC FACTORS

A Tentative Problem Typology

Studies of arithmetic problems make clear that the type of numerical operation required to solve the problem—addition or subtraction—is a poor predictor of (relative) problem difficulty (Bilsky & Judd, 1986). There is a general consensus that the critical features in problem solving are the conceptual and semantic features involved in increments, decrements, combinations, and comparisons of sets.

Recognition of the importance of these features has prompted researchers to define a problem taxonomy (Carpenter, Hiebert, & Moser, 1981; Carpenter & Moser, 1982, 1983; Riley et al., 1983) that delineates three basic categories of problems:

- *Change* problems (join or separate), which call for at least one "temporal" change in the start state to arrive at the end state (e.g., Paul had 3 marbles. John gave him 4. How many marbles does Paul have now?)
- *Combine* problems that involve static situations (e.g., Paul has 3 marbles in his left hand and 4 marbles in his right hand. How many marbles does he have altogether?)
- *Compare* problems that involve static quantities that are related by phrases such as *more than* or *less than* (see Fayol, 1990; Riley et al., 1983).

This extensively used taxonomy does not, however, cover the entire range of word problems. An exhaustive compilation of potential situations can be found in Vergnaud (1982), who pointed out that problems can deal with measures and/or transformations combined by several types of relationships. For example, the following situation is difficult to classify in the Riley et al. taxonomy: "John won 6 marbles this morning. He lost 9 this afternoon. What happened all together today?"

This issue of exhaustivity aside, most researchers, nevertheless, agree that there are different types of additive problems. Problems tend to be categorized on the basis of the semantic features of the events described in the problem statement rather by the type of numerical operation or formula required. The real issue, obviously, is to decide whether these categories are psychologically relevant, that is, whether they can successfully account for differences in performance.

From Taxonomies to Solution Procedures

Several studies have reported data on success rates for 6- to 10-year-olds on a variety of arithmetic problems. Other studies go further and describe type of processing and transitions in type of processing over a specific age period. In terms of percentage, these results show:

- Change problems are easier, irrespective of whether the change in the problem statement is positive (an increase in quantity) or negative (a decrease).
- Compare problems are by far the most difficult.
- One of the major difficulties (as reflected in performance) lies in the type of unknown: Problems with unknown result states are easier than problems with unknown combine states, and performance is weakest for problems with an unknown start state.

One plausible explanation for these differences is that children, in fact, implement different types of problem-solving strategies for each type of problem. Carpenter (1985) and Carpenter and Moser (1983) investigated the procedures used by children to solve highly contrasted addition problems. They drew three conclusions: First, in both addition and subtraction problems, children employ a variety of procedures: actual physical matching (vs. separating) followed by counting, counting from the first cardinal in the problem or from the larger of the two, counting backward from a number or up to a number, one-to-one correspondence, and pure rote responses (see also Baroody, Ginsburg, & Waxman, 1983; Marton & Neumar, 1989). Second, certain strategies are highly correlated with certain types of problems. For example, for "John had 8 marbles. He gave 5 away," children tend to use a physical separation procedure. In contrast, for "John has 8 marbles. Tom has 5. John has how many more marbles than Tom?," the main strategy is one-to-one correspondence (see also De Corte & Verschaffel, 1987). Third, the correlation between problem type and type of strategy, which is extremely high in the youngest subjects, falls off rapidly in subsequent years. In third grade, two thirds of the answers are based on rote "number facts" (Ashcraft & Battaglia, 1978; Ashcraft & Fierman, 1982).

To summarize, younger subjects tend to use problem-solving strategies that mimic the actions described in the problem statements. At this stage children are more likely to fall back on schemes rather than to use arithmetic operations. The advantage of this is that children can "solve" problems without recasting the situation in mathematical terms. Schemes also have a number of disadvantages, however, the major one being that children may not be able to solve problems that cannot be acted out (e.g., problems with an unknown initial state). Commutativity, for instance, can be acted out to turn $3 + 5$ into $5 + 3$ when the numbers initially have equivalent "roles" (as is the case in combine problems) but not when they have different roles, where one refers to a state and the other to a transformation (see Fayol, in preparation).

The ability to count to oneself eliminates a number of difficulties, but ease of simulation doubtless still plays a role at this stage. The ability to perform calculations probably facilitates—through reflective abstraction—the shift from *applied* commutativity (because the load caused by counting has been lessened) to principled, *conceptual* commutativity (Baroody, 1987d; Baroody & Gannon, 1984). At the same time, storage and retrieval of number facts in long-term memory increases the potential for flexibility and broadens the range of strategies available to solve a given problem situation (Siegler & Shrager, 1984). These strategies are not only governed by the semantic or conceptual features, but are also affected by other types of constraints. One that deserves fuller attention is wording.

Impact of the Wording of Problem Statements

Researchers have been quick to point out that conceptual and semantic features of problem statements cannot fully account for performance, particularly in the youngest age bracket. Other more unexpected factors related to formulation of the problem statement seem to intervene (Kilpatrick, 1987): One difficulty is related to lexical items; the other concerns the order of presentation of information in the statement or its *rhetorical structure*.

Impact of Lexical Items.   The role of lexical items in the understanding of problem statements has been investigated in two theoretical frameworks.

In a series of studies on class versus collection effects in inclusion tasks, Markman (1973, 1978, 1979) indicated that the use of terms that draw attention to the elements of a class (e.g., *trees, children,* and *soldiers*) result in differences in performance on the inclusion task (Inhelder & Piaget, 1964a) as compared to the use of collection terms that refer to a global entity (*forest, family,* and *army,* respectively). For example, children were asked to look at a family of frogs: the mother frog, the father frog, and the baby frogs. They were then asked to compare the set of the baby frogs either to the whole set of the frogs (class term) or to the family of frogs (collection term) (Markman & Seibert, 1976, p. 567). The results showed that performance on part–whole comparison is better when collection terms are used instead of class terms. Because part–whole relationships are so important in the solving of addition problems (Nesher & Katriel, 1977), one difficulty in the solving of certain addition problems may be caused by word choice. However, there is no clearcut evidence that the Markman effect extends beyond the inclusion task (Fuson, Pergament, & Lyons, 1985; Hodges & French, 1988).

The most abundant evidence on the impact of lexical items in problem solving comes from studies on the effects of relational terms. These studies show that terms such as *more than* and *less than* (see Donaldson, 1978) are difficult at all ages, but particularly for young children. Hudson (1983) has shown that rewording inclusion task problems in ways that made it easier to construct mental models results in significant improvement in performance.

In a more recent recall task paradigm, Dellarosa-Cummins, Kintsch, Reusser, and Weimer (1988) showed that relational terms are often understood in a non-relational way. For example, "John has 4 marbles. Mary has 3 more" is often misinterpreted as "John has 4 marbles, and Mary has 3 marbles." They also report that *altogether* is often misconstrued to mean *each*, which obviously changes the part–whole relationships in a problem and affects the type of numerical operations children will use to solve it.

De Corte, Verschaffel, and De Win (1985) described cases of miscomprehension caused by the type of presupposition in the problem statement. For example, on a word problem such as "Peter has 3 apples. Anne gives him 5 more apples," one child was reported as stating that "Anne cannot give any apples because she doesn't have any." Strictly speaking, the child is right, but this type of information is typically implicit in canonical word-problem formats.

Thus, the impact of lexical items, although often considered to be minor, is, in fact, of crucial importance in the solving of word problems. Recent computer simulations (in particular, Dellarosa-Cummins et al., 1988; but also Briars & Larkin, 1984; Dellarosa, 1986; Escarabajal, 1987; Fletcher, 1985; Kintsch & Greeno, 1985) confirm the importance of wording, and indicate that it may be more important than the semantic structure or conceptual organization of the problem (further justification of Kintsch's, 1988, simulation of comprehension problems).

Effect of Order of Presentation

Lexical items, in particular items that express relationships, are difficult to understand. The rhetorical structure of a problem, that is, the way a problem statement is phrased, also affects comprehension.

Rosenthal and Resnick (1974) asked 8- to 9-year-olds to solve word problems containing transformations (win or lose) in which the order of presentation of information was varied. As has been observed in other fields (Ferreiro, 1971), children did better when the order of presentation matched the sequential order of events. Rosenthal and Resnick also obtained a highly unexpected interaction between type of transformation (win vs. lose) and the nature of the unknown (start state vs. end state). In contrast to typical findings, calculation of the start state was easier when the transformation was a lose rather than a win. Similar data have also been obtained by Fayol and Abdi (1986).

In a related experiment, Fayol, Abdi, and Gombert (1987) asked 6- to 10-year-olds to solve word problems with unknown start or end states. The placement of unknown was varied by putting the question at either the beginning or the end of the problem. For all ages and for all problems, placing the question at the start of the problem resulted in better performance than placing the question in its canonical location at the end of the problem. In addition, this improvement in performance was accentuated on the most difficult problems. Performance varied as a function of changes in order of presentation of information in the problem statement, but more importantly, changes in presentation order were associated with changes in strategy. When the numerical information was more difficult to process and when the question was located at the end, the difficult word problems (those with an unknown start state) were handled as though the problem was to find the end state. This type of "simplification" has been observed on several occasions (Dellarosa-Cummins et al., 1988; Escarabajal, 1987).

What can account for these effects? I have argued elsewhere (Fayol & Abdi, 1986; Fayol et al., 1987) that they may be due to the efficiency of bottom–up or top–down strategies. Bottom–up strategies primarily tax working memory because the event structure is built up in accordance with the order of occurrence of events in the problem statement. Bottom–up processing is thus constrained by the limitations mentioned earlier: More top–down processing operates by the activation of schemata in long-term memory, and combines search and problem-solving procedures.

This interpretation is only partially satisfactory, however, in that it fails to explain either how problem schemas are developed or how they are activated. Nevertheless, it is useful in that it raises issues of individual differences in arithmetic problem solving. Individuals have a certain amount of prior knowledge that can be applied to an oral or written presentation of a problem statement. Subjects need to understand the situation and pinpoint those parts of the statement that can be used to find the correct answer. Clearly, understanding and problem solving are affected by constraints related to the limitations of working memory. As a function of prior knowledge, the wording of the problem statement, and limitations on working memory, individuals will either succeed or fail to solve a problem. These three features can be combined in a single model.

AN ADDITION PROBLEM-SOLVING MODEL

Regardless of the type of addition problem—change, combine, or comparison—problem solving always calls for the association of numerical data and a part–whole structure (Kintsch, 1988; Resnick, 1989). Once this mapping procedure has been initiated, the problem can usually be solved, although calculation errors are always possible. The problem—for theorists—is that the mapping of data and roles can take place in a variety of different ways and, above all, at different levels of abstraction. This can account for the high success rates in young subjects reported in some studies (Donaldson, 1978; Hudson, 1983) and the reports of persistent failure in others (Vergnaud, 1982).

The model accounts for both the wide range of problem-processing requirements in a single underlying structure (the inclusion schema), by assuming first that solving an addition problem is based on prior construction of a representation of the situation described in the problem. As the studies already mentioned have shown, relative ease of schema construction is dependent on two main factors:

The Nature of the Problem Situation.   Problems containing a transformation are apparently easier than comparison problems. Similarly, problems with unknown start sets are particularly difficult. In general, problems are more difficult for subjects to solve when they deal with unfamiliar situations or situations that are difficult to relate to familiar ones. This shows up in several ways. When children are asked to recall the problem after completing problem solving (e.g., delayed recall) the most difficult problems are recalled as simpler ones, as though the youngest subjects had "understood" another problem than the one given to them and had interpreted the target problem by assimilating it to one (or several) easier problems. Immediate recall however does not reveal the same pattern: It tends to coincide with the initial problem statement.

In adults, errors and assimilations to simpler problems obviously occur much less frequently, but fine-grained analysis—for example problem-solving times (Reusser, 1989)—show that problems dealing with familiar situations (or "scripts"; see Fayol & Monteil, 1988) are solved more quickly than those referring to abstract entities or sequences of events.

One possible interpretation of these data is the following: Problem solving calls for construction of a *mental model* (Johnson-Laird, 1983) or a *situation model* (Kintsch, 1986, 1988; Reusser, 1989). Situations that parallel ones the individual is familiar with and take place in a normal fashion (i.e., adhering to a typical order of occurrence) lend themselves more easily to the construction of mental models. Mental models can be constructed rapidly for tasks dealing with familiar situations in a familiar order. Problem solving simply requires mapping onto the part–whole structure. In contrast, when the occurrences (or states) are semantically impoverished, individuals are deprived of their "interpretation clues" and probably need to re-represent the numerical information by assigning part–whole roles and carrying out the appropriate computations. This would account for higher error rates and longer problem-solving times.

The Wording of the Problem Statement. Understanding relational terms (*more than, less than*) is not only a problem for children. Lewis and Mayer (1987) reported that college students have comparable difficulties. For example, students make more mistakes on problems like "John has 3 marbles. He has 5 less than Tom" than on problems like "John has 3 marbles. Tom has 5 more than John" (p. 364; see also Huttenlocher & S. Strauss, 1968). Similarly, data on story comprehension (Black, Turner, & Bower, 1979) show that establishing and maintaining a point of view facilitates information integration; Reusser (1989) reported similar findings for problem statements. This is, in fact, an illustration of the now classic result reflecting identification and implementation of given information, which is then complemented by new information (Clark & Haviland, 1977).

Problem statements thus present the same difficulties as those reported for text comprehension in general. Language is not simply a form of representation of reality. It is also a means of communication that is affected by pragmatic constraints and constraints on working memory capacity.

This makes it easy to grasp the importance of wording. The more a problem statement violates "given–new contract" rules (Clark & Haviland, 1977)— maintenance of a single topic, using a restricted number of presuppositions, and so on—the more the reader will experience difficulties in elaborating a coherent and complete representation of the situation (see Kintsch & van Dijk, 1978; Vipond, 1980). It also explains the facilitating effect (and improvement in performance) reported by De Corte, Verschaffel and De Win (1985) of reducing the number of presuppositions in problem statements, such as "John won 3 marbles. Now he has 5 marbles. How many marbles did he have at the start?" In all likelihood, better performance is the result of a better constructed representation of the situation presented in the problem statement.

Wording effects, even when observed in very young children (Hudson, 1983) can, in all likelihood, be attributed to the differential ease of constructing a representation of a situation model. Some forms of presentation are better than others to maximize the speed and reliability of constructing the mental model. Other forms of presentation make model building more difficult: problems with an unknown start set (discussed earlier) or problems that make high cognitive demands even before processing can begin (Fayol et al., 1987).

Explicit mention of the states or events referred to in the problem statement, and frequent exposure to certain types of problem statements (De Corte et al., 1985) contribute to better performance because they enable the child to build more relevant situation models. Once the relevant model has been elaborated, the child can associate numerical information to the corresponding part–whole roles in the problem.

SUMMARY

Thus, semantic and conceptual variables, and variables related to wording all have an impact on the solving of arithmetic problems. All affect the construction of a situation model which forms the interface between problem statement and computation. The situation model will vary in level of abstraction as a function of the states or events described in the problem, and as a function of type of wording of the problem statement. Very roughly, there are three levels of abstraction:

At Level 1, the ability to produce fairly accurate immediate recall of the problem makes it possible to act out the situation described in the statement. Regardless of whether this is done by using materials (e.g., blocks) or fingers (Marton & Neumar, 1989), subjects can match a state or action with a statement or proposition. Processing is sequential and is based on lexical meaning and order of occurrence. However, there is not necessarily any integrated overall representation. The answer is derived from the action and is thus totally dependent upon the extent to which the problem can be recast as a series of actions. In other words, at Level 1 there is no elaboration of a mental model. In Piagetian terms, this level corresponds to an externalized scheme, where the subject can succeed without understanding (Piaget, 1974). This results in systematic failure when simulation through action is unfeasible: for example, when the start state is not quantified, when the word order in the problem statement does not adhere to order of events, and so forth. It can also result in early success when the problem statement "follows" the order of events in sequence. Level 1 is fairly similar to Stage 1 in Briars and Larkin's (1984) simulation model: The program solves problems exclusively through action.

At Level 2, representations are gradually internalized, and there is internal building up of a situation model. Nevertheless, models do not emerge of a piece and do not generalize to all situations. Model construction is affected by wording (degree of explicitness of relationships and presuppositions, sequence order, etc.) as well as by familiarity with the situation described in the problem statement. This results in inconsistent performance (Escarabajal, 1987; Wilkinson, 1984). It also results in steady improvement in performance: Greater knowledge of the physical and social world and broader exposure to different types of problems statements all positively affect the construction of integrated situation models. The development of situation models authorizes numerical data operations, such as commutativity and empty sets, which facilitate problem solving. Performance, however, is still dependent to a great extent on the individual's ability to represent the problem. The youngest subjects at Level 2 still find unknown start state problems difficult. The oldest Level 2 subjects still do poorly on combine and transform problems (Vergnaud, 1982).

At Level 3, which subjects attain at variable rates as a function of both age and the problem situation, the sequence of data in the problem can be recoded in a fairly static re-representation version of the inclusion scheme. Elaboration of this re-representation is dependent on the type of problem (see Barrouillet, 1989; Bideaud & Houdé, 1987; Houdé, 1989). It is, however, necessary to problem solving when the problem statements are linguistically and semantically impoverished (Reusser, 1989). In cases of this type, subjects need to have an available inclusion scheme and must be capable of careful control over instantiation of part–whole relationships through assignment of roles to the numerical data. In short, the subject needs to understand to succeed.

Empirical data and classroom experience both show that the transition from Level 1 to Level 3 takes place gradually, over an extremely long period of time, from ages 4 to 11 or 12. Even in adults, certain types of problems (combine and transformation problems, in particular) prompt recourse to re-representation in the form of a cognitively costly and fragile inclusion scheme. However, the findings of Carpenter et al. (1981) and Willis and Fuson (1988) suggest that metacognitive training in systematic use of the inclusion scheme and careful checking of the assignment of numerical data to positions in the scheme improve performance and can transfer to related situations. However, interpretations of the effects of comprehension aids on performance remain speculative.

11

The Appropriation of the Concept of Number: A Lengthy Process

Gerard Vergnaud
LaPsydee

The study of the concept of number furnishes an excellent illustration of several key notions in the psychology of higher cognitive functions. It shows that the process of appropriation and construction of knowledge is a lengthy one, that the wide range of properties associated with a given concept are extremely diversified, and that acquisition of these properties is extremely slow. On a theoretical level, investigation of the concept of number points clearly to the impossibility of isolating the study of development from the study of learning, and the need to tie cognitive psychology and the epistemology of emergent knowledge and ability together.

By *epistemology* I am not referring to a general theory of knowledge but rather, on a more modest level, to recognition of the role of a given piece of specific knowledge—the relationship of given concepts and abilities—to the practical and theoretical problems that the solution of these problems is based on.

Although the most elementary aspects of the concept of number begin to be grasped by the age of 3 or 4, most individuals do not have a full understanding of signed (i.e., positive and negative) numbers and rational numbers before the age of 15 and they have a long way to go before they understand all the properties of real numbers, complex numbers, and the many other categories of numbers mathematicians have developed throughout history.

Few psychologists have taken an empirical interest in the learning of mathematics: The general feeling is that it is not of direct concern to psychologists. However, very young children—both in school and out—encounter situations for which analysis employing the concepts of signed, rational, and real numbers is relevant. In addition, children soon develop fairly good intuitions about these situations: For example, a number of studies in education show that by the age of 9 children are able to understand the concept of unlimited approximation by a decimal number of any fractional number, provided that they are placed in a situation that makes the question meaningful and age-appropriate.

Clearly, we cannot dismiss the learning of mathematics when exploring the development of children's number skills. These skills form a constantly evolving repertory that reflects the growth of skills mastered in ever-widening numerical domains; the automatization of the schemes underlying these skills; the understanding of new classes of problems and new relationships; and the conceptualization of new facets of physical, economic, social, and technological experience in which number plays a major role.

FIRST PROBLEMS, FIRST SKILLS, FIRST CONCEPTS

The first problems that have meaning for young children, the ones for which they can assign a functional value to the concept of number, are compare, combine, and transform problems on discrete sets:

- Who has the most? Who has the least? How many does each person have? How many more? How many less?
- How much are there when two sets are combined?
- What will my collection of marbles or candies be like if someone gives me some or I buy some, or someone takes some, or I lose some or I eat some?

The two main notions that are the foundations for the concept of number are *cardinality,* the measurement of discrete quantities, and addition. Without addition there can be no number, because addition gives numbers their distinctive properties. Naturally, order properties are important (5 is larger than 3), but order is not restricted to numbers: The letters of the alphabet and the days of the week also exhibit order properties (*d* is after *b,* Tuesday is after Monday). However, although it is true that $4 + 3 = 7$, it is meaningless to state that $c + d = g$, when they represent letters and not unknown numbers.

The two key criteria for the construction of the number concept, then, are:

- *cardinality,* which is manifest when children repeat the last number word in a count sequence ("one, two, three, four; four!"), when they stress the final number word by a change in intonation ("one, two, three, *four!*"), or when they are able to answer the "how many?" question correctly, without recounting, simply by repeating "four."
- mastery (for small sets) of the basic axiom of the *theory of measure:*
  card $(A \cup B)$ = card (A) + card (B),
  where $\cup$ = the union of disjuncted sets.

There is a general consensus that children who use the number fact $4 + 3 = 7$ hold this theorem-in-action to be true. This is also the case for children who do

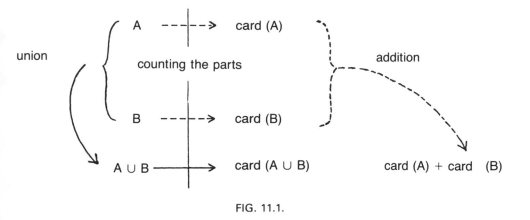

FIG. 11.1.

not count the whole (A ∪ B) after having counted its constituent parts, A and B, but rather count forward from the cardinal measure in the first set A the number of steps forward that are in the second set B. In fact these children are implicitly using the isomorphism between the set of collections and the union operation on the one hand, and the set of whole numbers and the sum operation on the other. No re-counting of the whole, however, reflects awareness of the identity of the two procedures shown in Fig. 11.1: uniting and counting the whole (solid lines) versus counting each part and operating on the numbers so obtained (dotted lines).

The construction or the recognition of a homomorphism is perhaps the most powerful means of enriching the knowledge base. I give more examples of this further on. What needs to be pointed out at this juncture is that the analysis just presented is far from satisfactory because situations involving the union of two parts into a whole are not the only prototype for addition. Another prototype, described by Gelman and Gallistel (1978), Vergnaud and Durand (1976), and others, consists of diachronic situations (see Fig. 11.2) in which addition is perceived as a process that increases (e.g., through acquisition or receipt), and subtraction is seen as a process that decreases (e.g., through loss, giving away, or consumption).

This leads immediately to the issue of signed numbers, because transformations can be either positive or negative. Some 5- and 6-year-olds can combine transformations with opposite signs without information on the initial state: I add 2; I take 1 away; how much is that?

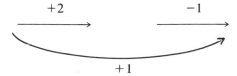

addition prototypes

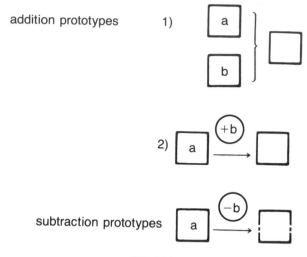

FIG. 11.2.

This theorem-in-action $(+2) + (-1)$ is the basis for an understanding of numerical sequences, as is the combination of the first quantified comparison relationships: If A has 2 more than B, and B has 1 less than C, then A has 1 more than C.

By the age of 6 or 7, children must cope with situations in which they need to use various forms of number knowledge—including the cardinality principle and the addition axiom—reaching a final state by counting forward (or backward) a given number of steps. Combinations of transformations and combinations of quantified relationships broaden the range of skills associated with the emergence of number: Conservation of discrete quantities is thus one of many building blocks of number knowledge, and not necessarily even the cornerstone, or at least, not the only one.

The list of skills is further expanded to include double counting (forward and backward), knowledge of addition and subtraction tables, and the knowledge of commutativity, that when two numbers are to be added, starting from the smaller number and starting from the larger give equivalent results:

Example: How much is $3 + 6$?
  3 . . . 4,5,6,7,8,9.
  6 . . . 7,8,9.

The use of the second procedure, which is more economical and reliable than the first, presupposes the implicit awareness that it is equivalent to the first.

  $3 + 6 = 6 + 3$ commutativity-in-action

The Expanding of Additive and Multiplicative Structures

The data collected since the 1980s have shown that six addition relationships can generate an astounding range of classes of problems, but few researchers have explored this phenomenon. Figure 11.3 schematizes the six elementary relationships that are necessary to analyze all addition and subtraction problems.

From a purely structural point of view (momentarily disregarding numerical values and potentially relevant domains of experience), the first three relationships alone can generate 14 separate classes of problems. There is evidence (Vergnaud & Durand, 1976; Carpenter, Moser, & Romberg, 1982; Nesher, 1982; Riley et al., 1983) that such problems differ considerably from one another in complexity. Most 15-year-olds are unsuccessful on some problems derived from relationships in the latter three classes, and the typical procedures used by children also vary from class to class.

There are several factors that can make a problem difficult. Take, for example, the problem of finding an unknown initial state.

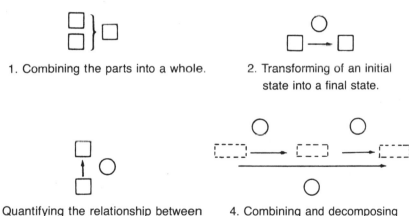

1. Combining the parts into a whole.

2. Transforming of an initial state into a final state.

3. Quantifying the relationship between referent and referred quantities.

4. Combining and decomposing of transformations.

5. Combining and decomposing of relationships.

6. Transforming of a relationship.

FIG. 11.3. Elementary additive relationships.

Jean just earned $7 by going on an errand for a neighbor. She now has $15 How much money did she have before she went on the errand?

This problem can be difficult for several convergent reasons.

- Conceptual difficulties related to reversal of the direct transformation:

    $F = T\,(I) \Rightarrow I = T^{-1}\,(F)$, where F = final state, T = transformation, and I = initial state

- Obstacle created by a primitive conception of addition as gain and subtraction as loss: 7 cannot be subtracted because it corresponds to a gain.
- Inability to count from an unknown initial state and the need to transform the problem to find the answer by counting.
- Difficulty in counting backward 7 steps from 15.
- Difficulty in counting the number of steps from 7 to 15.

Knowledge and ability are so closely knit that it is impossible to differentiate procedural from declarative knowledge (as is often—and erroneously—done). The solving of addition and subtraction problems is clearly procedural, but is necessarily based on theorems-in-action, which can be described in declarative sentences. In particular, these theorems make it possible to transform target procedures into other ones. For example, one possible line of reasoning for calculating by counting from the initial state is shown in Fig. 11.4.

Additive structures can only be fully conceptualized with signed numbers. Thus, there is some justification to the claim that discussing them with respect to children under 10 is inappropriate because signed numbers are not on the curriculum, in many places, until high school. However, the reasoning processes used by children in the reversal of transformations and relationships (e.g., if A has 2 more than B, then B has 2 less than A), and processes used in the decomposition of a transformation into two transformations with opposite signs (e.g., if Terry won 12 marbles in all and lost 7 on the second round, he won 19 on the first round) involve simultaneous processing of signs and absolute values. Children's pathway to knowledge of the number concept thus calls for some conceptualization of positive and negative numbers. This conceptualization is extremely fragmentary, but certain features are observable even before the age of 6 in some children.

Multiplicative structures are never taught before the age of 7. The conceptual

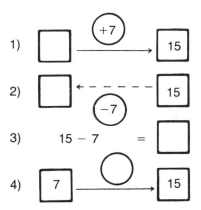

FIG. 11.4.   Solution: Count the number of steps from 7 to 15

explosion they produce is impressive: Proportion problems, in particular, give meaning to fractions as operators and as quantities. By the age of 8 or 9, children understand simple ratios, such as half and twice as much, and then more complicated ratios, such as one fourth. Children grasp the concept of ratio through situations that require comparing quantities (or continuous magnitudes) of the same type. At about the age of 10 or 11, most understand that orangeade tastes as sweet if you mix two glasses of orange syrup and four glasses of water, or if you mix one glass of syrup and two glasses of water (Noelting, 1980). Children at this age are also able to solve three classic problems with Archimedean fractions 1/x, if x is small (e.g., less than 10; Vergnaud, 1983):

- Find the referred quantity when the referent and the ratio are known.
- Find the ratio when the referred and the referent are known.
- Find the referent when the referred and the ratio are known.

In short, children encounter relational properties of numbers and master some of these considerably before they receive formal instruction in negative numbers or rational numbers.

These skills can be observed when children are in situations that confer meaning on these relational properties; it is also possible to develop instructional techniques to promote learning. Douady (1980) for example has designed situations in which children aged 9 to 10 are guided in finding the width of a rectangle with an area of 7 and a height of 5 or in finding the side of a square having an area of 27. The children are taught to find the answer by successive approximations by under- or overshooting, to the rational 7/5 or the real $\sqrt{27}$. For the $\sqrt{27}$, for example,

$5 < x < 6$		27 is closer to 25 than to 36
$5 + 1/4$	$(5 + 1/4)^2 > 27$	too big
$5 + 1/5$	$(5 + 1/5)^2 > 27$	too big
$5 + 1/10$	$(5 + 1/10)^2 < 27$	too little
$5 + 3/20$	$(5 + 3/20)^2 < 27$	too little

$5 + 3/20 < x < 5 + 1/5$ then $5 + 7/40 < x < 5 + 1/5$
then $5 + 19/100 < x < 5 + 1/5$ then $5 + 19/100 + 1/1000 < x$.

Exploring the origins of the concept of number is inseparable from concomitant exploration of the way that children's experiences lend new meaning to their understanding of the various properties of numbers. Psychologists can learn a great deal about children's skills by trying to teach them new skills and concepts, and by analyzing what they can and cannot assimilate.

One key to our understanding of the origins of the concept of number is identification of the obstacles some children face when learning number words and addition, subtraction, multiplication, and division algorithms. It is equally crucial to define which conditions facilitate their coming to view numbers as measures (cardinality), as order and quantified relationships (2 less, 4 times as many), and as transformations (increment or decrement of x). The notions of parity, multiple, and divisor are not only used by older children, but are partially accessible to children in elementary school. Furthermore, children this age like to play with geometric progression like 2, 4, 8, 16, 32, 64, 128. In short, the child's conceptual path leads him or her down many roads, some of which will eventually intersect.

Number concepts and number skills thus form a kind of partially structured lattice, which has some relatively stable and coherent parts and some unstable outcroppings, which are the natural targets for teaching.

A number of studies (e.g., Comiti, Bessot, & Pariselle, 1980) have shown that properties that are easily grasped for small numbers are not transferred to larger numbers, and that the feeling of obviousness that normally accompanies intellectual mastery only affects familiar areas of experience here. Furthermore, some primitive intuitions are the foundations for later acquisitions, whereas others constitute obstacles: For example, understanding the additive iso-morphism leads to grasping the proportional relationship between the number of objects purchased and their price, the basis for understanding the multiplicative isomorphism.

$$P(n) = P(1)_1 + P(1)_2 \ldots + P(1),$$
$$P(n) = n (P) (1)$$
then $P(nx) = n P(x)$

In contrast, familiarity with multiplication and division with whole numbers leads to the expectation that multiplication transforms an initial number into a larger one and division makes it smaller. Thus, multiplication and division by numbers less than 1 yields answers that children perceive as counterintuitive and, hence, wrong. In such a situation, they frequently change their first answers and decide to divide rather than to multiply and conversely (Greer, 1987).

CONCLUSION

The concept of number is context-bound, and cannot be separated from the operations and relations authorized by the context. Depending on the nature of the problem that number use helps solve, a number can be a measure of discrete quantities and continuous magnitudes, a means of ordering objects or sets, a relationship between measures, or a transformation that operates both positively and negatively. It is also a scalar operation (or a ratio) between quantities or magnitudes of the same type and a constant coefficient between two proportional variables (in most cases differing in nature) such as duration and distance covered, or the number of objects purchased and the corresponding expense. The concept of rational number arises from a synthesis of the two more primitive concepts of division and multiplication operators (which combine multiplicatively as fraction operators) and fractional magnitudes (which can be added and subtracted). Another line of research, which has not been touched upon in this chapter but which is nevertheless primordial, is the symbolic representation of numbers, in decimal notation, in another base, in other numerical systems, or by dots along the number line. Construction of this latter representation is particularly arduous (Vergnaud, 1987). In summary, the concept of number stems from the totality of concrete situations and theoretical problems that give this concept meaning, the properties and relationships the child discovers or is taught in these situations, and the symbolic representations that enable the child to represent numbers, their relationships, and the operations authorized by them. Children encounter a wide variety of opportunities, both in school and out, for thinking about and integrating number into their actions and reasoning schemes. They, thus, begin the rich and complex process of constructing the concept of number much earlier than is generally believed, and it is a process that is probably never completed.

III THEORIES AND METHODS: CRITICAL APPROACHES

12 The Multiple Roots of Natural Numbers and Their Multiple Interpretations

Remy Droz
University of Lausanne

THE GENETIC EPISTEMOLOGY OF NUMBER: PIAGET'S VIEW

Piaget repeatedly stated that the genetic epistemology of the notion of natural number can be attributed to a psychological process: namely, the operative synthesis of class structures (class inclusion, to be precise) and order relations (i.e., serial relations).[1] This position entails several epistemological and developmental problems.

From an epistemological point of view:

1. How does one explain to the reader how the notion of "one" moves from a given system of embedded classes to the specific system where the most embedded class only contains one element? In other words, there is a need for a clear account of the transition from species (or concept) to the individual. In my opinion, Piaget did not deliberately disregard this problem. Rather, he did not perceive the importance of the basis of the unit in the construction of number

---

[1] After his first formulation in 1939, Piaget often wrote about this (e.g., Beth & Piaget, 1961; Piaget, 1942, 1949, 1967, 1970b; Piaget & Inhelder, 1966b), but as usual, Piaget constantly introduced slight variations in his definitions. One comprehensive interpretation for this is that Piaget's writings should not be considered to be rational or logico-formal, but rather be considered to be analogico-intuitive. For a more tightly worked criticism, see Thérien (1985).

and, as a consequence, believed he could get around this through ad hoc reasoning founded on a plausible argument rather than a rational construction[2]

2. The reader needs to be told what is meant by *operative synthesis* from a formal or logical point of view. Piaget always dodged this by using a notational trick that overlays the equation for inclusion and the equation for order relations. However, to captivate us or, even better, to gain our allegiance, the essence of an operative synthesis cannot reside in a notational artifice.

From a developmental point of view:

1. Piaget reported no experiments on the development of the concept of singular class (Piaget & Inhelder, 1959, p. 123).

2. He presented no empirical data on the transition from the universal to the particular (from the species to the individual).

3. Piaget did describe one experiment in which he showed that children master cardinal and ordinal numbers simultaneously (Piaget & Szeminska, 1941, p. 154), and another (p. 136) where it can be conceded that there is joint use of class and serial structures, but he presented no experiments that prove in any way the (necessarily) synthetic nature of natural numbers.

4. Finally, Piaget did not make the concept of operative synthesis explicit from a psychogenetic point of view (or even from a psychological one). He never explained the the nature and the functioning of the notions that bear the most resemblance to this idea of operative synthesis (Piaget, 1936)—like the "new combination of schemes" and the "reciprocal assimilation of schemes"—in a way that pertains to the level of operational thinking.

Piaget's major contribution thus does not reside in the fact that he demonstrated—above all, experimentally—the nature of natural numbers and how children construct number.

The value of Piaget and Szeminska's studies and their incredible heuristic prolixity is that they showed, on the basis of experiments, that the domain of the quantitative is not tightly linked to the domain of number and counting. This accounts for the appeal of these experiments, which deal with the conservation of continuous and discontinuous quantities, the comprehension of two-way correspondences and their spatial invariance, and so on. Second, they showed bril-

---

[2]Grize (1960, 1967; and the 1972 edition of Piaget, 1979, under the direction of Grize) has made praiseworthy attempts to perform the squaring of the circle by trying to reconcile the requirements of a logician's approach without distorting Piaget's psychogenetic aims. To do so, Grize subordinates what can be said about child behavior on the basis of available observations to what should be said for the argument to hold for logicians. Unfortunately, the result is not entirely convincing either from the point of view of children or from the point of view of logicians.

liantly that the use of number is not necessarily connected to counting, in contrast to what all researchers before them believed.

In addition, Piaget sensitized us to careful examination of what are, or could be, cognitive activities, especially the mathematically inclined ones. Piaget terms these *logico-mathematical* activities, and they always deal, according to him, with collections of objects as collections, rather than with objects.[3] A list of these activities could take the following form:

- *Classify:* notice resemblances or equivalences among objects.
- *Order, seriate:* notice differences between objects.
- *Count:* enumerate, count objects.
- *Operate, arrange:* assemble (several objects into a whole, separate a whole into its parts).
- *Transform:* change (the characteristics of an object).[4]
- *Label:* act or name an object or a collection of objects.[5]

Piaget later acknowledged that his operative synthesis took place much later than he originally believed—in fact, he finally admitted that this synthesis was probably not terminated before the beginning of formal operations, hence, between the ages of 12 and 14—and was much more laborious, such that children's mastery of number develops very gradually and does not extend instantanously (at whatever point in development) to the set of natural numbers (Gréco, Grize, Papert, & Piaget, 1960). This overdue admission would have benefitted from a specific effort to clarify the true nature of what could be, in this new perspective of prolonged and slow genesis, a synthesis. In fact, we are dealing with a construction that is more or less synchronous, but above all interactive as regards the entire set of logico-mathematical operations.

THE ROOTS OF NATURAL NUMBERS

Everybody uses numbers and we do so from the cradle. As a result, we find it difficult to recollect when we discovered number of how we went about capturing it. Because of this, when we try to say what numbers are and where they

---

[3]In particular, see Apostel, Mays, Morf, and Piaget (1957, especially pp. 40–85), where a major attempt at theoretical explanation is made. In my opinion, it is unfortunate that this had little long-term impact on the later works of Piaget, which would have gained considerably in clarity and transparency if Piaget had taken his own writings a little more seriously.

[4]The focus here is on the set of characteristics, the invariants and the conditions for transformation, see Piaget, Grize, Szeminska and Vinh-Bang (1968).

[5]In my opinion, Piaget only acknowledged the importance of semiotic functions in the cognitive organization of the individual extremely late and in a partial way.

come from, we invent answers that are more or less plausible or appealing, but without knowing just how to go about getting the real answer, but what does *real* mean here, anyway?

There are claims that number arises from experiences with the universe of concrete objects and actions on them: By handling enough pebbles or candies we finally take an interest in their quantity and, so, discover number.[6] Others, in contrast, claim that numbers are the endproducts of the fantastic intuition of the human mind, but there is disagreement as to the nature of this intuition. Some speak of pure intuition. Although this is totally meaningless, it contrasts well with those who refer to spatial intuition, temporal intuition, or even spatiotemporal intuition.[7] Even within these schemas, however, the ideas are confused. For example, Aristotle thought that it is the idea of number that accounts for the idea of time and makes it possible, whereas Kant thought, to the contrary that time is one of the preconditions for number. Either the thinkers are confused, or their object appears confused, because it is polymorphous.

From another standpoint, others are convinced that it is possible to reduce number to a sort of first principle like logic, for example, or language,[8] but this does not go over with those (like Piaget) who want to demonstrate that number is, on the contrary, an original construction of the subject.

Finally this epistemological imbroglio has generated the bemusement of the wise, including those who take no position and those who think that, from any angle, numbers are only the signifiers of an idea and the signifiers for action.[9] There are still others, who followed Kronecker, and thought that it was God who made the natural numbers. Why not? But then why did He mix up our ideas so much about His work? Numbers do not exist, or in any case, are not concrete entities; only the signs that represent them are.

This luxuriant garden of ideas about everyday reality gives pause to ponder. Are all these ideas true? And if so, are they compatible with each other? Ob-

---

[6]This clearly evokes sensualism and the empiricist positions from Locke to John Stuart Mill to Helmholtz.

[7]The idea of pure intuition is Kant's, but can also be attributed to Poincaré, but there is no reason why it cannot be given another interpretation in which the issue is intuition connected to the subject's own actions: walking and the analogy with the next step and the idea of $x + 1$. Spatial intuition is central to the Gestaltist concept of number and numerosity. Temporal intuition of number (in fact, intuition of order) was defended brilliantly by Hermann Weyl (1949) while Ernest Cassirer (1910/1977, 1923/1972) stressed the importance of the spatiotemporal dimension, despite his fundamentally synthesist position.

[8]On the one hand is Russell (1930 and his reductionist logic; on the other are the remarkable analyses by Cassirer (1923/1972). Both make a remarkable number of excellent arguments that may prompt the reader to devote at least a short period of time to thinking about the relationships that could exist between the capturing of reality by numbers and the capturing of this same reality through words.

[9]This is the idea defended by conventionalism, founded by Hilbert (1900), and adopted by many other modern writers (e.g., Lorenzen, 1962; Lorenzen & Schwemmer, 1975).

viously they are not, so how should we proceed to make them so? If we cannot, is there at least one of these ideas that is true, or are there several that each contain a tiny bit of truth? Given that each of these ideas was produced by respectable and presumably intelligent individuals, were some wrong and others right? And so on, to infinity.

What happens is that you get tempted by those ignominous perspectivists from Nietzsche to Ortega y Gasset, who were simply subjectivists cloaked to give themselves academic airs. It's difficult to side with Vahinger's Als-Ob (As-If) and those who claimed (to ease their consciences) that scientific discourse is nothing more than metaphor. We end up with Leibnitz because that at least gives you a smathering of dignity: "In the same way that the same city viewed from different angles seems to be entirely different, as though multiplied in perspective, because of the infinity of simple substances, there are as many different universes, which are however only perspectives of a single one, from different standpoints" (Leibnitz, 1975, p.173).

But we have yet to reach bottom.

THE NATURE OF NATURAL NUMBER

The period between the middle of the 19th century and the start the 20th was an era of heated controversy: What are numbers? What can we do with them?[10] From the outset, the distance separating the debaters was a striking one: While Russell, for example, was writing his *Principia* and striving to found his cardinal number,[11] Binet plunged, in all candor, into the origins of spontaneous counting in his daughters and caused all the pedagogy of calculation to revolve around the abyssal question: Should children be taught to count (Zählmethode) or to perceptually recognize pluralities (Zahlbildmethode)?[12]

In fact, the question of the nature of natural numbers is as confused as the one concerning the roots of ideas on number.[13] On the one hand, we have mathematicians in the logical thought school such as Cantor, Frege, and Russell, who based

---

[10]For Dedekind (1888/1932) to ask with impunity and with all the trapping of candor, "Was sind und was sollen Zahlen?" (in the title of a short volume) these questions must already have covered a lot of ground: As long as we really don't know, we need to reassure ourselves, and people will take on knowledgeable stance.

[11]Frankly, the cardinalist position, which Piaget and many others attribute in such a natural way to Russell, is somewhat caricatured. Although it is true that Russell summarized his position in this way in a popular version of it (1926), it should not be forgotten that in a more technical work (1930) he gave ordinal numbers a thorough treatment.

[12]The initial attempt at synthesis of these two apparently unreconcilable approaches was put forward by the educator Johannes Kühnel (1916/1921).

[13]For a brilliant historico-critical overview of this issue, see Gericke (1970), which presents a detailed description of the mathematical points of the views I develop here.

the notion of natural number on the idea of the quotient of a set or a class and on the search for classes containing equipotent classes as elements. Their "natural number" is, thus, quite naturally a cardinal number. The natural numbers Peano deals with (and which both von Neumann, 1925, and Weyl, 1949, were each to adopt in their own way) are clearly not cardinal numbers, yet they are natural numbers nevertheless. What fascinated them was the unending parade of numbers following upon numbers: For these thinkers, the idea of an order remains permanently in the background (in the same way as a positive attitude toward the idea of maintaining a temporal component in an abstract structure). Hilbert was not fundamentally interested in the nature of number, and rather focused on actions that are made possible by numbers: computation, arithmetic, and algebra. What needs to be understood is that placing stress on either cardinality or ordinality of number can only be done at a cost: It is easy to calculate with numbers but to calculate with cardinal numbers you need to take major logical precautions, and the arithmetic that operates on ordinal numbers is, in fact, fairly baroque.

The only interpretation of number that no longer interested anyone at this time was the one that predominated from antiquity to the end of the 18th century, from Euclid to Euler: that is, that number expresses the relationship between two magnitudes or between two quantities. No one recalls that the great Herbart (1835/1894) founded his psychopedagogy of calculation on an idea of number as operator: According to Herbart, the idea of 12 chairs does not imply a mental representation of a dozen chairs (this would, in addition, clutter the mind with as many backdrops as an Ionesco play). Rather, there is a representation of one chair and the number 12, which acts as an operator—$\times\ 12$—on the quantity "chair" and its cardinal unit "a chair."

It is useful here to sum up this state of affairs in a schematic way so as to show clearly the simultaneous coexistence of several perspectives that are, at least legally, incompatible: A given number cannot be entirely cardinal *and* ordinal *and* a ratio of magnitudes, and so on, but we can use number to imagine realities in an independent or successive way. Better still, we can use number to understand one of the aspects of the idea of number: that number is multiple. Thus,

Number is:	Theoretical Perspective of:
cardinal	Cantor, Frege, Russell
ordinal	Peano, v. Neumann, Weyl
algebraic	Hilbert
constructive	Lorenzen
operator/ratio	Euclid, Euler, Herbart
outcome of counting	E. Cassirer

By referring to children's logico-mathematical cognitive activities this way, we obtain a schematic outline that clearly illustrates that the idea of number gives numbers a polymorphous and polysemic character:

Subject's Activity:	Number is:	Theoretical Perspective of
classify	cardinal	Cantor, Frege, Russell
compare, seriate	ordinal	Peano, v. Neumann, Weyl
write and combine	algebraic	Hilbert
write and count	constructive	Lorenzen
transform	operator/ratio	Euclid, Euler, Herbart
count	product of counting	E. Cassirer

Everyday, ordinary counting does not interest the epistemologist or the mathematician, except to show that it cannot generate ideas worthy of natural number. As Russell pointed out in 1926, the operation of counting is, in fact, extremely complex, and those who believe that counting is the logical source of number are revealing their lack of analytical powers. Russell argued that when we say, "one, two, three" when counting, we cannot find the number of objects counted unless we attach a meaning to the words *one, two, three.* As Russell stated, a child can learn the number words in their correct order like the letters of the alphabet, without assigning a meaning to them. This type of child can count correctly from an adult observer's point of view, without having any idea of number. The operation of counting can only be carried out in a meaningful way by someone who already has an idea of what numbers are, which entails that the operation of counting not yield the logical basis of number (see Russell, 1926, p. 194). The first convincing formalization of this was not put forward until Lorenzen (1962; Lorenzen & Schwemmer, 1975). It has immediate appeal in that it shows that the numbers that are used for counting are extremely easy to construct and understand, if you're willing to see it this way.

What emerges is the realization that the tragedy has repeated itself. We saw earlier, in examining the range of viewpoints for the study of the roots of natural numbers, that the multiplicity of positions was inevitable although profoundly problematic. The same tragedy has come full swing here, too, because one can, apparently, legitimately defend highly divergent points of view on what constitutes natural number.

Seen in this way there is no doubt that Piaget and Szeminska's research goals and program were truly revolutionary, or in any case innovative. They aimed at substituting for a debate that can be construed as purely semantic a series of experiments, and thereby introduced an empirically based response—one, and not several—as an argument in a theoretical debate. Pure genius.

Unfortunately, Piaget did not really take the trouble to obtain accurate and exhaustive information on the bases for this ideational quarrel. In fact, he was fairly unfamiliar with Russell's ideas, had never heard of Hilbert, was not interested in Frege, and if he ever read Herbart, must have been totally bored by his pompous tone. Piaget was not really equipped to take a full-fledged stance in this debate either from the point of view of the history of ideas (what I call *roots*) or from the point of view of ideas in mathematics. By postulating his "operative synthesis," he solved a problem he alone had cast in this way (Beth & Piaget, 1961; Piaget, 1950, 1967), and his methodological and experimental design was too fragmentary to do justice to the magnitude of the problem. What is even more unfortunate, in my opinion, is that the Piagetian art of providing the answer before asking the question led Piaget and Szeminska to commit two major methodological faux-pas.

First, although Piaget and Szeminska studied a host of richly variegated behaviors, they chose to ignore numerous spontaneous behaviors. It is one thing to scorn nursery rhymes or concocted ones, and it may be valid to claim that many children's games that involve number in one way or another are purely imposed by adults. These are value judgments. It is, however, quite another thing to pretend that these behaviors simply do not exist, and that no one had ever seen them. The work of Piaget and Szeminska would have gained considerably from at least a solid introduction to anchor the book in its sociocultural context.

Second, one aspect of Piaget and Szeminska's (1941) book should astonish the reader. It is amazing that Piaget and Szeminska, when they described, for example, an experiment in which children are asked to equalize two collections of 8 and 14 elements respectively by transferring elements from one collection to another (pp. 236–243) report no instances of counting and no behavior that would warrant the supposition that the subject proceeded by silent counting. Moreover, in the third stage, none of the children mentioned proceeded by successive counting of the two collections, which are gradually equalized by transfer of elements to prove their equality. I do not doubt that Piaget and Szeminska succeeded in obtaining behavior of this type. What I do find puzzling are the reasons they observed only these types of behavior. I have administered this task many times and I have always found that many children simply count (Droz & Paschoud, 1981). My impression is that Piaget and Szeminska either manipulated their subjects, for example, by promising them a reward if they succeeded in solving the problem without counting (I have tried this. For this age bracket, children can easily perform a one-to-one correspondence, but without being prompted specifically to use this solution they do not often do it spontaneously.), or they simply discarded protocols of children who counted at one point or another in their procedure, considering these behaviors too banal to be included in a book that, after all, had scientific pretensions. It is crucial to realize that children readily count, and that they often count with much more savvy than scientists tend to grant them.

CHILDREN'S NUMBERS

In fact, what children are capable of doing with numbers and with ideas that could become numbers if they were brought to fruition bears an uncanny resemblance to what the mathematicians and thinkers I mentioned previously have formulated. Children do everything and anything with numbers and things that look like numbers. Above all, they do what they need at a specific point in time. Obviously children handle words and thoughts more awkwardly than adults and at times do not know what they want, but what is crucial to understand for this parallel is their profound interest in a general structure that can be interpreted as a function of need and that affords counting, seriation, composition, counting, quantification, and so forth.

In my opinion, from the outset children treat numbers and what resemble numbers as expressions of a polymorphic and polysemic structure that can be implemented every time their use seems warranted without having doubts as to their bases. If children were told how they went about using number and the structures that purportedly underlie them, they would be as astonished as Monsieur Jourdan (of Molière's *Le Bourgeois Gentilhomme*) when he was told that he spoke fluent prose, without ever having studied it. A few examples selected from the restricted field of counting should suffice to get an idea of the variety possible.

I have always believed that the real mastery of number and plurality takes place when the child makes the transition from the omnipresent *one* to *two*. The remaining steps only call for mustering enormous efforts at generalization. Once the child has mastered the upright position, standing up without holding on, he or she suddenly has two free hands to possess the pleasures of this world. With one hand holding on, there is only one hand left to hold the cookie. With two free hands, the ability to hold cookies doubles.

At 18 months, L. is sitting on his father's lap. He indicates one of the buttons on his shirt and says, "ta" (Droz, 1981). His father says, "It's a button." The operation is repeated for the eight buttons in view on the shirt, then immediately afterwards on the six buttons on his mother's blouse. A few days later, L. indicates his left foot and says, "ta." His father says "It's a foot." L. then points in succession to his other foot, his father's two feet, his mother's two feet, and the dog's feet, labeling them "ta" each time, and manifestly waiting for parental confirmation that they are indeed feet. Expectations are confirmed. In the next few days, the game is repeated, with extensions, to the feet of a horse and sheep. Overcoming their linguistic hesitations, the parents confirm that all these "ta" are indeed feet. Similar observations have been made with another child, Y., and by other observers on children of the same age.

At 29 months, J. is exploring a succession of plastic geometric shapes. She moves the pieces successively from her left to her right and lines them up saying, "and one, and another one, and another one." A little later she plays the same game with a set of tokens, "toc and toc and toc and toc."

This type of observation calls for several comments:

1. In the course of activity, very young children spontaneously form collections of concrete objects (by colligation) that are also conceptual (or preconceptual) objects and that are uncannily like equivalence classes.

2. In addition, these children obviously enjoy "enumerating" the elements in these collections. In fact, they are establishing extension definitions by doing so.

3. They point to identical objects while minimizing the nature of the object and stressing a specific quality of "being one of the same kind" or "belonging to a defined set."

Many children like the names of numbers. They invent little poems and nursery rhymes, which then become ritualized. Children use number early to give a cadence to their rhythmic activities. They do not use number to count, at least not at the start. They use number to sing, to walk, to go to sleep, to bang against the sides of the crib. To really start to count, children need to be able to coordinate sequential pointing of objects associated in a collection, and be able to recite, in an invariant order, the names of the numbers (Droz, 1981). This is much more difficult. Once this coordination has been mastered, the child knows how to count, more or less correctly. In any case, this opens up a whole new world.

A., aged 2, counts four buttons "one, two, bu - tton" and four horses "one, two hor-se" (che-val, in French, in the singular). This child can even count up to five: "one, two three, one, two."

L., aged 3 years, 5 months, is administered the Piagetian task on bi-univocal correspondence (Piaget & Szeminska, 1941, chap. 3). He forms two equivalent collections of red and blue tokens by juxtaposing a blue and a red element each time. The experimenter puts all the red tokens into a pile. To make sure there is conservation of numerical equivalence of the collections, L. asks permission to count. He counts while pointing. The task is repeated twice more. L. stops pointing, but he still counts. On the third trial, L. has reached a conclusion: "You know, you can put those thingumajigs any way you like; there will always be the same a lot of things." Experimenter: "Even if I put them in my pocket?" L: "You think I'm dumb?"

R., also aged 3 years, 5 months (Droz & Paschoud, 1981) has two numerically nonequivalent collections of tokens in front of him. He has just observed, through count-pointing that there are six blue elements and four red elements. The experimenter says to him, "I would like there to be as many reds as blues." R. re-counts the blue tokens, "So one, two, three, four, five, six" and then the red tokens "and that one, two, three, four, so (the red ones) "plus a little, and that (the blue tokens) plus a lot." The experimenter says, "Yes." R. adds another red token: "If I had another red one, I would have "one, two, three, four, five, and that (the blue tokens): one, two, three, four, five, six—still more." The Experimenter says, "Yes, there are still more." R. adds another red token: "So I add a red one, and then (he counts the blue tokens) "one, two, three, four, five, six" and (counting the red tokens) "one, two, three, four, five, six. The same now!" The Experimenter says, "Is there the same thing now?" R.: "Yes." R clearly does not have a good mastery of number, as shown by his need to re-count his tokens constantly to make sure that the quantity has not suddenly changed, but he knows how to compare two numbers to know which is larger and he has mastered an operation that gives him fantastic powers: Given two unequal quantities, he knows that it is sufficient to iterate the operation $(+1)$ on the smaller of the two quantities and to recount the new quantity obtained each time to have good chances that at a given point in time the two collections will become numerically equivalent. The procedure may appear archaic, but it is efficient, and R. is still very young.

Alex, aged 4, was observed extensively by Mosimann, Bovay, Dällenbach, and Droz (1982) in a series of situations where he had the opportunity to count all sorts of things and to think about a variety of situations.

1. Alex puts four yellow marbles in one receptacle and counts, "Yellow, yellow, yellow, yellow, one, one, one, yellow, two, one yellow, two yellows, three yellows, four yellows, one, two, three, four." This is an impressive demonstration of the abstraction process Alex puts laboriously into play to coordinate two preoccupations concerning this collection: making sure that the marbles are all of the same color, proving it, and establishing how many marbles are present.

2. Having chosen and threaded four big blue beads on a string, Alex says, "There are four"; a little later he threads eight beads on a string and counts each of the beads while pointing, "One, two, three, four, six, seven, eight, nine; there are . . . 9 (Alex rarely uses the number *five* but because he forgets this number frequently his counts are often "right"—with a constant error of 1). In these two examples, Alex counts but he also draws a conclusion from his counts: There are a given number of elements. He does not only count, but assigns a cardinal-to-target collection. Reciprocally, he can first state the cardinal number, then count the collection as though he needed to prove that the cardinal was right.

3. Given two collections composed, respectively, of six small and six big marbles, Alex underscores and reinforces the numerical correspondence between the elements in the two collections by a form of simultaneous double counting of the two collections "One-one, two-two, three-three, four-four, six-six, seven-seven." Counting serves to establish the numerical equivalence between the two collections and at the same time to demonstrate this by a fairly original proof.

When I was in kindergarten, we played a game called "Emperor, emperor, what can I do?" The emperor stood facing a wall and looked behind him at his subjects in a row. Each subject in turn asked the emperor for permission to move. The emperor, if he so desired, granted the wish and the subject could then move forward toward the emperor. The Emperor's goal was to make his subjects move forward as slowly as possible, whereas the subjects cheated as much as they could to get to him as fast as possible. The emperor was allowed to turn around to see whether his subjects were cheating or not and if he caught them they had to go back to the starting line.

From a standpoint of analysis of children's number, the interest of the Emperor game is in the repertory of permissible movements. There were "giant steps," "ant steps," "steps backward," "spins," and a strange movement that was called the "bathtub" (consisting of lying face down and then getting up), and so on. Each movement could be performed several times, as a function of the emperor's orders: "one bathtub and three ant steps," "two giant steps and a spin," "two spins and a giant step backward," and so on. Sophisticated players used fraction operators.

This game uses number as an operator. What is crucial is that the operators do not apply to a single type of measure, but to a disparate assembly of measures. The complexity of the game is comparable to the complexity of the English money system before decimal conversion.

PROBLEMS FOR A SCIENTIFIC APPROACH

The incredible wealth of children's behaviors related to number and with number, generated *ad libitum* both spontaneously and in elicited situations, as well as the remarkable diversity in mathematical status of numbers and protonumbers that children use lead to the assumption that the notion of number is as polymorphous as the psychogenesis of this notion. In fact, to proceed cogently, it would be more appropriate to speak of the psychogenesis of notions relative to natural numbers. This would, in any case, allow us to understand why research on the development of number in the child has been plagued by four problematic features:

First, the models elaborated by researchers to explore the development of number have relatively few features in common. Rather, there is not only weak convergence across models, but more generally, a low level of interest in what exactly constitutes the numbers they plan to have children implement in the studies they designed. Researchers behave as though they expect the reader to have an immediate grasp of what they meant by *number*. In the end, the impression one gets is that many investigators treat the issue of number in the child as though it were a linguistic issue—understanding numbers is knowing how to use the appropriate words to say them—and a behavioral issue—using numbers is knowing how to converse with the special jargon that is formed by number names. This naturally has the advantage of skirting epistemological discussions that would be awkward and uncomfortable because they would deal with a historical reality that is as fuzzy as it is polymorphous. In this context, it seems to me that Piaget's epistemological intent and goal have been profoundly misunderstood: His intent was not to show how children arrive at socially normative counting and school arithmetic, but rather to shed light on the genesis and status of number (or numbers) in children's thinking. Further, Piaget did not let himself be overly influenced by the adult (naive or sophisticated) thinking of the time that set up norms for children to reach after a more or less lengthy pathway. Rather, he clearly postulated that children's thinking had the right to be qualitatively different from adult thinking. If Piagetian thought had not contained this epistemological openness, it would not have produced the consistent, decisive impact it did on attempts at reform in the area of elementary mathematics education.[14]

Second, investigative approaches have been characterized by a tendency to focus on current fads (for a fairly exhaustive overview, see Rauh, 1972), and although trends are always with us, they should be taken seriously each time they re-occur. In the distant past, people were naively interested in counting, something that has recently attracted attention again in a new sophicated version by Gelman and Gallistel (1978). Later, people got interested in classes and sets. The predecessor of Piaget in this area was a German Gestalt psychologist named Johannes Wittmann (1929), who developed a highly original approach to teaching set theory to children: The idea was to arrange a pile of concrete objects with similar shapes (such as tokens) into an articulated and spatially oriented configuration. Thus, Wittmann was a groundbreaker, in that he tried to introduce one way of seeing sets into elementary education, and one of the first to explore subitizing, as others had (almost) done, except that they had called it *colligation* (Spaier, 1927). For a certain period of time, it was chic to "replicate" Piagetian experiments in a purely psychological perspective, without the slightest epistemological concern. Undeniably, advances are made in research, but the impression one gets is of the rather limited benefits drawn from earlier work.

Third, in any scientific endeavor, there is a need for critical examination of the context in which the study takes place, the explicit and implicit premises raised by the researcher, and the specific goals to be accomplished by carrying out the study. It is my opinion that in many studies, a clearer presentation of aims would serve to clarify the rationale and the justification for both the hypotheses put forward and the methodological approach.

When we know the reasoning underlying an investigation, assessment of the study can move quickly from more or less academic considerations to a thematic and focused reading of the work. The criteria for evaluating the degree to which a study accomplishes its goals, of necessity, will vary with the study: Surveying the skills or performance of children on a problem that has been well-defined operationally, and investigating the possibilities for improvement of the teaching of a given technique (calculation) or a mode of scientific thought (mathematics) will clearly differ from exploring the range and wealth of the set of modes of mathe-

---

[14]The appeal of Piaget and Szeminska's work on numerous mathematical theories in the 1950s does not lie only in the intrinsic mathematical quality of the studies or in the models presented in them (grouping structures). Rather, it resides in the irresistible impression that there are, in necessarily extremely disparate formulations, major convergences between the thought of mathematicians dealing with the foundations of mathematics and the mode of thinking of young children.

matical (or mathematicoid) functioning that children employ in their spontaneous or social games with peers.

Finally, given that researchers tend to confirm rather than disconfirm their hypotheses—in contrast to what they should do if they followed Popper's canonical recommendations—it seems that we have accumulated a vast number of studies that are excellent technically but highly unsatisfactory in either their theoretical impact or their heuristic power. In a nutshell, X confirms that we have found an additional pathway that has not yet been falsified (and never will, for that matter) but X has made a meager contribution to the construction of knowledge of a theoretical nature.

MY PROBLEM

All this leads me, finally, to state my problem. I am guided in this by the following observations:

1. Neither philosophers or mathematicians have been able to determine unequivocally what numbers are, where numbers come from, or what they are for, because numbers are multiple and because they can be put to a multitude of purposes.

2. Children neither construct one notion of number nor one approach to number, but rather many notions and many approaches to multiple numbers that are known and unknown; that interact, overlap, and interpenetrate; and that can both complete each other and cancel each other out.

3. Investigators in child development reduce this richness to one perspective, often highly congruent with what they find appropriate at a given point in time for reasons often known only to them. Their perspective is never entirely independent of what children know how to do (if they are asked nicely), but this is neither the only perspective that they have nor the only one they are capable of having.

4. Researchers in child development describe their aims poorly: Are they trying to shed light on children's performance by comparing them to adult performance, are they trying to identify the best ways to teach mathematics (or what passes for mathematics, given the tender operational age of the children involved), or are they trying to continue in the path of Piaget and Szeminska, giving a psychogenetic analysis of spontaneous genesis in the multiple forms it can take on?

Given the foregoing, I am of the opinion that research on the psychogenesis of notions concerning number and on the more or less cohesive ideas that precede these notions will necessarily remain punctilious, and will betray, in all likelihood, both from a qualitative as from a quantitative point of view, the generosity, the originality, and the richness of children's thinking and activities in this domain.

Personally, I am convinced that number should be a Platonic idea, one both extremely simple and incredibly awesome: It is the possibility to continuously extend interpretations of number and the semanticizations of these interpretations of number and numbers that must fascinate so many children.

13 Number Transcribing by Children: Writing Arabic Numbers Under Dictation

Xavier Seron
Université de Louvain

Gérard Deloche
Hôpital de la Salpêtrière

Marie-Pascale Noel
Université de Louvain

The development of children's numerical and arithmetical abilities has been analyzed by the Piagetian school from the point of view of the logico-mathematical structures sustaining children's performances. These logical structures are assumed to lead to the elaboration of the concept of number (Piaget & Szeminska, 1941). The Geneva school's work spurred a growth of research in this area (Brainerd, 1982; Carpenter, Moser, & Romberg, 1982; Ginsburg, 1983) and has had wide influence in the United States and Great Britain. Originally, the works published in English had two main focuses: the child's behavior in his or her first numerical activities at school and an attempt to establish more precisely the role of language development in different arithmetic abilities, such as oral and object counting, acquisition of arithmetical facts, and problem solving. More precisely, it has been demonstrated that number names constitute, early on, a specific lexicon distinct from language at large. Moreover, the distinction between the numerical and non-numerical lexicons is acquired precociously, both in comprehension and in production (Fuson et al., 1982; Gelman & Meck, 1983). Production of the sequence of number names has been shown to be governed by rules generated by children from their knowledge of the morphosyntactical structure of the numbers from 1 to 21. The acquisition of the number lexicon and its organization in an ordinal sequence have been studied in depth by Fuson et al. (1982), who described some regularities in the sequences produced by children at different stages of their development. Siegler and Robinson (1982), who have also worked in this domain, analyzed the stopping points during the learning sequence. These works have enabled the articulation of various characteristics of the mechanisms that intervene during the learning of the number sequence: simple and unidirectional next-one succession, application

245

of composition rules indicating the knowledge of the organization of the number verbal lexical system (structure of the 10s lexicon, principles of the formation of the ten-plus-unit couple, regularities in the passage from one decade to the subsequent one, etc.), and knowledge of the Arabic system (Resnick, 1983; Siegler & Robinson, 1982). Simultaneously, other research has been done on the role of oral counting in the acquisition of elementary arithmetical principles that intervene in object counting (Gelman & Gallistel, 1978), in number conservation (Fuson et al., 1983), and in calculation algorithms (Fuson, 1982; Fuson et al., 1982, for addition; Carpenter & Moser, 1982; Fuson, 1984, for subtraction).

Oddly, little work has been devoted to the acquisition of the two different written systems used to code quantities. Some work has been done on the emergence of natural numerical notations in children (Hughes, 1986; A. Sinclair, Siegrist, & H. Sinclair, 1983), but little research has concentrated on the transcoding from one written code to another (see, however, Bacquet & Gueritte-Hess, 1982). This absence of research is striking if one considers that children, in the process of learning arithmetic, are confronted by a twofold system of number notation—the alphabetic system and the Arabic one—and that the acquisition of this double notational system represents a prerequisite not only to the reading and writing of numbers, but also to the learning of the written calculation algorithms (Resnick, 1983). This study examines transcribing abilities in children by analyzing the way second and third grade children pass from the phonological code to the Arabic written one, in the following way:

1. We presented sequences of number words containing all the lexical primitives from the two lexicons (phonological and Arabic written, see Table 13.1), the main rules of number composition in the verbal and the Arabic system, the sum and product relations in the verbal system, and the intercalary zeros in the

TABLE 13.1
Lexical Structure of the Phonographic and Digital Number Codes

Position Within the Category	Digital Code	Phonographic Code		
		Units	Teens	Tens
First	1	un	onze	dix
Second	2	deux	douze	vingt
Third	3	trois	treize	trente
Fourth	4	quatre	quatorze	quarante
Fifth	5	cinq	quinze	cinquante
Sixth	6	six	seize	soixante
Seventh	7	sept		septante
Eighth	8	huit		quatre-vingts
Ninth	9	neuf		nonante

Deloche and Seron, 1982a.

Arabic system. All of these particularities have been implicated in the origin of difficulties in transcribing activities with adult aphasics (Deloche & Seron, 1982a, 1982b; Seron & Deloche, 1983, 1984).

2. We presented numerical structures not yet learned in school by the children, in order to assess whether they use rules that they have already learned on simpler numbers forms (and if so, which rules) to transcribe new forms.

Children's performances were compared at three different times to see if the evolution of their performances could reveal a logic in the process underlying their transcribing.

Given that this work is the first one devoted to such a topic, it remains of an exploratory nature. We discuss here children's transcribing errors by referring to some criteria of analysis we have developed with brain-damaged aphasic adults.

METHOD

Population

The population was composed of 60 Belgian French-speaking children: There were 30 second-grade and 30 third-grade children, with 15 boys and 15 girls in each grade. None of the children had been noted for having specific difficulties in calculation. At the first testing, the mean ages for the groups were 7 years, 7 months (range: 7 years, 1 month to 10 years, 1 month) for the second-grade group and 8 years, 8 months (range: 7 years, 1 month to 10 years, 6 months) among the third-graders. The pupils were examined from two schools, both of high sociocultural level.

In the Belgian school system, children learn to write Arabic numbers; from 0 to 100 during the second grade and from 100 to 1000 during the third grade.

Tasks

Two tasks were administered: reading Arabic numbers aloud and writing numbers in the Arabic code under dictation. The reading task was done individually; the writing task was conducted in groups, with attention paid to eliminating any possibility of the children copying from one another. During the testing the examiner strongly urged the children to answer all the items of the task, even if they had not yet learned the numbers they were presented with.

The tasks were administered during three separate periods, with a 2½-month delay between them: the beginning of January, the middle of March, and the end of May. The writing task always preceded the reading task. Only data from the writing task are presented here.

Structure of the Battery

The results obtained from the first testing caused us to enlarge the initial battery for the second and third testing. Thus, two different batteries were used: a basic battery and an extended battery. The basic battery (first testing: T1) contained 72 items; the extended one (second and third testing: T2 and T3) contained 116 items, the 72 items from the first battery plus 44 new ones. In each battery the items' presentation order was randomized.

The Basic Battery. This contained 72 items selected according to various lexical and syntactical characteristics of the two coding systems. These were:

1. The whole set of lexical primitives, that is, the Units (U) from *un* (1) to *neuf* (9), the Tens (D) from *dix* (10) to *nonante* (90) and the Teens (T) from *onze* (11) to *seize* (16),[1] *cent* (C; 100), *mille* (M; 1,000) and *zero* (0), yielding a total of 27 items.[2]

2. Numbers inferior to *cent* (100) of simple ten-unit structures (DU)—13 items.

3. *Cent* (100) and *mille* (1,000) in *Sum relation,* that is, not preceded by a multiplier in the verbal system (e.g., *mille vingt* [1,020], which means *mille* [1,000] *plus vingt* [20]), or in a *Product relation* (e.g., *deux cents* [200], which means deux [2] TIMES CENT [100]). There were 10 items in each relation. (For the linguistic formalization of the sum and product relations in the number verbal sequences, see Power & Longuet-Higgins, 1978).

4. *Mille* (1,000) preceded by *un* (1)—5 items, in order to compare the transcoding of *mille* in 1,000 and in 101,000.[3]

5. The complex tens *quatre-vingts* (80) alone or integrated with other primitives (10 items).[4]

6. Numbers with intercalary zeros (10 items).[5]

---

[1]Given the structure of the French verbal number system, the teens end at *seize* (16), with the French names for 17, 18, and 19 being two-word strings: *dix-sept, dix-huit,* and *dix-neuf* (literally: *ten-seven, ten-eight,* and *ten-nine*).

[2]As it is necessary to represent number verbal structures with letters, and given that in English *thousand, ten* and *teen* began with the same letter *T,* we adopted the following conventions: Hundred and Thousand are represented by their corresponding Roman letters *C* and *M,* respectively, whereas to distinguish Teens from Tens we decided to represent the *teens* by their first letter (as for Units) and the Tens by a D (from Decade). With such conventions the following notations result: Unit = U, Tens = D, Teens = T, Hundred = C, and Thousand = M. Furthermore when the transcribing of a specific number is referred to, it is presented in French, but accompanied with the digit notation in parentheses.

[3]Note that in French 1,000 is transcribed *mille* (*thousand,* and not *one thousand*), whereas 101,000 is transcribed *cent un mille* (*hundred one thousand*).

[4]In French 80 is a two-word structure that can literally be translated as four twenties.

[5]The total of the items by category is greater than 72, because some items pertain to more than one category (e.g., 1,010 is in the sum *mille* category and also in the category with intercalary zeros).

The Extended Battery.   These 116 items elaborated on the original 72 in order to allow us to examine the children's performances on simpler structure items and increase the interpretative possibilities. Thus, items of the type CU (*hundred-unit*), CD (*hundred-tens*), CT (*hundred-teens*), and UC (*Unit-Hundred*) were added; in the same way, various structures with *thousand* were also included: MU, MD, and MT, and UM, DM, and TM, with 4 items for each of these two-word structures.

RESULTS

We first analyze the results in a quantitative way, by calculating errors rates; we then examine the errors according to some structural parameters.

Global Analysis

In this analysis, any type of erroneous transcoding was scored as an error. A mixed ANOVA with four factors—grade (second vs. third), gender (male vs. female), testing period (T1, T2, T3), and task (reading vs. writing)—was carried out on the 72 items of the basic battery.

Emerging from the data were three main effects: grade, $F(1,56) = 23.82, p < 0.001$; testing period, $F(2,55) = 78.64, p < 0.001$; and task, $F(1,56) = 159.73, p < 0.001$), as well as two first-order interactions: Grade $\times$ Testing period, $F(2,55) = 13.18, p < 0.001$, and Task $\times$ Testing period, $F(2,55) = 4.66, p < 0.025$. The main task effect indicated better scores in reading Arabic numbers (mean of 64.03 correct responses out of 72) than writing Arabic numbers (mean of 59.9 correct responses of 72). The grade effect indicated lower scores in second grade than in third grade (mean of 65.6 correct responses in third grade compared to 56.9 in second). Only the main effect of the testing period had to be nuanced by an interaction with the grade variable. Thus, whereas the second-grade pupils improved their performances at each subsequent testing session, the third-grade children progressed only between the first (mean correct responses of 65.3) and the second testing session (mean correct responses of 66.2), probably due to a ceiling effect.

Structural Analysis

These analyses were conducted in reference to the structure of the verbal number forms. At this level, except for lexical primitives, the analyses are limited to the second and third testing sessions and to sequences containing only two lexical primitives.

Lexical errors were distinguished from syntactical ones (McCloskey & Caramazza, 1987; Deloche & Seron, 1982a, 1982b). An error was considered lexical when it concerned the production of isolated items in the number (i.e., an isolated digit or word), but maintaining a syntactically correct assembly of the elements and thus the correct length. For example, the transcribing of *quatre mille vingt cinq* (4,025) as 3,025 is a lexical error, whereas the same sequence transcribed as 4000 25 constitutes a syntactic error.

Lexical Errors

The distribution of lexical errors occurring on the lexical primitives is presented in Table 13.2. Already by the middle of the second grade (T1), lexical errors were infrequent, and they diminished progressively at the subsequent testing sessions. Paradoxically, a moderate increase of lexical errors was observed at the beginning of the third grade. These results concern two different groups of children, however, and are therefore not strictly comparable.

A qualitative analysis of the errors produced on *quatre-vingt* (80) and *mille* (1,000) is of particular interest. All the errors produced on *quatre-vingts* (80) indicated a nonintegrated or a partial processing of the Tens complex structure. Of the whole set of errors, 420 was the most frequent one (8 errors), that is, a separate transcribing of *quatre* (4) as 4 and *vingts* (20) by 20, but other forms were also observed, such as 820 (2 errors), 84 (2 errors), and 4,020 (1 error). Partial processing, such as 20 (2 errors) or no response (1 error), also occurred. Similar errors have been observed with adult aphasics (Deloche & Seron, 1982a, 1982b). Errors on *mille* (1,000) were also interesting because the transcribing of *mille* (1,000) has not yet been learned in second grade. In fact, the absence of formal learning raised few difficulties for the majority of children, and by the middle of the second grade, 26 of 30 children correctly wrote the Arabic string for mille (1,000). The four errors consisted either of producing one zero too few, (100; 3 instances) or of not responding (1 instance). With regard to errors on

TABLE 13.2
Distribution of the Lexical Errors Produced on the Lexical Primitives
Per School Year and Testing Periods in Each Category

Category	n	Second Graders			Third Graders		
		T1*	T2	T3	T1	T2	T3
Units	300	5.3%	2 %	1 %	0.7%	0 %	1 %
Tens**	240	4.6%	2.5%	0.4%	2.5%	2.2%	0.4%
Quatre-vingts	30	13.3%	3.3%	3.3%	23.3%	0 %	6.6%
Teens	180	4.4%	1.1%	0 %	1.7%	1.1%	0.6%
Cent (hundred)	30	3.3%	6.7%	6.7%	0 %	0 %	0 %
Mille (thousand)	30	13.3%	13.3%	6.7%	3.3%	0 %	3.3%
Mean		5.4%	2.6%	1.1%	2.3%	0.9%	0.9%

*T1, T2, and T3 are the first, second, and third testing periods, respectively.
**Quatre-vingt is not taken into account in the tens.

Units, Tens (except *quatre-vingt,* 80) and Teens, we checked the data on brain-lesioned patients in Deloche and Seron (1982a) to see if "stack" or "position" errors were found in written number transcribing tasks. The *position error* is characterized by the fact that the erroneous response belongs to the same lexical category as the correct answer: for example, *vingt* (20) transcribed as 30, *four* (4) transcribed as 5, or *douze* (12) transcribed as 11. Conversely, when the response belongs to another lexical category but shares a common position in its stack by comparison to the stimuli, it is called a *stack error:* for example, *vingt* (20, occupying the second position in the Tens category) is transcribed as 2 (second position in the Unit category), *trois* (3) transcribed as 13, or seize (16) transcribed as 60.

Table 13.3 reveals a clear difference in the distribution of error types according to grade. Among second graders, mixed errors represented more than one third (35.9%) of the lexical errors, whereas they were much less common in third graders (17.4%). Third graders' lexical errors tended to make errors in only one category: Stack (34.8%) and position (21.8%) accounted for over half (i.e., 56.6%) of their lexical errors. The small number of lexical errors overall, however, prevents any statistical analysis of the variations in error type.

These tendencies may well reflect a progressive structuration of the number names into a lexicon structured in stacks. We return to this point later on.

Syntactic Errors

The distribution of the syntactic errors is presented in Table 13.4. The sequence DU was mastered at the beginning of the second grade, and presented no difficulties for the third-grade children. The sequences with *cent* (100) and those with *mille* (1,000) are analyzed separately.

The Sequences With cent (xC and Cx).   In second graders, sequences with *cent* in the sum relations (CU, CD, and CT, combined as Cx) seemed to be

TABLE 13.3
Typology of the Lexical Errors:
Distribution (%) According to School Year

Type of Error	Group		
	Second Graders	Third Graders	Total
Stack	18.9	34.8	23.7
Position	26.4	21.8	25
Not processed	13.2	26	17.1
Mixed	35.9	17.4	30
Paralexias	5.7	0	3.9

TABLE 13.4
Distribution of the Syntactical Errors Produced
on the Two-Lexical Primitives Sequences

Sequences	n	Second Graders				Third Graders			
		T2		T3		T2		T3	
DU	240	13.3*	2**	6.7	1.3	0	0	3.3	0.4
CU	120	36.6	25.8	16.7	10	3.3	0.8	13.3	4.2
CD	120	56.7	31.7	33.3	20.8	3.3	1.7	10	3.3
CT	120	50	35.8	33.3	26.7	13.3	4.2	3.3	2.5
UC	120	26.7	15	13.3	15	0	0	6.7	2
MU	120	56.7	37.5	46.7	26.7	26.7	13.3	20	7.5
MD	120	63.3	48.3	63.3	38.3	26.7	16.7	20	13.3
MT	120	66.7	54.2	53.3	43.3	26.7	20.8	33.3	19.2
MC	30	63.3	63.3	50	50	30	30	23.3	23.3
UM	120	40	20	20	14.2	10	5	6.7	2.5
DM	120	63.3	48.3	56.7	40.8	53.3	39.2	46.7	31.7
TM	120	63.3	55.8	50	39.2	50	37.5	50	34.2
CM	120	76.7	76.7	70	70	43.3	43.3	46.7	46.7

*Percentage of subjects producing at least one error.
**Percentage of errors in that category.

mastered less well than in the unique product relation, UC (also referred to as xC). In the second testing session (T2), the mean percentage of errors for the three sum relations was 31.6 versus 15 for the product relation; which is statistically significant, $t(29) = 3.197$, $p < 0.002$. This difference was no longer significant at T3: The mean error percentage was 19.2 for the sum relations versus 12.5 for the product relation, $t(29) = 1.164$, ns. Finally, the number of errors was negligible in the third graders (from 0% to 4.32%).

Qualitative analyses of errors produced by the second graders suggests some hypotheses regarding the organization of the children's performances. Three main classes of errors can be distinguished.

1. *Lexicalizations*, which consist of the transcoding of each verbal primitive by its counter digit part:

CU: cent neuf (109)   →   1009
CD: cent trente (130)   →   10030
CT: cent seize (116)   →   10016

It should be noted that, despite their name, these errors are not of a lexical type, as they do not result from the confusion between lexical primitives, but rather are of syntactical type because they affect the number's length.

2. *10x errors*, which consisted of producing an extra *0* between the *1* corre-

sponding to cent (hundred) and the digit counterpart of the lexical primitive (Tens or Teens) that followed:

| CD: | cent trente (130) | → | 1030 |
| CT: | cent seize (116) | → | 1016 |

3. Other errors, which were not frequent, were often inversions of lexical primitives.

The error distributions for the second graders on the xC and Cx sequences are shown in Table 13.5. At T2, the children could be characterized, on the basis of their error types as follows:

- 5 children were *lexicalizators:* They produced lexicalization responses for every sequence with *cent.*
- 2 children were partial lexicalizators: They produced lexicalisations for the Cx, but not the UC, sequences.
- 9 children produced 10x responses.
- 11 children made no errors.

TABLE 13.5
Error Distribution on xC and Cx Sequences in Second Graders

| | | Errors | | Categorization | | |
| | | | % of the total of errors for | Lexicalization | | |
Category T2	n	Number	the C pair	Number of Error (%)	10x	Others
xC						
UC	8	18(15)[a]	13.6	15(83.3)	—	3(16.7)
Cx						
CU	11	31(25.8)	23.5	24(77.4)	—	7(22.6)
CD	17	40(33.3)	30.3	24(60)	15(37.5)	1(2.5)
CP	15	43(35.8)	32.6	29(67.4)	14(32.6)	—
T3						
xC						
UC	4	15(12.5)	17.9	12(80)	—	3(20.0)
Cx						
CU	5	12(10)	14.3	12(100)	—	—
CD	10	25(20.8)	29.8	14(56)	14(40)	1(4.0)
CP	10	32(26.7)	38.1	16(50)	16(50)	—

[a]Percentage of errors for the pair considered.

It is important to note that all the children who emitted 10x responses also produced correct responses in transcribing CU. In other words, erroneous 10x transcribings such as 1011 for *cent onze* (111) or 1030 for *cent trente* (130), were present only in children who correctly transcribed at least once (but more often three or four times) the sequences *cent deux* (102, *cent neuf* (109), *cent six* (106), and *cent un* (101). The occurrence of erroneous 10x transcribings thus seems to be dependent on (at least partial) mastery of the CU sequences. The extra 0, which appears in the CD and CT sequences could thus be an erroneous generalization of the correct 0 required between the 1 and the Unit digit in the transcoding of the CU sequences.

At T3, the third testing, we observed the following improvement:

- 3 children were lexicalizators.
- 1 child was a partial lexicalizator.
- 7 children made 10x responses.
- 18 children produced no errors.

The analysis of the evolution of the response types from one testing session to another (from T2 and T3) led to other interesting observations:

1. Among the 5 lexicalizators at T2, 3 remained in the same category at T3, 1 became a partial lexicalizator (mastery of UC), and 1 mastered UC and CU and produced 10x responses on CD and CT.
2. The 2 partial lexicalizators at T2 became error-free at T3.
3. Of the 9 children who produced 10x responses at T2, four remain at the same level at T3, and the five others made no further errors.

Finally, a global analysis of the Cx and xC sequences indicated that there were significantly fewer lexicalization errors at T3 than at T2 ($t(29) = 2.43; p < 0.01$).

Interpretation of the Transcoding of Cx and UC Sequences. The transcribing of verbal sequences containing *cent* (100) seemed to follow a succession of stages that could be summarized as follows:

1. At the beginning children are unable to integrate the elements of the sequence; at this stage each element in the Cx and UC sequences is lexicalized.

2. Children then begin to transcode the product sequence UC correctly, but the sum relations are still lexicalized.

3. Among the sum relations, the first one to be learned is the sequence CU. At this point, some children construct by inference the transcoding of CD and CT relations by applying to these structures the rules they have just learned for CU. This results in erroneous transcodings of the type 1011 and 1030 for *cent onze* (111) and *cent trente* (130).

Other arguments strengthen this evolutionary schemata:

- The strategy of total lexicalization was present in 5 children at T2 and only 3 at T3.
- The precocity of the correct transcribing of UC is attested by the fact that at both T2 and T3 this sequence, by comparison with the other sequences, is responsible for fewer errors in fewer children.
- When all the sequences are no longer lexicalized, it is usually the sequence UC that is the first one to be correctly transcribed (see, however, the single case MV described later on).
- The 10x responses were elicited from only those children who gave correct answers to CU sequences. The CU sequences were responsible for fewer errors at T2 and T3 than the sequences CD and CT. Such a difference was statistically significant at T2 (Friedman test, $X^2(2) = 8.18$, $p < 0.025$; Wilcoxon two by two comparisons: z (CU-CD) $= -1.77$, $p = 0.04$; z (CU-CT) $= -2.03$, $p = 0.03$, and z (CD-CT $= -1.16$, ns), as well as at T3: Friedman test, $X^2(2) = 7.6$, $p = 0.025$, z (CU-CD) $= -1.84$, $p = 0.03$, z (CU-CT) $= -2.52$, $p = 0.005$, and z (CD-CT) $= -1.93$, $p = 0.03$.
- From T2 to T3 an inverse progression was never observed. Indeed, at T3, there was not one child at the level of total lexicalization who had emitted at T2 either partial lexicalization or a 10x response. Similarly, not one of the partial lexicalizators at T3 gave a 10x response at T2.

It should be noted, however, that the method used does not allow the affirmation of an obligatory passage through the three response levels (total lexicalization, partial lexicalization, and 10x) described here. Thus, some of the total lexicalizators at T2 gave correct responses at T3, and it is not clear whether between the two testing periods, they would have emitted responses belonging to the intermediary levels.

Sequences With mille (xM and Mx)

In second grade—with the exception of the UC product relation, which seemed well transcoded (22.5% and 14.2% of errors at T2 and T3, respectively)—the sum relations (MU, MD and MT) raised no more difficulties (46.1% errors at T2, 36.1% at T3) than did the Product relations (DM and TM; mean error rates of 50.4% at T2 and 38.75% at T3), Wilcoxon, Mx versus xM, at T2: $z = -.871$, ns; at T3: $z = -.643$, ns. See Table 13.6. In the third graders, there was perceptible progress in all sequences, but the error rate was still about 15%. At this time, the sequence UM was nearly always correctly transcribed (only 5% and 2.5% of errors at T2 and T3 respectively).

Qualitative analysis of the children's errors provided information about the difficulties incurred and allowed us to identify some response strategies:

TABLE 13.6
Errors Distribution on xM and Mx Sequences in Second Graders

Pairs		n	Errors % of the sequence	Errors % of the total	Categorization Lexical-ization	100x	D00/T00	D10/T10	Others
T2									
	MU	17	37.5[a]	14.3	36[b]	—	—	—	11
Mx	MD	20	49.2	18.6	35	13	—	—	11
	MT	18	51.7	19.7	39	11	—	—	12
	UM	13	22.5	8.6	21	—	—	—	6
xM	DM	19	50.0	19.1	35	—	20	2	3
	TM	18	50.8	19.4	34	—	22	3	2
T3									
	MU	14	26.7	13.3	17	—	—	—	15
Mx	MD	19	38.3	19.2	15	19	—	—	12
	MT	16	43.3	21.7	18	22	—	—	12
	UM	6	14.2	7.1	8	—	—	—	9
xM	DM	17	38.3	19.2	21	—	14	3	9
	TM	16	39.2	19.6	16	—	18	4	8

[a]percentage of errors for the considered sequence
[b]number of errors in that category.

1. Lexicalization errors: for example, *sept mille* (7,000) transcribed as 71000 and *mille nonante* (1,090) as 100090.
2. 100x errors: They consist of writing two zeros after the digit 1 corresponding to *mille,* before writing the digits corresponding to the lexical primitive in the MD and MT sequences (e.g., *mille vingt* (1,020) transcribed as 10020 or *mille treize* as 10013.
3. D00 or T00 errors: These consist of writing two zeros after the two digits corresponding to the tens or the teens word in the string (e.g., *vingt mille* [20,000] transcribed as 20 00, or *quatorze mille* [14,000] by 14 00).
4. The D10 and T10 errors: Here, the transcribing of the tens or teens word is followed by the digits 10 (e.g., *vingt mille* [20,000] transcribed as 2010 or *quatorze mille* [14,000] transcribed as 1410).

The Sum Relations: Mx. At T2, the error distribution on the sum sequences evidenced a majority of lexicalization errors (65%); for one third of the children, the majority of errors were of this type. The sequence MU seemed better transcribed than the sequences MD and MT, but this difference was not significant, Friedman Test, $X^2(2) = 3.1$, *ns.* An equal number of lexicalization errors were observed on these three sequences. By contrast, MD and MT sequences gave rise mainly to errors of the type 100x. As was observed with the 10x errors on the *cent* sequences, the 11 children who made 100x errors produced at least one, and often more, correct responses at MU sequences. Thus, the 100x errors seem to be a generalization of a correct transcribing procedure of MU on the sequences MD and MT.

At T3, there is a decrease in total errors (130 at T3 compared to 168 at T2, $t(29)$, $= 1.74, p < 0.05$), essentially due to an important decrease of lexicalization errors: 110 at T2 compared to 50 at T3, $t(29) = 2.65, p < 0.02$; 100x errors, however, increased: 24 at T2 versus 41 at T3. Here, too, the 12 children producing 100x errors all produced correct responses for the transcribing of MU sequences. As at T2, the sequence MU is better transcribed than the other sequences; this time, the difference was statistically significant, Friedman Test, $X^2(2) = 7.033, p < 0.05$. Other errors—a majority of them due to three cases AC, MV, and LT—are discussed further.

The transcribing of the sequences with *mille* in a sum relation seems to follow an evolution similar to the one previously described involving the cent sequences.

1. At the beginning, lexicalization responses are made for all Mx sequences.
2. Then, some children begin to correctly transcribe the sequences MU.
3. Finally, some of the children apply the rule learned with MU on the MD and MT sequences, producing 100x errors.

Here, too, the comparison between T2 and T3 indicates that in no case did the evolution of the children's abilities reverse direction: The lexicalizators at T2 either did not change or produced correct responses at T3; similarly, the children producing 100x responses at T2 either did not change or produced correct answers at T3.

The Product Relations: xM.   At T2, the distribution of errors on the product relations indicated a majority of lexicalization errors (60.8%): Eleven children produced a majority of errors of this type. The sequence UM was better transcribed than the other product relations: Friedman Test, $X^2(2) = 11.524; p < 0.01$; Wilcoxon comparisons, two by two: z(UM-DM) $= 3.13, p < 0.001$; z(UM-TM) $= -2.97, p < 0.002$; Z(DM-TM) $= 0.14, ns$. Actually, of the 11 children with a majority of lexicalization errors, 3 correctly transcribed the sequences UM. Furthermore, errors of the D00 and T00 type appeared on the DM and TM sequences. These 42 errors were made by 8 subjects who correctly transcribed all items for UM. Finally, 2 children produced D10 and P10 errors.

At T3, there was a decrease in total errors: 109 at T3 compared to 148 at T2 $t(29) = 1.57, p < 0.15$, essentially due to a decrease of the lexicalization errors

(45 at T3 versus 90 at T2), while the other error categories remained stable. None of the 7 children that committed T00 or D00 errors made errors on the UM sequences. Finally, only 17 errors were produced by 6 children on the sequence UM. Moreover, this sequence was better mastered than the other product sequences: Friedman Test, $X^2(2) = 16.30$, $p < 0.001$; Wilcoxon paired comparisons: $z(\text{UM-DM}) = -3.20$, $p < 0.001$; $z(\text{UM-TM}) = 3.03$, $p < 0.002$; $z(\text{DM-TM}) = 0$, ns.

The transcribing of the xM product sequences also seemed to follow successive stages:

1. A lexicalization period comes first.

2. Then, some subjects correctly transcribe UM, while still producing lexicalization errors at DM and TM sequences,

3. A typical pattern of errors next begins to appear on DM and TM sequences in which a sequence of four digits is produced: the first two being the correct transcribing of the two multiplicand lexical primitives (D or T), and the two subsequent ones being two zeros. This error seems to result from an overextension of the rule learned with UM: production of a four-digit string with the leftmost positions occupied by the digits corresponding to the transcribing of the multiplicand lexical primitive.

There were three children, however, who presented erroneous transcribings that seemed to be organized differently than the errors in the pattern described. Indeed, they showed rule generalizations involving the sum and product relations simultaneously. For example, some errors in which *mille* was transcribed as 10 were encountered in the Product structure (e.g., 13,000 as 1310) Two interpretations are possible: Such an error on a product structure could either be an extension of a rule learned with the correct transcription of *mille* in sum relations MD and MT (e.g., *mille vingt* [1,020] as 10 20 and *mille onze* [1,011] as 10 11) to the same forms but in product relations (*vingt mille* [20, 000] → 20 10 and *onze mille* [11, 000] → 11 10, or it represents an intermediary step in the evolution of the lexicalization strategy, in which the lexicalization is applied so that *vingt mille* (20, 000) is transcribed as 201000 or *onze mille* (11,000) is written as 111000, and are progressively shortened on their right side by the application of the rule requiring four digits in a verbal sequence with *mille* (a rule which is, of course, adequate only for MU and UM).

We now describe the cases of the children presenting this type of response pattern. They are interesting in that they illustrate the existence of some diversity in the use and extension of rules in number transcoding.

Case 1: LT (a second-grade girl, 8 years old) produced, during the two testing sessions (T2 and T3), the set of errors presented in Table 13.7.

It is possible to interprete all the responses produced by LT with a set of very simple rules:

TABLE 13.7
Transcriptions Produced by LT on the Mx and xM Sequences

Type	Combination	Incorrect Response	Number of Occurrences
MU	Mille deux (1,002)	1,200	2
	Mille sept (1,007)	1,700	2
	Mille six (1,006)	1,600	2
	Mille cinq (1,005)	1,500	2
MD	Mille quarante (1,040)	1,400	2
	Mille cinquante (1,050)	1,500	2
	Mille nonante (1,090)	1,900	2
	Mille dix (1,010)	1,100	1, the other one is correct
MT	Mille onze (1,011)	1,110	2
	Mille douze (1,012)	1,120	2
	Mille quinze (1,015)	1,150	2
	Mille treize (1,013)	1,130	2
UM	Sept mille (7,000)	correct	2
	Huit mille (8,000)	correct	2
	Deux mille (2,000)	correct	2
	Quatre mille (4,000)	correct	2
TM	Treize mille (13,000)	1,300	2
	Onze mille (11,000)	1,100	2
	Quatorze mille (14,000)	1,400	2
	Quinze mille (15,000)	1,500	2
DM	Septante mille (70,000)	7,000	2
	Vingt mille (20,000)	2,000	2
	Dix mille (10,000)	1,000	2
	Nonante mille (90,000)	9,000	2

1. Transcribing is done from left to right.
2. *Mille* at the beginning is transcribed by *1;* in other positions, it is not transcoded.
3. Every sequence with *mille* is transcribed by a four-digit string,
4. If the written string does not have a length of four digits, add the required number of zeros at the right end.

With these four rules, LT correctly transcribed the UM sequences (e.g., *trois mille,* 3,000). Indeed, she wrote the digit corresponding to the Unit lexical primitive, then added to the right end the three zeros required to obtain a four-digit length. Nonetheless, the systematic application of these procedures provoked systematic errors in the transcribing of the other sequences of the xM type: For DM sequences (e.g., *septante mille* (70, 000), she wrote 70 00 by transcribing *septante* (70) as 70 and applying her length adjustment rule, which added 00, and for TM sequences (e.g., *quinze mille,* 15, 000, she wrote 15 00. The application of the same rules to Mx sequences gave such erroneous transcribings as *mille cinq* (1, 005) transcribed as 1 5 00 (*mille* at the beginning, yields 1 by rule 2, followed by cinq, 5, and by the length adjustment, 00, *mille treize* (1, 013) transcribed 1 13 0 and *mille cinquante* (1, 050) transcribed as 1 50 0.

Case 2: The whole set of transcribing sequences with *mille* by AC (a second-grade boy) is presented in Table 13.8.

In this case, the observed evolution from one testing period to the subsequent one is especially interesting. At T2, there were a variety of errors: Apart from two lexical errors (e.g., 5 for 6 in *mille six* 1,006 → 10,005), there was a clear tendency to lexicalize all the elements of the verbal string (13 errors out of 22), and *mille* was nearly always transcribed by its lexical value (17 cases of 22). However, some responses to *mille* diverged from this general schema, and on five items *mille* was transcoded as 100 (see the correct responses 100 2, and the errors 100 70, 100 10, 100 120 and 13 100). These kinds of transcribings just appearing at T2, emerged clearly at T3. All these errors and also a majority of

TABLE 13.8
Transcodings of the Sequences with *Mille* by AC at T2 and T3

		Reponses	
Items to Transcribe		*T2*	*T3*
MU	Mille deux (1,002)	correct	correct
	Mille sept (1,007	10,070	correct
	Mille six (1,006)	10,005*	correct
	Mille cinq (1,005)	10,001,000	correct
MD	Mille dix (1,010)	10,010	10,010
	Mille quarante (1,040)	10,004	correct
	Mille cinquante (1,050)	10,004	correct
	Mille nonante (1,090)	100,090*	10,090
MT	Mille onze (1,011)	10,110	10,011
	Mille quinze (1,015)	100,015*	10,015
	Mille treize (1,013)	100,013*	10,013
	Mille douze (1,012)	100,120	10,012
UM	Sept mille (7,000)	71,000*	7,100
	Huit mille (8,000)	81,000*	8,100
	Deux mille (2,000)	correct	2,100
	Quatre mille (4,000)	41,000*	4,100
TM	Treize mille (13,000)	13,100	13,100
	Onze mille (11,000)	111,000*	11,100
	Quatorze mille (14,000)	141,000*	14,100
	Quinze mille (15,000)	151,000*	15,100
DM	Septante mille (70,000)	71,000	70,100
	Nonante mille (90,000)	901,000*	90,100
	Vingt mille (20,000)	201,000*	20,100
	Dix mille (10,000)	101,000*	10,100

* = total lexicalization.

correct answers could be interpreted by a simple rule: Mille has to be written 100 in the digit string. This simple rule explained the correct transcribing of the MU sequences and all the errors produced at T3. Only two correct responses on MD did not correspond to this rule.

It is also plausible, but we do not have any direct evidence for it, that this rule was learned by the child through the transcribing of MU sequences, sequences for which the application of such a rule gives correct responses. This case highlights the fact that some children may extend the rules in an undifferentiated way on sum and product relations.

Case 3: MV (a second-grader) demonstrates an instance of simultaneously using two systems of rules: one for the sequences with *cent* and another one for the sequences with *mille*. Table 13.9 represents MV's errors at T2 and T3.

TABLE 13.9
Transcriptions on the Sequences with *Cent* and *Mille* by MV
(second grade) in T2 and T3

Items to Transcode	T2	T3	Items	T2	T3
CU			MU		
Cent un (101)	1,001	correct	Mille deux (1,002)	10,002	102
Cent deux (102)	1,002	correct	Mille sept (1,007)	10,007	10,070
Cent neuf (109)	1,009	correct	Mille six (1,006)	10,006	correct
Cent six (106)	1,006	correct	Mille cinq (1,005)	10,005	correct
CD			MD		
Cent dix (110)	10,010	correct	Mille dix (1,010)	100,010	correct
Cent trente (130)	10,030	10,013	Mille quarante (1,040)	100,040	10,040
Cent quarante (140)	10,040	10,040	Mille cinquante (1,050)	100,050	10,050
Cent septante (170)	10,070	1,070	Mille nonante (1,090)	100,090	10,090
CT			MT		
Cent onze (111)	10,011	1,011	Mille onze (1,011)	100,011	10,011
Cent douze (112)	10,012	1,012	Mille douze (1,012)	100,012	10,012
Cent quatorze (114)	10,014	1,014	Mille quinze (1,015)	100,015	10,015
Cent seize (116)	10,016	1,016	Mille treize (1,013)	100,016	10,016
UC			UM		
Cinq cents (500)	5,100	510	Sept mille (7,000)	71,000	17,010
Neuf cents (900)	9,100	910	Neuf mille (9,000)	91,000	900
Trois cents (300)	3,100	correct	Quatre mille (4,000)	41,000	40,100
Huit cents (800)	8,100	810	Huit mille (8,000)	81,000	8,100
			DM		
			Septante mille (70,000)	701,000	70,100
			Nonante mille (90,000)	901,000	90,100
			Vingt mille (20,000)	201,000	2,000
			Dix mille (10,000)	101,000	10,100
			TM		
			Treize mille (13,000)	131,000	13,100
			Onze mille (11,000)	111,000	11,100

At T2, all the sequences containing *cent* and *mille* were lexicalized. By contrast, at T3 the transcribing of CU was correct, and the errors on CD and CT were either lexicalizations (two times) or, more often (five times) 10x errors. The point of interest here is that the product relation UC was also introduced in the child's system of rules so that regardless of the semantic relation, *cent* was transcribed as 10. As concerns *mille,* its transcribing was identical to the one described in the preceding case, where *mille* was always transcribed as 100. MV seems, thus, to have used essentially two rules, one for *cent* and one for *mille.* These rules probably result from an over-generalization of the rules that generate the correct transcribing of CU and MU to all the product and sum relations. Although these rules were applied incorrectly (except for MU and CU), they indicated the existence of a discrimination in the transcribings of *cent* and *mille.*

The CM and MC Sequences

The sequences containing both *cent* and *mille* were incorrectly transcribed by all the children: Indeed, in the second graders MC gave rise to 63.3% of the errors at T2 and 50% of the errors at T3, whereas CM provoked 76.7% and 70% of the errors at T2 and T3, respectively. For the third graders, these structures remained difficult: CM still rendered 43% and 46.7% of the errors at T2 and T3, respectively, and MC rendered 30% and 23.3%, respectively.

Among the more frequent errors, we found total lexicalizations to account for 50% of the errors in the second graders and 39.6% of the errors in the third graders: *mille cent* (1, 100) → 1000 100 and *cent mille* (100,000) → 100 1000.

CONCLUSION

The analysis of the transcribing errors produced by normal second- and third-grade children deserves comment.

As with brain-damaged adult subjects, two main types of errors (lexical and syntactical as well as mixed errors, those involving the two types simultaneously) were observed. Lexical errors were not numerous, but were not random, either. Although mixed errors were predominant in the second graders, some stack and position lexical errors were already appearing. The existence of position errors could indicate the emergence, during that time, of an organization of the lexical primitives for number in different lexical categories. The low percentage of stack errors (18.9%) suggests a weakness in the sequential organization of the items within each of the lexical categories. Third graders showed a decrease in mixed errors concomitant with an increase in the proportion of stack errors (up to 34.8% of all the lexical errors). This evolution in error distribution suggests a progressive elaboration of the verbal lexicon for number: There might first be a categorization into three classes, followed by a progressive organization of stacks within each of these classes. This interpretation should be verified among younger children, because the few lexical errors occurring in our groups did not permit the necessary statistical analysis of their distribution.

Concerning syntactical errors, in the two-word verbal sequences, those with *cent* and those with *mille* were distinguished. For the *cent* sequences, beyond the level of lexicalization responses their correct responses first appeared on the product relation UC. For the sum relations, it was the sequence CU that was the first to be correctly transcribed, but its partial or total mastery provoked the appearance of an organized pattern of errors on the product structures containing *cent* (CD and CT): the 10x errors. We have interpreted the fact that all the children who committed 10x errors made some correct transcriptions on CU sequences as the application to CD and CT of a rule elaborated from the correct transcription of CU sequences.

For the two-word sequences with *mille,* a similar schema is applicable: At the lexicalization level, errors were equally distributed on product and sum relations. Within the class of sum relations, the MU sequence were the earliest to be correctly transcribed, and the rules elaborated with this sequence were then generalized, giving rise to errors of the 100x type on MD and MT sequences. With respect to the product relations, UM served as a prototype for the D00 and T00 errors. It seems then, that for *mille* as well as for *cent,* errors due to over-extension of rules remained located within the product or sum relations.

Most of the children's errors, thus, resulted from overgeneralization of rules, rules that were correctly elaborated on simple sequences but were then misapplied on others. The fact that these generalizations spread selectively within the sum or product relations does not necessarily mean that the children were sensitive to the meaning (plus or times) of these relations. It is equally plausible that the positional regularities of the words *cent* and *mille* relative to the other lexical primitives in the sum and product relations played the leading role in the rule extensions. Indeed, in the two-word sum sequences, *mille* and *cent* occupy the first position in the string, whereas in the product relations they always occupy the last one. A complementary examination of the children's semantic representations underlying the sequences they transcribe would be the only argument necessary to choose between one of these interpretations.

Three children, however, did not follow this general schema. A careful analysis of all the transcriptions produced by these children (using the single-case methodology used in cognitive neuropsychology) allowed an interpretation of these productions, both the errors as well as most of the correct answers. We suggested that these children applied a finite set of simple rules without taking into account the differences between the sum and product relations. If these children did not follow the general pattern of evolution, their responses nevertheless indicated that they also transcribed by generalizing correct rules to incorrect contexts. The differences between these children and the whole group was that either the rule they produced was different or they applied the same rule to a different gradient of generalization. One may wonder why some of the structures with *cent* or *mille* were correctly transcribed before some others. It could be that such an order of acquisition mimics the order of presentation at school. If so, one would expect UC to be systematically transcoded first as this is taught first. It could also be that UC was more easily transcribed because it constitutes the only structure of the product relation, as compared with the Cx sequences, under which three different lexical structures (CU, CT, and CD) are subsumed.

Finally, the exploratory nature of this study must be stressed. We emphasize the limitations of a longitudinal approach of examining children's performances at different periods, which we now see were probably spaced too far apart in time. A more fruitful procedure with respect to testing would assess the children more frequently or even continuously over the testing period. Furthermore, the study would benefit from being conducted with small groups of children, who could be asked for justifications of their productions. Such a revised methodology would yield a clearer understanding of the chronology of the developmental stages in children's transcribing.

Moreover, the discovery of the rules system developed by children from their knowledge of the transcribing of some simple structures is of great interest for the pedagogist who, before trying to correct these errors, should take advantage of the opportunity to gain an understanding of their underlying logic.

14 Understanding the Microgenesis of Number: Sequence Analyses

Madelon Saada-Robert
Université de Genève

MICROGENETIC REPRESENTATION AND THE
SEQUENTIALITY OF NUMERICAL BEHAVIOR

This chapter has two objectives. The first is to demonstrate the methodological interest of segmentating sequences of observational data and analyzing how they chain in the microgenetic construction of numerical and protonumerical procedures. The second is the application of microgenetic analysis to numerical representations. The general psychological framework is the structural approach to the ontogenesis of number (stage level markers, filiation, and connected constructions; Piaget & Szeminska, 1941) and the principles of genetic epistemology. The analysis of numerical microgenesis is specifically situated within the context of the study of representation, as formulated in cognitivist developmental psychology (Cellérier & Inhelder, 1991). *Representation* is defined as the organizational framework of knowledge activation in models. This knowledge is made meaningful through its specification in context and is oriented through the sequencing of procedures.

Understanding the microgenetic construction of representations (i.e., models) presupposes an in-depth and fine-grained analysis of the sequencing of behavior. This is a lengthy endeavor, which, as has been shown in work on adults' (Vermersch, 1984) and in children's problem solving (J.-M. Richard, 1989), can be accounted for in a rigorous fashion. The sequencing of behaviors, their order of occurrence, and the type of chaining that connects them (linear, progressive, inclusive, or hierarchical) can be identified by segmenting the continuum of observable behaviors into organized sequences. Several methods of data analysis can then be applied to these segments. Thus, case observation and analysis are no

265

longer merely the first step in the construction of hypotheses to be tested. Rather, they constitute a fullfledged experimental approach dealing with the sequencing of behavior. J.-M. Richard and Poitrenaud (1988) attempted to validate this approach through simulation. The observation of prototypical cases in which behavior is analyzed in sequences (see Saada-Robert, 1992) has shown that this approach is well suited to the study of cognitive functioning. By extension, analysis of prototypical cases makes it possible to elaborate explanatory hypotheses concerning the relationships revealed by quantitative analysis.

Analysis of behavior sequencing raises the issue of the criteria for segmentation. One solution is task analysis, which defines a priori units based either on task variations or on temporal criteria. Alternatively, one may segment units based on the subject's own plan. In this case, sequences link different behaviors having a common goal. In both cases, only an explicit presentation of the methodology can serve to evaluate its potential contribution. This chapter is an illustration of the second approach, applied to numerical and protonumerical behaviors. It should contribute to shedding new light on the understanding of number.

THE CONSTRUCTION OF OBSERVABLE DATA AND INFERENCES ON REPRESENTATIONS

The data and their segmentation into sequences are drawn from a protocol. The definition of sequences adheres closely to the subject's underlying representations. The chaining of these sequences is then analyzed.

The protocol from Katia (aged 4 years, 9 months; Robert, Cellérier, & Sinclair, 1972) was obtained without audiovisual equipment, so the analysis of her protocol does not have the explanatory power of the functional analyses of cases conducted subsequently, due to the lack of sufficiently fine-grained and complete diachronic and synchronic indices (Saada-Robert, 1992). Nevertheless, although the transition from the description of behavior and its interpretation is not always explicit, there is a twofold interest in this protocol: The first is the nature of data segmentation and the type of descriptors used. The set of data and descriptors must be well-defined as long as the study does not apply an existing theoretical framework. Use of an existing framework in the case of this protocol would have been reduced to identifying the structural level of behavior in terms of preoperational figural collections (Piaget & Szeminska, 1941). Second, Katia's chaining of segments in this situation are illustrative of the construction of numerical representations: the construction of shared and individual properties of elements, the breakdown of these properties, the substitution of a numerical identity for these properties (via one-to-one correspondence), and finally the counting.

Katia was presented with a set of animals: three red fish, four swans, and a duck. When placed in two lines, the three fish covered the same space as the four swans. The duck, different and singular, could be used as a marker of the differences between the two collections, or associated with the fish if there was to be one-to-one correspondence between the two collections. The instructions were as follows: "Here are some animals. You can play with them as you like, any way you like."

Behavioral data were coded on the basis of action descriptors and sequence segmentation. The descriptors were the following: (a) take two objects (one in each hand) and hold them together either face to face or side by side without putting them down; (b) take one object, take several objects, or take one by one; (c) place or arrange objects in a row (side by side) or in a line (in a file) with the presence or absence of orientation marks. Each one can be alternately vertical, horizontal, or oblique; (d) add one object, add several, or add them one by one; (e) remove an object, move them closer, farther away, or separate them; (f) undo a row or a line and (g) reiterate an action. The child's behavior is thus described in terms of elementary unit-schemes constructed and used by the child to form a resultant configuration (a row or a line with heterogeneous objects, or a collection, or an alternation; a double or triple row-line, a same vs. different orientation, etc). Each sequence was considered to be a functional unit for the subject, corresponding to her intentions and representations. The action sequences that are linked together by Katia can be classified on several levels as a function of a combination of more or less elementary schemes: Make a collection or an arrangement of several sets, make elements alternate, make two collections alternate, establish a procedural correspondence (e g , a pairing) between elements, and control for resemblance or difference either verbally or procedurally (by touching, pointing, or pairing) or spatially (different meaning for rows and lines, orientation of each element, position in the configuration).

Katia's Protocol

The Experimenter places the animals in a heap in front of the child and asks her to play with them. Katia starts by active pairing (she has two animals in her hands, brings them together, moves them apart, brings them beak to beak, etc.) and by creating configurations in lines or rows, either horizontal, vertical or oblique where the elements are arranged in separate alternating collections. She then turns to double configurations (two lines, two rows), with insertions of diverse forms of pairing.

Sequence 11: After the singularity and difference of the duck has been clarified, Katia constructs a row configuration composed of three different groups: the three identical fish are on the right (f), a space, two identical swans (s), a space, the last group composed of the two remaining swans and the duck (d), on the extreme left (denoted as dss ss fff). Each group is individualized (three different, two identical, three identical), yet nevertheless connected to the two others by at least one factor: by resemblance (fff - ss) or by number (three identical - three different). The singular duck marks one end.

Sequence 12: Katia moves all the objects closer to form a continuous row and starts vaguely to count them, without pointing to each object: "*There are 6!*" The numerical aspect of the configuration thus becomes the only way for Katia to compensate for the loss of qualitative differences resulting from bringing the groups together.

Sequence 13: She moves the animals down one by one to the edge of the table while maintaining their position in the row. This ordinal-iterative characteristic of her behavior gives procedural meaning to the elements and prepares for the change from row to line. This is a necessary transition when a given figural identity that is assigned to elements by their position in the configuration cannot be immediately expressed in another figural identity: in this case, there is a return to a procedural identity that re-confers a neutral meaning on each element (Saada-Robert, 1979).

Sequence 14: Katia successively forms two vertical lines. The left one is made up of the three fish placed head to tail the long way; the right one is made up of the four swans and the duck at the top. The three fish and the four ducks arranged in this way form two lines the same length, that is, with the same boundaries; the duck extends over (Fig. 14.1). As soon as she finishes her arrangement, Katia again counts the elements beginning with the duck, then the line of swans, then the line of fish by pointing to each element, "One, two, three, four, five . . . one, two, three."

Sequence 15: She removes the duck, looks at the lines, and re-counts the two collections, "Four . . . three". The counting and the figural correspondence begin to conflict.

Sequence 16: She looks once more at the two lines and removes a swan. By doing so, she disrupts the figural correspondence while introducing a numerical correspondence. The specificity of the figural and numerical tags is thus established explicitly. Each element can be treated procedurally, figurally, and numerically. The numerical modality newly established by Katia integrates into the two other modalities: She ends her game by making a single collection where the elements of the two collections are placed in one to one alternation.

This protocol is characterized by three types of identification that exhibit complex interconnections in the progression:

1. Procedural identification: manipulation of pairs of elements and iteration of the same action on the elements taken one by one.
2. Figural identification: arrangements and configuration operations (line and row), and figural notation of logical classes.
3. Numerical identification: counting.

Segmentation into sequences and sequence analysis shed light on the nature of these interconnections and their importance. Here, again, figural features are

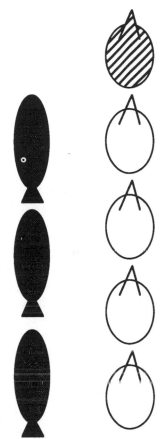

FIG. 14.1. Katia in Sequence
14 forms two lines in parallel.

shown to play a crucial role. Structural analysis has shown the ways in which figural features can act as a source of distortion, particularly with regard to boundaries between collections in number conservation. An analysis focusing on the coherence of behavior sequencing, however, shows to what extent the spatialization of number is a necessary construction because it authorizes a figural notation of inferences that already goes beyond successive procedural tagging, even though it is still not conceptual.

In other words, construction of figural notation is critical in very young children for the elaboration of classes and logical relations, and in their representations of number. Lawler (1985), in a study of spontaneous approaches to addition using case analysis, reported a wide range of procedures linked to specific contextual representations, which can be either procedural, figural, or conceptual. Von Glasersfeld's (1982) investigation of protonumbers shows that there are different "experiential routes," one of which has figural dominance. Seen in this way, interindividual décalages, or more general décalages linked to context specifically take on a new meaning vis-á-vis the notion of number representation (see Bideaud, 1980, and Fayol, 1985, for reviews of the diversity of number representations).

Sequential analysis of this protocol shows, furthermore, that the progression of knowledge is mediated by functional conflicts. This form of conflict has yet to be included in researchers' inventories of epistemological, cognitive, sociocognitive, and didactic obstacles to knowledge acquisition (Brousseau, 1989). Two examples of these conflicts appear here: The first is the "deconstruction" of progressively constructed qualitative properties of objects. This deconstruction is a prerequisite to assigning a numerical identity to these objects. The second example is the figural base (Katia's explorations of the diverse configurations in which the relational position of objects is crucial) on which numerical identity is constructed, even though it is discarded once identity has been established.

THE CONSTRUCTION OF A CONCEPTUAL FIELD

Segmentation of data and elaboration of concepts are dialectically linked in the initial phase of the construction of a theoretical model, even when researchers define one or the other as the major point in their investigation. The units of analysis that form the basis for this theoretical model result from the identification of both observational units (segmentation of the world environment investigated in the study) and conceptual units (definition of the conceptual field of the study).

This type of analysis on a prototypical case in different situations was the major preoccupation for several years of the Geneva cognitive developmental psychology group (headed by B. Inhelder and G. Cellérier; see Saada-Robert, 1992).

The construction of a conceptual field, characteristic of the approach by this group to the study of representation as a cognitive regulator, is applied here to numerical representations. It shows, first the existence of different routes in problem solving and their interconnections; the following analysis of protocols focuses on number and measurement sequences that have been shown to exhibit homomorphistic relations (Vergnaud, 1981). It then explores the microgenetic construction of problem solving, defined as changes in meaning.

Different Routes in Problem Solving and Their Interconnections

The experimental paradigm I used for investigating number and measurement sequences is described in Saada-Robert (1986). Briefly, the child is placed in a situation where he or she must construct a miniature, three-dimensional, inclined road using small slats of wood (for the road) and wooden blocks (for the pillars).

The experimenter places a slat and a block in the correct position and asks, "How many slats like this one, and how many little blocks like this one do you need to build the road?" (The correct solution is 5 slats and 15 blocks: Fig. 14.2.) The child is given a variety of tools: a long wooden stick, spaghetti, string, scissors, matches, tokens, paper, and a pencil. The spatial arrangement presented to the child as well as the instructions actualize two distinct universes of knowledge: measurement and number sequence. They form two possible problem-solving models that are empty universes at the start (with no contextual content), universes that the child will fill by specifying the situation concretely through the use of appropriate procedures. Neither of the two models is sufficient to solve the problem because, during initial specification, the subject is invariably led back to the problem of how far to continue the number sequence (measurement requirement) or realizes through measuring, that, *"Oh, yes, of course: It's one, two, three, four, five."* Each model refers to the other, and they thus give rise to a process of analogy where one is seen as a "type" of the other. The problem solving of this task can be defined by two dominant strategies. The dominance and the way they are linked together define individual differences.

Measurement Strategy.

1. Place the stick between the beginning and end points, cut the strands of spaghetti the same length as the slats, and cover the distance measured with the strands of spaghetti (5 units).
2. Set up the one slat to one block correspondence (5 pillars).
3. Measure the block and define the height of the end point. This yields the number of block units for the last pillar. Take away one unit for the pillar preceding it, up to the first block pillar.
4. Count the number of block units.

Number Sequence Strategy.

1. Place the stick on the table and align the slat with the stick.
2. Establish the one slat to one pillar correspondence.

FIG. 14.2. Solution for the slope.

3. Apply the number sequence: first pillar, one block, second pillar, two blocks, and so on, up to fifth pillar, five blocks.
4. Add up the blocks.

Microgenetic Construction as a Change in Meaning

The problem solving of Laurent (age 8 years, 11 months) is noteworthy because his solution chiefly uses the number sequence, and his functional specification efforts can be reconstructed step by step. This contrasts with typical problem solving in which the measurement procedure which is "grafted" too quickly for analysis to the number sequence procedure. The slow process of specification exhibited by Laurent reveals changes in meaning, and are a·major key to our understanding of cognitive functioning.

Sequence 1: Laurent places the stick between the car and the box-building (Fig. 14.3) and says, "You need to put one, two, three, four, five in," while marking each number with a point in the empty space between the car and the box. The end of the stick is not touching the car, and it can be assumed that Laurent does not intend to measure by placing the stick, but rather is trying to concretize the route of the slope. This is his way of establishing the problem space. The hypothesis of assignment of "one, two, three, four, five" to the number of blocks and not to the slats is confirmed by the manipulation that follows.

Sequence 2: He places the block as low as possible underneath the stick, then slides the block toward the box at several points without lifting it up, checking in this way the number of blocks he will need by an initial procedural specification. In doing so he may become aware of the need for segmentation of slats/ pillars, i.e. the basic construction unit.

Sequence 3: Laurent takes a sheet of graph paper and draws a box on the left, a car on the right and the board (stick) between them. Using the grid on the sheet as elements of his own schema, he counts them vertically, from the base to the end line of the stick, "One, two, three, four, five, six, seven." This is a second specification of the number sequence—after the procedural moving in the pre-

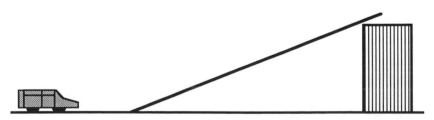

FIG. 14.3.   Laurent in Sequence 1 places the stik between the car and the box.

ceding sequence—but here it is figural, and reveals the unmastered particularities of this form of representation. Reassured by all the problem data that can be represented simultaneously, the schema must cope with double constraints: two-dimensional space and the graph paper with a grid that is too similar to the blocks to prevent confusion.

We term a specification of this type a *routine,* to describe the relevance of a scheme in relation to the objects, and its automatic and rigid use. But unless there is immediate goal attainment, the full specification of this scheme calls for greater recognition in relation to the goal; that is, the scheme becomes a basic component to the solution (in this case, we term it a *primitive*). It also presupposes combining the scheme with other key problem primitives, and then we refer to situation *procedure.* These are the three meanings assigned to schemes over the course of their specification (Saada-Robert, 1989). The more procedures are automatized, the more they are subsequently used as routines. The less procedures are automatized and if they are at the same time sufficiently general, the more they will be used later in the form of primitives (unless they can be directly implemented in the form of a procedure, in situations that are recognized as highly analogous). Laurent "identifies" with his counting routine on the grid so well that he now refers to squares rather than to blocks, even after having drawn the pillars and the block supports. He forms pillars with five blocks but he is not at all sure of the number of slats (six or five). He cannot deduce this from his drawing of the blocks because he has not yet constructed the one-to-one slat to pillar correspondence. He finally reaches the answer of *five* by measuring the slat on the stick, and only establishes the relationship between the number of pillars and the number of slats at the end. It is via this one slat to one pillar relationship that he sets up the analogy between the measurement model and the number sequence model that, until then, had remained disjoint because they applied to different objects: measurement to slats, and numbers to blocks.

The segmentation of behavior into sequences, and above all, the analysis of their sequencing thus captures the specification of the number scheme through the diversity of problem-solving routes and through the changes in meaning assigned to this scheme.

THE MICROGENESIS OF PROTONUMERICAL BEHAVIORS

Analysis of action sequences and of their chaining is applied here to protonumerical behavior. The analysis is designed to show, on the sensorimotor level, as well as on others (Katia on the preoperational level in the construction of numerical identity, Laurent on the operational level with specification of the number sequence), that the specification of number arises to a greater extent from the multiplicity of meanings constructed by the subject on actions and objects, than from a self-generating unitary concept.

The protonumerical behaviors observed reveal the complexity and richness of the connections associating schemes whose content relevance differs across situations. "Numerous classes of situations and numerous activities, some of which contain clearcut sensorimotor features" are the foundations for number (Vergnaud, 1985). As well, a solid anchoring of the protonumerical characteristics can be found in spatial and causal activities. The study of these behaviors also highlights the critical role of iteration, and the role of variation in order of repetition in elementary number schemes. This is what is shown by a sequential analysis of behaviors of two babies, aged 9 and 20 months, when presented with a range of familiar objects from their home or nursery environments.

Jerome, aged 9 months, plays house with material provided by the experimenter. The material is composed of nine boxes and 15 corks. Three familiar objects, a smurf, a mechanical teddy bear, and a rubber ball are also in the room. The corks are all identical but the boxes differ. There are four closed cylindrical boxes 15 cm high, three of which are full (one full of corks, one full of shells, and one full of matches), one smaller closed cylindrical box that is empty, one fake cardbox open at the two ends, two boxes of matches (one empty and one full) and one small red heart-shaped box.

Jerome's Protocol

Jerome is standing up, holding on to a low table. He turns around, looks at the objects, glances at the experimenter, and then looks at the objects again. He laughs, moving his whole body.

While holding on to the table, he leans over and picks up the smurf with one hand. He straightens up and puts the smurf into his mouth, takes it out, puts it back, takes it out again, and throws it on the floor. He then looks at it.

He gets on the floor and heads off on all fours . . . toward other objects. He lies on his stomach, and looks at the experimenter before taking the box with the corks. He throws it, takes a second box (the box with the matches), and throws it. By turning slightly, he takes a cork and throws it, takes another cork and throws it, then looks at the experimenter and laughs.

He takes a box by shifting position slightly and bangs it on the floor. Without letting it go, he takes two corks in his other hand and throws them together. He drops the box. Then he takes the full matchbox, shakes it, giggles, shakes it several times, and looks at the experimenter. Still on all fours, he pivots around and goes back to the first box he touched. He makes it roll and looks at it as the box moves away. He takes a cork in one hand while crawling, then takes the box of shells and pushes it with the other hand; he watches it move away. He takes the full box of matches, shakes it, and looks at the experimenter. He crawls off, picks up several corks one by one and throws them successively. He gets on his stomach, picks up the full matchbox, starts crawling again, sits, then takes a cork that he rolls. He watches it move away. He lies on his stomach, takes the full matchbox again, puts it into his mouth and sucks it, takes it out, shakes it again, and throws it.

Jerome tries to stand by pulling himself up on the low table. He fails and lets himself sink into a sitting position on the floor. The teddy bear (a battery-driven toy) is next to him. He touches it, picks it up, moves it slightly, presses a button, pulls on it, and shakes it. Then he loses interest and crawls off down the hall and comes back toward the corks.

He takes several, one by one, and throws them, one after the other. He takes the box of shells, makes it roll in several directions, and crawls after it. Then he throws it with one hand and laughs.

He heads toward the ball, presses on it with one hand, takes it in both hands, throws it, and crawls after it. He throws it and sends it under a piece of furniture. He tries to get it, tries several times, fails, and gives up. He goes back to the box of shells and rolls it while he watches it. Then he finds the ball (that his older brother had gotten out from under the furniture). He pinches it with two fingers, throws it while pushing it, and sends it under the same piece of furniture. He crawls out of the room.

Sequence Analysis

Three actions from Jerome's repertoire were specified: *a,* throwing; *b,* shaking; *c,* rolling *Sequence 1:* Entrance into activity using a familiar action with a familiar object.

Smurf: In/out of mouth, twice.
      Throw on the floor.
      Look, position on floor.

Sequence 2: Familiar activity prompted by sequence 1, on a new object. The child gets on the floor himself and moves toward other objects. He lies on his stomach (to free his arms to act on objects), looks at the experimenter (for approval or disapproval) and takes a full box.

Cork box: Throw.
Match box: Throw.
Cork 1: Throw.
Cork 2: Throw.

Sequence 3: Two actions at the same time, a new one and a familiar one, on different objects; then a succession of new actions on objects in his possession: establishment of prototypical relationships between procedure *x* and object *y.*

Box: Bang on floor (one hand) with cork 1 and cork 2 in other.	
Box: Throw (second hand).	a
Full matchbox :Shake (noise).	b
Full matchbox : Shake several times.	b
Cork box: Make it roll.	c
Watch: Moves away differently than when he throws.	
Cork 1: Take.	neutral
Shell box: Make it roll, watch.	c
Matchbox: Shake.	b
Cork 1: Throw.	a
Cork 2: Throw.	a
Cork 3: Throw.	a
Full matchbox: throw.	a'
Cork 1: Make it roll, watch.	c'
Matchbox: Shake.	b'
Matchbox: In/out of mouth, shake, throw.	b' + a'

After successively building up three prototypical relationships (routines) a, b, and c, there is a succession of these same routines following a neutral action (take) but in the opposite order: c, b, a. Next, the prototypical relations are disbanded and new actions are tried out on different objects (i.e., primitives a', b', c'). Two points call for comment. First, variations from one relationship to another follow an ordered progression: The child starts with a double action that incorporates the familiar and the novel, and then continues with a new action on a new object and ends with a familiar object and a new action. Second, variations between actions and objects only take place after prototypical relations have been established. The permeability of the prototypical relation (the routine) appears to be fundamental for microgenetic progression, in particular, because it allows for the combination of the initial primitives with other possible primitives to form a complex procedure, which is not the case when they are functionally defined (i.e. associated) by the object.

Sequence 4: Interlude with familiar object (bear).

This acts as a fundamental resource in that it recontextualizes the ongoing progression in a well-mastered cognitive area.

Sequence 5: Partial repetition of Sequence 3.

Prototypical relations are consolidated here with slight variations within the relation.

Cork: Throw.	a
Cork: Throw several times.	a
Shell box: Make it roll, followed by body movement.	c
Shell box: Make it roll, by pushing also with foot.	c

Sequence 6: End of activity involving familiar procedures with familiar object; integration of the novel.

  ball: press.
  ball: pinch.
  ball: make roll like shell box.
  shell box: make roll.

What is observed here is a microgenesis with the following prime characteristics:

1. A progression from Sequence 1 to Sequence 3, with a maximum of discoveries and combinations in Sequence 3 (showing a transition from routine to primitive).
2. A loop connecting the beginning and end of the activity, in which familiar activities with familiar objects are stressed. The practically implicit appeals to the experimenter are apparently an important feature in the unfolding of the activities, particularly with regard to the degree of the child's cognitive involvement.
3. The establishment of prototypical relationships between certain actions and certain objects (i.e., elaborating routines). These routines are then fragmented to combine with other resolution primitives and are defined by their meaning with respect to the solution, not just through their functional relationship to the object.
4. A numerical kernel in activities that have spatial or causal dominance. These consist of iteration of basic actions with variations in the order of repetition, which makes it possible to assign a procedural identity to objects. The network of difference and similarity relations constructed thus appears to be one of the building blocks of the construction of number, preceding numerical identification itself.

It is precisely this identity that Amina, aged 20 months, explores in relation to the cardinality of a collection obtained by the ordered iteration of one plus one elements.

Amina's Protocol

Amina is playing with some other children in a small room of the day-care center she attends. The experimenter gives her some playthings the children have not used for several weeks: A box full of a large number of different colored 2 cm ×

3 cm rectangles made of plastic with two holes in them; nine plastic cups of different colors and different shapes; 12 "flowers" of different colors with a hole in the center, and a stick that could be fitted into the hole in the flowers.

Amina is seated on a rug. She gets up and dumps the box full of multicolored rectangles on the floor. She stirs the rectangles with both arms. She takes a cup in her left hand and stirs the rectangles with the cup. She looks up, looks at the experimenter, and smiles. She continues to stir the rectangles with the cup.

She looks at the experimenter. She puts a finger into one of the two holes in a rectangle. Her finger doesn't go in. She takes the stick, then puts it down. She tries again with her finger, by pushing harder into the hole. She manages to get it in; she takes it out. She puts the stick in the hole in the rectangle, but she is holding the objects horizontally and the rectangle falls off the stick. She stirs the rectangles with the stick, but she is holding the wrong end, the narrow end that goes in the holes. She looks at another child. She puts the stick in her mouth and takes it out. She takes a rectangle and tries to put the hole around the stick.

She bangs the stick on the heap of rectangles. She then takes three rectangles together and puts them on the head of another child. She takes them off and puts them in a cup. She bangs the stick on the rectangles. She looks out the window (without moving). She bangs on the rectangles, stops, bangs, stops, bangs, stops, bangs, looks at another child passing by, bangs, looks at the experimenter, and bangs. All the rectangles are now scattered all over the room. She looks outside, then bangs. The experimenter asks her to stop and explains that the rectangles are going to break.

Amina takes a rectangle in her hand, looks at it, puts it down. She takes the stick and holds it by both ends with her two hands. She puts it down, stands it up, stands in the box, and steps out. She picks up two rectangles and puts them in the recipient. She takes four rectangles, piles them up and puts them in the box. She takes a rectangle and tries to put her finger in one of the holes. She takes it out, puts the rectangle down, takes another, and then does the same thing quickly.

She takes a flower and puts it on the stick. She takes four flowers together and puts them on the stick one after the other. She puts the stick in her mouth. She adds another flower on the stick, puts it in her mouth again, adds a flower, and puts the stick in her mouth. She puts on another flower, the wrong way (between the petals), says something inaudible, and takes the flower off so as to put it on correctly. She puts on a rectangle, but it doesn't stay. She takes a flower again and puts it on, and does this with another and still another. Amina turns the stick upside-down, and all the flowers fall off. She takes the stick in both hands, threads a flower, and takes it off by letting it slide down the stick. She takes three flowers together and threads them together on the stick. She turns the whole thing upside-down while holding it with her two hands, takes another flower, and wants to put it on the stick by holding it upside-down. She removes her hand, and all the flowers fall off.

Amina takes a handful of rectangles and throws them into the box. She gets up, goes to look in the hall, comes back, and sits down. She takes three rectangles, puts them in a cup, and empties the cup into the box. Then she takes several rectangles, one by one, and puts them in the box. She gets on all fours in front of the box and then sits down. She throws the cup, puts both hands flat in the box, stirs the rectangles, then gets up, and goes to get a hug from the caretaker.

Sequence Analysis

Sequence 1: Exploration of the collection of rectangles by the same action, with two agents, the body and an object.

> Box tips over; all the rectangles fall out.
> Stirs rectangles with both arms.
> Stirs rectangles with cup.

Sequence 2: Exploration of the stick on the rectangles as an additional agent other than the body.

> Puts finger in hole of rectangle.
>> The exploration of the rectangles continues, not as a set of objects to be acted on, but rather as having a specific property: holes.
> Takes stick (intention to put stick in hole); puts it down.
> Puts finger in hole of rectangle.
> Puts stick in hole of rectangle.
>> As in Sequence 1, the finger acts as an active intermediary in the discovery of object properties; before another object becomes an agent for action instead of the body.
> Stirs rectangles with stick (upside-down).
>> This is a third way to stir the rectangles.
> Puts stick in mouth.
> Places hole of rectangle on stick.
>> This is the opposite of the stick in the hole of the rectangle, with the same effect: The stick is threaded on the hole of the rectangle.

Although Amina is working on the same passive objects, the rectangles, the important part of the discovery process concerns the function of the stick, a causal action agent, like the hand in Sequence 1. She continues to extend her exploration of the functions of the stick.

> Stick: Bangs on rectangles.
> Takes 3 rectangles: Places them on head of another child.

Places several rectangles in cup.
The cup becomes both a stirring agent and a receptacle.
Stick: Bangs on rectangles; looks elsewhere.
Stick: Bangs on rectangles; brief pause.
Stick: Bangs on rectangles; brief pause.
Stick: Bangs on rectangles; looks elsewhere. twice.
The rectangles are now dispersed in all directions.

Sequence 3: Exploration of the "putting in" procedure, with variations on content and containers.

Rectangles in hand: looks, puts them down.
Stick in hand: looks, puts it down.
Steps into box.
Places 2 rectangles in box (1 in each hand, put simultaneously, then separately).
Piles 4 rectangles (successively, $1 + 1 + 1 + 1$), then places them in the box simultaneously.
Puts finger in hole of rectangle (put in, threaded), then immediately puts rectangles in box (put in, positioned).

Sequence 4: Exploration of flowers and the stick by the "putting in and thread" procedure, with variations on the procedure: by order (succession) or cardinality (simultaneity).

Flower threaded on stick.
This is similar to the stick threaded in the flower, which is what she previously did with the holes of the rectangles.
Takes 4 flowers together in her hand, and threads them, one by one, onto the stick.
Puts 5th flower on stick, then stick in mouth.
Puts 6th flower on stick, then stick in mouth.
Puts 7th flower on stick wrong.
Puts 7th flower on stick correctly.
Puts rectangle on stick (through hole); rectangle does not stay on.
Puts 8th, 9th, and 10th flowers on stick, successively.
Stick put upside-down; all flowers fall off.
After putting several on, one by one, she takes them all off in one move by reversing the position of the stick.
Flowers on stick taken off by sliding them toward top (putting one on, taking on off).
Puts 3 flowers together in one hand, then on the stick simultaneously.
Note relation to 4 flowers taken together and put on one by one.

Stick upside-down, holds the flowers.
> The intention is to chain the sequence—take, put, take off—with the whole collection.

Tries to thread 4th flower on upside-down stick.
> This is an exploration of the reversed procedure—take, take off—in relation to the reversed position of the stick.

Lifts stick; all flowers fall off.

Sequence 5: End of game by a return to the rectangles and a synthesis of the "put in" procedure.

Takes handful of rectangles in two hands and throw into box.
Piles up 3 rectangles, one by one, in cup.
Empties full cup in box.
> This shows procedural transitivity as well as relativity of the cup, which is both larger than rectangles and smaller than the box.

Places several rectangles, one by one, in box.
Takes cup and throws it.
Places hands flat in box.
Rectangles are all together. Stirs with both hands.
> The end of the game is a repeat of the procedure used at the start, with the same objects used as agent and patient.

In sum, two features of this protocol stand out: First, the start–end game cycle involves body actions on objects, whereas the microgenetic progression involves more complex relations between objects. As in the preceding analysis, it is likely that the appropriation of new relations constructed in interaction with the situation must be re-placed into the context of a familiar procedure. These new relations arise from the familiar procedure, but lead the subject in other directions. The disequilibrium thus created calls for a return to the point of departure. Through this reprise, the subject can also evaluate the progression between the point of departure and his or her furthermost point. This progression is threefold; it can be explicated in terms of:

1. The inventory of procedures with each object. These procedures set up similarity and difference classes between objects.
2. Relations between objects, of which body–object relations are the precursor. These relations are based on the "stir," "put in," and "put on" procedures.
3. Exploration of number, linking ordinal/serial, and cardinal/simultaneous features. These are carried out in conjunction with upside-down versus right-side up relations, with do and undo procedures, and with the active and passive function of objects.

These microgenetic analyses on three different structural levels are illustrative of the same functional diversity of numerical constructions.

Structural analysis of number (Gréco et al., 1960; Piaget & Szeminska, 1941) has shed light on the nature of the relations between infralogical and logical aspects of number, numerical filiations, and connections between logical and mathematical features of number. In the structural framework, the mechanisms of the construction of number are primarily accounted for by the concept of optimizing equilibrium (Piaget, 1975) and reflective abstraction (Piaget, 1976). In an attempt to gain a better grasp of construction mechanisms in a more functional perspective, cognitive developmental psychology studies have considered knowledge in terms of representations that can be specified for a given situation. The study of cognitive microgeneses was motivated by this perspective, and was applied to number. Analysis was based on the segmentation of data into functional sequences defined by the subject's intention, and inferences which presuppose a parallel investigation of the representational sequencing.

Structural analysis, on a macrogenetic or stage level, indicates that there is an obligatory and exclusive step by step progression of a concept, only defined by its logico-mathematical content (e.g., sensorimotor actions followed by figural collections preceding operational behavior). In contrast, functional analysis, which occurs on a microgenetic level, shows that there are different pathways to number, pathways that can be multimodal (procedural, figural, or conceptual), that can involve changes in the meaning (routine, primitive, or procedural) of number schemes, or that entail connections that, for structural (Inhelder, Sinclair, & Bovet, 1975) as well as contextual reasons, create functional associations between representations. Work on the diversity of pathways in other areas of the acquisition of knowledge is now in progress: in learning to read (Rieben & Saada-Robert, 1989, 1991) and in the regulation of written language production in classroom environments (Allal & Saada-Robert, 1991).

ACKNOWLEDGMENT

The author extends her thanks to the staff of the Ecole des Professions de la Petite Enfance, and the students enrolled in her course on observation in educational practices for authorizing the use of some of the protocols cited in this chapter.

15

Learning Addition and Subtraction: Effects of Number Words and Other Cultural Tools

Karen C. Fuson
Youngshim Kwon
Northwestern University

There are thousands of different systems of number words; on the island of Papua New Guinea alone there are over 700 languages (Lancy, 1983; see also Ifrah 1981/1985; Menninger, 1958/1969; Zaslavsky, 1973). Many cultures, especially those surrounding and within the Pacific Ocean, even have several different number-word systems that are used for different purposes or for counting different kinds of objects. The features of a system of number words affect how easily it can be learned and used to add and subtract numbers less than 10, to add and subtract numbers between 10 and 100, and to add and subtract numbers larger than 100. This chapter will focus on some of the features that affect these different aspects of numerical learning. The concentration will be on a comparison between European systems of number words, which are irregular up to 100 (with English used as the main example), and the Asian systems that are based on Chinese, which are totally regular. Most of the points made also generalize to a wide variety of other systems of number words, and examples will be given where available. Nonlinguistic cultural supports for learning addition and subtraction, especially the different uses of fingers as countables, will also be discussed.

Asian number-word systems that are based on Chinese and most European number-word systems are named-value systems in which the values are successive powers of 10: there are words for the numbers 1 through 9, and larger numbers are made by saying one of these number words followed by a power-of-ten-value word that tells the value of the 1 through 9 word. One says 5353 in English as five *thousand* three *hundred* fifty three, in French as cinq*mille*trois-*cent*cinquante*trois, and in Chinese as five *thousand* three *hundred* five *ten* three (using English words to show the values of the Chinese words; the actual Chinese

283

words are wu *chien* san *bai* wu *shi* san). Most European languages are irregular (in many different ways) up to 100 but are regular named-value systems after 100, whereas Asian systems based on Chinese are regular named-value systems, explicitly naming the *ten* beginning with 11 (*ten one*) and continuing to 100 (e.g., 16 is *ten six*, 24 is *two ten four*). Mandarin Chinese, Japanese, Korean, and Burmese are totally regular named-value systems, and many other Asian languages have only minor irregularities in the second decade (words for 11 through 19) and in some decade words (e.g., Thai, Vietnamese, Bahasa used in Indonesia, Tagalog used in the Phillippines, at least some versions of Maori used in New Zealand, and Austronesian languages used on the coast and islands of Papua New Guinea). Some African languages also have regular named-value systems based on successive powers of 10 (e.g., Dioula).

LEARNING THE SEQUENCE OF NUMBER WORDS

How difficult it is to learn a sequence of number words depends on the features of the number-word sequence; the nature of errors made in saying a sequence depends on these features. Deaf children learning the number-word sequence of American Sign Language gestures make errors on the signs that are difficult for their fingers to form and show confusions about the rules used to make the separate related parts of the sequence for 1 to 5, 6 to 10, 11 to 15, and 15 to 20 (Secada, 1985). Most English-speaking children in the United States learn the English number words to twenty largely as a rote sequence in which the words between *ten* and *twenty* are not related to the words below *ten* (although some children do show awareness that these words are teen words and may overgeneralize and say "eight, nine, ten, eleventeen, twelveteen, thirteen"). The errors children in the United States make are largely omissions of words rather than reversals, and the portions of the sequence from which words are omitted may be stable for a long time (Fuson et al., 1982). English-speaking children do show awareness of the decade structure (the pattern of x-ty, x-ty one, x-ty two, . . . , x-ty nine), but they take a long time (as much as a year and a half) to learn the decade words in their correct order. Children learning Italian show particular difficulties with the reversal from 16 to 17 (the *ten* is said second for 11 through 16—*undici*, . . . , *sedici*—but is said first for 17 through 19—*diciassette, diciotto, diciannove*) (Agnoli & Zhu, 1989). Korean children, whose language has a formal and and informal system of number words, show more errors in decade words when counting in their informal system, in which all decade words are new different words, then when counting in their formal system based on Chinese, in which decade words are regular named tens (Song & Ginsburg, 1988).

The Asian systems based on Chinese (see Table 15.1) are very easy for children to learn. They only need to learn the first nine words, the words for the

TABLE 15.1
French, English, and Chinese Systems of Number Words

	French	English	Chinese — English words	Chinese — Chinese words
1	un, une	one	one	yi
2	deux	two	two	er
3	trois	three	three	san
4	quatre	four	four	si
5	cinq	five	five	wu
6	six	six	six	liu
7	sept	seven	seven	qi
8	huit	eight	eight	ba
9	neuf	nine	nine	jiu
10	dix	ten	ten	shi
11	onze	eleven	ten one	shi yi
12	douze	twelve	ten two	shi er
13	treize	thirteen	ten three	shi san
14	quatorze	fourteen	ten four	shi si
15	quinze	fifteen	ten five	shi wu
16	seize	sixteen	ten six	shi liu
17	dix-sept	seventeen	ten seven	shi qi
18	dix-huit	eighteen	ten eight	shi ba
19	dix-neuf	nineteen	ten nine	shi jiu
20	vingt	twenty	two ten	er shi
21	vingt et un	twenty-one	two ten one	er shi yi
22	vingt-deux	twenty-two	two ten two	er shi er
23	vingt-trois	twenty-three	two ten three	er shi san
24	vingt-quatre	twenty-four	two ten four	er shi si
25	vingt-cinq	twenty-five	two ten five	er shi wu
26	vingt-six	twenty six	two ten six	er shi liu
27	vingt-sept	twenty-seven	two ten seven	er shi qi
28	vingt-huit	twenty-eight	two ten eight	er shi ba
29	vingt-neuf	twenty-nine	two ten nine	er shi jiu
30	trente	thirty	three ten	san shi
31	trente et un	thirty-one	three ten one	san shi yi
39	trente neuf	thirty-nine	three ten nine	san shi jiu
40	quarante	forty	four ten	si shi
50	cinquante	fifty	five ten	wu shi
60	soixante	sixty	six ten	liu shi
70	soixante-dix	seventy	seven ten	qi shi
80	quatre-vingt	eighty	eight ten	ba shi
90	quartre-vingt-dix	ninety	nine ten	jiu shi
99	quartre-vingt-dix-neuf	ninety-nine	nine ten nine	jiu shi jiu
100	cent	one hundred	one hundred	yi bai
101	cent-un	one hundred one	one hundred one	yi bai ling yi
125	cent vingt cinq	one hundred twenty-five	one hundred two ten five	yi bai er shi wu
4,313	quatre mille trois cent treize	four thousand three hundred thirteen	four thousand three hundred ten three	si qian san bai shi san

285

powers of 10 (shi, bai, qian, etc.), and the order in which words are said (from the largest value to the smallest). Chinese children make many fewer errors in saying the words to 19 than do English-speaking children in the United States (Miller & Stigler, 1987), and Chinese children show earlier learning of the sequence between 109 and 200 than do English-speaking U.S. or Italian children (Agnoli & Zhu, 1989). Errors reflecting imperfect knowledge or use of the decade structure, which the Chinese, English, and Italian number words all possess, were made by children speaking all three languages: They jumped to the wrong decade, forgot the current decade they were saying, and had trouble at transition points in counting backward (e.g., erroneously saying 72, 71, 70, 60, 69, 68 . . .). Fuson et al. (1982) and Siegler and Robinson (1982) also reported such difficulties for English-speaking children in the United States.

Most European languages clearly say neither the *ten one, ten two, . . . , ten nine* structure for 11 through 19 nor the *two ten, three ten, four ten, . . . , nine ten* pattern for the decade names, but most of them show some traces of both of these structures. In many languages, some words have lost their original meaning. For example, the English twelve for 12 comes from the Anglo-Saxon *twa-lif* meaning "two remain" (presumably two remain over ten; Greenberg, 1978), and *eleven* probably has a similar derivation (e-lif-un: "remain one" or even "ten left one"). The multisyllabic nature of European languages (compared to the single syllables used in Chinese) has, over time, led to the omission of parts of words, to changes in consonants, and to the addition of short syllables in order to facilitate pronunciation of the underlying words for 11 through 19 and for the decade words from 20 to 90. These phonetic changes then make it difficult for children to see the underlying structure of many European words as composed of *x* tens and *y* ones. Examples in English are the use of *thir* in *thirteen* (13) and in *thirty* (30) instead of *three,* the use of *fif* in *fifteen* (15) and *fifty* (50) instead of *five,* the use of *-teen* for 13 through 19, and *-ty* for 20 through 90 instead of *ten.* These phonetic substitutions and the quantitative meaning of these substitutions may not be understood even by adults; many of the first author's university undergraduates have never realized that -teen and -ty sound like *ten* and mean "ten"; they just used these syllables in a counting pattern without ever reflecting on their meaning. French and most other European languages have several such examples of phonetic changes: for example, *quatre* (4) becomes *quator* in 14 and *quar* in 40. Some Asian languages that have a regular structure except for a few irregularities also exhibit such phonetic changes: *isa* means "one," but *sam, san,* and *sang* are all used to mean "one" for larger numbers in Tagalog (Philippines); *satu* means "one" in Bahasa (Indonesia), but *se* is used when forming larger numbers that require "one"; and *tit* means "one," but *ta* is used with larger numbers in Burmese. All of these phonetic changes make it more difficult for children learning the language to understand and use the underlying tens and ones structure.

The preceding discussion has only focused on the nature of the patterns involved in producing (and, thus, in learning) a number-word sequence and has ignored any quantitative aspects of the actual words used in a sequence. Any number-word sequence can, of course, be learned as a totally arbitrary sequence of sounds like saying the alphabet (A, B, C, D, E, F, G, . . .). Because the native sequence of number words is so overlaid with quantitative meaning for adults, a useful technique for understanding what children must learn for a given language is to generate a particular number-word sequence using the alphabet. The patterns revealed by such alphabetic sequences are given in Table 15.2 for three European languages, Chinese, a Papua New Guinea language using some body parts, and an African language using a base of 20 and subtraction. The base-ten pattern is the pattern of the written base-ten positional numerals. Note the similarities and differences between the base-ten and Chinese patterns: the tenth symbol (*j*) is "zero" in base ten and is "ten" in Chinese (10 reuses the first symbol 1 and needs a new symbol 0 while shi in Chinese is just another new word) and the values are not named in base ten (e.g., 55 is *ee* [*five five*] in base ten rather than *eje* [*five ten five*] as in Chinese). It is clear that some patterns would be easier than others to learn, and the patterns lead to predictions about where errors might occur. Some languages use a word that has a quantitative meaning—like *hand* for five or *man* for twenty—for a particular number. Such meanings may be ignored in the original learning of the sequence, but they may facilitate the linking of quantitative meaning to related words when the sequence is used for cardinal purposes. Thus, languages may vary in how easily individual words and patterns can be related to cardinal meanings. These differences have important implications for addition and subtraction

RELATING SPOKEN NUMBER WORDS
TO WRITTEN NUMERALS

Written Numerals Having Sequence/Count Meanings

Children learn associations between written numerals and spoken number words, and these written numerals take on the meanings of the spoken number word. For small number words, the meanings may be cardinal (3 may mean three cookies) or sequence meanings (3 may mean what is said after two and before four), but for most larger words, children have few cardinal meanings. Thus, the meanings of the number words and of the numerals are initially only sequence meanings (8 means the word coming after seven and before nine). The pattern in the sequence of written numerals used in most languages is a simple one: It is just the regular Chinese pattern with the value words omitted and a 0 numeral used for any missing value, so that all the values stay in their correct relative position. This numeral pattern is given in Table 15.2 as the base-ten pattern. Children can learn the sequence of written numerals by its pattern, but in order to say a given written

TABLE 15.2
Patterns in Different Number-Word Systems

Number	Base Ten	Chinese	English	French	German	Kilenge[a]	Yoruba[b]
1	a	a	a	a	a	a	a
2	b	b	b	b	b	b	b
3	c	c	c	c	c	c	c
4	d	d	d	d	d	d	d
5	e	e	e	e	e	hand	e
6	f	f	f	f	f	hand a	f
7	g	g	g	g	g	hand b	g
8	h	h	h	h	h	hand c	h
9	i	i	i	i	i	hand d	i
10	aj	j	j	j	j	b hands	j
11	aa	ja	k	km	k	b hands a only	ak
12	ab	jb	l	lm	l	b hands b	bk
13	ac	jc	mn	nm	cj	b hands c	ck
14	ad	jd	dn	om	dj	b hands d	dk
15	ae	je	on	pm	ej	c hands	l
16	af	jf	fn	qm	fj	c hands a	d reduces m
17	ag	jg	gn	jg	gj	c hands b	c reduces m
18	ah	jh	hn	jh	hj	c hands c	b reduces m
19	ai	ji	in	ji	ij	c hands d	a reduces m
20	bj	bj	pq	r	mn	one man	m
21	ba	bja	pqa	rsa	aomn	one man a only	a on m
29	bi	bji	pqi	ri	iomn	one man hand d	i on m
30	cj	cj	rq	t	cn	one man a b hands	o
31	ca	cja	rqa	tsa	aocn	one man a b hands a only	a on o
39	ci	cji	rqi	ti	iocn	one man a b hands hand d	i on o
40	dj	dj	dq	uv	dn	one man b over	mb
50	ej	ej	oq	ev	en	—	j reduces mc
55	ee	eje	oqe	eve	eoen	—	e reduces mc
60	fj	fj	fq	wv	fn	one man c over	mc
70	gj	gj	gq	wvj	gn	—	—
80	hj	hj	hq	dr	hn	one man d over	—
90	ij	ij	iq	drj	in	—	—
91	ia	ija	iqa	drkm	aoin	—	—
99	ii	iji	iqi	drji	ioin	—	—
100	ajj	ak	ar	x	p	—	me
101	aja	akla	ara	xsa	pa	—	—
125	abe	akbje	arpqe	xre	peomn	—	—

[a]Kilenge is a Type III Papua New Guinea language typical of 40% of the languages (Lancy, 1978); not enough information was available to fill in all the numbers.

[b]Yoruba is a West African language based on 20 that uses subtraction frequently (Zaslavsky, 1973); not enough information was available to fill in all the numbers; k is an abbreviation for "on ten" or "in addition to ten," l is an abbreviation of "e reduces m," and several other higher forms are slightly abbreviated in actual use but are given in the table as if they were not.

numeral, they must relate the pattern in the numerals to the pattern in their own number-word sequence (or learn a very large number of numeral to number-word associations by rote).

Clearly, the ease with which children can relate the numeral and number-word patterns depends on their number-word sequence. Chinese (and Japanese and Korean) children have a very simple relationship to learn, because the patterns share many features and have no special irregularities. For European languages, this relationship is much more complex. The English words do not even signal a pattern break at 10 because the first 12 words are rote, arbitrary words. For many languages (e.g., French, Spanish, Italian, German, English, and Swedish), all or part of the words for the numerals between 11 and 19 have a number-word order opposite to the numeral order: One says the *four* first (*quatorze* or *catorce* or *quattordici* or *vierzehn* or *fourteen* or *fjorton*), but writes the *four* second (14). Some languages switch the order of the *ten* and the *ones* words at 15 or 16, but the written numerals keep the single ten-then-one order. Many European languages have the decade word before the ones word (*vingt et un, twenty-one, ventuno*) as in the written numerals, but in German all words between 20 and 100 are ordered opposite to the written numerals, with the ones words before the tens word (e.g., *einundzwanzig* is *one and twenty*).

The difficulties European children sometimes have in learning the sequence of number words and in relating this sequence to the pattern of written numerals is illustrated by a report by Neuman (1987) about an 11-year-old Swedish boy in a remedial math class who, after some work on structuring by tens, made a drawing of rows of numerals so that 1 through 10 were lined up, with 11 through 20 lined up just below, and 21 through 30 lined up just below that. This boy shouted out excitedly,

> You see . . . I sat the other day and thought about numbers . . . and so . . . so I wrote on a bit of paper like that . . . and then I *saw* . . . you see? . . . Look!! . . . Have you ever noticed? . . . That one comes under one the whole time, and two comes under two . . . and three under three . . . Then it's much *easier* to count!! (pp. 318–319)

This boy had been in school for 4 years and undoubtedly had had the tens and ones structure of the numerals "explained" to him many times, but he still had not seen the numeral pattern or related this pattern to the Swedish number words. For some European children, the easier regular pattern of the numerals may provide the structure necessary to understand the pattern of an irregular system of number words.

Written Numerals Meaning Tens and Ones

Children need to understand the quantitative meaning of written numerals as tens and ones and not just learn the nonquantitative alphabetic pattern of the numerals. Evidently, children speaking regular, named-value Asian languages, which name the "ten," learn these tens and ones meanings much more easily than do English-speaking children in the United States. Miura (Miura, 1987; Miura, Kim, Chang, & Okamoto, 1988; Miura & Okamoto, 1989) has reported, in a number of studies, that Chinese, Korean, and Japanese kindergarten and first-grade children chose to show two-digit numerals as combinations of ten-unit blocks and unit blocks, whereas their English-speaking age-mates in the United States showed the same numerals only with unit blocks (e.g., they counted out 42 unit blocks by ones instead of choosing 4 ten-unit blocks and 2 unit blocks). This was true even though the Japanese first-grade children had had no instruction on tens and ones in school and the U.S. first-graders had (Miura & Okamoto, 1989). Children in the United States have considerable difficulty in replacing their unitary sequence meaning of numerals by a meaning in which the first digit means "ten." Many first and second graders, and even substantial proportions of fifth graders, show the meaning of the *1* in *16* as one object and not as ten objects (C. K. Kamii, 1985, 1986). The *1* may be said by children to "teen" the *6,* that is, to make the *6* be *sixteen* instead of *six,* but there is no comprehension of 16 being composed of a ten and a six. M. Kamii (1981) argued that this "glued-together" pattern meaning of numerals is similar to spelling: *16* and *61* are reversals, just as are *dog* and *god,* and each of the glued-together composites in the pair has a different meaning, but the *1* and the *6* within *16* and *61* do not have quantitative meaning aside from their single-digit meanings as "one" and "six." The path to quantitative named-value multiunit meanings (e.g., the hundreds-digit telling the number of hundred-units) is a difficult one for English-speaking children, and many of them do not negotiate this path successfully. They may, at best, be able to use verbal named-value labels, that is, to tell which numeral in a four-digit numeral is called the hundreds digit. The very strong unitary meanings of number words and written numerals continue to create difficulties for English-speaking children in carrying out single-digit and multidigit addition and subtraction (see Fuson, 1990, in press-a, in press-b).

Even though the pattern of regular named-value number words relates fairly easily to the regular pattern of positional base-ten numerals, these systems do have several differences that can cause difficulties (see Fuson, 1991, for a discussion of the difference between named-value number words and the positional base-ten written numerals). It is quite common to write incorrect named-value numerals that mirror the named-value words (e.g., writing 300408 for *three hundred forty-eight*). English-speaking children make such errors (Bell & Burns, 1981). Europeans first changing from Roman to Arabic numerals also made such named-value errors (Menninger, 1958/1969), and Dioula and Baoule African children also do so (Ginsburg, Posner, & Russell, 1981b). We know of no evidence concerning how frequently Asian children may make such named-value number-word intrusion errors when first learning to write numerals.

SINGLE-DIGIT ADDITION AND SUBTRACTION

Cardinal Meanings for Number Words

In order for number words to be used for addition and subtraction, they must take on cardinal meanings; that is, they must tell how many there are. The structure of the system of number words, and the number words themselves, affects which cardinal meanings are easily understood. In Table 15.2, the Kilenge system supports cardinal meanings for 5, 10, 15, and 20 because the *hand* and *man* words can have quantitative meanings. In Chinese, once a cardinal meaning for *shi* (10) is understood, the cardinal meanings for 11 (*ten one*) through 99 (*nine ten nine*) follow quite readily. In English there is little similar support for these meanings for two-digit numbers. The words through *twenty* are just a linear sequence of piles of entities that get one larger, and the words between *twenty* and *one hundred* are just a similar sequence of very large piles that suggest, at most, a composition of a large plus a small pile of things (57 is 50 and 7 of the same single units, not 5 tens and 7 ones). Features of number-word (or number-gesture) systems can even interfere with the construction of these cardinal meanings. Papua New Guinea Oksapmin children, who learn a body-parts number sequence in which a succession of body locations constitute the numerical sequence, show cardinal confusions between similar body parts (e.g., left elbow and right elbow) even though these are quite separated in the sequence (Saxe, 1981). Some number-gesture systems have many clear cardinal references, whereas others do not (Zaslavsky, 1973).

Most number-word systems have a considerable number of words with no cardinal meaning: These words take on cardinal meaning through counting objects. The last counted word tells how many there are in (i.e., has a cardinal reference to) the pile of counted objects. How children first make this connection between counting and cardinal meanings of number words is discussed by Fuson (1988; this volume, chap. 6), including the developmental sequence of continuing relationships children construct to relate sequence, counting, and cardinal meanings. Once children can move from a count meaning to a cardinal meaning and vice versa, they can add by "counting all" and subtract by taking away or separating. In *counting all,* a child counts out objects for the first addend, counts out objects for the second addend, and then counts all of the objects. In taking away or separating, the child does the reverse: Counts out objects for the known sum, counts some of those sum objects up to the known addend and moves them away, and then counts the remaining objects to find the unknown addend objects.

Developmental Paths to More Advanced
Addition Procedures

These original object counting procedures become increasingly abbreviated and abstract. Fingers are frequently chosen as the objects to be counted, and children eventually begin to learn finger patterns that make certain numbers. At this point there are at least three developmental paths children can take through addition and subtraction of single-digit numbers. Different cultures seem to support certain paths, although there is also individual variation within a culture. Fingers are used in conceptually different ways in these different paths. These differences seem to be related to the way a particular culture shows the numbers 1 through 10 on fingers, although other factors may also be involved. On all of these paths, children construct relationships among sequence, count, and cardinal meanings of numbers words, but the meanings that predominate differ. These paths describe children in the United States (the pertinent research is summarized by Fuson, 1988; 1990, in press-a; in press-b; and this volume, chap. 6), in Sweden, (Neuman, 1987), and in Korea (Fuson & Kwon, in press-a, in press-b). Some examples of these paths that occur in other cultures will also be given. These paths clearly depend on fingers and not the structure of the number words because English and Swedish number words have identical structures. The regular Korean words do confer some advantages even beyond the Korean finger methods.

Sequence Counting. In one path, taken by many children in the United States, the number words themselves eventually become the objects that present the addends and the sum within addition and subtraction situations (see Table 15.3 for steps along this path), and the fingers are only used to keep track of the second addend. One begins this path by using fingers on one hand to count out one addend and fingers on the other hand to count out the other addend; all of the fingers are then counted to find the sum. When counting, fingers are typically raised beginning with the finger closest to the thumb and moving across the other fingers to the smallest finger; the thumb is raised last.[1] The child holds both hands up in the air, usually with the palm toward the face. Children eventually learn patterns for each number from 1 through 5 on either hand; they can then just raise finger patterns for each addend and count all of the fingers (Baroody, 1987c; Siegler & Robinson, 1982). Children eventually learn that they do not have to count all of the fingers in the sum count, but can begin the counting from the first addend word, that is, they can count on from the first addend. This is not a rote procedure but requires them to shift from the cardinal meaning of the first addend word to a counting meaning of that word (see Fuson, this volume, for a more detailed discussion). Finally, children do not need the perceptual support of the fingers to see the addends and the sum; they simply say the number words in sequence, and these sequence words themselves present the addends and the sum

---

[1]No claim is made in this chapter that the finger patterns shown in Table 15.3 are those used by all children or adults in the United States, Sweden, or Korea. Data concerning the range of finger patterns that may be used in different geographic and subcultural areas of these countries are not now available. The patterns shown are those reported in the references cited.

TABLE 15.3
Three Developmental Paths Through Single-Digit Addition

Fingers Keep Track of Sequence Counting	Fingers as Count Names	Cardinal Finger Counting
Count All	Count All	Count All
Pattern Count All	Count Name Errors	Pattern Count All
Pattern Count On		Pattern-Count-Pattern
Sequence Count On: Cardinalized Number-Word Sequence	Finger Count On: Cardinalized Finger Sequence	
fingers raised successively		
Sums Over Ten: 8 + 6	Sums Over Ten: 8 + 6	Sums Over Ten: 8 + 6
Two-handed finger pattern		
fingers raised successively	Number Line	
One-handed finger pattern		
6 = thumb (5) + 1		

$4+5=5$

$2+7=7$

$2+7=8$

$10+4=\boxed{14}$

$=\boxed{14}$ ten four folded unfolded

8 folded 2 folded

4 unfolded

Note. $\boxed{4}$ means a cardinal meaning for four, 4 means a count meaning for four, ④ means a sequence meaning for four, $\boxed{14}$ means a ten and four meaning for 14. Only the folding down Korean methods are shown.

to the child. If the second addend is very large, some method of keeping track of how many sequence words have been said is required. Fingers are the most usual means of keeping track. Here, the fingers function as a cardinal finger pattern that is matched to each sequence word as it is said: Fingers are raised in succession with each word (rather than being put out before and then counted as in object or pattern counting on), and the sequence counting stops when the desired finger pattern has been made (see Table 15.3). New Guinea Oksapmin children use such sequence counting on for addition problems that exceed their native body-parts sequence, which only goes to 27: They count on in English and use their body-parts sequence to keep track of the second addend (Saxe, 1985).

The Fingers as Count Names.   In a different path, taken by many Swedish children (Neuman, 1987), each finger takes on a particular count name from *one* through *ten;* see Table 15.3 for steps along this path. Swedish school entrants were interviewed by Neuman; in Sweden children begin first grade at age 7. These children counted on their fingers by placing both hands on the table in front of them with the palms down and the thumbs in the middle and counted from left to right (some counted similarly with their hands raised in the air). When adding two small numbers, they did not put the second addend on the second hand, but counted it continuing across the fingers, beginning with the finger to the right of the last finger used for the first addend. All fingers were then counted to find the sum by beginning from the left and counting to the right. With this method each finger always receives a standard word during the counting of the first addend and the sum: The left little finger is always *one,* the left thumb is always *five,* the right thumb is always *six,* the right little finger is always *ten,* and the middle fingers take on the words between these words. The word received by a given finger always varies during the second addend count because those words depend on the size of the first addend. Through repeated standard counting, each finger takes on its own count name from *one* through *ten.*

Many children stay in this count-name stage for a considerable period of time (a substantial proportion of these school entrants displayed this level) and make errors in adding and subtracting that result from their failure to connect these count names to a cardinal meaning for these names: Thus, for example, the word *four* is the count name for the index finger on the left hand, but *four* does not also have a cardinal meaning as referring to all of the first four counted fingers. Children therefore make the three kinds of mistakes shown in Table 15.3.[2] For example, 4 + 5 is found to be 5 by using the count meaning of 5: 4 fingers (or possibly, the finger named four) plus the finger named 5 (the thumb on the left hand) is 5 fingers; 2 + 7 = 7 by using count meanings for both *two* and *seven:*

[2]Children at this level were frequently not very articulate about the meanings they were using, so increased understanding of the conceptual bases for these mistakes awaits further research.

The finger *two* and the finger *seven* go along the fingers to finger seven. Also, 2 + 7 = 8 because each count finger is just one finger: "the *seven* finger plus one more finger (which happens to be named *two*, but this name does not matter) equals finger *eight*." Children showed a strong predisposition at this level to add by beginning with the larger number regardless of which number was given first in the problem.

Eventually, the fingers became a cardinalized finger sequence in which the second addend word has a cardinal value as the number of fingers counted past the first addend. Children may first pass through a period in which they estimate the second addend by counting an approximate number of words past the first addend but do not actually keep accurate track of the second addend. Neuman (1987) does not provide much information about how Swedish children come to keep track of large second addends, because almost all of her problems had a small addend that could just be subitized when counting on. The obvious way to keep track of the second addend accurately is to use number words to count the second addend fingers; the fingers then show the sum. This is opposite to the use of fingers and spoken words in the first path, where the spoken words present the sum and the fingers present (or keep track of) the second addend.

New Guinea Oksapmin children follow this second path in solving addition problems within the range of their 27-unit body-parts number sequence. They count on from a given body location while calling each counted-on location a body part from the second addend body part list (Saxe, 1985). The number line used in some textbooks is structured like this second path: the written numerals present both the first addend and the sum, and the spoken number words present the second addend as children go up the number line. Chisenbop, the Korean method of finger calculation that attracted national attention in the United States in the 1970s, is also structured as in the second path: Finger patterns on one hand present 1 through 9 (the thumb pressed to a surface is 5, so the thumb plus the index finger—the *one* finger—is 6, etc., through the thumb and all four fingers, which equals 9), the first addend is put onto the right-hand fingers, number words are spoken aloud to present the second addend as each successive finger number pattern is made, and the fingers then present the sum (if the sum is over ten, tens are made on the left hand). These one-handed finger patterns can also be used successfully by first graders learning to add by counting on in the first path: Words say the sum, and the one-handed finger patterns show the second addend and match the sum count to stop it at the correct sum (see Table 15.3; see also Fuson & Secada, 1986). In that study we used the one-handed finger patterns rather than the two-handed finger patterns usually used by children in the United States for second addends over 5 because children frequently put down their pencil in order to use two-handed finger patterns, slowing their addition considerably.

The first path is easier than the second path to carry out for sums over 10 because the fingers can easily show any single-digit number through 9 as the second addend (either with one-handed or two-handed finger patterns, see Table 15.3), whereas the second path requires that fingers be reused in some way to show any sums over 10 because the fingers show the sum. Table 15.3 shows one possibility for doing this: moving the fingers for 1 through 5 (the left hand) over to the right of the right hand and reusing them. This has the advantage of clearly showing the tens and ones structure: Eleven is two hands (ten) and the named *one* finger, 12 is two hands (ten) and the named *two* finger, and so on. This, however, requires a move of the second hand for sums over 15, which might get too complex for some children. Neuman (1987) did not report how Swedish children use their named fingers to solve sums over 10, so it is not clear how children solve (or how the culture solves) this reusing problem. In her experimental teaching, Neuman used Cuisenaire ten-rods and one-rods for teaching sums over 10 rather than using fingers. It would also be possible for children to shift to the first path and say the sum words while keeping track of the second addend with the named fingers. How difficult this shift would be is not clear.

Cardinal Fingers Reused Over Ten.   A third path through addition is a cardinal approach, in which fingers are counted or patterned to make finger patterns for 1 through 10 and fingers are reused to make numbers between 11 and 19. In this approach, the 10 fingers support the construction of addition methods based on structuring numbers by 10. This path was evidenced by first-grade Korean children interviewed to ascertain how they solved single-digit addition and subtraction problems (Fuson & Kwon, in press-a), and it is the path supported by Japanese teaching tiles structured around 10 (Hatano, 1982).

When a Korean child is counting all, the hands are held up facing the person with the thumbs out, as in the first path. However, the counting starts with the thumb and moves linearly across the fingers to the little finger, then continues onto the other thumb, and moves across to the little finger on that hand (see Table 15.3), or counting may be done in the reverse fashion beginning with the little finger and moving to the thumb. Some children begin on the left hand and move to the right, and some begin on the right hand. Children may count all by folding down fingers as each count is made, or they may begin with folded fingers and unfold the fingers while counting.[3] The first step in finding sums by counting all is like the second Swedish path: The first addend is counted as the fingers are folded, the second addend is counted as the next fingers are folded (the second addend does not begin separately on the second hand), and then all of the fingers

---

[3]Koreans typically show small cardinal finger patterns for age or small numbers of objects (e.g., three apples) by raising their fingers. *One* may be shown by the thumb or by the index finger, 2 may be shown by the thumb and index finger or by the index and second finger, 3 may be the shown by the thumb and next two fingers or by the three fingers other than the little finger, 4 is shown by the four fingers, and 5 is the thumb and four fingers. In the pattern-count-pattern procedure shown in Table 15.3, 4 might be made with the four fingers rather than with the thumb and three fingers, as in the earlier unfolded finger counting all.

are counted to find the sum. Children then may learn finger patterns of folded fingers so that they can fold fingers for the first addend without counting, count and fold fingers for the second addend, and then recognize the folded fingers for the sum. Counting all by unfolding is done in the same way (the unfolding second addend fingers are next to the unfolded first addend fingers), and unfolded finger patterns are learned for pattern adding.

To find sums over 10 by counting all in the folding-down method, all 10 fingers are folded (i.e., counted to 10), and then the fingers are unfolded beginning with the little finger of the second hand and moving across the fingers toward the thumb (i.e., the last fingers folded are the first fingers to be unfolded). A child using the method of unfolding fingers would count numbers over 10 by folding fingers again beginning with the last finger unfolded. With either method, the sum over 10 is easily said in the ten-structured Korean words as *ten* (all the fingers were used) *the-number-of-fingers-reused* (e.g., ten four in Table 15.3).

Korean children learn in first grade the over-ten method for adding sums over 10. In this method, addition (usually) begins with the larger addend and the smaller addend is broken up into (a) the number that will make ten with the first addend and (b) the remaining number. So eight plus six equals eight plus two (which makes ten) plus four (the rest of the six) = *ten four*. This method is easy to do in Asian languages in which 11 to 19 are said *ten one, ten two, . . . , ten nine,* because the sum is said as just ten and the rest of the second addend over ten. In English one has the extra step of finding this ten sum as a teen word (e.g., ten plus four is fourteen). Many first and second graders in the United States do not know these ten sums and have to count on from ten to find the sum (e.g., they find ten plus four by saying, "ten, eleven, twelve, thirteen, fourteen"). The Korean finger methods of folding and unfolding fingers support the learning of the over-ten method because (a) they make it easy to learn all of the complements to ten (i.e., the pairs of numbers that equal ten) just by looking at or thinking of the folded versus unfolded fingers, and (b) the counting of the second addend by folding and then unfolding fingers gives visual pattern support for breaking the second addend into the part that makes ten and the rest over ten. Most of the Korean first graders interviewed in Fuson and Kwon (in press-a) used the over-ten method even before they had been taught this method in school, and most of them knew, without calculating, which number made ten with a given number.

The second and third paths, thus, begin in the same way: counting all by showing the second addend on fingers following the first addend fingers. Korean first graders interviewed midway through the school year did not show any of the count-name errors shown by Swedish children just entering first grade: The Korean children were considerably more advanced in their addition methods, so it is possible that younger Korean children might show such count-name errors. Alternatively, the visual salience of the folded (or unfolded) fingers and the common reusing of fingers in the folding and unfolding methods may help

Korean children keep the cardinal view of fingers paramount and avoid count-name errors. This reuse of fingers was demonstrated in two other ways, both of which fall along the first developmental path. A couple of Korean children counted all by unfolding fingers for the first addend while counting them and then folding some of those same fingers to make the second addend while counting them; this unfolding and folding were then repeated while counting all. A couple of children also made one addend on one hand by unfolding and then folding fingers (e.g., made 7 by unfolding 5 fingers and folding 2), and the other addend on the other hand by unfolding 5 and folding 3 fingers, and then stated the sum as *ten* (the 5 fingers unfolded on each hand) *five* (the sum of the 2 and 3 folded fingers).

Some Korean children did show methods from the first path. The examples of reusing fingers just described both use addends in this nonsuccessive way. A few Korean children also counted on by the first method, saying the sum words for the second addend. Their method of keeping track of the second addend was usually not evident, but either folded or unfolded finger patterns could have been used. Ascertaining whether some children follow the whole first developmental path or only adopt some steps within it (e.g., count on before learning the over-ten method) requires more research.

In Japan many first-grade teachers use tiles that show the numbers 6 through 9 as $5 + 1, 5 + 2, 5 + 3$, and $5 + 4$ (Hatano, 1982), just as the one-handed finger patterns do and as the two-handed finger patterns can do if one thinks of the first hand as 5 (Neuman, 1987, reported that Swedish children do think of 6 as the 5 finger plus 1 more finger, 7 as the 5 finger plus 2 more fingers, and the 9 finger as 1 finger less than the *ten* finger). These tiles support the over-ten method, and the over-ten method is taught to all Japanese children (or at least appears in all Japanese textbooks; Fuson, Stigler, & Bartsch, 1988).

Stucturing Sums Around Ten

These paths have different advantages and disadvantages for supporting methods of finding sums that are structured around ten (such methods are advantageous for multidigit addition and subtraction as well as being effective general methods). The first path entails no difficulty in one's finding sums over ten, but its usual application by children in the United States is in a unitary sequence counting on in which ten plays no special role: The sum count moves across ten without marking ten with the fingers or with the words, because the English language moves across ten without showing any strong difference in the words below and above it. Sequence counting on could support an over-ten method if the finger pattern for the second addend was separated into two parts: the words counted up to ten and the words over ten. Thus in $8 + 6$, for example, fingers on one hand could be raised for the words nine and *ten*, and fingers on the other hand could be raised for the words *eleven, twelve, thirteen, fourteen,* showing a total of 6 fingers, but separated into the two that made ten and the four that make

14 (i.e., ten four). Using an English version of Chinese words would also structure sequence counting on around ten: As the six fingers go up in 8 + 6, the words would say *eight, nine, ten, ten one, ten two, ten three, ten four* (14), thus showing the two fingers to make ten and saying the four fingers over ten. In the second path, the need to reuse fingers on both hands for sums between 10 and 19 has already been discussed. Such a reuse can support an over-ten method because the fingers for the first 10 count names allow a child to learn the complements to ten visually and kinesthetically, and the second addend is broken into the two needed parts visually (see Table 15.3). The number line, as used in schools, is always taught as a unitary procedure, in which the second addend jumps to make ten and the jumps over ten are not differentiated, but the number line could potentially be used to support an over-ten method. Both children and teachers show considerable difficulty with a number line, using it as a count model (and, thus, sometimes ending up with answers off by 1) rather than as the measuring model it actually is: Each number is shown by the length from 0, not by the number itself. A better support for the second path might be a number list of the written numerals (a count model like the Swedish row of finger numbers), in which the numerals over 10 were written in a different color to make the shift more salient (the numerals do mark the different structure before and after ten better than do English words). Some children might temporarily show the same use of count meanings of the numerals unconnected to the cardinal meanings seen in Swedish children (i.e., the numeral 4 would be the only meaning for *four* rather than *four* also having the cardinal meaning of the first four numerals), but they would presumably move on to connect the count and cardinal meanings.

An alternative method of structuring addition by ten could be carried out by using the first method of putting each addend on a separate hand if each addend over 5 is presented on one hand as a pattern involving 5 (e.g., 7 = 5 + 2). For two such numbers, their sum is easily found by combining the two fives to make ten and combining the parts of each over 5 to make the *x* in *ten x* (in Asian words). The use of this method by two Korean children was described earlier. Two first graders in the United States who learned one-handed finger patterns in one of the first author's instructional studies also invented the same approach by putting one number on each hand: 7 + 8 would be the thumb plus two fingers on one hand touching the desk (7) and the thumb plus three fingers on the other hand touching the desk (8), so the two thumbs made ten (5 + 5 = 10) and the 2 + 3 fingers down made 5, for a sum of 15. Roman numerals also support this 5-based approach, with 7 + 8 = VII + VIII = XV. The Japanese tiles have this five sub-base and therefore can also support this method.

Subtraction

Subtraction can be carried out in all three paths by both forward (adding up or counting up) and backward (taking away or counting down) methods. The drawings in Table 15.3 can be interpreted as showing the forward subtraction procedures for each path: In each drawing the first addend and the sum are known, and the second addend is the unknown number to be found. For the top drawings this means that the order of the counts is reversed; for the lower drawings, the feedback loop governing the stopping of the counting depends on the sum word or the sum finger pattern being reached, and the unknown addend is then read from the second addend words or fingers. There is insufficient space here to present and discuss backward procedures along each path. These backward procedures for the first and second paths are more difficult than are the forward procedures, because they require counting backward (which is much more difficult than is counting forward; Fuson et al., 1982) and because two alternative counting-down procedures can be carried out and children sometimes confuse them (e.g., Steinberg, 1984). The backward procedure for the third path is not so difficult because it is supported just by looking at the fingers; the most difficult part of the procedure (the separation of the second addend) involves forward rather than backward thinking. For example, to carry out the down-over-ten method that is the reverse of the addition over-ten method for $14 - 6$, one just makes "ten four" on the hands, looks at the folded four fingers, thinks of how much more makes 6 (an additive procedure), and then takes that away from ten by folding down two fingers from ten unfolded fingers or by thinking of the complement of 2. Korean children also use a take-from-ten method in which the known addend is subtracted from ten and the difference is added to the amount over ten: $13 - 6$ (ten three minus six) is thought of as ten minus six is four plus the three is seven (Fuson & Kwon, in press-a).

ADDITION AND SUBTRACTION
OF MULTIDIGIT NUMBERS

Addition and subtraction of multidigit numbers requires that the same values be added to each other or subtracted from each other. Thus, to add 2,489 and 3,765, the thousands are added to each other, the hundreds are added to each other, the tens are added to each other, and the ones are added to each other. When there are too many of a given value, 10 of them must be given over (or carried, or traded, or regrouped) to the next larger value; when there are not enough of a given value to subtract from, 10 of them must be given over from the next larger value (or borrowed, or traded, or regrouped) to make enough to subtract. There is nothing explicit in the written multidigit numerals either to show the values, i.e., to show what should be added to or subtracted from each other, or to show that 10 must be given over sometimes. Therefore, understanding how to add and subtract multidigit numbers must be supported in some way.

Systems of number words vary in the extent to which they support these two different understandings crucial to understanding multidigit addition and subtraction. Regular named-value systems support these understandings, while irregular systems do not. For example, the Dioula language used in West Africa is a regular named-value language that names tens, and adult unschooled Dioula merchants add two-digit numbers mentally by adding the tens, then adding the ones (often by an over-ten method), and then adding the ones sum to the tens sum (Ginsburg, Posner, & Russell, 1981a). Unschooled Oksapmin adult store owners adapted their unitary body parts counting system to early Austalian currency that used 20 shillings to the pound by counting up to 20 (the inner elbow on the second side of the body) and then beginning the count again at 1; with this base-20 system, pound and shilling amounts could be added or subtracted by adding the shillings within this 20-value and then adding the pounds (Saxe, 1982).

Asian named-value systems, which are regular, make it very easy to see that one adds and subtracts like values. They also support transferring 10 when there are too many or not enough because sums over 10 are actually said as tens and ones. Thus, when adding 2,489 + 3,765, 9 + 5 is *ten four,* which indicates that there are 4 ones left and 1 ten to be added to the other tens. We found, in interviewing Korean second and third graders (Fuson & Kwon, in press-b), that some of them used named-value conceptual structures for the tens (and also for the hundreds) so that, in 489 + 765, a child would say, "eight tens plus six tens is hundred four ten"[4] (found perhaps by using an over-ten analogue within the tens: eight tens plus two more tens from the six tens make one hundred and the four tens left from the six tens make one hundred four tens). Other Korean children used conceptual structures in which the numbers in each column were said without values, but the values were kept in mind and used for correct giving of tens when a sum was greater than 10 or a value of a minuend needed to be larger in order to subtract from it: In such a case a child said, "eight plus six is ten four" and wrote down the four and traded the ten over to the next column to the left. Some children used mixed conceptual structures within the same sum ("eight plus six is hundred four ten"), using or not using the named-values very freely. For both addition and subtraction, the Korean children showed remarkable accuracy and could explain and justify their procedures. For example, in sharp contrast to children in the United States, many of whom say that 1 written at the top of an addition problem to show a carried ten or hundred is a one (rather than saying it is a ten or a hundred), every Korean child said that the 1 written in the tens column was a ten, and only one Korean child said that the 1 written in the hundreds column was a one. Thus, these Korean children were aware of and used the different values of the numerals when they added and subtracted multidigit numbers, whereas many children in the United States do not show such awareness.

Children in the United States have great difficulties in learning place value

---

[4]There are no singulars or plurals in the Korean language, and Koreans say only *hundred,* and not *one hundred.*

(i.e., learning the values of the written numerals and how these values relate to the English words) and in carrying out multidigit addition and subtraction accurately (much of this evidence is reviewed in Fuson, 1990). Many build neither named-value conceptual structures for the English words nor positional base-ten conceptual structures for the written numerals. Either of these are conceptual structures adequate to support understanding of multidigit addition and subtraction. Differences between named-value systems of words, including most European and Asian languages, and the positional base-ten system of written numerals used in most countries are discussed in Fuson (1990). Many children in the United States instead construct inadequate conceptual structures for written multidigit numerals in which numerals are interpreted as concatenated single digits: numbers from 1 through 9 placed adjacent to each other. These children make many errors in multidigit addition and subtraction that reflect this inadequate single-digit conceptual structure (see Fuson, 1990). French-speaking Canadian children show many similar difficulties with place value and multidigit addition and subtraction (Bednarz & Dufour-Janvier, 1986; Bednarz & Janvier, 1982).

The irregularities in the English language and characteristics of the mathematics curriculum in the United States seem to contribute to the failure to construct adequate conceptual structures and adequate multidigit procedures. First, most children in the United States find sums over 10 by using unitary conceptual structures that do not involve tens and ones. Thus, when they get too many in a given column, neither the English words for the sum nor their conceptual structures for this sum suggest giving over the ten to the tens column: for 489 + 875, a child would find or know 9 + 5 to be *fourteen* but this would not be thought of as a ten and four ones. Such children have to switch between using unitary conceptual structures for finding sums over 10 to named-value tens and ones structures to trade when there are too many. This switch is exemplified by the step invented by first graders who had used base-ten blocks (see further on) to understand multidigit addition (this step was also used by many second graders who were shown it in a study the following year, Fuson & Briars, 1990). When these children attempted a problem without the blocks, they would add a column (by using a known fact or one-handed finger patterns to count on) to find the sum (e.g., "eight plus six is fourteen"), and then they would write this sum (14) out to the side by using their pattern relationship between 2-digit numerals and counting words, look at the written 14 as a tens and ones structure because they knew they had to break the 14 down into a ten and the left-over ones in order to trade the ten, and then write the 4 in the ones column and write the 1 ten in the tens column. They could explain what they were doing and used named-value conceptual structures for multidigit addition and subtraction, but they needed the written support of the numerals to switch from their unitary meaning of the sum word *fourteen* to a tens and ones structure for this word (they did not automatically know that fourteen meant 1 ten and 4 ones). In contrast, regular Asian languages automatically provide sums over 10 in a tens and ones structure, so children speaking these languages either do not have to switch meanings as they add or the switch is a very easy one.

Second, the curriculum in the United States gives children only 2-digit addition problems with no trades for a long time. The English language cannot support named-value meanings for these problems because the words are irregular for the tens. Furthermore, because no trades are required, the tens meaning of the digits on the left is not evident: they look and act like single digits that are added to and subtracted from each other rather than looking or acting like tens and ones values. These children may not add or subtract 3-digit numbers until the third grade and 4-digit numbers until the fourth grade (Fuson, Stigler, & Bartsch, 1988), so the support of the regular named-value English words for hundreds and thousands is not available until quite late. Finally, the support provided in textbooks is insufficient for children to construct named-value conceptual structures: Multidigit addition and subtraction is approached as a rule-based manipulation of written digits in most textbooks (Fuson, in press-a).

English-speaking children can construct adequate conceptual structures that enable them to understand multidigit addition and subtraction and carry out these operations accurately and meaningfully. Base-Ten blocks[5] (Dienes, 1960) show the values of the English words and of the positions of the written numerals. Second graders of all ability levels who linked procedures with the blocks tightly to procedures with the written numerals learned to add and subtract 4-digit numbers, could justify their procedures (e.g., they never said that a traded-over 1 was a one but said its actual value), and many generalized these procedures to addition and subtraction of 10-digit numbers (Fuson, 1986a; Fuson & Briars, 1990).

The unitary sequence methods used to find single-digit sums and differences can be extended to find 2-digit sums and differences: One can count up or count down by ones to find 26 + 37, and many children initially do this even though it is time-consuming. One can also structure such counting by constructing tens units within the counting, and can then count on, count up, and count down by tens and ones (e.g., 47 + 35 is 47, 57, 67, 77, 78, 79, 80, 81, 82 or, separating the values, 40, 50, 60, 70, 77, 78, 79, 80, 81, 82). Many children invent such counting procedures to solve two-digit sums or differences not presented in vertical form. Almost all invented procedures reported in the literature involve such sequence procedures (Labinowicz, 1985). However, such procedures are difficult for many children, and their counterparts for three- and four-digit numbers are difficult, because these sequence procedures do not generalize well to general multidigit addition and subtraction. Therefore, educators in the United States and Europe, who use languages that are irregular for two-digit numbers, face a choice: (a) spend time allowing children to construct ten-unit items (count-

---

[5]A ones block is a cubic centimeter, a tens block is 1 cm × 1 cm × 10 cm, a hundreds block is 1 cm × 10 cm × 10 cm, and a thousands block is 10 cm × 10 cm × 10 cm.

ing up and down by tens) within their sequence conceptual structures and use these for solving two-digit addition and subtraction; later, shift to some other support for named-value conceptual structures to add three-digit and four-digit and larger numbers in a meaningful way; or (b) move directly to supporting children's construction of named-value conceptual structures for three-digit and/or four-digit numbers by using perceptual multiunit supports such as base-ten blocks. The former seems to be done in the Netherlands: Second graders use only mental methods of adding and subtracting two-digit numbers, and written multidigit addition and subtraction and three-digit numbers are delayed until third grade (at least as reported by Beihuizen, 1985). Some U.S. educators advocate supporting counting approaches for two-digit numbers, even if this means delaying two-digit subtraction until third grade, because such subtraction procedures are difficult for many second graders (e.g., C. K. Kamii, 1989). The classroom base-ten block research by Fuson (1986a; Fuson & Briars, 1990) suggests that alternative (b) leads to accelerated performance compared to alternative (a), similar to that shown by children in Asian countries (i.e., strong multidigit competence for four-digit numbers in second graders). These alternative educational paths will probably continue to be debated, and it will be interesting to compare the paths for children in different countries.

Different mental and written algorithms (or repetitive procedures) are used to add and subtract multidigit numbers in different countries. Some of these support conceptual understanding better than others, and some are more efficient or easier to carry out. For example, in the base-ten block studies (Fuson, 1986a; Fuson & Briars, 1990), a subtraction algorithm was used in which any necessary trading was done for all columns first, followed by single-digit subtraction for each column; this eliminated the need to shift back and forth between a named-value conceptual structure for trading and a unitary conceptual structure for the single-digit subtraction (done by counting up from the known addend to the known sum; Fuson, 1986b; Fuson & Willis, 1988). Korean children learn a written subtraction algorithm in which they write a *10* above any column that requires a ten traded over to subtract; this written *10* supports both types of single-digit subtraction methods structured around 10 (Fuson & Kwon, in press-b). However, little research exists in English that compares children's understanding using different algorithms and even less that relates aspects of an algorithm to aspects of English number words that may make a given algorithm easier or harder for children to understand.

OTHER CULTURAL SUPPORTS
FOR ADDITION AND SUBTRACTION

It is clear that systems of number words that are regular and that name the values used in the system support, in many different ways, the construction of concepts of number and facilitate the learning of addition and subtraction. Cultures also provide other experiences that can support or interfere with the construction of number concepts structured around 10 and around multiples of 10. Most countries in the world use the metric system, which provides many examples of 1-for-10 exchanges of value within and between different kinds of measures. Some countries have systems of money that have regular 1-for-10 exchanges. A traditional calculator based on 10—the abacus—has had widespread use in many Asian countries and in the Soviet Union. The United States has none of these supports: the English system of measure, with its many irregular, non-10 trades is still used, and the system of money has irregular intrusions of nickels and quarters (5¢ & 25¢) and of $20 and $50, which interfere with the tens and ones structure within the monetary system. Therefore, children in the United States need considerable support from materials and special activities within the classroom in order to construct multiunit named-value or base-10 positional conceptual structures, and they often do not get that necessary assistance. Children in other countries in North, Central, and South America and in Europe who speak one of the irregular European systems of number words do at least have the support of the metric system, but the systems of money in these countries vary in how much they are structured only by tens. Whether and how various countries choose to attempt to redress the linguistic disadvantage of their irregular number words is an interesting question for future comparative research.

CONCLUSION

This chapter has focused heavily on various consequences of the difference between the regular named-value Asian number words and the irregular European number words. Of course, the superiority in mathematical performance of Japanese and Chinese children over children in the United States (e.g., Stigler, Lee & Stevenson, 1990; Stigler & Perry, 1988) is due to many factors other than the systems of number words: more time spent in mathematics learning; higher teacher status; more activities in the classroom using particular concrete materials; more focus on understanding, explanation, and alternative solution procedures; and more emphasis on the role of effort in childrens', and parents', and teachers' views of mathematics learning (see Fischer, 1991, for a review). Although some of these cultural differences may be relatively difficult to change, providing support to compensate for the irregularities in English number words may be easier, and may result in considerable increases in children's understanding of numbers and of addition and subtraction. Our work with counting on and counting up with one-handed finger patterns and with base-ten blocks indicates that children in the United States can perform considerably more like Asian children, at least in single-digit and multidigit addition and subtraction situations.

Three different developmental paths through single-digit addition and subtraction have been identified here. These paths seem to be supported by different uses of fingers to show addition and subtraction. These different uses of fingers may then lead to different addition procedures even when the number-word sequences are similar (as English and Swedish are). Therefore, understanding how children in a given culture construct concepts of, and procedures for, addition and subtraction may require knowing how that culture uses fingers to show numbers, as well as knowing the structure of its number-word sequence. Exploring how teaching children finger or number-word practices that support their construction of useful concepts and procedures also seems likely to prove fruitful.

IV DIFFICULTIES AND REMEDIATION

16 Remedying Common Counting Difficulties

Arthur J. Baroody
University of Illinois at Urbana-Champaign

Counting is the basis of much of young children's mathematics. The development of oral counting skills begins very early—in some cases even before a child is two (Baroody & Price, 1983; Fuson, 1988; Fuson & Hall, 1983; Gelman & Gallistel, 1978; Wagner & Walters, 1982). At first, counting may be nothing more than a "sing-song" (Ginsburg, 1982)—a pattern of sounds uttered without any apparent purpose. In time, however, children extend this skill to the task of object counting. Moreover, children count or use their mental representation of the number sequence to compare collections or numbers. Difficulties with counting skills can seriously hamper a child's mathematical progress in school. It is important, then, to identify and remedy young children's counting difficulties quickly. This chapter focuses on the sources of common difficulties and some possible remedies in three areas: oral counting, object counting, and numerical comparison.

ORAL COUNTING

Children may first learn the *forward sequence* (*one, two, three* . . .) as a sound string, like *onetwothree* (Fuson, 1988), not realizing that the number sequence is composed of separate words. Children pass quickly, however, from this *string* level to the *unbreakable-list level,* where they differentiate among the number words. Even so, they cannot begin counting from any point in the number sequence other than one and must recite the whole sequence to produce a particular number word. Only later do children attain the *breakable-list level,* in which they can count from an arbitrary point within the sequence. Later still, children achieve the *bidirectional-chain level,* where they can proceed backward as well as forward in the number sequence.

As children become familiar with the number sequence, they can master *next-term* skills, which involve specifying the term after or before a given number. They can automatically cite the term after a given number at the breakable chain level and the term before a given number at the bidirectional chain level. Once children can cite the term before a given number, they can engage in *counting backward.*

Forward Sequence

Difficulties.   At first, children may not realize that numbers follow a particular order. It seems, though, that they quickly sense this and set about mastering more and more of their culture's standard sequence of terms (Baroody, 1987b; Fuson, 1988). Children throughout the world learn the first 10 or so arbitrary number terms by rote memorization. They typically learn the rest of the number sequence to 100 by discovering patterns (e.g., Ginsburg, 1982). The ease with which this can be done varies greatly from language to language. Oriental languages such as Korean (see Table 16.1) are highly regular, in that they correspond to a written base-10 system (e.g., *twelve* is said *ten* and *two, twenty* is *two tens, fifty-three* is *five tens and three*).

Other languages vary in their regularity and in the extent to which they correspond to the written base-10 system. In English, for example, the underlying base-10 nature of the numbering system is disguised by terms such as *eleven* and *twelve.* Moreover, the teen terms after *twelve* are not entirely regular. Unlike other teen terms, *thirteen* and *fifteen* break with the pattern of combining a single-digit term with *-teen* (e.g., *six + teen = sixteen*). Not surprisingly, they are the most frequently missed teen terms by English-speaking children just entering school or those with learning difficulties (e.g., Baroody, 1986b; Fuson, 1988; Siegler & Robinson, 1982).

In English, deciphering patterns is further complicated by the fact that the pattern for multidigit numbers beyond the teens changes (Fuson, in press-c). Instead of combining a single-digit term with a decade-identifying term, as is the case with the teens, the terms beyond *nineteen* do the opposite: They combine a decade term with a single-digit term (e.g., *twenty + three*). To complicate matters even more, the pattern of the decade terms is not entirely regular: Except for *ten,* the decade terms are designated by the suffix *-ty.* Similar to the teens, *forty* and *sixty* to *ninety* are formed by the straightforward rule: Combine a single-digit term with *-ty. Twenty, thirty,* and *fifty* are irregular versions of this rule.

To count to 100, children need to understand several things about the number sequence. First, they need to understand, at least implicitly, that *nine* signals a transition (Baroody, 1989). For example, they need to realize that *nineteen* signals the end of the teens and the beginning of a new series. Otherwise, they make

TABLE 16.1
A Comparison of Two Oral Count Systems

Arabic Numeral	English Count	Korean Count*
1	One	Eel
2	Two	Ee
3	Three	Sahm
4	Four	Sah
5	Five	Oh
6	Six	Yook
7	Seven	Chil
8	Eight	Pal
9	Nine	Goo
10	Ten	Sip
11	Eleven	Sip-eel
12	Twelve	Sip-ee
13	Thirteen	Sip-sahm
14	Fourteen	Sip-sah
15	Fifteen	Sip-oh
•	•	•
•	•	•
•	•	•
•	•	•
19	Nineteen	Sip-goo
20	Twenty	Ee-sip
21	Twenty-one	Ee-sip-eel
•	•	•
•	•	•
•	•	•
30	Thirty	Sahm-sip
40	Forty	Sah-sip
50	Fifty	Oh-sip
•	•	•
•	•	•
•	•	•
90	Ninety	Goo-sip

*According to Song and Ginsburg (1988), Koreans have two count systems. The one delineated above is highly regular and is the main system employed in formal mathematics instruction. A second system is more irregular and is usually learned informally during the preschool years or in kindergarten and first grade.

errors like that of 4-year-old Arianne: ". . . eighteen, nineteen, *ten-teen.*" They also need to know the next decade (or *transition*) term (e.g., *twenty* follows *nineteen*), which is complicated by the irregularities already noted. Moreover, they need to realize that the number sequence is a repetitive system. That is, they need to appreciate the rule that specifies that the *twenties* and subsequent series are generated by combining the decade term with, in turn, each term in the single-digit sequence. For example, 4-year-old Alexi could count to *twenty* but did not know what came next. After his father modeled the *twenty, twenty-one* link a number of times over a 2–week period with little apparent effect, Alexi suddenly counted up to *twenty-nine*.

Instruction.   Regular exposure to, and practice of, the rote portion of the sequence is important for mastery. Stories and rhymes are entertaining ways of cultivating a familiarity with the count sequence to *ten* or *twelve* (e.g., see Baroody & Hank, 1990). Many children find that counting with objects is more interesting than oral counting alone (e.g., Fuson & Hall, 1983). Games that involve counting objects, then, can provide oral-counting practice that is meaningful and interesting. Children may enjoy error-detection games, where they have to spot another's mistake (e.g., a hand puppet's count of "one, two, three, five"). All of these activities can help reinforce a child's use of the standard sequence. The error-detection activity is particularly well-suited for encouraging a discussion of the fact that numbers follow a particular order.

For fostering learning beyond the rote portion of the number sequence, instruction should focus on encouraging children to discern patterns: *Nine* always ends a series, the decade sequence *ten* to *ninety* parallels the *one* to *nine* sequence, and new series (other than the teens) consist of the decade combined with the *one* to *nine* sequence. A number chart in which the 0 and the decades begin each row can be used to highlight such patterns (Spitzer, 1954). Children can, for example, color all the squares in which a 9 appears in the ones place and then discuss the location of these colored squares: that they always appear at the end of a series, right before the next decade.

Exceptions to rules, such as *fifteen* in English, may require special attention. One interesting way to work on both patterns and exceptions is a modified version of the error-detection activity. In this version, the child is given only a sample of the number sequence to evaluate (e.g., "Is counting 'seventeen, eighteen, nineteen, *tenteen*' right or wrong?"; "Is counting 'ten, eleven, twelve *threeteen,* fourteen' right or wrong?").

Recording children's oral counts on a tape recorder can be used to help them master both the rote and pattern-governed portions of the number sequence. Listening to the tape can provide an opportunity to note and correct errors. Moreover, the tape recorder can be a motivational tool. Some children may enjoy using or learning to operate a tape recorder and may be naturally interested in hearing themselves on it.

Next Term

Difficulties.   When asked what follows a given number, children initially have to count from *one* to determine an answer (e.g., Fuson & Hall, 1983). For "What comes right after *six*?"), for example, they may have to count: "One, two, three, four, five, six, *seven.*" After the sequence becomes highly familiar, children can immediately cite the term after a number without a "running start" (counting from *one*). For example, when asked what number comes after *seven,* 3-year-old Alison quickly replied, *"Eight."* Before they turn 6, most children can efficiently cite the term after a number up to *nineteen* or even *twenty-eight* (Fuson et al., 1982).

Citing the term before a number is more difficult, because one has to operate on the number-sequence representation in the direction opposite the one in which the sequence was learned. Moreover, the word *before* may be relatively unfamiliar to children and interpreted as *after* (cf. Donaldson & Balfour, 1968).

Instruction. First ensure that children can count to a term with some ease. If necessary, introduce the term-after-a-number skill by giving a child a running start (e.g., "When we count, we say, 'one, two, three, four, five,' and then comes . . . ?" As the child catches on, keep shortening the running start (e.g., "Three, four, five, and then comes . . . ?") until it is eliminated altogether (e.g., "When we count, we say, 'five' and then comes . . . ?"). Then have the child practice citing the next term after a number until it is automatic.

A variety of games can provide entertaining practice (e.g., see Baroody, 1987b; 1989; Bley & Thornton, 1981; Wynroth, 1986). For example, Number-After Dominoes (Wynroth, 1986) is played like dominoes except that the added domino must be the number after the end item, rather than the same number. This is a good game for introducing the term-after-a-number skill, because counting the end domino gives a child a running start (e.g., "The end domino has one, two, three, four dots, so I've got to look for a five"). An error-detection game is also useful for practicing this skill.

Games and activities that use a number list are useful for children who can read numerals. In the most basic version, the teacher points to a number and a child has to cite the term after it. Note that the number list can be used to give the child a running start. An intermediate version entails using a separate card for each numeral and placing all but, say, three cards face down in order. The child is then encouraged to use these three numbers as a (shortened) running start to identify the next (face-down) card. In the advanced version, all the cards but one are turned over and the child has to state the next term after the number shown. Note that this version does not clue the child with a running start.

For children who have not mastered the term-before-a-number skill, use a representation of the number sequence (e.g., a number list) to show that a number has two neighbors: one that comes before and one that comes after. For example, point to 5 and ask how many neighbors *five* has and where they are in respect to *five.* Help children summarize the facts that *four* is the term before *five* and *six* is the term after *five.* By contrasting the relatively unfamiliar term *before* with the relatively familiar term *after,* children should better be able to distinguish between the two terms and attach an accurate meaning to the term *before.* The games and activities used to foster the term-after-a-number skill can be adapted to practice the term-before-a-number skill. For example, Number-

After Dominoes can, by a simple change of the rules, become Number-Before Dominoes.

Counting Backward

Difficulties.   Some children may learn to count backwards from 10 by rote as a result of repeated exposure to this sequence (e.g., from children's television programs like Sesame Street or from televised space shots). Even so, they may not be able to count backward from other numbers, like *nine*. Once children can cite the term before a number, the stage is set for the general skill of counting backward. Counting backward from a number beyond 10 is relatively difficult because, in part, the teen portion of the sequence is less familiar to children than the sequence to 10 (Baroody, 1987b).

Instruction.   First, ensure that the more basic forward sequence and next-term skills are automatic. Initially, have the child count backward with a number list present. Once the child has an idea of what the count-backward task entails, use only a partially visible number list as a cue. This can be done with the activity "Peek." Insert a 1-to-10 number list into a sheath left-end first so that only the 10 on the number list shows. Before uncovering the next number, ask the child to predict what comes next when you count backward. Note that this activity can also be used to practice the term-before-a-number skill. Proceed in this manner until you reach 1. As soon as the child is ready, remove prompts like the number list. Do not have the child count backward starting with numbers larger than 10 until he or she can do so easily starting with numbers up to 10.

OBJECT COUNTING

Object counting includes *enumeration,* which entails labeling an existing set (e.g., given six pennies, a child identifies how many pennies there are) and *production,* which entails creating a set (e.g., asked to get six pennies, a child counts out a set of six from a pile of pennies). Both enumeration and production entail understanding *cardinality principles:* the rules governing the naming of sets with numbers. Object-counting skills cannot develop until children achieve the unbreakable-list level of counting.

Enumeration

Difficulties.   To enumerate collections of objects correctly, children must be able to generate the correct number sequence with ease. They must understand— at lest implicitly—the one-to-one principle: One and only one number-sequence term (tag) is applied to each object in the collection. One-for-one counting also requires keeping track of counted and uncounted objects, so that each object is, in fact, tagged once and only once.

There are three basic kinds of enumeration errors (Gelman & Gallistel, 1978):

1. If children do not know the correct number sequence, they will make *sequence errors* when counting objects. For example, a child may tag three blocks: "One, two, ten."

2. *Coordination errors* involve a breakdown between mouth and eyes: a difficulty coordinating, in a one-to-one fashion, the processes of saying the number sequence (oral counting) and indicating to which object in a collection the tag applies (pointing). Pointing can be done with the eyes or with the aid of, say, a finger. Children who have not constructed a one-to-one principle will make no effort at one-for-one counting and may, for example, simply spew out numbers as they pass a finger over a collection. Typically though, children construct an understanding of the one-to-one principle relatively early—well before they begin kindergarten. Even so, they often have trouble executing it accurately. They may point to an object and assign it either too many tags or no tag at all. A child just learning to enumerate sets or one with learning difficulties, in particular, may have difficulty starting or stopping the oral-counting and pointing processes at the same time (Baroody, 1986b; Gelman & Gallistel, 1978). As a result, the child may point to the first item and say nothing but thereafter honor the one-to-one principle. Likewise, the child may get to the last item of a set and let several tags slip out before stopping the oral count. Children are especially prone to coordination errors when they rush their counting.

3. Although children can coordinate saying one number word for each object pointed out, they may still make *keeping-track errors*, failing to keep track of which objects have been counted and which need to be numbered and thus skip an object or count it more than once. Such errors are the most common type of enumeration error among children just starting school. Apparently, some preschoolers fail to devise effective keeping-track strategies, such as creating a separate pile for counted items (Fuson, 1988). Keeping-track errors are also more likely if a child rushes.

Enumeration difficulty is greatly influenced by the arrangement of the set and set size. For example, it is easier to keep track of objects in a line than those in a disorganized array. By the time they enter kindergarten, most children can accurately enumerate collections up to 5, even in disorganized arrays. With larger sets, they may be able to enumerate those in a linear array but have difficulty with those in a disorganized array.

Instruction.   The nature of enumeration training depends on a child's specific difficulty. If children make sequence errors, they need help in mastering the standard number sequence. Generating the number-sequence words automatically will facilitate their effort to coordinate this activity with pointing.

If children do not appear to make any effort at one-to-one counting, they need help in constructing the one-to-one principle. Begin with a pointing exercise, using a relatively easy set of objects (e.g., three blocks in a row). Have a child point once and only once to each object in the set. After the child has mastered this skill, introduce enumeration. If necessary, first say the numbers for a child while he or she points to each block. The child should then say the number sequence while pointing to the blocks.

If the child understands the one-to-one principle but has difficulty with one-for-one counting, such as starting (or stopping) the oral-counting and pointing processes simultaneously, emphasize the importance of accuracy and encourage the pupil to count slowly and carefully (e.g., Strauss & Lehtinen, 1947). This applies equally to children who make keeping-track errors.

For a child who basically uses one-for-one counting effectively and counts carefully but still makes errors, focus on keeping-track strategies. Point out that counted objects can be put in their own pile far enough away so that they are not confused with uncounted objects. For sets of objects that are fixed, start in a well-defined place, such as a corner or an end, and count in a particular direction. For pictured collections, cross out items as they are counted.

Error-detection activities can readily be adapted for enumeration training. Model correct enumeration and various enumeration errors (examples and non-examples of the one-to-one principle). Children can then evaluate the correctness of the count and, if incorrect, indicate what was wrong. For example, count the fingers on a child's hand but make sequence errors (e.g., count five fingers with, "One, two, three, nine, ten"), coordination errors (e.g., point to the first finger and say, "One, two," and then complete the count with, "Three, four, five, six"), or keeping-track errors (e.g., skip a finger or go back and count a finger a second time). Such exercises make an excellent vehicle for pointing out and discussing the one-to-one principle underlying enumeration and how to implement this principle correctly.

Enumeration practice can be accomplished with numerous games (including Number-After Dominoes already described). For example, Animal Spots (Wynroth, 1986) requires players to throw a die with 0 to 5 dots to determine how many pegs ("spots") they can take for their leopard or giraffe (an animal figure cut out of wood with holes drilled for pegs). (The game can also be played with 0- to 10-dot cards.) The first child to fill his or her animal with spots is the winner. Any board game that uses a die to determine the number of spaces players move can provide enumeration practice as well.

The size and complexity of the dot arrangement on the die can be varied according to children's readiness. For very young children just beginning to master enumeration, use a linear array of dots. This minimizes the demands of keeping track of the starting point and which items have already been counted (as long as a child starts at one end and counts in one direction). With somewhat more experienced counters, arrange the dots in patterns like this:

These arrangements require some keeping-track effort. For relatively advanced children, use a die with irregular arrays that require more complex keeping-track strategies.

Cardinality Principles

Difficulties. Early on, children learn that enumeration tells how many objects are in a collection (the cardinal designation of the collection). Typically, children learn how to respond to "How many?" questions very quickly. To indicate how many they have counted, preschoolers soon learn that they do not have to repeat the whole count (e.g., "One, two, three, four, five" for a set of five pennies) but need only repeat the last term of the enumeration process (e.g., "*five*"). This shortcut is called the *cardinality principle* (Gelman & Gallistel, 1978; Schaeffer, Eggleston, & Scott, 1974).

An understanding of cardinality does not stop with mastering the cardinality principle. A deeper sense of cardinality requires understanding the *identity-conservation principle:* that the number in a set remains the same even though its appearance changes (Elkind, 1967). For example, a set designated as *five* continues to have the same number even though it is lengthened and looks "bigger."

With counting experience, children discover another important aspect of cardinality: As long as the one-to-one principle is observed, a collection can be enumerated in any order, and its cardinal designation will not change: For example, you can count a row of objects from left to right or from right to left, and the outcome is the same. This property of the numbering process is called the *order-irrelevance principle.*

Nearly all children spontaneously construct the cardinality and identity-conservation principles through their everyday counting activities. Indeed, even the order-irrelevance principle, which is a relatively sophisticated concept (Baroody, 1984), is typically acquired before children enter kindergarten (Gelman & Gallistel, 1978; Gelman & Meck, 1986). Some preschoolers, however, do not have the informal experiences that support such discoveries. Such children need intensive intervention and regular practice with a variety of counting activities.

Instruction. Before introducing the cardinality principle, first ensure that a child can count orally to at least *five* and has some appreciation of the one-to-one principle. Examples and non-examples (correct and incorrect applications) of the cardinality principle can be demonstrated and discussed by using an error-detection game. The Hidden-Stars Game (Baroody, 1989) is another high interest teaching device. To introduce the game, model the principle by counting, say, two stars pasted on a 3 × 5-inch card ("one, two") and then announce, "So there are *two* stars." Next, turn the card over and ask, "How many stars am I hiding?"

If the child seems confused or indicates none, ask, "How many stars did I count?" If the child still does not respond correctly, uncover the card, count the stars and note, "See, there are two stars." Afterward, have a child count a different small collection and ask, "How many stars did you count?" Then cover this collection and ask, "How many stars am I hiding?" (or "How many stars did you count?"). This exercise will be sufficient for most children to master the cardinality principle. If the child does not learn the principle quickly, continue the modeling-and-practice procedure in conjunction with pattern-recognition activities involving collections of one to three items. Provide the child with many opportunities to enumerate collections—particularly small ones.

Instruction on the identity-conservation and order-irrelevance principles should not begin until children understand the cardinality principle. *Mathematics Their Way* (Baratta-Lorton, 1976) has a number of activities that help children construct these number-invariance concepts. For example, in Spill the Beans, a number of beans are counted, placed in a bag, and passed around a circle of children. The child holding the bag when a bell rings, spills out the contents of the bag. The children are then asked to predict how many beans there are and to count the set to check their predictions. This process is repeated several times to demonstrate that the number of items is always the same despite the different configurations.

It may be helpful to have a child count a collection and to ask questions, such as, "Now, if I rearrange these things into another shape, will there be the same number of things?" or "Do you think you will get the same number if you count the other way?" An error-detection activity can provide an opportunity to illustrate and discuss valid and invalid applications of the identity-conservation principle or the order-irrelevance principle. For example, children can watch a puppet count a collection of five correctly in one direction, surreptitiously count it in the opposite direction, and conclude there are now four (or six) items. A discussion can bring out that both counts of the collection should be the same.

Production

Difficulties.   Preschool children also learn to count out (produce) a specified number of objects from a group of objects. Production of a given number is more difficult than labeling an existing set (enumeration), because it requires the child to remember how many objects have been requested and to stop counting when that many objects have been reached (Resnick & Ford, 1981).

A common error, especially among very young children, is continuing to count out objects even after the specified amount has been reached (Resnick & Ford, 1981). For example, given a pile of 10 pennies and asked to count 5, a child may simply count all the pennies available. Children make such "no-stop" errors because (a) they do not understand the task (i.e., that they are supposed to stop at the requested amount); (b) they forget the requested amount; or (c) they forget to stop at the requested number. Another error that may occur is counting out an incorrect number of items but tagging the last item with the requested number (Baroody, 1986b; Wagner & Walters, 1982). For example, asked to count out five pennies, Brian—a primary-grade student classified as mentally handicapped—tagged three pennies "One, two, five." Children make such end-with-the-requested-number errors because they (a) do not understand the task, (b) do not know the standard sequence, or (c) do not care to make the effort to complete the production process. The latter can be checked by asking the child to take a specified number of highly desired items to keep.

Less serious errors include minor errors in counting out objects in a one-to-one fashion or in keeping track of counted items and those still available to count. If children do not have an efficient keeping-track strategy, they may come up with one or two too few (if counted items are recounted) or too many (if uncounted items are included in the counted pile).

Instruction.   First ensure that a child can enumerate small collections. If a child continues to make no-stop errors, ask what the requested number is. If it appears that the child is having difficulty remembering the requested amount, point out the importance of remembering the requested number and how he or she can remember the number (e.g., by rehearsing the number several times before getting involved in the counting-out process). If the child makes end-with-the-requested-number errors, efforts need to focus on encouraging the use of one-to-one counting until the requested number is reached (rather than helping the child to remember the requested amount).

With all types of errors, help the child to acquire efficient keeping track strategies. For example, when practicing the production of sets, have the child put already-counted items in a jar lid or plate to separate them from the pile of uncounted items. Again, error-detection activities can be useful in modeling and discussing correct and incorrect production procedures.

Production of sets can be practiced with a game like Animal Spots, described earlier (see Baroody, 1987b; 1989; Wynroth, 1986). After the child has counted the dots on the die, retrieving the corresponding number of pegs ("spots") from the dish of pegs is a production task. Games where a child has to move a specified number of spaces also provide practice. (In such cases, the "things" produced are the spaces moved.)

NUMERICAL RELATIONS

Unlike object-counting competencies, which involve a single collection, numerical relationships involve two (or more) collections or numbers. The concepts of equality and inequality are fundamental to understanding number and operations on number (Piaget, 1941/1952a). A *magnitude-comparison* ability—the facility to determine the larger of two collections or numbers—is an integral aspect of a number sense. For the most part, such relational knowledge develops later than object-counting concepts and seems to depend largely on counting experiences.

Equality and Inequality

Difficulties.   A primitive ability to judge the equality or inequality of two collections is based on direct perception and may be present before children can enumerate accurately. Even 2-year-olds can readily recognize whether or not two very small sets are equivalent. For example, they can *see* that ○ ○ and °○ have the "same number" but are different from ○ or ○ ○ ○ (Wagner & Walters, 1982). With collections larger than three or so, children base their judgments of equivalence on appearances. For instance, if two rows of objects have the same length, children conclude that they are equal. However, appearances can be deceiving: Although the lines at two check-out counters have the same length, this does not guarantee that there are exactly the same number of people in each.

In time, children learn that numbers can be used to compare quantities, and that counting is more reliable than depending on appearances: If two collections have the same number label, then the collections are equivalent (have the same number of objects), despite differences or changes in appearance (e.g., Gelman, 1972). Conversely, if two—even similar appearing—collections have different number labels, they are unequal. Establishing the equality or inequality of collections up to five or so is less difficult than doing so for larger collections (Klahr & Wallace, 1973; Schaeffer et al., 1974), because children generally can enumerate such collections more accurately. In arrays like the following, children are also much more likely to subitize (automatically recognize the numerical value) of small, more familiar patterns like A or B than they are larger, less familiar patterns like C or D:

A	B	C	D
○ ○	○ ○	○	○ ○ ○ ○
	○	○ ○ ○	○ ○ ○ ○
○ ○	○ ○	○ ○ ○	

Moreover, especially when comparing larger collections, children may fail to establish their equivalence because they do not think to count the collections, or because they do not want to expend the effort necessary to do so.

Children eventually learn a noncounting method for gauging same or different with collections larger than about three (Elkind, 1964; Gelman & Gallistel, 1978; Lawson, Baron, & Siegel, 1974; Zimiles, 1963). Children have little difficulty in learning a one-for-one matching method, like putting out one item for each item of an existing set. Although they readily recognize that the two rows are equivalent in number, young children still base this conclusion on appearances (the rows are equally long), not the one-to-one matching. Thus, when one of the rows is lengthened—as in a number-conservation task—they no longer believe the rows are equal, because they fail to realize that the equivalence relationship established by matching is unaffected by changes in appearances (e.g., Piaget, 1941/1952a). In time, children will count each row and conclude that the initial match still holds despite the fact that one row looks like more (e.g., Apostel, Mays, Morf, & Piaget, 1957, cited in Flavell, 1963; Green & Laxon, 1970). Eventually, they do not even have to count; it is obvious that nothing has been added or taken away, and so the initial match is "conserved" despite changes in appearance (e.g., Lawson et al., 1974). A mature concept of matching sets (number conservation) implies this last stage of logical certainty (Piaget, 1941/1952a) and represents a relatively sophisticated or abstract understanding of numerical relationships (Gelman & Gallistel, 1978).

Instruction.   First ensure that the child can efficiently enumerate collections of at least three items. Instructional efforts should then focus on how counting and numbers can play a role in comparing collections. To foster an understanding of equality and inequality, encourage the child to play with very small sets that can be readily recognized as the same and can be enumerated easily. In this way, he or she can attach number labels (e.g., *three*) to different-looking collections that are clearly equal (e.g., *three* applies to $\circ{}^{\circ}\circ$ and $\circ \, \circ \, \circ$). This can promote the understanding that it is a number label that is important in comparing collections, not appearances (e.g., von Glasersfeld, 1982). One vehicle for such instruction is the game Same Number or Different. Begin by asking the child to compare collections that are obviously the same in number (1 vs. 1, 2 vs. 2, and 3 vs. 3) or obviously different (1 vs. 6, 2 vs. 8, 3 vs. 9). Then proceed to less obvious cases (e.g., 4 vs. 4, 3 vs. 4, 4 vs. 5), which may require the child to count. Later, games such as Dominoes Same Number or Lotto Same Number are useful (e.g., see Baroody, 1987b; Wynroth, 1986). For the first game, use a variety of regular and irregular arrangements for each number—unlike the standard dominoes game, which uses one regular pattern for each number. To play the lotto game, children first blindly select a number of squares (say, three) from a pile of squares with different numbers and arrangements of dots. The pile of squares is then turned face up. From this pile, players try to find a square with the same number of dots as a square drawn earlier. Clue (see Fig. 16.1) is another game that can be used to teach a same-number concept (Carrison & Werner, 1943; Descoeudres, 1928). If necessary, explicitly point out that counting can be used to determine if two collections have the same number.

For the more abstract matching skills, instruction efforts can begin with asking the child to take out the same number of objects as in a pre-existing set. Begin with sets that naturally go together and that highlight the one-to-one correspondence (e.g., sets of plastic tea cups and saucers). Then introduce sets with no functional match (blue and white sets of blocks) or with pictured sets of objects (e.g., drawings of girls and dresses).

Some children may need help in learning how to match sets one-to-one. Some

Make up cards like that shown below.

Cover the bottom half of the Card A, show it to the child, and say: "You have to figure out how many dots I'm thinking about. Here's a clue to help you figure out just the right number of dots I'm thinking about [point to the dot that is showing]. Now [uncover the bottom half of the card], am I thinking about this many dots [point to the two dots], this many [point to the three dots], or this many [point to the one dot on the bottom half of the card]?" If the child makes no attempt to respond, point to each choice in turn and say: "Does this have the same number of dots as the clue up here [point]?" Continue in the same way with Cards B to E.

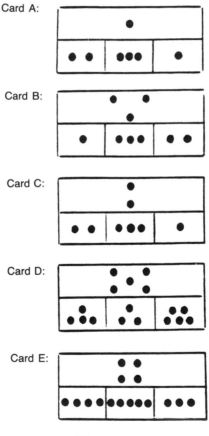

FIG. 16.1.

children will simply put out a row of the same length but with too few, for example:

sample row: O   O   O   O   O
child's row: O   O   O   O

Some put out a row of the same length, but with too many items:

sample row: O   O   O   O   O
child's row: O O O O O O O

If need be, help the child to line up the corresponding elements. Point out that to match up two collections, there must be one and only one item in one collection for each item in the other collection.

Next, give the child two sets in which the items are not arranged in any order, and have the child match the two sets to see if rows can be put in one-to-one correspondence or if one set has items left over. During the initial phase of training, children should be encouraged to check their answers by counting.

Once children can make one-to-one matches, remedial efforts can focus on helping them to see that changes in physical appearance do not affect equivalence relationships, but that addition or subtraction transformations do. (See Baroody, 1987b or Gelman & Gallistel, 1978, for a description of the Magic Show, which can be used to demonstrate these ideas.) Although direct instruction on number conservation is not necessary, it can be hastened. Begin by matching collections sufficiently small that children can easily enumerate or subitize the numbers involved. Change the appearance of one row and, if necessary, encourage a child to count each row. Later, proceed to larger collections. Children will frequently transfer number-conservation learning with small collections to larger collections (Gelman, 1982a).

Magnitude Comparisons

Difficulties.   Children quickly learn to identify as "more" the larger of two collections that differ in appearance. Many have considerable difficulty, though, determining which of two collections is "less," in part, because they rarely hear or apply the term (Donaldson & Balfour, 1968; Kaliski, 1962; Weiner, 1974).

For collections that are not obviously different, children must learn how to use counting to make comparisons. At first, they do not realize that numbers are associated with magnitude. For instance, they do not realize that *three* stands for a quantity that is more than *two*. From their experiences with small sets and numbers, children construct a magnitude-comparison rule: A number that comes after another in the number sequence is more than its predecessor (Schaeffer et al., 1974). They can then count a collection of, say, eight items and one of six and conclude that the first has more because, "*Eight* comes later when I count."

Children also use their mental representation of the number sequence to determine which of two stated or written numbers is more (or less). They can first use their magnitude-comparison rule to compare two numbers relatively far apart in the sequence. Only later can they compare numbers closer together. Those that differ by one (adjacent numbers) are especially hard for children to compare: They may know that 9 is more than 2 but may be confused about whether 9 is more than 8 (Schaeffer et al., 1974).

Children may have difficulty comparing collections or numbers, then, for several reasons: First, they may not have constructed a magnitude-comparison rule. Second, they may not think to use their magnitude-comparison rule and knowledge of the sequence. Third, they may not use this knowledge because it is not sufficiently automated and requires too much effort. Finally, they may not be sufficiently familiar with the numbers involved in the comparison to use the rule: A child may not know that *nine* comes after *eight* in the number sequence. Only after the breakable chain level of counting can a child readily determine the term-after-a-number and, thus, make such comparisons efficiently (e.g., reason that "*Nine* comes after *eight* when I count so 9 is more").

Most children entering school can use their representation of the number sequence to determine which of two adjacent numbers indicates the larger quantity for numbers up to 5, and many can do so for numbers up to 10 or more. However, children with relatively little informal mathematical experience or those with learning difficulties may not develop this number-comparison ability (Baroody, 1988). Unfortunately, this important skill is often overlooked in the evaluation and teaching of kindergartners (Baroody, 1991).

Instruction.   A child should be able to count orally and enumerate objects proficiently before beginning efforts to remedy numerical-relationship difficulties. Then ensure that the child realizes that the number sequence represents increasingly larger quantities—that a number further along in the counting sequence is more. This can be done concretely with the Staircase Activity: using interlocking blocks to build a staircase model of the number sequence and noting, for example, that the *six* step comes after and is bigger than the *five* step (Baroody, 1987b). In a similar vein, Stern (1949) suggested using a counting board into which proportionally sized blocks can be fitted.

Other games, such as Moon Invaders (Baroody, 1987b), which use interlocking blocks, can be used to compare two collections. In such activities, appearances (the length of each collection) cues which collection is larger. Counting or attaching number labels to each noticeably different collection reinforces the idea that numbers differ in magnitude. This can be fostered directly by counting the smaller collection and then noting that this number is passed when the larger collection is counted. For example, a teacher might say, "This row has one, two, three—three blocks. And this row has one, two, *three,* four, five— five blocks. We counted past three, so five [pointing to the longer row] is more than three [pointing to the shorter row]."

A game like High Die (Baroody, 1989) is an enjoyable way to practice and master small-number comparison. In this game, each player rolls an oversized 0-

to 5-dot die. The players determine the number of dots they rolled by counting or subitizing. The first two children then compare their roll. The child with the larger roll then compares his or her roll with the third child and so on. The player(s) with the largest roll scores a point.

A number of activities or games can foster reasoning out answers by counting or using number-after knowledge as well as extending comparisons to collections of larger numbers. Consider Wynroth's (1986) Cards More Than, which is essentially the card game War using cards with 1 to 10 pictured geometric shapes in irregular arrays. In this game, the players count the number of items on their drawn card to see who counts the furthest. The player with the largest draw wins the cards. If players tie for the largest draw, they draw again to break the tie. The winner is the player with the largest number (a) at the time the first child loses all of his or her cards or (b) after a predetermined amount of time.

Once children can count to determine the larger of two collections and once they have mastered the term-after-a-number skill, they are ready to compare two numbers mentally. Any game that involves comparing numbers or scores to determine a winner can be used to practice this skill; for example, one can play Cards More Than with numeral cards instead of dots cards. Another interesting game for practicing this skill is the Hit-The-Target Game (Baroody, 1989). In this game, players throw a bean bag or other object at a target outlined in tape on the floor. The geometric shapes or concentric circles comprising the target are each labeled with a number. The player(s) hitting the highest number win a point.

Similar activities and games can be used to each *less than*. Initially, it may be helpful to substitute *not as many as* for the relatively unfamiliar term *less* (Kaliski, 1962). *Mathematics Their Way* (Baratta-Lorton, 1976) has a number of activities that can be helpful in helping children master a concept of "less." For example, in the Handsful Activity two players each grab a handful of differently colored blocks. Then one player predicts whether his or her blocks are less than the opponent's. The players check the prediction by placing one set of blocks on one side of an egg carton and the second set on the other side. The row of blocks that is shorter has less. Note that this method ties the term *less* to the perceptual cue of length (appearances). Later, children can be encouraged to count each set of blocks and use their mental representation of the number sequence to determine the set with fewer.

CONCLUSION

Children can be helped to develop oral-counting, object-counting, and numerical-comparison skills in a meaningful and enjoyable manner. Occasionally, verbal instruction and feedback can be helpful—especially when children ask questions or seek help. However, most of the instruction and practice can be achieved in the context of games and everyday activities, which are children's natural media for learning.

17

Some Unforeseen Variants on the Number Construction Scenario

Claire Meljac
Centre Henri Rousselle

This chapter has a twofold purpose. The first is to discuss hypotheses regarding the processes used by the child in the mastery of number, and to describe the departures from the standard path that may occur for a variety of reasons. The second is to examine the relevance of these hypotheses in the light of case studies of children with severe numerical learning disabilities.

Over the course of development, the "normal" child discovers number and enriches his or her initial discoveries by continual interaction with the environment. He or she gathers information while performing activities that have numerical content. Achievements in this field are a source of considerable satisfaction: The child is happy to have solved a problem and enjoys the resultant praise. What he or she "thinks" about number is, thus, subjected to constant restructuration and undergoes continual enhancement. In striking contrast—and one of the aims of this chapter to show why—children with learning disabilities must wage an increasingly arduous, uphill battle. When principles are not correctly established early, the mental foundation is unstable at the outset, leading to spates of errors and feelings of failure, which are reinforced by a total lack of gratification. This can result in more flaws in regulation, and (more damagingly) can impair the mental frameworks that are essential to cognitive restructuration. Without the scaffolding formed by these frameworks, there can be no firm basis for the development of numerical representation.

The hypotheses presented here incorporate these maladjustments as gaps, holes, or aberrations in the course of development. They are also part of the methodological and theoretical approach whose main thrust I outlined further on. It is my hope that this approach can help to guide clinical psychologists who find themselves disoriented by the current upheavals in theory. The Piagetian system, which inspired pratically all research for 50 years on child development and, in particular, studies of the construction of number, is no longer the mandatory reference point, so many have no star to guide them.

THE CLINICAL PSYCHOLOGIST AND THE TOOL BOX: TOWARD AN INVENTORY OF THE "KIT" AND A BETTER UNDERSTANDING OF DISABILITIES

The benefits psychologists have derived from the Piagetian model are well known: The Piagetian model has enabled psychologists to describe child development in terms of neatly defined stages. The idea that the construction of number was linked to the development of elementary logical structures has clarified an extremely complex problem. Researchers who based themselves on classic Piagetian definitions (e.g., "number is formed exclusively of classes and asymmetrical relationships"; Piaget, 1950/1973, p.104 in the 1973 edition) and on the concrete operations stage, long believed it was legitimate to infer a general structure from performance simply by making the right combination of partial, meaningful observations. (For a general discussion of the issue of structure, see Bideaud, 1988, 1990.) Although there is obvious utility to this type of approach, not enough emphasis has been placed on the windfall the Piagetian approach was to the lay clinical psychologist. After administering the conservation task, plus some classification and seriation tasks (Piaget & Inhelder, 1959), the clinical psychologist did not hesitate, despite repeated warnings from Geneva, to draw firm conclusions about the child he or she had tested, or to make pronouncements about the child's state of knowledge and "numerical structuration" (which had not been directly evaluated). The Piagetian method was, for better and worse, a real saving in terms of time and personal thought.

Recurrent failures (e.g., an inability to detect why a child with no difficulties continued to stagnate while another, who appeared to be at a much lower Piagetian stage, made spectacular progress) and theoretical upheaval, however, led to changes in the way the Piagetian or neo-Piagetian psychologists viewed their clinical practice. Although, as Bideaud pointed out in 1988 (p. 389), "the Piagetian structure suggests one possible behavior, which can emerge in situations where this possibility is not a necessity," it is clear today that neither the psychological tester nor the remedial psychologist can apply pre-established profiles without questioning their reliability.

In research, Pierre Gréco argued as early as 1960 and 1962 that number construction could be investigated by other means than class, logic, and relationships: ways that were both more specific (analyses dealing with numerical properties, per se) and more general, going beyond the linear schema organized around well-defined structures. In his latest publication (Gréco, 1988), Gréco presented what he humoristically termed *kit theory*. According to Gréco, the cognitive tool kit "contains few specialized, ready-made instruments for a given task, but rather contains parts (in particular, spare parts, a critical feature) and assembly instructions" (p. 16). These considerations should prompt the psychologist to change his or her outlook on testing. Rather than seeing the tasks as "means of revealing structure," they should be seen as problems for the subject to solve (Bideaud, 1988, p. 395). This focus on the individual and the problems he or she is asked to solve draws attention to new features. Individual differences in meaning, which were long considered to be "noise" unworthy of comment, are no longer discarded. Rather, the current approach makes explicit attempts to design tasks that create difficulties for one child and facilitatory effects for another (Lautrey, 1990; Lautrey, de Ribaupierre, & Rieben, 1981; Rieben, Lautrey, & de Ribaupierre, 1983). These are now considered to be different facets of "normal" development.

Tackling the obstacles encountered by some children is one step toward understanding disabilities; looking at the surprises of "ordinary children's" performance permits insight into the field of pathology. Piaget himself was not particularly attracted to the study of "exceptional" development, although other members of the Geneva school were, at times, extremely interested in certain disorders (e.g., Inhelder, 1943). It is easy to understand why researchers focus on exceptional types of behavior, because disturbed performance in one area can shed light on underlying processes. In turn, the development of robust theoretical frameworks should increase our understanding and remedial efforts with the handicapped. In principle, no one challenges methodology in this area.

The current empirical work in early mathematical learning, however, shows almost no real acknowledgment of the value of this approach: Spiers (1987), in a volume dealing primarily with a neuropsychological approach to brain damaged adults, reported that little is known about disabilities in mathematics.

To my knowledge, there are no theories that truly take into account difficulties emerging over the *course of development,* and not from diagnosed damage. Instead of adhering to what is assumed, in the adult, to be a linear schema—normality, damage, observable disability—the clinical psychologist who works with children has two totally contradictory models available. One centers on schooling, and mainly places the blame on "underprivileged" environments, such as overpopulated classrooms, insufficient teacher training, and so on (see Allardice & Ginsburg, 1983; Hughes, 1986). The other deals with the outcomes of suspected brain damage. In this latter case, the aim is to show (on the basis of case studies) that children's difficulties are due to specific, rare forms of brain damage (Hasaerts-van Geertruyden, 1970, 1975; Hasaerts-Van Geertruyden & Delfosse, 1972; see also Klees, 1983). Even the *Diagnostic and Statistical Manual,* (DSM-III, 1985) contains a section on arithmetic learning disabilities.

Since the early 1980s however, different questions have been raised and the issues are now closer to those found in cognitivism (for a discussion of "renewed" theoretical issues, see Grigsby, Kemper, & Hagerman, 1987; Shalev,

Weirtman, & Amir, 1988). Questions now focus on type of computation, memory store, processing mechanisms, and so forth. Sharing a common denominator with cognitive functions has led to increasingly closer ties between pedagogy and medical screening.

A critical examination of the ways in which of certain types of handicapped individuals use the basic principles of counting of Gelman and Gallistel (1978) constitutes another direction for the analysis of developmental disorders.

Recent articles by Baroody (1986a, 1986b, 1988) and Gelman (1982b; Gelman & Cohen, 1988) have been extremely stimulating in this respect. Their findings show that counting is the most highly affected area in obviously retarded children, in whom the "principles" of counting are not always present and operational. What accounts for these deficiencies? Can the results of these studies on the (non-) application of these principles serve as complete contradictions of the Piagetian constructivist model? Some researchers, such as Gelman, have shown that such studies may serve as a springboard for the examination of a fundamental theoretical issue: testing the validity of those aspects of a well-defined model of knowledge structures related to the understanding and the use of number. Aside from their theoretical interest, these studies could, if they focus on pivotal features, lead to better clinical practice.

The need for this type of approach should be obvious to psychologists interested in knowledge acquisition. There are benefits to be derived from recognizing the relevance of this approach to this field. Obviously, this does not require or imply recourse to Gelman's theories, or the adoption of her "principles" as compulsory guidelines.

In the sections that follow, I present a different approach, which draws on work by Mounoud (see Mounoud, 1983). Although Mounoud deals more with motor behavior than number, his views transfer easily to the field of early mathematical learning.

PATHWAYS, BARRIERS, DEAD ENDS, AND INTERSECTIONS

According to Mounoud (1983), the forms or general structures of actions (their coordination) and reasoning (their logical operations) are prewired from a basic mechanism for processing and coordination.[1] Development is dependent on the emergence of new abilities for the encoding of information, which is the source of representations. Individuals do not construct new general structures over the course of development but, rather, elaborate new internal representations (models, memories, or schemas). Mounoud viewed these representations as the prod-

---

[1]In an entirely different perspective, drawing more heavily on psychoanalysis, Gibello (1984) used the term *thought contents* to designate what I believe to be a similar entity.

ucts of the structuring and organization of content. Mounoud and Vinter (1985) defined representation as "the outcome of analysis or sampling activities and an association of different dimensions of objects and their variants through the use of coding and processing systems" (p. 256). Thus, representations organize or structure the content of reality within the individual. They are part of object identification, recognition, and retrieval. Within this same system, representations can be specified in terms of their type: They are global, partial, totally rigid, and totally decomposable, in that order. Structures, according to Mounoud and Vinter, cannot be dissociated from the representations that activate them.

In my view[2] of the child's mastery of number, a decisive step forward is made when representations dealing with numerical content, or pre-numerical content, reach a certain level of *stability,* the first prerequisite, or general condition, for the emergence of the quantification process.

For a representation to achieve a certain degree of robustness (which differs from the rigidity mentioned earlier) and be seen as stable, it must, in my opinion, use a primitive form of invariance as a pivot: the *identical result principle.*[3] If, under exactly the same conditions, the same event recurs, and if, as expected, the second outcome of the sequence is the same as the first, and so on,[4] the result is clearly not a random occurrence, but rather arises from necessity. This leads directly to the problem of normative facts. What can be said in this respect about counting, which is expressed by the cardinal of a collection? The response, for an adult, is obvious: The second evaluation of the same set will lead to the same number, and if not, there has either been a numerical transformation or a mistake. However, even if we endow the child with a cognitive framework that leads him or her to predict an identical outcome in the case of re-counting of the same collection (when it has not been transformed; see Gelman & Gallistel, 1978), this expectation—before any explicit identification of the invariant—is dependent on intuition, which must, in a given situation, be confirmed. Piaget spoke of a "phase . . . in which experimentation is necessary for discovery and verification of arithmetic truths" (1950/1973, p. 132 of the 1973 edition).

However, it is not easy to master the art of how to count. As long as one-to-one correspondence wavers, the cardinal answers vary, and mistakes of one to

---

[2]I deliberately choose *view,* instead of *model,* despite the current rage for notions of models, to avoid using a word that is much too precise and rigorous.

[3]Perfetti (1989) also stressed the importance of redundancy effects in the case of reading. The differences between number and reading are sufficiently great for it to be immediately apparent that these redundancies cannot be identical in nature; nevertheless, the general idea is common to both: a piece of information needs to be compared and contrasted with others for it to be grasped easily and assimilated.

[4]This notion immediately brings to mind Baldwin's (1895) concept of *circular reaction,* which was later used by Piaget (1936). This involves related ideas, but what I have just described requires metacognitive features as well: A child who expects to obtain an identical result through repetition *knows* that he is expecting this result and can, to a certain extent, express this.

two units above or below are common. The simpler the rules required to complete the task, the fewer the chances of getting lost; this is the case when the number of objects to be counted is small, or when the response can be obtained simply by subitizing. At this step it is crucial for the child to confirm his belief that "if nothing changes, and I do what I did before, I will get the same answer as before." If these beliefs are consolidated, the child will always feel he or she is dealing with a coherent world, regulated by the principle of noncontradiction.

Thus, an identical result is obtained in the most elementary conditions: by pure repetition. In a more subtle way, and at the cost of more elaborate rules, this result can also be obtained by *concordance*. The picture now becomes increasingly complex. Two procedures, for example, subitizing and counting, can now intersect. I have shown elsewhere that this intersection plays a crucial role (J.-P. Fischer & Meljac, 1987). The notion of number derives its coherency and its normative properties from the fact that very early on, cardinalization can be the outcome of two fundamentally different cognitive operations (as long as the child is operating on a small set, having fewer than four elements). With respect to what was later to be termed the *order irrelevancy principle* (Gelman & Gallistel, 1978), Piaget described the stupefaction of one of his friends—a future mathematician who was to be reknowned for his epistemological work—who, as a child, found that he always got the same answer if he counted a row of pebbles in one direction or in the other, from left to right or from right to left (Piaget, 1950/1973; p. 132 in the 1973 edition). In both cases (fusion between counting and subitizing and fusion of the results of one trajectory and another), there are what can be termed *afferent* or *confluent* concordances. The child grasps that he or she can use different procedures to arrive at the same result. It is also useful to look more closely at *efferences:* processing the same statements in different ways, breaking them down, putting them together, adding, removing, saying, writing, and knowing that these acts are derivatives of the same initial action. Sinclair (1988) touched on problems of this type in transcription. Clearly, a child must elaborate systems of this type well before beginning to deal with reversibility. The discoveries that follow are crucial ones. Concordance in itself is probably not the basis for number, but it is doubtless one of the building blocks. A child acquires the first notions of commutativity through experiments in this area (starting with *a,* going on to *b,* and then doing the reverse), and a little later by discovering the equivalence between completing a set and counting backward (Fuson, 1988) and between repeated additions and multiplications and so on. The need for concordance is so strong that it sometimes even leads the learner to overgeneralize its domain (e.g., children—some for a long time—may believe that subtraction is commutative).

A child who uses two different approaches in succession, with the implicit assumption that they are equivalent, is trying to "find the same thing," and is vaguely troubled, without being able to explain why, if the findings do not match. Structured reasoning is for later on; what happens here are special "Eureka!" moments. Most adults can search back in their memories and recall having had such insights, which become the impetus for the reshaping of notional fields. The astonishment of Piaget's friend in counting his rows of pebbles is one. I personally remember, at the age of 5 or 6, panicking after I put a handful of change into my pocket: I had been given one amount of money to make two purchases (*a* and *b*) in the same store. After a moment of total confusion, I realized that I didn't need to differentiate the coins I should use to buy *a* and the coins to buy *b*, but that, on the contrary, each portion of the change could be used at any time to buy either *a* or *b*.

The mastery—presumably much later—of an alternative pathway to identity (after repetition and concordance) leads to a much more high-level awareness of the interchangeability of certain cognitive procedures. This new field of maneuver enables the child to incorporate previously "illegal" combinations. He or she understands, for example, why 5 − 8, which is not the equivalent of 8 − 5 (as long as the problem remains on the level of simple concordance and subtraction taught at primary school), is still closely linked to it. He or she also grasps why multiplications, when the multiplier is less than 1, are the equivalent of divisions, which are known to be "the opposite." And so on. These considerations go beyond the scope of the present chapter.

The mastery of number can, thus, be *partially* described in terms both broader and more varied; over the course of time, fusions of these pieces of knowledge make progressively richer procedures possible. Rigid performances, which at the start only take into account elementary relationships between certain facets of the environment (e.g., contiguities—see Mounoud's comments on early representations, already cited), gradually become flexible and differentiated. Operations can be executed in either direction on material that is grasped with increasing accuracy. Elementary masses are "transformed" into piles, which can be broken down into separate objects. Each of these objects can be labeled by simply repeating the same phoneme (e.g., "ta, ta"). Somewhat finer organization then turns these objects into elements in a colligation, which can be pointed to with a finger in interchangeable ways (see the fine-grained descriptions by Droz, 1981, Droz & Paschoud, 1981; and Mosimann, et al., 1982, on the inception of counting). When pointing goes along with the first number words, the beginning of a fusion between external coordination (pointing and objects) and internal fusion (pointing and words) takes place (Chichignoud, 1985). The fusion between subitizing and counting may be a more advanced form, or an extension, of known unions, whereas the fusion between cardinalization and the vicariance of units (the order-irrelevance principle) shows that number has attained the rank of an operant concept (see Fig. 17.1).

At this point, the child reaches the generalization phase, which allows him to carry out more frequent, diversified operations in increasingly varied situations

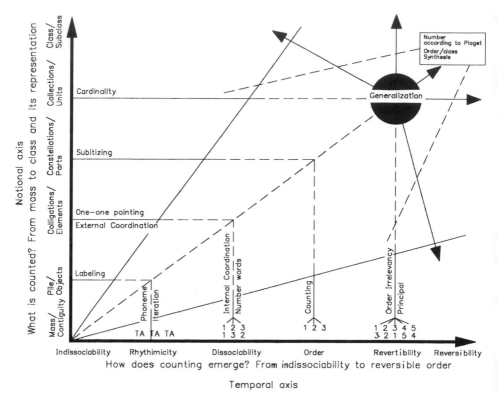

FIG. 17.1.   A Partial Representation of Number Acquisition

(Meljac, 1979). This stage of number construction develops in the coherent way described by Piaget—the way one imagines the construction of number when reading his works.

The developmental schema (Fig. 17.1) for numerical concepts was mainly based on observations on normal children, and is consistent with data published recently on the subject (for an overview see Fayol, 1990, as well as this whole volume). One should not, however, confer properties on this schema that it does not have. In particular, the linearity and the hierarchy of the stages are presentation artifacts, and it is obvious that steps in the process are intertwined. Children's performance varies as a function of context, task, task sequence, and degree of motivation.

The second purpose of this chapter, as I stated earlier, is to test the relevance of this tentative framework in the light of pathological case studies. Cases like those that follow provide a whole host of counter examples that can serve to challenge the robustness of the assumptions presented earlier. How can cases of severe disability be integrated into the framework I have described?

The main argument presented earlier is that the earliest (and, doubtless, the most acute) cases of severe disability in number construction should be viewed as the result of gaps, holes, or distortions in the identical result principle and then later in the concordance system. A child with gaps has been prevented from feeding his prewired systems with meaningful content. Instead, these prewired systems have becomed filled with noise that twists them and destroys their natural pattern. What are the causes of this noise? The reasons vary, but all are linked to weaknesses in modes of information processing. There may be weaknesses in implementation, or weaknesses stemming from more complex strategy systems located at higher levels. Rather than gaining in coherency, then, the prewired systems become fuzzier. Later, they become useless, because lack of development through lack of significant experiences have progressively weakened them.

Should these failures be given the same weight as successes? In other words, will a positive experience with identical results or concordance weigh as heavily in the construction of number as a failure will in its destruction? My experience with children with severe disabilities suggests not. To the extent that a positive outcome fits in an uneventful way with expectations and within pre-established frameworks, it does not truly constitute a major occurrence (with the exception of "Eureka!" moments, which are probably extremely rare). In contrast, incoherencies in child environment interactions make deep inroads in the organizational network. Successes can thus be seen as enhancers and clarifiers of representations, whereas failures have direct effects on the prewired structures.

The sections that follow chart the ways in which prewired structures are progressively undermined. My remarks are drawn from brief observations made during testing (i.e., over the course of a microgenesis). In cases of significant and repeated failures, children find themselves in an extremely precarious situation: They have lost the tools younger children use to structure their first encounters with the universe of number, and they have nothing to replace them with save memories of dissonant experiences that caused pain and frustration.

I now turn to a description of three categories of children I am very familiar with and with whom I have worked for several years. I then present excerpts of clinical evaluation protocols.

THREE GROUPS OF EXCEPTIONAL CHILDREN

The children described here are not retarded, as in the Baroody and in Gelman studies cited earlier: All have normal IQs on standard measurement tests (usually the Wechsler Intelligence Scale for Children-Revised; WISC-R). What distinguishes them is their inability to use number, as shown by their low level of performance in this area. These children are "exceptional" in that they are outside the norms for at least one facet of development. They certainly cannot be termed "extraordinary," because profiles similar to theirs are frequent in the literature.

Although these groups are not the only ones that present difficulties in number operations, they were selected because they are the ones I have had the most clinical experience with, and because they are (in my opinion) the most representative.

Children With Cerebral Palsy.   Group 1 is composed of children with cerebral palsy (CP) being treated at Kremlin-Bicetre Hospital.[5] Individuals with cerebral palsy (infirme moteur cérébral [IMC] in Tardieu's terminology) are all characterized by neonatal brain lesions that have resulted in varying degrees of motor impairment. However, this type of cerebral palsy leaves mental or relational abilities totally or almost totally intact, and most such individuals with normal IQs. The current joint study was designed to evaluate the mainstreaming of these children. One of the major findings for one subgroup was the frequency and severity of deficiencies in the in early mathematics foundations, in particular, the notion of number. Characteristic features of this group are described further on.

Dyspraxic Children.   The French research community is familiar with dyspraxias in children. In Anglo-Saxon countries there is a tendency to refer to minimal brain damage (MBD) or to learning disabilities (LD). (For critical comments on this notion, see Allardice & Ginsburg, 1983.) My position is that *dyspraxia,* which does not directly imply a neurological cause, is more prudent term than MBD or LD. Dyspraxic children have normal or high Verbal IQs, but also have major motor disabilities or problems on tasks requiring some degree of spatial organization (Stambak, L'Heriteau, Auzias, Bergès, & de Ajuriaguerra, 1964). These children are referred to clinicians for a variety of reasons: lack of coordination, writing problems, and school problems, of which the most prominent is their spectacular failure in mathematics at the most basic level; this feature is discussed in Meljac (1979).

Nonreaders.   The third group is composed of what we term *nonreaders,* a new rubric coined by our research term to avoid the connotations associated with *poor readers* or *dyslexics. Nonreaders* seems a more appropriate term for this group, who present major, persistent lexical deficiencies, as differentiated from children with minor, transitory problems. These children were aged 9 and older (including several 13- to 17-year-olds), and of average IQ. (All scored 85 or more on one of the two WISC-R scales.) These children do not come from particularly impoverished backgrounds. All had attended schools "normally" (in quantitative

---

[5]They are part of an ongoing study financed by the MIRE (de Barbot, Meljac, Truscelli, & Henry-Amar, 1989).

terms) in France since kindergarten, and none exhibited signs of language impairment. Nevertheless, as the term suggests, they do not read; that is, their performance in this area is no better than performance observed in first graders.[6] In contrast to the other two groups, the motivation for referral by the families (or teachers) of nonreaders is not their lack of numerical knowledge: Their deficiencies in reading are so dramatic that they tend to mask all the others. Nevertheless, careful examination shows that well before these nonreaders experienced difficulties with mathematical problem statements, they had encountered severe difficulties in the field of number transcriptions.

The cases I have chosen to present here are illustrative of each of these groups. I have included selected portions of the clinical examination that have the greatest bearing on the focus of this chapter. My aim is to specify the relationships between these children's knowledge bases and their concrete use of number.

Methodology

In order to determinine how children appropriate notions of number so as to define their specific disabilities, I have chosen the most obvious approach: observing and analyzing the way individual children *use* number. It is well known, however, that psychologists have often been tempted to proceed otherwise. What are disparagingly termed *achievement tests* have received little attention (Fayol, 1990, underscores this lack of interest). These are generally administered collectively, providing little opportunity for in-depth examination, or they are relegated to new, inexperienced members of the staff.[7] The testing manual I have developed (Meljac, 1980) makes it possible to examine the mathematic facets of number construction in a more accurate and functional way without discounting Piagetian issues of logic (classification, seriation, etc.) or conservation. The main issue is this: When and how does a given child come to use number spontaneously? By *spontaneously,* I mean without prompting by others through "How many?" questions or commands, such as "Count!" Apparently this is a key question that I touched on (Meljac, 1979), although few researchers have dealt with it (with the exception of Michie, 1984). It seems that there is a critical period—regardless of precocity of the underlying principles of counting (Gelman & Gallistel, 1978)—when the child appropriates certain words, instru-

---

[6]A number of papers have been devoted to studies of this group, and an ongoing research program is being financed by an INSERM contract (see, e.g., Bergès et al., 1986; Kossanyi, Waiche, & Netchine, 1986; Meljac, 1988; Preneron & Salazar-Orvig, 1987; Sprenger-Charolles & Khomsi, 1989).

[7]Psychologists' (either new or experienced). The total ignorance of this area by psychologists can be accounted for by the fact that, to my knowledge, there are no official diploma courses in French universities that provide specific, in-depth instruction in this field. Professional reading specialists are at the same disadvantage.

ments, and concepts from the adult universe (see Durkin, Shire, Riem, Crowther, & Rutter, 1986; Fuson, 1988; Wagner & Walters, 1982).

I illustrate this here by presenting a glimpse into the type of testing and observation I do. The following represents a subset of the tests in the battery.

Cards and Tokens Task.   Sets of blue gummed stickers (from 21 to 3, presenting first 21, down to 3 stickers) are pasted on file cards in three types of configurations: random, with a good Gestalt, and in a row. The observer notes whether the child spontaneously uses the numerical dimension to describe the cards in his or her response to the instruction, "Tell me exactly what you can see." For children who count, their procedures are noted (see Chichignoud, 1985; Fuson, 1988; and Fayol, 1990, for different quantification procedures).

Bananas and Oranges Task.   Subjects are presented with a reference set (e.g., miniature plastic bananas) which is never modified, that can be used to evaluate changes in a second set (e.g., plastic oranges) placed in one-to-one correspondence with it. Children are observed for their ability to assess changes and for their responses to change. The most common version of the task involves removing objects from the ends of one row, from the middle, or in a discontinuous fashion (see Fig. 17.2).

Dolls and Dresses Task   (use of quantification in the absence of a reference set). The child is presented a set of dolls (cut out of cardboard and all identical in height, measuring 15 cm). The number of dolls can range between four and nine, depending on the age and level of performance of the individual child. Dresses (clearly more dresses than dolls, but all the right size) are arranged on the other side of the room. The extremely repetitious instruction is to "get just enough dresses to dress the dolls." The task is based on a suggestion in Gréco (1962) to observe the operational use of number, that is, when and how it occurs to a child to count the dolls (and the dresses) in order to be able to accomplish the task quickly and correctly. There is also a "handbag" variant on this task, in which the child must bring back just enough handbags for all the dolls, and a "slippers" variant, in which the child must bring back twice as many socks as dolls.

All these tasks are described more fully in Meljac (1979; 1980), and age-related changes in performance on these tasks has been charted: At roughly 4 to 5 years of age, children have no difficulty determining the sets of bananas and oranges in one-to-one correspondence. Children succeed on the doll task much later (at about 6 for nine dolls). The cards and tokens task, despite its apparent simplicity, does not prompt children to use number until considerably later; in fact, nothing in the instructions or in the situation itself requires children to use number.

The crucial point here is that these different uses of number do not manifest

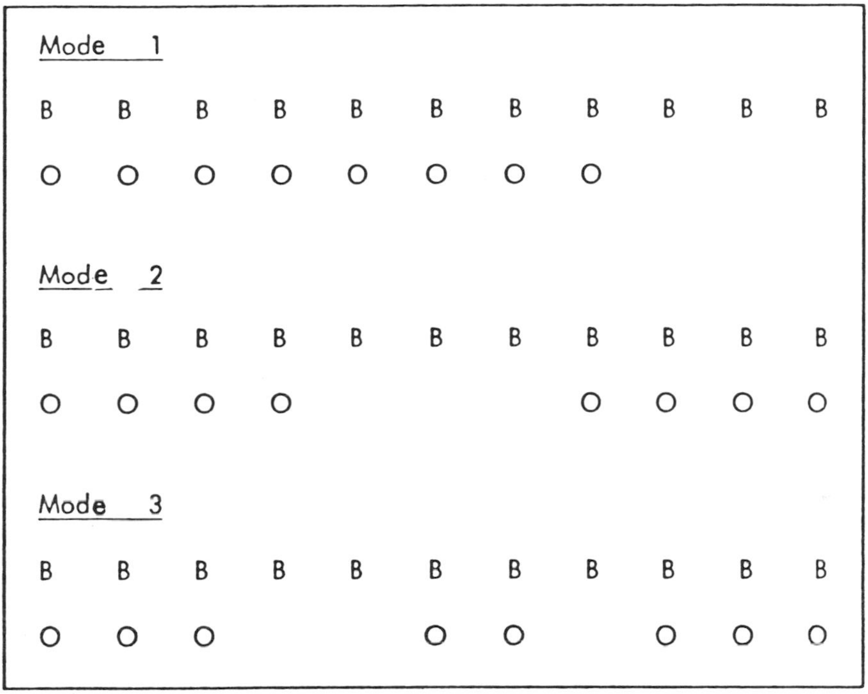

Mode   1

B	B	B	B	B	B	B	B	B	B	B
O	O	O	O	O	O	O	O			

Mode   2

B	B	B	B	B	B	B	B	B	B	B
O	O	O	O				O	O	O	O

Mode   3

B	B	B	B	B	B	B	B	B	B	B
O	O	O		O	O		O	O	O	

FIG. 17.2.   Modes of Presenting Oranges and Bananas (after Subtracting Oranges)

themselves as direct functions or immediate outcomes of acquired knowledge.
Children often begin to use number for these tasks spontaneously, well after
having learned to count, and may do so as a function of constraints other than
those connected to pure reproduction of a previously learned and practiced procedure. This type of behavior is related to the generalization phase described
earlier.

The test procedure also makes it possible to compare spontaneous counting
and induced counting (i.e., explicitly requested counting).

*Observation of transcription of dictated numbers and the reading of numbers
of varying complexity (forms of transcoding).*   The procedure used is similar to
the one described by Deloche and Seron (1987). In French there are many
irregularities, in particular in numbers up to 100 (more even than in English!).
The sequence from 70 to 100 is particularly irregular: *Seventy* is said *soixante-dix*
(*sixty-ten*), *eighty* is said *quatre-vingts* (*four-twenty*) and *ninety* is said *quatre-
vingt-dix* (*four-twenty-ten*).

SOME OBSERVATIONS OF CHILDREN: UNFORESEEN VARIANTS ON THE NUMBER-CONSTRUCTION SCENARIO

This section presents typical performances observed in the three groups described earlier. Rather than providing statistical data, I have opted for the case-study method. This type of presentation is more appropriate for accounts of procedures and observations of microgenesis. Each of the case studies I have chosen serves, in its own unique way, to shed light on the long-term effects of defective modes of processing. These cases provide some clues as to how intuitions, or "prewired" notions, which are present at the start of the observations, disappear, drained of their meaning by repeated disillusioning experiences.

Prewired Notions and Techniques in Children with CP

Matthew (aged 5 years, 2 months), who often thinks about counting spontaneously without actually counting, was asked to say how many stickers were pasted on a card (an irregular arrangement of 3 stickers). Immediately, by subitizing, he answers, "Two." We thus see that "three" is not subitized with complete certainty as is the general rule for children of his age who recognize 3 as a familiar quantity. I ask him to count. He points to nonexistent objects and recites the words of a counting rhyme without corresponding pointing. He is clearly not able to carry out internal and external coordinations jointly (see Chichignoud, 1985; Fuson, 1988). He answers, "Four." This is not an isolated example of a mistake. The other quantitative estimates he made during the same session were equally unsure. Is this a case of a child whose difficulties in simple motor coordination affect pointing activities or vocal production? Apparently not. His disorder is not limited to a particular action as such, but resides in the order of progression of organized and reliable sequences. Matthew constantly gives the impression of being lost. Nevertheless, he knows the rhyme by heart and can recite it. His performance is in the "normal" range for other tests of intellectual ability, such as classification, which Piaget believed to be tightly connected to the construction of number. Matthew is supposed to start first grade in a few months and there is concern as to how he will fare as long as his subitizing and counting yield results that are at least one unit away from the cardinal from the right answer. Two years later our fears are confirmed: Matthew is sent to us for severe calculation problems.

John (aged 5 years, 10 months) refuses to apply all the "how to count" rules, that is, Gelman and Gallistel's (1978) first three counting principles. He is able to recite the number sequence for the first few decades, but when asked to quantify a set, he relies on intensive subitizing, which often leads to wild estimates. During his first use of pointing, in an attempt at counting four objects, he uses an extremely idiosyncratic technique (described at 18 months by Mosimann et al., 1982) consisting of "There, there." This technique is a primitive, simple enumeration, which eliminates the problem of adjustments and coordinations with the words of the counting rhyme, leaving only the coordination of object, uncertain finger movement, and iterative speech production.

In this group of cerebral palsy children, all of whom exhibit severe numerical learning deficiencies, the most remarkable case is Arnaud (7 years, 10 months), who is in what roughly corresponds to second grade in a school for exceptional children. I will comment in more detail on his behavior, which was videotaped. (Unfortunately, this was not feasible for the other children.)

Arnaud is asked to identify the transformations in a set of oranges originally placed in one-to-one correspondence with a set of bananas

The bananas and oranges are initially arranged in simple one-to-one correspondence (11 elements in each set). Arnaud immediately states they are "the same," that is, that there are as many elements in one row of fruit as in the other. The one-to-one correspondence is, thus, the proof of equality. The examiner asks him to close his eyes; he continues to point to imaginary objects in the air. The examiner removes 3 oranges from the end of a row (leaving the bananas unmodified). The configuration now corresponds to Arrangement 1 in Fig. 17.2. Arnaud is disconcerted.

"There are still as many" (*autant,* in French), he says. His spontaneous use of the word *autant* is interesting, because the word is acquired late, and is usually related to access to concrete operational thought in Piagetian terms (Pierard & Thuvelle-Delahaye, 1985). "No, there aren't as many," he says, looking despairingly at the examiner. "You put one orange less" (another despairing look).

E: So what did I do ? I took oranges away . . .
A: Two, you took two away. . . . There were as many . . .
E: How did you know that it was the same?

Arnaud feverishly counts the unchanged set of bananas and arrives at the correct answer: 11 bananas. He looks at the ceiling (and not the sets).

A: You took two bananas away!
E: I took two bananas away? You mean oranges.

Arnaud continues to look at the ceiling.

A: Oranges. There should be 11. There are 9.

Gazing upward, Arnaud had clearly subtracted $11 - 2$, because he just stated that 2 oranges had been removed, and he did not look at the array.

Encouraged, he hesitantly re-counts the objects present and tries, with extreme difficulty, to coordinate objects, pointing, and the counting sequence: 8 (number of oranges), 11 (number of bananas).

With his fingers in his mouth, he taps on his lips. He triumphantly takes his fingers out of his mouth and says, "You took 3 away! There are 8 and to make it all [11] there should be 3."

During this last sequence, Arnaud looked only at the examiner and never at the set. He arrived at the answer by numerical operations (probably by a count plus extension technique) and never based his responses on the configuration. He never estimated what was missing by looking at the reference elements, although he was clearly conceptually aware of what one-to-one correspondence means. He showed this by stating immediately that there were as many in one set as in the other. Is recourse to counting a preference or a disability? In other words, is calculation a more positively valued activity than simple visual inspection (which might be seen as too "easy" to do)? Apparently not: The rest of the examination showed that Arnaud was not able to count when the first counting number does not correspond to the first (i.e., the left-most or right-most) element in the set. This disability was particularly apparent when an item was removed from the center of a row. In this case he would start to count the unchanged set, and then took the loci and not the objects into account in counting the changed set (yielding an answer of 5 for 3 missing objects). In such a case, he probably confused the "hole" in the middle of the set of oranges—where the oranges had been removed—with the interval spaces between each pair of items in the set of bananas, which served to indicate item discontinuity. The "find the gap" rule that applies to a given (transformed) set for specific spatial locations (from which the objects corresponding to the reference items were missing) was transferred to the unchanged set, so that the gap became the locus. (Other children with CP also exhibited this type of behavior.)

Guiding Arnaud's hand helped him to point. He had the most trouble with discontinuous gaps, that is, when the set of oranges had 2 "holes," such as Arrangement 3 in Fig. 17.2 where three oranges (2 + 1) were removed. Because Arnaud stated that the experimenter had taken 9 oranges, it was clear that he was still counting the spaces. Therefore, the rule was explained to him: "Look at each banana and then find the bananas that don't have an orange facing them." This helped him attend to, and prompted him to use, one-to-one correspondence. He dropped this procedure rapidly, however, as though it were a disrupting constraint.

Arnaud's errors are characteristic of this group of children, and are indicative of the disparity between a good hunch (intuition) and disability with regard to efficient information processing. Arnaud's first responses may be *prewired,* in Mounoud's terms. This prewired pattern prompts Arnaud to use numerical processing. Arnaud clearly grasped the role of quantitative features, such as one-to-one correspondence, but inadequacies in information gathering had a direct impact on the construction of representations, which remain vague and non-operational and yielded no results that could be confirmed by experience. The prewired form, isolated in this way and self-contained, cannot be fed by coordinated and operational representations. Some children, after a few unsuccessful attempts, simply cease to have recourse to number and take refuge in archaic behaviors, such as guessing. Arnaud, however, carried out a simple complement task (which is ordinarily solved after a mere glance at age 4 or 4½) by using a much more complicated operation requiring more knowledge than is available by simply scanning the configuration. This operation remained viable as long as the goal was restricted and the linear information was continuous. As soon as the information became more complex, or when the goal was fuzzier, the higher level numerical operation could no longer be accomplished. This is in no way surprising. The real question is how this operation could take place on simple sets without any guidance from one-to-one correspondence.

Operationalization of Number in a Dyspraxic Child

Nadine was 8 years, 8 months when she was tested for the first time, several months older than Arnaud. A complicated clinical history, (hypotonia) and specialized examinations led us to classify her as dyspraxic (for details on the clinical examination, see Meljac, 1979). Nadine scored normally for her age bracket in reading and spelling. Her overall IQ was normal but her performance was mediocre on the WISC-R Performance scale. In terms of mathematical acquisition, the number sequence was recited correctly, read correctly, and transcribed correctly. The number facts were known by heart (declarative knowledge), but recitation seemed to be devoid of meaning and unrelated to any procedure (for the distinction between procedural and declarative knowledge as concerns number, see J.-P. Fischer, this volume). Following are excerpts from her protocol.

I give Nadine the Dolls and Dresses task. Although she had immediately counted the cards with the colored stickers in the Cards and Tokens task, she is completely at a loss as to how to proceed when asked to "get just enough dresses to dress the dolls." First, she takes all the dresses. After she has dressed all nine dolls she was given, it is pointed out to her that she did not follow the instructions. So, on the second trial, she leaves a (random) handful of dresses. On the third trial, she starts to count, and says, "I thought (about) how many dolls (there) were," and she brings back the right number of dresses.

Nevertheless, when presented with different materials (handbags instead of dresses) she again brings too many back: "I won't tell you (how I went about it)," she says, "I thought about not taking the bags I shouldn't take." This is not pursued, and she is then asked to put slippers on the same set of dolls (i.e., two nonlateralized slippers per doll). This time she is completely lost. After repeating the instructions to herself—"Bring back just enough slippers, just enough"—

she takes a pile of 14 slippers (for nine dolls). It is at this point that she mentions the need for counting for the first time, saying, "I'm going to count the dolls." Undoubtedly, she had already counted the dolls in the preceding variant on the task, although the counting was not explicit. Thus, Nadine has a need to re-count despite the fact that she has no retention problems. Most likely, now that the instructions have been changed, Nadine is no longer sure of the permanence of the result: Can the number of individuals who need slippers be the same as the number of individuals who needed dresses? However, she makes a counting mistake. Like Arnaud, she finds it extremely difficult to fuse internal and external coordination. She points to nonexistant objects while reciting the numbers in an inappropriate rhythm and arrives at 11 (for 9 dolls). Disoriented (perhaps, after all, she hoped she would arrive back at 9), she re-counts, after changing the position of the dolls to make counting clearer (a row of 4 and another row of 5). This time she gets the right answer, and she takes 9 slippers! The technical difficulties were such that she lost touch with the problem. She puts the slippers on the dolls and half the set are barefoot. The remainder of the session, which was characterized by Nadine's growing discomfort, are not be described here because it yielded no new information.

Nadine presents what can be seen as the logical extension of the performance observed in the youngest children with CP described earlier. The implication is that the range of erratic cases may, in fact, be extremely small. Nadine counts hesitantly and is entirely unsure when counting (something she tries to hide as long as possible) and tries to solve the task by the available means. She is never sure—and rightly so—of getting the correct answer or getting the same answer that she did before. This is true to such an extent that any change in context (bringing back handbags, getting slippers after having dressed the dolls) forces her to start the procedure all over again, and the procedure absorbs her to such an extent that she forgets what the purpose of the procedure.

The two most frequent types of errors in this type of child are mistakes in estimating the number of dolls, and mistakes in estimating the number of dresses. My purpose here is to chart behavior of these children, and to examine the result and its psychological impact on them.

Mistakes Concerning the Number of Dolls.

1. Description of the erroneous sequence: Given six dolls, the child correctly applies the rule "first count the number of dolls," but because of flawed adjustments, arrives at the wrong answer: eight dolls.

    He or she correctly uses the rule "the last cardinal should be transferred to the dresses" but, having counted eight dolls, takes eight dresses. The child dresses the dolls, but is left with two dresses in hand.

2. Result: Immediate perception of failure.

3. Impact: The child is disoriented: Correctly applied rules lead to an incoherent result.

If a child does not check, which is often the case when the child is disoriented and/or when he or she is not convinced (perhaps through repeated errors) that identical results to an identical problem always occur, there is no way for the child to rectify the situation. This means that errors will snowball.

The end result is a fragilization of the notion of number, and a loss of confidence in the results expected from recourse to experience. The idea to have recourse to concrete experience was certainly there at the start of the experiment as a framework or general architecture. However, encounters with outside reality have destroyed this avenue of exploration. The "necessary" experience of verification described by Piaget (1949) indeed took place, but contrary to his claims, could verify nothing.

Mistakes Concerning the Number of Dresses.

1. Description of the erroneous sequence: Given six dolls (as before), the child applies the first rule and counts the dolls correctly. He or she then correctly applies the second rule to the dresses but makes a mistake in counting, only bringing back five.
2. Results: The child is missing one dress, although the procedure was correctly applied.
3. Impact: The conclusions the child will draw from this failure will probably be identical to those mentioned in the previous example.

What emerges from these transcriptions is that children who "know" the rule and its sequence may nevertheless fail entirely because they are unable to apply the counting techniques correctly, because they have not mastered the complex coordinations they require. This application flaw, in turn, undermines the understanding of the rule. This points directly to the need for the stabilizing effects of recurrence and concordance. These serve to reinforce initial intuitions, confer meaning, and structure representations.

If the child has not had the experience of such gratifications, it is easy to see why he or she will have problems becoming oriented: This is the case of the "beginner". The children described here, however, are clearly in a much more problematic situation. They have had plenty of experience, perhaps even too much. Their expectations are never confirmed, they have lost their anchor points and all hope of mastering the quantitative universe. This disorientation should be kept in mind when testing children whose repeated failures generate continual discomfort. These children need to have situations specially designed for them that will enable them to be receive gratification and comfort. If a child has no experience of successes in this area during development—successes that play a major role in the process of number operationalization—and only encounters incoherencies along the path, the concept itself will remain an empty shell that will shatter at the first opportunity. I recall, for example, one 28-year-old for whom the sum of 10 + 8 yielded everything—including 19 but never *dix-huit* (ten-eight), although the number words make the answer explicit in French.

Trancoding "Slips" in Nonreaders

Coding ability plays a crucial role in the course of development. Transitions between different types of expression—action, speech, reading, writing—lead directly to the notion of transcoding. These transcodings, their anchoring and their activation, in addition to other features I cannot deal with here, are the major missing elements in child nonreaders.

Simon was brought for a consult for the first time at the age of 9 years, 1 month. Although his IQ is normal, he does not come from a particularly impoverished background, and he attends a regular school, he is totally unable to read any words at all. He cannot understand a text when reading silently or orally. I will only touch here on his approach to number. Note first that he presents none of the difficulties described so far. Sets are counted correctly, and number is operationalized with ease. The only obstacle concerns memorizing his answers, even in the short term. For example, he says "I am missing the number" (when getting slippers for the dolls), although he has just correctly counted the feet and knows which rule to apply, because he uses the word *number*.

The observations presented here is devoted to the way in which Simon knows the number sequence, writes it, and reads it.

Simon knows how to recite the number sequence up to 19 without too many hesitations. He is then asked to write down what he knows. At the crucial point—going from one decade to the next—he makes his first mistake. Instead of 11, the first number that contains a repetition of two identical figures in its transcription, Simon writes 12, and then corrects himself. According to Deloche, Seron, and Noel (this volume; see also Deloche & Seron, 1987), this is a lexical error, because it only affects the writing of one constituent and no change in category. After 19 however, Simon has no mastery. He writes 213, clearly intending 21 (instead of 20, the shift to a new decade), then 3 (reconstituting the 1, 2, 3 sequence or indicating a shift to the next higher decade: 30).

In reading, confusions also occur, even for the first two decades. Note that Simon gives answers referring to higher numbers in the sequence: for example, 15 (*quinze*) is read *cinquante* (50). This is a lexical stack error, in the Seron and Deloche's terminology: The same relative position in the stack is preserved; 19 (*dix-neuf*) is read *twenty-nine* (lexical position error), 18 is read *twenty-eight* (same type of error). In the other direction: *Quinze* (15) is transcribed as 25. The most astonishing is for *seize* (16), which is written *66* (a double stack error?). This error clearly expresses the fact that *seize* is a complicated and transformed *six* (6).

Simon is seen again at the age of 10 years, 8 months. His reading skills have not improved significantly. He always fiercely rejected any suggestions of remedial work. He knows the number sequence up to 100, but now makes inversions in the written forms of numbers that were not present earlier; *7*, in particular, is written as its mirror image. In addition, his transcription errors now concern earlier numbers. The numbers marking the transitions to "complex" or "special" decades, after 60, in French are not identified. In addition, there are syntactic errors of the 10x type: *trois-cent-vingt-six* (326) written as *3026*, and of lexicalization: quatre-vingt-dix-neuf (99) written as *891* (see Seron et al., this volume).

When he is seen for the third time, Simon is 11 years, 4 months. His difficulties with transitions between decades, particularly for the irregular decades after 70, are even more apparent. The crucial question is the reading of 0; that is, is it possible to account for a number by simply announcing the tens place when the ones place is occupied? Simon thinks so, because he reads 94 by omitting the 4 at the end.

Simon does not make random substitutions; his confusions occur between the two "special numbers" with combinations of 10: *soixante-dix* (70) and *quatre-vingt-dix* (90). A triple complexity (*quatre, vingt, dix*) expressed by a single figure (9) is simplified by reduction to a double complexity (*soixante, dix*). This does not imply that he can read *70* correctly; he reads it as 71 (*soixante et onze*)—a confusion with the next number. His reading level for texts is of approximately a second-grade level. He still refuses remedial help. At age 14, Simon has enormous problems in just reaching the third-grade level.

Is this a case of application of rules (at times erroneous) of transcoding, such as those described by Seron and Deloche (1987)? What emerges, above all, in the case of Simon and most other child nonreaders is the effects of a search to establish a perfect correspondence (which does not exist between written and spoken French, or English for that matter) between what is said and what is written. This leads to lexicalizations. This same interpretation also applies to certain simplifications (quatorze, 40, for quatre-vingts, 80) driven by lexical errors, whereas position errors seem to testify to poorly focalized centrations: that the most important element is said first (e.g., *cinq*uante, 50, for quinze, 15). "Don't overlook anything and immediately emphasize the most salient features": This is the obligatory rule for nonreaders. It produces contradictions, however, and results in the (apparent) permanence of certain mistakes. The number sequence that is known and applied remains small; this severely restricts explorations of numbers over 100. Even in the portion of the sequence that is known, changes in modality (written vs. oral) create enormous difficulties, particularly when several number words (the compounds for numbers between 70 and 90, in

French) are expressed in writing by a single figure. Young children make similar errors during acquisition. Quickly, however, a direct route is charted between the number word and the written form, and vice versa. After a certain amount of time, for 90, for example, the three number words (*quatre, vingt, dix*) are probably no longer differentiated (children are stupefied when they are told that *quatre vingts*, 80, is literally 4×20). Simon, who has grasped the law of number construction: (because he writes sequences—if he can base himself on a preceding number), is still uncertain, and his direct approach remains inconsistent, even at the last observation. Simon relies on sound-to-sound, word-to-word transcoding, and it is easy to imagine the difficulties associated with a system of this type.

CONCLUDING COMMENTS

The cases presented here and the obstacles encountered by these children are illustrative of cleavage and its consequences. There is cleavage between one moment and another, between an action and its recurrence, between a procedure and its equivalent (with respect to type of information obtained), between one response modality and its transcription in another modality, and among different types of information processing. All of these features, which interact over the course of development, could be seen here, as in the laboratory, acting alone. These microcleavages finally create a major fissure between a prewired system and a concept. The earlier the break, the more the foundations for systems of meaning, which give number its status as a notional tool, are undermined. Disorganizations of spatial representation and action spaces lead to primitive disconnections: the iteration of identical sounds (ta, ta, ta) followed by number words that do not fuse with the pointing operations, later uncertain subitizing that yields results that differ from erratic counting. There is a dysfunctionality in this system of recurrence because performance on a given sequence, with no other changes, yields a variety of cardinals. Distortions in concordance then appear, which, when threatened by experience, fail to be firmly established. The obstacles that emerge during early transcodings (and in later phases of generalization) apparently have less debilitating effects, to the extent that they do not threaten the first system of meaning but rather hinder transitions between different modalities of expression. Performances whose registers cannot become interchangeable tend to reify. It is then impossible to make the transition from written to oral, from the procedural mode to the declarative mode, and so on.

What may take place is a reverse of the itinerary described by Nelson (1985, 1988) and commented on by Bideaud (1990). Conceptual categories (one of which is number) or abstract paradigmatic structures act in this system like derivatives of scripts or syntagmatic structures, derived from the world of experience. This derivation mechanism, which fills in the blanks in the script over the course of ontogenesis, seems to be hindered dramatically for certain realms of behavior in some of the children I have described. Nelson also referred to *substitutability* in a given empty cell between one (or several) scripts, where substitutability is the key relationship between different members of a given conceptual class. In terms of the acquisition of numerical relations, one example is the different compositions of a number.

The cleavages observed in children with severe disabilities is likely to prevent them from forming substitutions of this type. These cases of "exceptional" development lead to new mathematical and theoretical questions. The first conclusion we can draw is that the cases described here lend weight to the hypothesis that conceptual development is highly dependent on context, and the reinforcements that the context can provide, and is highly susceptible to damage from defective procedures that are the outcomes of poor information processing. The crucial issue raised by observations of these "hindered" children is obviously how we can reach and help them. I hope the descriptions I have provided suggest some possible avenues of exploration for psychologists and educators. To move ahead, however, we need to know more about the repair processes children discover by themselves, regardless of whether they are consistently failing or not. In an often surprising way, some of these children, who seemed to be "stuck" for good, are able to overcome the obstacles, but most tend to founder. Should we give them cognitive and technical crutches that will give them step-by-step guidance and thereby eliminate these problematic situations? This is the explicit goal of some remedial researchers, who are satisfied to fill in Nelson's blanks with paradigmatic structures having valences that are limited because they are highly circumscribed, and operate with the hope that, in the end, the appropriate generalizations will take place.

Other teams start out with more ambitious goals. They prefer to work on and refine the performances of these children in areas where they have demonstrated certain abilities. This work consists of identifying these "strong points" and using them as springboards. The picture we have of the learning disabled child is becoming more subtle: He or she not only has gaps or deficiencies, but has specific assets as well.

Even though research communities have turned a deaf ear on controversies of this type, the clash in conceptions and the heated debate are far from over on the practical level. Researchers, teachers, and clinicians, and above all, children would gain from greater collaboration and exchange on a more active and permanent way between daily practice and fundamental research.

ACKNOWLEDGMENTS

My thanks are extended to the editorial board—Jacqueline Bideaud, Remi Brissiaud, and Jean-Paul Fischer—for their help in all stages of the writing of this chapter. I also wish to thank Jacqueline Bigeargeal and Majid Safouane.

CONCLUSION

18 Assessment and Perspectives

Jacqueline Bideaud
Université Charles de Gaulle, Lille III

The chapters making up *Pathways to Number* are ample testimony to the variety of routes to mastery of number that are potentially open to the child, and how they are authorized as a function of external or internal constraints. More specifically, this volume is illustrative of the heterogeneity of viewpoints adopted by psychologists to study the processes of acquisition and its unpredictable turns. This heterogeneity is in one sense reassuring, in that it is indicative of the complexity of the genesis of number. It is, however, more apparent than real, because most of these studies can be assigned to one of the two major contemporary theoretical and methodological trends: Anglo-Saxon cognitivism (information processing) or neostructuralism. In this closing chapter, I try to define what I feel to have been the contributions and the limits of Piagetian structuralism—the obligatory reference—developmental cognitivism, and neostructuralism. I then attempt to show how new pathways can branch out from the intersection of the most seminal theoretical concepts in each of these approaches.

PIAGETIAN STRUCTURALISM AND THE ONTOGENESIS OF NUMBER

The contribution of Piagetian operational theory to number is not restricted to the (1941) volume by Piaget and Szeminska. Reflection was taken much further in the 1960s through joint efforts associating mathematicians, logicians, epistemologists, and psychologists, such as Beth, Grize, Papert, Gréco, Matalon, Morf, and others in the stimulating environment of the Centre International d'Epistemologie Génétique (International Center for Genetic Epistemology:

ICGE). It cannot be stressed enough that operational theory, and its role in the genesis of number, cannot be apprehended outside this context, that is, outside its own epistemological and biological frame.

The specificity of Piaget and the Geneva school lies in having demonstrated that the historico-critical and psychogenetic approaches are indissociable, by showing that normative systems that validate our knowledge of reality evolve and are constructed in the child in the same way as they are in the logician or the mathematician "who invents his systems intuitively before being able to formalize them" (Piaget, 1967, p. 383). This points directly to the major role played by what Papert (1990, p. 9) termed "the search for a link with what is basic to the mathematical sciences" in Piaget's works.

However, understanding Piaget's approach calls for simultaneous reference to his biological groundings. By going beyond the Bergsonian opposition between intelligence and vital forces—a forerunner of contemporary neurobiological metaphors—Piaget postulated that human intelligence, because of the variety of its adaptive forms, is inscribed in a more general vector (or thrust) of Life. Human intelligence on the cognitive level is the expression of a "general tendency toward endogenous reconstruction (by new variations and "intraselection") of unstable, exogeneous acquisitions" (Piaget, 1974, p. 75)—a Piagetian biological *tertium* between Lamarckism—direct action of the environment on the organism and transmission of characteristics and (neo)Darwinism—accidental variations and selection. Intelligence is defined by the end goal of this internal reconstruction, the optimal level of adaptation, called the higher thought processes, the logico-mathematical operations congruent with the hereditary biological core, or the process of assimilation–accommodation and reflex schemes. In short, intellectual development is the development of endogenous adaptive behaviors whose structural organization gradually comes closer (isomorphic) to the forms elaborated by logic and mathematics, which themselves are in evolution.

In a theory as specific as this one, which was to become even more explicit in the 1960s, it is easy to grasp the importance of the construction of number as the basis for mathematical thinking. Its importance was underscored by the publication of three specific works: volumes XI, XIII, and XIV of the Etudes d'Epistemologie Génétique (Gréco et al., 1960; Gréco & Morf, 1962; Beth & Piaget, 1961, respectively). These volumes presented new experimental evidence for Piaget and Szeminska's claim that the number sequence emerges through the operational synthesis of classification and seriation. This remarkable reassessment was conducted in three steps: a review of new experimental data, comparison of these data against implications derived from a variety of axiomatizations of number, and formalization of the resultant synthesis.

New Experimental Data

In papers published from 1959 to 1962, a whole series of studies consolidated the pioneering experiments by Piaget and Szeminska on several points.

1. They lent additional weight to the assumption that there is strong parallelism at the three stages of development between classification, seriation, and number (conservation tasks). This parallelism, according to Piaget (in Beth & Piaget, 1961, p. 279) ". . . is a first indicator in favor of their interdependence and tends to discount an initial autonomy of number."

2. The validity of this indicator is reinforced by analysis of errors committed by Stage I number-construction subjects (no correspondence), and Stage II subjects (one-to-one correspondence without conservation). One of these errors involves the relationship between class and number. This occurs, for example, if when given two equal sets $A = A' = 7$ drawn, respectively, from two unequal sets M and N (where $M > N$), a child believes that there are quantitatively more A drawn from M than A' drawn from N. This is an illustration of a lack of differentiation between extension (7 elements) and intension (membership of subsets in their original sets). Further, this lack of differentiation is precisely what characterizes the figural collections formed by children in the corresponding substage of development of classification (Piaget & Inhelder, 1959).

Another difficulty in the construction of number can be traced to the underlying system of seriation. This is shown in a well-crafted study by Morf (Gréco & Morf, 1962) on the origins of connectedness of the number sequence. The principle behind the experiment was the following: The experimenter lets roughly 30 blocks (N elements) roll, one by one, down an inclined plane. He asks the child whether, between this total and zero, they will necessarily pass through equality with a reference set K composed of only a few blocks. The results show that before the age of 6, children do not believe it is necessary to refer to the intermediary of K. Moreover, although children readily agree that by adding units to the start set N, a number $N' > N$ will be reached at some point, they find it hard to accept that it is then possible to pass through the equality $K' = N'$. It is well known that the relation that governs the elements in one series (e.g., rod seriation) is simultaneously asymmetrical, connective, and transitive. The whole number sequence is clearly connective as a series, but is also connective in a specific way, because each whole number is separated from all other whole numbers by a unit or a multiple of 1. What the Morf data show is that the number sequence is first constructed like preoperational qualitative seriation, and that it only becomes specified later through the construction of iteration.

3. Although these data, as well as others, argue for a synthesis integrating (by surpassing) the systems of classes and seriation, a fine-grained analysis of commutativity conducted by Gréco on children aged 4 years, 9 months to 8 years, 3 months shows that this construction is laborious (Gréco & Morf, 1962, pp. 151–224). The number sequence is acquired gradually, by portion, from 1 to 7, 8 to 15, and then 15 to 30; the remaining nonarithmetized portions continue to retain, as Piaget himself pointed out in the preface to the third French edition of La Genèse du Nombre in 1967 (p. 11), ". . . their properties of simple classes or simple serial order, as long as the synthesis has not been generalized."

4. Along these same lines, another study by Gréco (1962, pp. 1–70) on the construction of number as assessed by the standard conservation task, demonstrates an intermediate stage between one-to-one correspondence and conservation of quantity. This is the stage of the conservation of *quotity:* the "counted" end amount is conserved before the quantity. Gréco attributed this to a counting effect: ". . . the 'serial aspect' inherent to the act of counting itself serves to determine numerical equivalence classes, even before concrete operational thought has constituted systems of quantitative invariants. Thus, quotity should be assigned a somewhat cardinal, quasinumerical status rather than a pseudonumerical one . . . naturally, because . . . the nesting system that is the basis for true operational cardinality is still absent" (p. 67). The true foundation for cardinality is the iteration operation.

All of these data strengthen the initial hypothesis that the construction of number is built up from the construction of elementary systems, which it surpasses by integrating them.

The Axiomatics of Number: Implications, Confrontations and Formalization

Examination of the different natural number postulates, from Peano's five axioms to Quine's, via those developed by Poincaré and Russell, show that ". . . these different models correspond to possible but highly different ontogenetic models, in such a way that the real problems of number construction are raised much more precisely if we start by comparing the respective implications of these various formalizations." (Piaget, in Beth & Piaget, 1961, p. 270).

Critical comparison of these implications and experimental data, such as the ones just presented lend weight to the Piagetian interpretation. It is clear that the intuition of $n + 1$ (or iteration) is not the primitive given in Poincaré's conjecture. Rather, this intuition develops progressively, and iterative inferences are used by 70% of subjects only at about age 8 (Gréco et al., 1960; p. 104).

The assumption of Whitehead and Russell that ordinals and the number sequence are independent also fails to be confirmed by the data. If the ordinals and cardinals were, in fact, derived from independent formative mechanisms, then, as Piaget stated ". . . the sequence itself would be problematical, as would be the coordination of cardinals and ordinals, but any high number could be structured independently of any other and recurrence, equated to an ordinary serial inference, would be found at all the operational levels of development (hence as early as 7–8)" (Gréco et al., p. 25).

The data show otherwise. Although the constituents of number are clearly logical in nature, these logical constituents give rise to a new synthesis, which does not correspond fully to class composition or to serial composition, but rather to both at the same time. If we disregard qualities, the one-to-one correspondence that Russell drew on to construct class equivalence classes (the *12* months, the *12* Apostles, etc.) is no longer a qualified correspondence but rather a numerical correspondence—which is begging the question, because number has already been introduced to justify the equivalence that supposedly constructs it.

"In short, number is neither a simple system of class inclusion, nor a simple seriation, but rather an indissociable synthesis of inclusion and seriation . . ." (Piaget, 1964b, p. 96). Peano's axioms, where cardinals and ordinals necessarily correspond to and entail iteration, are congruent with the experimental evidence and the genetic psychology interpretation.

The formalization of this interpretation was the work of Grize (1960, pp. 69–96), who began by constructing formalized models of "grouping" of classes and "grouping" of asymmetrical relations. Because of their specific properties—equivalence of elements for the former and differences for the latter—these two groupings are not irreducible. However, Grize showed that the transformation of specified elements into element-units, by disregarding their inherent properties, entails that: (a) all singular classes corresponding to these elements are substitutable; and (b) a vicariant order is introduced, which makes it possible to distinguish classes formed in this way. These transformations ensure the fusion of the two groupings into a system that overcomes their original limitations (stepwise combination in the absence of combinatory rules): This is the number group structure, which confirms Peano's axioms. Thus, the process of number construction in the child, as the data apparently reveal, corresponds to a formalization that sharpens its contours further; a formalization that is indeed arduous, as Droz somewhat ironically points out in this volume, but could it be otherwise? Connes, the mathematician, compared specialists to explorers who "at the price of heroic efforts" finally demonstrate that the list of 26 finite, simple, sporadic groups is complete (Changeux & Connes, 1989, p. 37). Grize and Piaget were, in this sense, explorers and innovators.

Contributions and Limits of Piagetian Structuralism

It is obvious that the experiments, reflections, and debate that took place at the ICGE in the 1960s both reinforced and enhanced the hypotheses put forward by Piaget and Szeminska. It is equally obvious that these new contributions drew even more clearly than before on constructivist and structuralist epistemology. Work on number constitutes, in fact, in Piagetian history the best application of a method in which historico-critical epistemology and developmental psychology are postulated at the outset as indissociable. Recall that the method is based on normative facts, their construction processes, and their evolution. Numerical operations, like all other cognitive operations in the subject, model the physical world. As a special normative system, and because of its inherent symbolic nature, number *reconstructs* reality by quantifying it, by measuring it. This is clearly an example of a logico-mathematical "net" that, for purposes of mastery, "captures" matter, which tends to escape us (see Bideaud & Houdé, 1989). The arithmetization of content and the discrete is "tailor-made for nature" in Changeux and Connes's (1989) felicitous terms. "Don't worry what number is; worry what you can do with it": This is how Papert (1990, p. 11) characterized the Piagetian approach.

This constructivist position, associated with emphasis on the normative pole, accounts for the nature and orientation of the Piagetian investigations of the genesis of number. It also accounts for its major contribution. No one challenges that the construction of the number sequence is *also* based on logical foundations. In this volume, the labeling of Steffe's stages, from perceptual and figurative counting schemes to tacitly and then explicitly nested numbers, seems to fit the process formalized by Grize. This evolution can also be found in the transformation of the number sequence, as described magnificently by Fuson, into a nested, seriated, cardinalized, and unitized sequence.

Piaget's contribution, however, goes beyond the demonstration of underlying logical structures. It also lies in his extraordinary experimental ingenuity as found in the (overly?) well-known conservation of small numerical sets task, and the tasks devised by Morf, Gréco, and Inhelder (see Inhelder et al., 1974). The tasks used since then are, for the most part, variants on Piagetian situations.

A final point is worth making. The data on the precocity of conservation of quotity led Gréco, well before Gelman, to assign a major role to counting and to one-to-one correspondence. The actions of a subject who uses prelearned numeration, gestures, and glances to ensure full one-to-one correspondence, introduces an implicit order, which "plays a major role in number construction; it is in fact the foundation for distinctiveness, without which sets would only be classes or categories" (Gréco, in Gréco & Morf, 1962, p. 68). Here, however, we are already dealing with subject activity and not just operational structuration.

It is here that we encounter the limits of Piagetian investigations. Number is not only a normative system, constructed from weaker logical subsystems. Number is also a cultural object, the product of the same socio-historical evolution investigated by Piaget. The paradox is that Piaget only explored the mechanisms of the growth of scientific knowledge in terms of their evolution, overlooking the fact that these mechanisms produce permanent cultural representations, or knowledge "objects." This was the price he paid for a theory that privileged the structuration of knowledge to the detriment of the psychological functioning of the individual, and operations (i.e. computation) to the detriment of representation.

With regard to these points, *Pathways to Number* fills in certain gaps in operational theory. The volume does so by implicit or at times explicit use of conceptualizations and approaches that tend toward Anglo-Saxon and neostructuralist cognitivist positions.

ANOTHER SCIENTIFIC CONTEXT

In the years between 1940 and 1956, increasing importance was ascribed to ideas deriving from works by Turing, von Neumann, McCulloch and Pitts, and Wiener (see Introduction) suggesting that human intelligence works in a way so similar to that of the computer that cognition can be defined by computation of symbolic representations. This trend gained in momentum in the 1970s with the inception the cognitive sciences, which thrust into the mainstream new conceptualizations drawing on the metaphor of the computer.

New Concepts

Any cognitive actor—whether human or artificial—is endowed with symbolic representations on the state of the world, which form meanings that serve as the basis for computation and, hence, intelligent behavior. This conception led cognitive researchers to focus on forms of representations of knowledge in memory, and the use of this knowledge in problem situations. In line with the computationalist view, these issues were examined in terms of a cognitive architecture having three components: a knowledge base (long-term memory), a factual base (working memory), and an inference engine or control structure. With respect to this architecture, the most significant advances in cognitivism can be found first in the content of long-term memory, which can be activated in working memory, and second, in control structures and the functional constraints affecting implementation and processing of these mnemonic contents. The brief description that follows only highlights those features of direct concern to us here (for a fuller description, see Bideaud & Houdé, 1991).

Representation of knowledge in memory is specified at three levels: representational format (imaginal, verbal or linguistic, and propositional), types of knowledge (declarative or procedural), and modes of organization of knowledge (list structure and semantic networks, production systems and "structured mental objects" such as schemas—frames, scripts—and prototypes). Note that the propositional format, which corresponds to what is termed an *abstract* formalization of information in predicate logic, is located at the level of long-term memory as the infrastructure for imaginal or verbal symbolization. Further, declarative knowledge, whose representational archetype is the propositional format, is located at the level of facts or concepts, independent of actions likely to activate them; procedural knowledge, in contrast, is encapsulated in action.

This architecture as a whole is indicative of two major advances of cognitivism with respect to the Piagetian unitary model of normative and logical activity: (a) The same pieces of information can be represented in long-term memory in different formats, types and modes; and (b) the same problems can be solved through different processing modes as a function of format, type, and mode of representation, activated by a control structure (which explains the need for one). In addition, constraints connected to operationality of the cognitive system are taken into account and are, in a certain way, the counterparts of physical constraints on computational systems (e.g., the restricted capacity of working memory).

But the fundamental difference between the two perspectives lies in the hypotheses put forward to account for the dynamics of cognitive activity. In the Piagetian perspective and its constructivist view, operations and their semantics constrain or "feed" representations. In contrast, in cognitivism's computational view representations or symbols and their semantics constrain and "feed" operations. Thus both approaches can be criticized for polarizing one facet of cognition (operations or representations) and their omission of the other, with in addition, the major lack of a developmental perspective of cognitivism in its original form.

Current neostructuralist theories have rectified this omission (see Case, 1988; Demetriou & Efklides, 1988; K. W. Fischer & Farrar, 1988; Halford, 1988; Pascual-Leone, 1988, for the main representatives and most recent advances). Neostructuralism aims explicitly at articulating the contribution of Genevan structuralism (stages, structures, and developmental mechanisms) and original Anglo-Saxon cognitivism (representations, functional architecture, and constraints) to remedy the weak points in the Piagetian framework. It enhances operational theory on three points. First, the typology of mental representations is now more fine-grained and extended, which broadens the range of types of schemes and structures. Second, constraints on activity are now taken into account, for example, the restricted capacity of working memory. Third, the emphasis is on pragmatic transformation of representations into actions in problem-solving contexts (optimal or suboptimal contextual aids, etc.). In short, the ontogenetic subject is seen as a problem solver in a certain context, having a state of knowledge (problem representation) at each stage and for each problem situation, and one or a set of more-or-less well-defined goals, and more-or-less efficient strategies, as a function of current system constraints (the capacity of short-term memory and operational efficiency).

This emphasis on symbols and representations links neostructuralism to classic cognitivism. The ties are reinforced by the virtual elimination of the Piagetian focus on normative facts and logic. Nevertheless, it differs from cognitivism in that it is resolutely developmental (see earlier discussion). Importantly, a new research trend, developmental cognitivism, is aimed at examining the core issues of cognitivism in the adult (mental imagery, categorization) in a developmental perspective. What makes these models specific is that they are local, as compared to the more general frame of structural models (see Bideaud & Houdé, 1989).

Pathways to Number

This brief description of the main, current conceptualizations in psychology in the field of cognition serves to frame the ways in which each of the chapters in *Pathways to Number* fits into this context and into Piagetian theory.

It is worth stressing at the outset that all the chapters have a common feature: Number and its ontogenesis are approached as a well-defined topic area, without reference to current theories of cognitive development. This doubtless confers a certain unity on the whole. This gain in precision (which calls for further assessment) is probably also associated, however, with a loss in openness.

The remaining heterogeneity can be partially resolved by the fact that most of the chapters can be grouped under two headings as a function of whether the conceptualizations and the approaches tend toward developmental cognitivism or to diverse variants of a Piagetian neostructuralism.

Two chapters are, in my opinion, fairly clearly anchored in a developmental cognitivist perspective: the chapter by Brissiaud, which compares two systems of representation and processing of numerositiy (finger reference sets and number tagging) and the chapter by J.-P. Fischer, which specifies the processes underlying subitizing, with reference to the model of J. R. Anderson on relationships between declarative and procedural knowledge. Baroody's chapter can also be classified under this heading: He acknowledges his weakness for an interactionist position based on R. C. Anderson's schemas. The study of the transition from the representation of a numerical quantity expressed in a source code to the corresponding representation in an object code, presented by Seron, Deloche, and Noel is also part of this trend, and surely Fayol's chapter can be placed within this category as well, in that it integrates knowledge base with internal and external constraints (problem statements) in an additive problem-solving model.

Most of the other offerings aim explicitly at "completing" Piagetian structuralism and, because of this, can be classified as variants of neostructuralism. The first variant is characterized specifically by the search and description of processes subjects implement in specific problem situations. It is, in fact, this approach to algorithmic functioning of logico-mathematical structures—or psychological constructivism of the knowing subject—that underpins the Genevan postPiagetian transition from structures to procedures (see Inhelder, 1987). The chapters by Saada-Robert and Parrat-Dayan are clearly illustrative of this trend. The position taken by Steffe and Fuson can also be located here, in that they explicitly state that they work in a Piagetian framework. Lastly, the elegant study by Tollesfrud-Anderson, Campbell, Starkey, and Cooper enriches Piagetian works on number conservation.

Another variant is found in researchers who refer explicitly to other approaches. This is the case of Sophian, whose empirical data are part of a theory presented as a "synthesis of a Piagetian perspective on conceptual development with a theory of social transmission of procedural knowledge." This is also the case for the Gelman and Meck chapter, which combines a synthesis of nativism, a certain type of functionalism (from principles to procedures) and Piagetian historico-critical epistemology. Meljac's article also belongs under this heading: She describes a voyage that starts from a certain structural prewiredness, and then moves through the evolution of representations and procedures to the Piagetian construction of number.

These classifications under the two broad headings of cognitivism and neo-structuralism help define what we can gain from *Pathways to Number:* the volume is a complement to Piagetian conceptualizations and observations concerning the subject's involvement in the appropriation, interiorization, and procedural utilization of number as a cultural tool, and gives it its unity.

NEW PATHWAYS

This classification, although it gives the volume its unity, cannot, however, conceal the extreme diversity of topics examined. This diversity prompted Droz, who takes a lucid and somewhat playful view of things, to draw a pessimistic conclusion as to the future of research on the psychogenesis of number, which will, in his terms "necessarily be atomistic." It is true that the diversity of empirical data (in this volume, but even more, elsewhere) on counting procedures, linguistic factors, additive and subtractive problems, subitizing, algorithms, number conservation, and so forth would make any researcher feel he or she is dealing with puzzle pieces without having cues to the full picture. Having found certain configurations, and knowing how to recognize when one or several pieces are missing, he or she can even replace some, but it is hard to put the pieces together. In contrast, children, in ordinary learning conditions, form elegant number construction in several years' time. The search for new pathways is doubtless an attempt by psychologists to assemble disparate pieces of knowledge so as to clarify and better understand the polymorphous psychogenesis of number.

One path, in particular, should help place the psychogenesis of number into a more general theory of cognitive development. The major trends today can be found in the conceptually rich (and hence, more general) neostructuralist theories (of Case, K. W. Fischer, etc.), and in cognitive developmental theories that tend to be applied to more restricted fields, such as categorization, which is not entirely foreign to number. Integrating precise data on diverse facets of the psychogenesis of number into a broader conceptualization of cognitive development would, in itself, be a step toward a certain unification and would prompt investigators to formulate new hypotheses. It is practically impossible today to speak of declarative or procedural knowledge without integrating them into the architecture of cognition. The activation of knowledge and the range in types of processing is closely connected to their mode of organization (schemas, networks, lists, etc.) and to the formats in which they can be represented. On the other hand, numerical problem solving, goal recognition, and orientation (see Sophian, this volume) are dependent on the development of control structures (see, e.g., the control structures in Case, 1988, and Pascual-Leone's, 1988, modular attention structure). These few examples highlight the value of recourse to general theories of cognitive development.

A framework developed by Bideaud and Houdé (1991) to synthesize the contributions of cognitivism (meanings) and Piagetian structuralism (computation) in the area of cognitive development can reorient us toward other pathways, as it did in its application to the study of the psychogenesis of categorizations (Houdé, 1991). The central concept of this analytical framework is the Polymorphous Computation and Meaning System (PCMS), which specifies the notion of subject-in-context. Each PCMS contains two components, a Subject component and a Context component. The Subject component covers three subcomponents: a computation device, an integration and meaning-assignment device, and a control device. The Context component has two subcomponents corresponding to a pragmatic or a normative context. The following examples illustrate how these contexts are related to number.

The pragmatic context is the physical and social microgenetic context of a given individual in everyday problem-solving situations (in the broad sense of the word) that involve number: purchase situations (size of a garment, measurements of an object, price and change received, etc.), everyday number tags (street numbers, telephone numbers, etc.), problem statements in schoolwork, and so on. This context has a direct effect on the subject-in-construction (an effect that was overlooked by Piagetian theory but emphasized by most of the authors in this volume). The normative context has a dual influence: on the subject-in-development, through cultural transmission (syntax of the number sequence, teaching and learning of mathematics in school), and on the teacher and the psychologist who observe and theorize about the activity and the development of this same subject and who are influenced by current scientific "know-how." It is obvious that this distinction does not preclude the fact that the two contexts may overlap and be partially, if not totally, intertwined. This is the case of classroom problems, which are contextualized socially in terms of the problem statement and type of teaching, and call for "normative" mathematical operations.

Note that the subject in constructive evolution cannot be dissociated from two contexts: The analytical framework put forward here is that of constructivism-in-context. Nativistic positions, in addition, have been shown to be difficult to defend. Data from the neurosciences and connectionist models do not mesh with the hypothesis of a genetically determined structure, endowed with specified rules. Genes, apparently, do not determine the intricate branching of nerve cells: It is more likely that cerebral responses are selected by predictable stimuli present in the environment, which do not in themselves have a predefined meaning. The brain uses these responses to establish connections and specifications by structuring and categorizing its own activities (see Changeux & Connes, 1989; Edelman, 1987). The Piagetian approach, which acknowledges a predefined but also reconstructed world is not incompatible with these data. The polymorphous psychogenesis of number seems, in addition, to preclude the specifically pre-wired.

This polymorphism, which is incorporated (as its name suggests) in the analytical framework of the PCMS, is expressed in a given subject-in-context by a multitude of computational and meaning subsystems (CMS) each of which is characterized by specific weightings of the subcomponents of the PCMS (computation, meaning, and control; pragmatic context and normative context). Thus, if each subcomponent of the PCMS can be defined as a dimension, and if the position of each behavioral instance in the subject can be defined along this dimension, then the degree of subsystem (or structural) similarity between observed behaviors can be measured by an formula, such as:

$$S_{AB} = f\ [(p_c.C, p_m.M, p._{ct}.CT, p_p.P, p_n.N)]$$

where A and B are the behaviors that are compared; C, M, CT, P, and N are the five subcomponents of the CMPS (Computation, Meaning, and Control; Pragmatic Context and Normative Context), and p corresponds to the relative importance of the subcomponents in terms of their involvement in the behavior(s) in question. This is merely one way of formulating this relation, and it is obviously theoretical: The quantification of the weightings (p), of course, is difficult. This can, however, be represented in the initial steps in scale form. On the basis of an a priori inventory of the pragmatic and normative contexts, these contexts can yield a first approximation of the degree of (necessary or unnecessary) entailment of the computation, and meaning and control processes in the specific tasks given to the subjects.

Steps in the construction of number, as described by Steffe, Fuson, or Meljac, can be analyzed in terms of coordination of subsystems of computation and meaning (SCM). On the level of perceptual counting (Steffe), the "string" level (Fuson), or nondissociation (Meljac), high weight is attached to the Meaning (M) and Pragmatic (P) context subcomponents, and the use of number occurs most often within socially contextualized schemas. The transition toward dissociation, reversibility, and inhibition of number chaining calls for a higher weighting of the Computation (C), Control (CT) and Normative context (N) subcomponents. The emergence of these subcomponents would benefit from closer examination, in particular with respect to the control mentioned by Sophian in this volume (goals, strategies, focus, and inhibition). On the basis of a possible typology of the various P and N contexts in which number intervenes, it would be easier to specify on which points and in which optimal context progress takes place. In addition, at a given stage in development and as a function of learning procedures, different subsystems may operate separately or in synergy, with the emergence of the Computation and Control subsystems, whose weightings vary as a function of activated and activate-able subsystems. This is probably the case for the subsystems involved in the use of finger reference sets and number count tags compared by Brissiaud. An application of this grid to Meljac's observations could serve to pinpoint in a more precise fashion fissures already detected in learning disabled children.

These examples are merely a rough outline of what I see as an application of this analytical framework. It is obviously not a theory. The number of subsystems, their nature, and their interrelations remain unspecified. The framework is an open one, which allows it to integrate and treat the existing data by indicating to what extent they are complete or incomplete. This could be the point of departure for theory building, which while respecting the diversity and complexity Vergnaud stresses in this volume, could account for both the unity underlying the apparent heterogeneity of behaviors and the coordinations established by the child over the course of development of mathematical thinking.

References

Agnoli, F., & Zhu, J. (1989). One, due, san: Learning to count in English, Italian, and Chinese [Abstract]. *1p12Proceedings of the Biennial Meeting of the Society for Research in Child Development, 6*, 75.

Allal, L., & Saada-Robert, M. (1991a). *Les régulations en jeu dans une situation de production écrite: position des problèmes.* Unpublished manuscript.

Allal, L., & Saada-Robert, M. (1991b). La métacognition: cadre conceptuel pour l'étude des régulations en situation scolaire. (Unpublished manuscript).

Allardice, B. S., & Ginsburg, H. P. (1983). Children's psychological difficulties in mathematics. In II. P. Ginsburg (Ed.), *The developmenty of mathematical thinking* (pp. 319-349). Orlando, FL: Academic.

Anderson, J. R. (1983). *The architecture of cognition.* Cambridge, MA: Harvard University Press.

Anderson, R. C. (1984). Some reflections on the acquisition of knowledge. *Educational Researcher, 13*(9), 5-10.

APA (1985). *Manuel diagnostique et statistique des troubles mentaux* (DSM III). American Psychiatric Association (translated by J. D. Guelfi & P. Pichot). Paris: Masson.

Apostel, L., Mays, W., Morf, A., & Piaget, J. (1957). *Les liaisons analytiques et synthétiques dans les comportements du sujet* (Etudes d'épistémologie génétique, Vol. IV). Paris: Presses Universitaires de France.

Ashcraft, M. H. (1982). The development of mental arithmetic: A chronometric approach. *Developmental Review, 2*, 213–236.

Ashcraft, M. H., & Battaglia, J. (1978). Cognitive arithmetic: Evidence for retrieval and decision processes in mental addition. *Journal of Experimental Psychology: Human Learning and Memory, 4*, 527–538.

Ashcraft, M. H., & Fierman, B. A. (1982). Mental addition in third, fourth, and sixth graders. *Journal of Experimental Child Psychology, 33*, 216–234.

Audigier, M.-N., Clavier, Y., Clavié, C., & Clesse, C. (1985). *Enseigner les mathématiques au cours préparatoire.* Paris: Hatier.

Bacquet, M., & Gueritte-Hess, B. (1982). Le nombre et la numération: Pratique de rééducation. Paris: Isoscel.

Baldwin, J. M. (1897). *Le développement mental chez l'enfant et dans la race.* Paris: Alcan. (Original work published in 1895)

363

Baratta-Lorton, M. (1976). *Mathematics their way.* Menlo Park, CA: Addison-Wesley.

Barbot de, F., Meljac, C., Truscelli, D., & Henry-Amar, M. (1989). *Pour une meilleure intégration scolaire des enfants IMC: L'importance des premiers apprentissages en mathématiques.* Vanves: CTNERHI-MIRE.

Baroody, A. J. (1984). More precisely defining and measuring the order-irrelevance principle. *Journal of Experimental Child Psychology, 38,* 33–41.

Baroody, A. J., & Mason, C. A. (1985, April). *Early arithmetic thinking processes.* Paper presented at the annual meeting of the National Council of Teachers of Mathematics, San Antonio, TX.

Baroody, A. J. (1986a). Basic counting principles used by mentally retarded children. *Journal for Research in Mathematics Education, 17,* 382–389.

Baroody, A. J. (1986b). Counting ability of moderately and mildly mentally handicapped children. *Education and Training of the Mentally Retarded, 21,* 289–300.

Baroody, A. J. (1987a). *Children's mathematical thinking.* New York: Columbia University Press.

Baroody, A. J. (1987b). *Children's mathematical thinking: A developmental framework for preschool, primary, and special education teachers.* New York: Teachers College Press.

Baroody, A. J. (1987c). The development of counting strategies for single-digit addition. *Journal for Research in Mathematics Education, 18,* 141–157.

Baroody, A. J. (1987d). Problem size and mentally retarded children's judgements of commutativity. *American Journal of Mental Deficiency, 91,* 439–442.

Baroody, A. J. (1988). Number-comparison learning by children classified as mentally retarded. *American Journal on Mental Retardation, 92,* 461–471.

Baroody, A. J. (1989). *A guide to teaching mathematics in the primary grades.* Boston: Allyn & Bacon.

Baroody, A. J. (1991). Teaching mathematics developmentally to children classified as learning disabled. In D. K. Reid, W. P. Hresko, & H. L. Swanson (Eds.), *A cognitive approach to learning disabilities* (2nd ed., pp. 375–429). Austin, TX: Pro-Ed.

Baroody, A. J., & Gannon, K. E. (1984). The development of the commutativity principle and economical addition strategies. *Cognition and Instruction, 1,* 321–339.

Baroody, A. J., & Ginsburg, H. P. (1986). The relationship between initial meaningful and mechanical knowledge of arithmetic. In J. Hiebert (Ed.), *Conceptual and procedural knowledge: The case of mathematics* (pp. 75–112). Hillsdale, NJ: Lawrence Erlbaum Associates.

Baroody, A. J., Ginsburg, H. P., & Waxman, B. (1983). Children's use of mathematical structure. *Journal for Research in Mathematics Education, 14,* 156–168.

Baroody, A. J., & Hank, M. (1990). *Elementary mathematics activities: Teachers' guidebook.* Boston: Allyn & Bacon.

Baroody, A. J., & Price, J. (1983). The development of the number word sequence in the counting of three-year-olds. *Journal for Research in Mathematics Education, 14,* 361–368.

Barrouillet, P. (1989). Manipulation de modèles mentaux et compréhension de la notion d'inclusion au delà de 11 ans. *C.P.C.: European Bulletin of Cognitive Psychology, 9,* 337–356.

Beckmann, H. (1923). Die Entwicklung der Zahlleistung bei 2-6 jährigen Kindern [The development of number performance in the 2- to 6-year old children]. *Zeitschrift für Angewandte Psychologie, 22,* 1–72.

Beckwith, M., & Restle, F. (1966). Process of enumeration. *Psychological Review, 73,* 437–444.

Bednarz, N., & Dufour-Janvier, B. (1986). Une étude des conceptions inappropriées développées par les enfants dans l'apprentissage de la numération au primaire. *European Journal of Psychology of Education, 1,* 17–33.

Bednarz, N., & Janvier, B. (1982). The understanding of numeration in primary school. *Educational Studies in Mathematics, 13,* 33–57.

Beihuizen, M. (1985). *Evaluation of the use of structured materials in the teaching of primary mathematics.* Aspects of Educational Technology, New Directions in Education and Training Technology (pp. 246–258). New York: Nichols Publishing Co.

Beilin, H. (1968). Cognitive capacities of young children: A replication. *Science, 162,* 920–921.

Beilin, H. (1975). *Studies in the cognitive basis of language development.* New York: Academic.

Bell, M., & Burns, J. (1981). Counting and numeration capabilities of primary school children: A preliminary report. In T. R. Post & M. P. Roberts (Eds.), *Proceedings of the Third Annual Meeting of the North American Chapter of the International Group for the Psychology of Mathematics Education* (pp. 17–23). Minneapolis: MN: University of Minnesota.

Bergès, J., Fagard, J., Ferron, C., Meljac, C., Netchine, S., Pauchard, P., Preneron, C., Salazar-Orvig, A., & Sprenger-Charolles, L. (1986). *Les impossibilités persistantes de lecture chez les enfants âgés de 9 ans et plus.* Communication au Congrès International de Psychiatrie de l'Enfant et de l'Adolescent. *Paris, Juillet, Texte ronéot.*

Beth, E. W., & Piaget, J. (1961). *Etudes d'épistémologie génétique: Vol. XIV. Epistémologie mathématique et psychologie.* Paris: Presses Universitaires de France.

Bever, T. G., Mehler, J., & Epstein, J. (1968). What children do in spite of what they know. *Science, 162,* 921–924.

Bideaud, J. (1980). Nombre, sériation, inclusion: irrégularités du développement et perspectives de recherche. *Bulletin de Psychologie, 33,* 659–665.

Bideaud, J. (1988). *Logique et bricolage chez l'enfant.* Lille: Presses Universitaires de Lille.

Bideaud, J. (1990). Vous avez dit "structure"? *Archives de Psychologie, 58,* 165–184.

Bideaud, J., & Houdé, O. (1987). Représentation analogique et résolution du problème dit "d'inclusion". *Archives de Psychologie, 55,* 281–303.

Bideaud, J., & Houdé, O. (1989). Le développement des catégorisations: "capture" logique ou "capture" écologique des propriétés des objets. *L'Année Psychologique, 89,* 87–123.

Bideaud, J., & Houdé, O. (1991). *Développement et cognition: Boîte à outils théoriques.* Berne: Peter Lang.

Biemüller, W. (1932). Wiedergabe der Gliederanzahl und Gliederungsform optischer Komplexe [Reproduction of number and arrangement of the parts of optical complexes]. In F. Krueger & F. Sanders (Eds.), *Gestalt und Sinn* (pp. 163–283). München: Beck.

Bilsky, L. H., & Judd, T. (1986). Sources of difficulty in the solution of verbal arithmetic problems by mentally retarded individuals. *American Journal of Mental Deficiency, 86,* 395–402.

Binet, A. (1890). La perception des longueurs et des nombres chez quelques petits enfants. *Revue Philosophique, 30,* 68–81.

Black, J. B., Turner, J. T., & Bower, G. H. (1979). Point of view in narrative comprehension, memory, and production. *Journal of Verbal Learning and Verbal Behavior, 18,* 187–198.

Bley, N. S., & Thornton, C. A. (1981). *Teaching mathematics to the learning disabled.* Rockville, MD: Aspen.

Born, M. (1965). *My life and my views.* New York: Charles Scribner's Sons.

Bovet, M., Parrat-Dayan, S., & Deshusses-Addor, D. (1981). Peut-on parler de précocité et de régression dans la conservation? I. Précocité. *Archives de Psychologie, 49,* 289–303.

Brainerd, C. J. (1973). Judgments and explanations as criteria for the presence of cognitive structures. *Psychological Bulletin, 79,* 172–179.

Brainerd, C. J. (Ed.). (1982). *Children's logical and mathematical cognition.* New York: Springer-Verlag.

Bresson, F., & Schonen de, S. (1979). Le développement cognitif. Les problèmes que pose aujourd'hui son étude. *Revue de Psychologie appliquée, 29* 119–127.

Briars, D. J., & Larkin, J. H. (1984). An integrated model of skill in solving elementary word problems. *Cognition and Instruction, 1,* 245–296.

Briars, D. J., & Siegler, R. S. (1984). A featural analysis of preschoolers' counting knowledge. *Developmental Psychology, 20,* 607–618.

Bringuier, C., Gorlier, S., Perrot, G., & Ragot, A. (1989). *Atout math CP: Livre du maître.* Paris: Hachette.

Brissiaud, R. (1989). *Comment les enfants apprennent à calculer: Au-delà de Piaget et de la théorie des ensembles.* Paris: Retz.

Broadbent, D. E. (1975). The magic number seven after fifteen years. In A. Kennedy & A. Wilkes (Eds.), *Studies in long-term memory* (pp. 3–18). New York: Wiley.

Broughton, J., & Freeman-Moir, D. J. (1982). *The cognitive developmental psychology of James Mark Baldwin: Current theory and research in genetic epistemology.* Norwood, NJ: Allen.

Brousseau, G. (1989). Obstacles épistémologiques, conflits socio-cognitifs et ingénierie didactique. In N. Bednarz & C. Garnier (Eds.), *Construction des savoirs: Obstacles et conflits* (pp. 277–285). Ottawa: CIRADE Agence d'ARC Inc.

Brown, A., & Kane, M. J. (1988). Preschool children can learn to transfer: Learning to learn and learning from example. *Cognitive Development, 20,* 493–523.

Bruner, J. S. (1964). The course of cognitive growth. *American Psychologist, 19,* 1–16.

Bryant, P. (1974). *Perception and understanding in young children: An experimental approach.* New York: Basic Books.

Bryant, P. (1982). The role of conflict and of agreement between intellectual strategies in children's ideas about measurement. *British Journal of Psychology, 73,* 242–251.

Bullock, M., & Gelman, R. (1977). Numerical reasoning in young children: The ordering principle. *Child Development, 48,* 427–434.

Campbell, R. L., & Bickhard, M. H. (1987). A deconstruction of Fodor's anticonstructivism. *Human Development, 30,* 48–59.

Campbell, R. L., Cooper, R. G., Jr., & Blevins-Knabe, B. (1988).*The development of subitizing in preschool and early elementary school children* (IBM Research Report RC 14168). Yorktown Heights, NY: IBM.

Cantor, G. (1879–1884). Über unendliche, lineare Punktmannigfaltigheiten [On infinite, linear varieties of points]. *Mathematische Annalen, 15,* 1–7; *17,* 355–388; *20,* 113–121, *21,* 51–58; *23* 453–488.

Carpenter, T. P. (1985). How children solve simple word problems. *Education and Urban Society, 17,* 417–425.

Carpenter, T. P., Hiebert, J., & Moser, J. M. (1981). Problem structure and first-grade children's initial solution processes for simple addition and subtraction problems. *Journal for Research in Mathematics Education, 12,* 27–39.

Carpenter, T. P., & Moser, J. M. (1982). The development of addition and subtraction problem-solving skills. In T. P. Carpenter, J. M. Moser, & T. A. Romberg (Eds.), *Addition and subtraction: A cognitive perspective* (pp. 9–24). Hillsdale, NJ: Lawrence Erlbaum Associates.

Carpenter, T. P., & Moser, J. M. (1983). The acquisition of addition and subtraction concepts. In R. Lesh and M. Landau (Eds.), *Acquisition of mathematics: Concepts and processes* (pp. 7–44). New York: Academic Press.

Carpenter, T. P., & Moser, J. M. (1984). The acquisition of addition and subtraction concepts in grades one through three. *Journal for Research in Mathematics Education, 15,* 179–202.

Carpenter, T. P., Moser, J. M., & Romberg, T. A. (Eds.). (1982). *Addition and subtraction: A cognitive perspective.* Hillsdale, NJ: Lawrence Erlbaum Associates.

Carraher, T. N., Carraher, D. W., & Schliemann, A. D. (1985). Mathematics in the streets and in schools. *British Journal of Developmental Psychology, 3,* 21–29.

Carrison, D., & Werner, H. (1943). Principles and methods of teaching arithmetic to mentally retarded children. *American Journal of Mental Deficiency, 47,* 309–317.

Case, R. (1988). The structure and process of intellectual development. In A. Demetriou (Ed.), *The neo-Piagetian theories of cognitive development: Toward an integration* (pp. 65–101). Amsterdam: Elsevier North Holland.

Cassirer, E. (1977). *Substance et fonction: éléments pour une théorie du concept.* Paris: Editions de Minuit. (Original work published 1910)

Cassirer, E. (1972). *La philosophie des formes symboliques* (Vol. 1). Paris: Editions de Minuit. (Original work published 1923)

Changeux, J.-P., & Connes, A. (1989). *Matière à pensée.* Paris: Editions Odile Jacob.

Charness, N., & Shea, J. (1981, June). *Enumeration and the hemispheres: Is counting right?* Paper presented at the annual meeting of the Canadian Psychological Association, Toronto, Ontario.

Chi, M. T. H., & Klahr, D. (1975). Span and rate of apprehension in children and adults. *Journal of Experimental Child Psychology, 19*, 434–439.

Chichignoud, M.-P. (1985). *Le concept de nombre: Etude des structures additives et soustractives en relation avec la suite numérique chez des enfants d'âge préscolaire.* Thèse en vue de l'obtention du doctorat en Psychologie—EHESS—Laboratoire d'études des processus cognitifs et du langage.

Clark, H. H., & Haviland, S. E. (1977). Comprehension and the given–new contract. In R. O. Freedle (Ed.), *Discourse processes* (pp. 1–40). Norwood, NJ: Ablex.

Cobb, P., & Steffe, L. P. (1983). The constructivist researcher as teacher and model builder. *Journal for Research in Mathematics Education, 14*, 83–94.

Cockcroft, W. H. (1982). *Mathematics counts: Report of the committee of inquiry into the teaching of mathematics in schools.* London: HMSO.

Cohen, M. (1987). *A study of the use and "misuse" of the How Many? Exhibit at the Please Touch Museum.* Unpublished manuscript, University of Pennsylvania, University Park.

Comiti, C., Bessot, A., & Pariselle, C. (1980). Analyse de comportements d'élèves du cours préparatoire confrontés à une tâche de construction d'un ensemble équipotent à un ensemble donné. *Recherches en Didactique des Mathématiques, 1*, 171–217.

Cooper, R. G., Jr. (1984). Early number development: Discovering number space with addition and subtraction. In C. Sophian (Ed.), *Origins of cognitive skills* (pp. 157–192). Hillsdale, NJ: Lawrence Erlbaum Associates.

Cooper, R. G., Jr., Campbell, R. L., & Blevins, B. (1983). Numerical representation from infancy to middle childhood: What develops? In D. Rogers & J. A. Sloboda (Eds.), *The acquisition of symbolic skills* (pp. 523–533). New York: Plenum.

Cowan, R. (1979). Performance in number conservation tasks as a function of the number of items. *British Journal of Psychology, 70*, 77–81.

Cramaussel, E. (1908). *Le premier éveil intellectuel de l'enfant.* Montpellier: L'abeille.

Cuneo, D. O. (1982). Children's judgments of numerical quantity: A new view of early quantification. *Cognitive Psychology, 14*, 13–44.

Dantzig, T. (1930/1954). *Number: The language of science.* New York. The Free Press.

Davydov, V. V., & Andronov, V. P. (1981). [The psychological conditions for the origination of ideal actions] (Project Paper 81-2). Madison: University of Wisconsin, Wisconsin Research and Development Center for Individualized Schooling.

De Corte, E., & Verschaffel, L. (1987). The effect of semantic structure on first graders strategies for solving addition and subtraction word problems. *Journal for Research in Mathematics Education, 18*, 363–381.

De Corte, E., Verschaffel, L., & De Win, L. (1985). Influence of rewording verbal problems on children's problem representation and solutions. *Journal of Educational Psychology, 77*, 460–470.

Decroly, O., & Degand, J. (1912). Observations relatives à l'évolution des notions de quantités continues et discontinues chez l'enfant. *Archives de Psychologie, 12*, 81–121.

Dedekind, R. (1932). Was sind und was sollen die Zahlen? [What are numbers and what are they for?] In R. Dedekind, *Gesammelte mathematische Werke* (Vol.3, pp. 335–391). Braunschweig: Vieweg. (Original work published 1888)

Dellarosa, D. (1986). A computer simulation of children's arithmetic word-problem solving. *Behavior Research Methods, Instruments, & Computers, 18*, 147–154.

Dellarosa-Cummins, D., Kintsch, W., Reusser, K., & Weimer, R. (1988). The role of understanding in solving word problems. *Cognitive Psychology, 20*, 405–438.

Deloche, G., & Seron, X. (1982a). From one to 1: An analysis of a transcoding process by means of neuropsychological data. *Cognition, 12*, 119–149.

Deloche, G., & Seron, X. (1982b). From three to 3: A differential analysis of skills in transcoding quantities between patients with Broca's and Wernicke's aphasia. *Brain, 105*, 719–733.

Deloche, G., & Seron, X. (1987). Numerical transcoding: A general production model. In G.

Deloche & X. Seron (Eds.), *Mathematical disabilities: A cognitive neuropsychological perspective* (pp. 137–170). Hillsdale, NJ: Lawrence Erlbaum Associates.

Demetriou, A., & Efklides, A. (1988). Experiential structuralism and neo-Piagetian theories: Toward an integration model. In A. Demetriou (Ed.), *The neo-piagetian theory of development: Toward an integration* (pp. 173–222). Amsterdam: Elsevier North Holland.

Descoeudres, A. (1928). *The education of mentally defective children.* Boston: Heath.

Descoeudres, A. (1946). *Le développement de l'enfant de deux à sept ans* (3rd ed.). Neuchâtel: Delachaux & Niestlé. (Original work published 1921)

Dienes, Z. P. (1960). *Building up mathematics.* London: Hutchinson Educational, Ltd.

Donaldson, M. (1978). *Children's minds.* New York: Norton.

Donaldson, M., & Balfour, G. (1968). Less is more. *British Journal of Psychology, 59,* 461–471.

Douady, R. (1980). Approche des nombres réels en situation d'apprentissage scolaire: Enfants de 6 à 11 ans. *Recherches en Didactique des Mathématiques, 1,* 77–111.

Douglass, H. R. (1925). The development of number concept in children of pre-school and kindergarten ages. *Journal of Experimental Psychology, 8,* 443–470.

Droz, R. (1981). Psychogenèse des conduites de comptage. *Bulletin de l'Académie Nationale de Psychologie, 1,* 45–49.

Droz, R., & Paschoud, J. (1981). Le comptage et la procédure "(+1)-itéré" dans l'exploration intuitive de l'addition. *Revue Suisse de Psychologie, 40,* 219–237.

Durkin, K., Shire, B., Riem, R., Crowther, R. D., & Rutter, D. R. (1986). The social and linguistic context of early number word use. *British Journal of Developmental Psychology, 4,* 269–288.

Easley, J. (1983). A Japanese approach to arithmetic. *For the Learning of Mathematics, 3,* 8–15.

Edelman, G. (1987). *Neural Darwinism.* New York: Basic Books.

Elkind, D. (1961). Children's discovery of the conservation of mass, weight, and volume: Piaget replication study II. *Journal of Genetic Psychology, 98,* 219–227.

Elkind, D. (1964). Discrimination, seriation and numeration of size and dimensional difference in young children: Piagetian replication study VI. *Journal of Genetic Psychology, 104,* 275–296.

Elkind, D. (1967). Piaget's conservation problem. *Child Development, 38,* 15–27.

Escarabajal, M.-C. (1987). Quel problème l'enfant résout-il? In J. Vivier (Ed.), *Les problèmes de l'enfant à l'école élémentaire* (pp. 79–98). Caen: Ecole Normale du Calvados.

Fayol, M. (1985). Nombre, numération et dénombrement: Que sait-on de leur acquisition? *Revue Française de Pédagogie, 70,* 59–77.

Fayol, M. (1990). *L'enfant et le nombre.* Neuchâtel: Delachaux & Niestlé.

Fayol, M. (in preparation). *Commutativity and meaning: From counting-on from first to counting-on from larger.* Unpublished manuscript.

Fayol, M., & Abdi, H. (1986). Impact des formulations sur la résolution de problèmes additifs. *European Journal of Psychology of Education, 1,* 41–58.

Fayol, M., Abdi, H., & Gombert, J.-E. (1987). Arithmetic problems formulation and working memory load. *Cognition and Instruction, 4,* 183–202.

Fayol, M., & Monteil, J.-M. (1988). The notion of script: From general to developmental and social psychology. *C.P.C.: European Bulletin of Cognitive Psychology, 8,* 335–361.

Fernberger, S. W. (1921). A preliminary study of the range of visual apprehension. *American Journal of Psychology, 32,* 121–133.

Ferreiro, E. (1971). *Les relations temporelles dans le langage de l'enfant.* Genève: Droz.

Fischer, J.-P. (1981). Développement et fonctions du comptage chez l'enfant de 3 à 6 ans. *Recherches en Didactique des Mathématiques, 2,* 277–302.

Fischer, J.-P. (1984). *La dénomination des nombres par l'enfant.* Strasboug: IREM.

Fischer, J.-P. (1985). *Etude complémentaire sur l'appréhension du nombre.* Strasbourg: IREM.

Fischer, J.-P. (1986). *Eléments de psychologie pour l'apprentissage des mathématiques.* Strasbourg: IREM.

Fischer, J.-P. (1990). Pourquoi les élèves asiatiques surclassent-ils les américains (en maths)? In R. Duval (Ed.), *Annales de Didactique et de Sciences Cognitives* (Vol. 3, pp. 103–141). Strasbourg: IREM.

Fischer, J.-P. (1991). *Apprentissages numériques: La distinction procédural/déclaratif.* Nancy: Presses Universitaires.

Fischer, J.-P., & Meljac, C. (1987). Pour une réhabilitation du dénombrement: Le rôle du comptage dans les tout premiers apprentissages. *Revue Canadienne de Psycho-Education, 16*, 31–47.

Fischer, J.-P., & Pluvinage, F. (1988). Complexités de compréhension et d'exécution des opérations arithmétiques élémentaires. *Recherches en Didactique des Mathématiques, 9*, 133–154.

Fischer, K. W., & Farrar, M. J. (1988). Generalizations about generalization: How a theory of skill development explains both generality and specificity. In A. Demetriou (Ed.), *The neo-piagetian theories of development: Toward an integration* (pp. 137–171). Amsterdam: Elsevier North Holland.

Fletcher, C. R. (1985). Understanding and solving arithmetic word problems: A computer simulation. *Behavior Research Methods, Instruments & Computers, 17*, 565–571.

Flexer, R. J. (1986, November). The power of five: The step before the power of ten. *Arithmetic Teacher, 34*, 5–10.

Folk, C. L., Egeth, H., & Kwak, H. W. (1988). Subitizing: Direct apprehension or serial processing? *Perception & Psychophysics, 44*, 313–320.

Frege, G. (1884). *Die grundlage der Arithmetik: Eine logisch-mathematische Untersuchung über den Begriff der Zahl* [The foundations of arithmetic. A logico-mathematical research on the concept of number]. Breslau: W. Koebner.

Frydman, O., & Bryant, P. (1988). Sharing and the understanding of number equivalence by young children. *Cognitive Development, 3*, 323–339.

Frye, D., Braisby, N., Lowe, J., Maroudas, C., & Nicholls, J. (1989). Young children's understanding of counting and cardinality. *Child Development, 60*, 1158–1171.

Fuson, K. C. (1982). An analysis of the counting-on solution procedure in addition. In T. P. Carpenter, J. M. Moser, & T. A. Romberg (Eds.), *Addition and subtraction: A cognitive perspective* (pp. 67–81). Hillsdale, NJ: Lawrence Erlbaum Associates.

Fuson, K. C. (1984). More complexities in subtraction. *Journal for Research in Mathematics Education, 15*, 214–225.

Fuson, K. C. (1986a). Roles of representation and verbalization in the teaching of multi-digit addition and subtraction. *European Journal of Psychology of Education, 1*, 35–56.

Fuson, K. C. (1986b). Teaching children to subtract by counting up. *Journal for Research in Mathematics Education, 17*, 172–189.

Fuson, K. C. (1988). *Children's counting and concepts of number.* New York: Springer-Verlag.

Fuson, K. C. (1990). Conceptual structures for multiunit numbers: Implications for learning and teaching, multidigit addition, subtraction, and place-value. *Cognition and Instruction, 7*, 343–404.

Fuson, K. C. (1991). Research on learning and teaching addition and subtraction of whole numbers. In G. Leinhardt, R. T. Putnam, & R. Hattrup (Eds.), *Analysis of arithmetic for mathematics teaching.* Hillsdale, NJ: Lawrence Erlbaum Associates.

Fuson, K. C. (in press). Research on whole number addition and subtraction. In D. Grouws (Ed.), *Handbook of research on mathematics teaching and learning.* New York: Macmillan.

Fuson, K. C., & Briars, D. J. (1990). Using a base-ten blocks learning/teaching approach for first- and second-grade place value and multidigit addition and subtraction. *Journal for Research in Mathematics Education, 21*, 180–206.

Fuson, K. C., & Hall, J. W. (1983). The acquisition of early number word meanings: A conceptual analysis and review. In H. P. Ginsburg (Ed.), *The development of mathematical thinking* (pp. 49–107). New York: Academic.

Fuson, K. C., & Kwon, Y. (in press-a). Korean children's single-digit addition and subtraction: Numbers structured by ten. *Journal for Research in Mathematics Education*.

Fuson, K. C., & Kwon, Y. (in press-b). Korean children's understanding of multidigit addition and subtraction. *Child Development*.

Fuson, K. C., Pergament, G. G., & Lyons, B. G. (1985). Collection terms and preschoolers' use of the cardinality rule. *Cognitive Psychology, 17*, 315–323.

Fuson, K. C., Pergament, G. G., Lyons, B. G., & Hall, J. W. (1985). Children's conformity to the cardinality rule as a function of set size and counting accuracy. *Child Development, 56*, 1429–1436.

Fuson, K. C., Richards, J., & Briars, D. J. (1982). The acquisition and elaboration of the number word sequence. In C. Brainerd (Ed.), *Progress in cognitive development: Children's logical and mathematical cognition* (Vol. 1, pp. 33–92). New York: Springer-Verlag.

Fuson, K. C., & Secada, W. G. (1986). Teaching children to add by counting on with finger patterns. *Cognition and Instruction, 3*, 229–260.

Fuson, K. C., Secada, W. G., & Hall, J. W. (1983). Matching, counting, and conservation of numerical equivalence. *Child Development, 54*, 91–97.

Fuson, K. C., Stigler, J. W., & Bartsch, K. (1988). Grade placement of addition and subtraction topics in China, Japan, the Soviet Union, Taiwan, and the United States. *Journal for Research in Mathematics Education, 19*, 449–458.

Fuson, K. C., & Willis, G. B. (1988). Subtracting by counting up: More evidence. *Journal for Research in Mathematics Education, 19*, 402–420.

Gallistel, C. R. (1988). Counting versus subitizing versus the sense of number. The *Behavioral and Brain Sciences, 11*, 585–586.

Gallistel, C. R. (1989). Animal cognition: The representation of space, time, and number. *Annual Review of Psychology, 40*, 155–189.

Gallistel, C. R. (1990). *The organization of learning*. Cambridge, MA: Bradford Books/MIT Press.

Gallistel, C. R., Brown, A. L., Carey, S., Gelman, R., & Keil, F. (1991). Lessons from animal learning for the study of cognitive development. In S. Carey & R. Gelman (Eds.), *The epigenesis of mind* (pp. 3–33). Hillsdale, NJ: Lawrence Erlbaum Associates.

Gallistel, C. R., & Gelman, R. (1992). Preverbal and verbal counting and computation. *Cognition*.

Geary, D. C., Widaman, K. F., Little, T. D., & Cormier, P. (1987). Cognitive addition: Comparison of learning disabled and academically normal elementary school children. *Cognitive Development, 2*, 249–269.

Gelman, R. (1972). The nature and development of early number concepts. In H. W. Reese (Ed.), *Advances in child development and behavior* (Vol. 7, pp. 115–167). New York: Academic Press.

Gelman, R. (1977). How young children reason about small numbers. In J. Castellan, D. B. Pisoni, & G. Potts (Eds.), *Cognitive theory* (Vol. 2, pp. 219–238). Hillsdale, NJ: Lawrence Erlbaum Associates.

Gelman, R. (1982a). Accessing one-to-one correspondence: Still another paper about conservation. *British Journal of Psychology, 73*, 209–220.

Gelman, R. (1982b). Basic numerical abilities. In R. J. Sternberg (Ed.), *Advances in the psychology of human intelligence* (pp. 181–205). Hillsdale, NJ: Lawrence Erlbaum Associates.

Gelman, R. (1983). Les bébés et le calcul. *La recherche, 14*, 1382–1389.

Gelman, R. (1990). First principles organize attention to and learning about relevant data: Number and the animate–inanimate distinction as examples. *Cognitive Science, 14*, 79–106.

Gelman, R. (in press). Constructivism and supporting environments. In D. Tirosh (Ed.), *Implicit and explicit knowledge: An educational approach*. New York: Ablex.

Gelman, R., & Baillargeon, R. (1983). A review of some Piagetian concepts. In J. Flavell & E. Markman (Eds.), *Handbook of child psychology: Vol. 3. Cognitive development* (pp. 167–230). New York: Wiley.

Gelman, R., & Cohen, M. (1988). Qualitative differences in the way Down's syndrome and normal children solve a novel counting problem. In L. Nadel (Ed.), *The psychobiology of Down's syndrome* (pp. 51–99). Cambridge, MA: MIT Press/Bradford Books.

Gelman, R., Cohen, M., & Hartnett, P. (1989). To know mathematics is to go beyond thinking that "Fractions aren't numbers." In (Ed.), *Proceedings of the 11th Annual Meeting of the North American Chapter of the International Group for Psychology of Mathematics Education.*

Gelman, R., & Gallistel, C. R. (1978). *The child's understanding of number.* Cambridge, MA: Harvard University Press.

Gelman, R., & Greeno, J. G. (1989). On the nature of competence: Principles for understanding in a domain. In L. B. Resnick (Ed.), *Knowing, learning, and instruction: Essays in honor of Robert Glaser* (pp. 125–186). Hillsdale, NJ: Lawrence Erlbaum Associates.

Gelman, R., & Massey, C. (1988). The cultural unconscious as contributor to the supporting environments for cognitive development. *Monographs of the Society for Research in Child Development, 52*(2, Serial No. 216, pp. 39–151).

Gelman, R., & Meck, E. (1983). Preschoolers' counting: Principles before skill. *Cognition, 13,* 343–359.

Gelman, R., & Meck, E. (1986). The notion of principle: The case of counting. In J. Hiebert (Ed.), *Conceptual and procedural knowledge: The case of mathematics* (pp. 29–57). Hillsdale, NJ: Lawrence Erlbaum Associates.

Gelman, R., Meck, E., & Merkin, S. (1986). Young children's numerical competence. *Cognitive Development, 1,* 1–29.

Gelman, R., & Tucker, M. F. (1975). Further investigations of the young child's conception of number. *Child Development, 46,* 167–175.

Gericke, H. (1970). *Geschichte des Zahlbegriffs* [History of number concept]. Mannheim: Bibliographisches Institut.

Gibello, B. (1984). *L'enfant à l'intelligence troublée.* Paris: Le Centurion.

Gillièron, C. (1977). Serial order and vicariant order: The limits of isomorphism. *Archives de Psychologie, XLV*(175), 183–204.

Ginsburg, H. P (1982). *Children's arithmetic.* Austin, TX: Pro-Ed.

Ginsburg, H. P. (Ed.). (1983). *The development of mathematical thinking.* New York: Academic.

Ginsburg, H. P., Posner, J. K., & Russell, R. L. (1981a). Developmental and functional schooling and culture. *Journal of Cross-Cultural Psychology, 12,* 163–178.

Ginsburg, H. P., Posner, J. K., & Russell, R. L. (1981b). Developmental knowledge concerning written arithmetic. *International Journal of Psychology, 6,* 13–34.

Ginsburg, H. P., & Russell, R. L. (1981). Social class and racial influences on early mathematical thinking. *Monographs of the Society for Research in Child Development, 46*(16, Serial No. 193).

Gödel, K. (1931). Über formal unentscheidbare Sätze der Principia Mathematica und verwandter Systeme, I. [On undecidable formal propositions of the Principia Mathematica and related systems]. *Monatshefte für Mathematik und Physik, 38,* 173–198.

Gréco, P. (1960). Recherches sur quelques formes d'inférences arithmétiques et sur la compréhension de l'itération numérique chez l'enfant. In P. Gréco, J. B. Grize, S. Papert, & J. Piaget (Eds.), *Problèmes de la construction du nombre* (Etudes d'Epistémologie Génétique, Vol. XI) (pp. 149–213). Paris: Presses Universitaires de France.

Gréco, P. (1962). Quantité et quotité: Nouvelles recherches sur la correspondance terme-à-terme et la conservation des ensembles. In P. Gréco & A. Morf (Eds.), *Structures numériques élémentaires* (pp. 1–70). Paris: Presses Universitaires de France.

Geéco, P. (1988). Préface. In J. Bideaud (Ed.), *Logique et Bricolage chez l'enfant* (pp. 7–18). Lille: Presses Universitaires de Lille.

Gréco, P., Grize, J.-B., Papert, S., & Piaget, J. (1960). *Etudes d'épistémologie génétique: Vol. XI. Problèmes de la construction du nombre.* Paris: Presses Universitaires de France.

Gréco, P., & Morf, A. (1962). *Etudes d'epistémologie génétique: Vol. XIII. Structures numériques élémentaires.* Paris: Presses Universitaires de France.

Green, R. T., & Laxon, V. J. (1970). The conservation of number, mother, water and a fried egg chez l'enfant. *Acta Psychologica, 32,* 1–20.

Greenberg, J. H. (1978). Generalizations about numeral systems. In J. H. Greenberg (Ed.), *Universals of human language* (Vol. 3, pp. 249–297). Stanford: Stanford University Press.

Greeno, J. G., Riley, M. S., & Gelman, R. (1984). Conceptual competence and children's counting. *Cognitive Psychology, 16,* 94–143.

Greer, B. (1987). Non-conservation of multiplication and division involving decimals. *Journal for Research in Mathematics Education, 18,* 37–45.

Grigsby, J. P., Kemper, M. B., & Hagerman, R. J. (1987). Developmental Gerstmann Syndrome without aphasia in Fragile X syndrome. *Neuropsychologia, 25,* 881–891.

Grize, J.-B. (1960). Du groupement au nombre: essai de formalisation. In P. Gréco, J.-B. Grize, S. Papert & J. Piaget (Eds.), *Problémes de la construction du nombre: Vol. 11. Etudes d'Epistémologie génétique* (pp. 69–96). Paris: Presses Universitaires de France.

Grize, J.-B. (1967). Remarques sur l'épistémologie mathématique des nombres naturels. In J. Piaget (Ed.), *Logique et connaissance scientifique* (pp. 512–525). Paris: Gallimard.

Groen, G. J., & Parkman, J. M. (1972). A chronometric analysis of simple addition. *Psychological Review, 79,* 329–343.

Haake, R. J., & Somerville, S. C. (1985). The development of logical search skills in infancy. *Developmental Psychology, 21,* 176–186.

Halford, G. S. (1988). A structure-mapping approach to cognitive development. In A. Demetriou (Ed.), *The neo-Piagetian theories of cognitive development: Toward an integration* (pp. 103–136). Amsterdam: Elsevier North Holland.

Hasaerts-Van Geertruyden, E. (1970). Dyscalculie d'évolution. *Revue de Neuropsychiatrie Infantile, 18,* 5–18.

Hasaerts-Van Geertruyden, E. (1975). La dyscalculie chez l'enfant: Diagnostic différentiel. *Revue de Neuropsychiatrie Infantile, 23,* 665–677.

Hasaerts-Van Geertruyden, E., & Delfosse, F. (1972). Rééducation psycho-motrice dans un cas de dyscalculie: Importance de l'intégration gestuelle. *Revue de Neuropsychiatrie Infantile, 20,* 753–759.

Hatano, G. (1982). Learning to add and subtract: A Japanese perspective. In T. P. Carpenter, J. M. Moser, & T. A. Romberg (Eds.), *Addition and subtraction: A cognitive perspective* (pp. 211–223). Hillsdale, NJ: Lawrence Erlbaum Associates.

Heath, S. B. (1983). *Ways with words.* Cambridge, England: Cambridge University Press.

Herbart, J. F. (1894). *Principales oeuvres pédagogiques.* Paris: Alcan. (Original word published 1835).

Hiebert, J. (Ed.). (1986). *Conceptual and procedural knowledge: The case of mathematics.* Hillsdale, NJ: Lawrence Erlbaum Associates.

Hiebert, J., & Wearne, D. (1986). Procedures over concepts: The acquisition of decimal number knowledge. In J. Hiebert (Ed.), *The relationship between procedural and conceptual competence* (pp. 199–223). Hillsdale, NJ: Lawrence Erlbaum Associates.

Hilbert, D. (1900). Über den Zahlbegriff [On the concept of number]. *Jahresbericht der Deutschen Mathematikervereinigung,* 180–184.

Hitch, G., Cundick, J., Haughey, M., Pugh, R., & Wright, H. (1987). Aspects of counting in children's arithmetic. In J. A. Sloboda & D. Rogers (Eds.), *Cognitive processes in mathematics* (pp. 26–41). Oxford: Clarendon.

Hoc, J.-M. (1987). *Psychologie cognitive de la planification.* Grenoble: Presses Universitaires de Grenoble.

Hodges, A. (1983). *Alan Turing: The enigma of intelligence.* London: Burnett.

Hodges, R. M., & French, L. A. (1988). The effect of class and collection labels on cardinality, class-inclusion, and number conservation tasks. *Child Development, 59,* 1387-1396.

Houdé, O. (1989). Logical categorization and schemas: A study of their relationships in 6- to 11-year-olds. *C.P.C.: European Bulletin of Cognitive Psychology, 9,* 401–429.

Houdé, O. (1991). Le contigu, le substituable et le nécessaire: Etude développementale de la caté-gorisation. (Thèse de Doctorat). Paris V: Université René Descartes.

Hudson, T. (1983). Correspondences and numerical differences between disjoint sets. *Child Development*, *54*, 84–90.

Hughes, M. (1986). *Children and number: Difficulties in learning mathematics*. Oxford: Basil Blackwell.

Hull, C. L. (1943). *Principles of behavior theory*. New York: Appleton Century Crofts.

Huttenlocher, J., & Strauss, S. (1968). Comprehension and a statement's relation to the situation it describes. *Journal of Verbal Learning and Verbal Behavior*, *7*, 300–304.

Ifrah, G. (1985). *From one to zero: A universal history of numbers* (L. Bair, Trans.). New York: Viking Penguin. (Original work published 1981)

Inhelder, B. (1937). Observations sur le principe de conservation dans la physique de l'enfant. *Cahiers de Pédagogie Expérimentale et de Psychologie de l'Enfant* (Monograph 9).

Inhelder, B. (1943). *Le diagnostic du raisonnement chez les débiles mentaux*. Neuchâtel: Delachaux et Niestlé.

Inhelder, B. (1987). Des structures aux processus. In J. Piaget, P. Mounoud, & J.-P. Bronckart (Eds.), *Psychologie* (pp. 654–679). Paris: Gallimard.

Inhelder, B., Blanchet, A., Sinclair, A., & Piaget, J. (1975). Relations entre les conservations d'en-sembles d'éléments discrets et celles de quantités continues. *Année Psychologique*, *75*, 23–60.

Inhelder, B. & Cellérier, G. (Eds.) (in press). *Les Microgénèses cognitives: Le Cheminement des découvertes*. Neuchâtel et Paris: Delachaux et Niestlé.

Inhelder, B., & Piaget, J. (1964a). *The early growth of logic in the child: Classification and seriation*. New York: Norton. (Original work published 1959).

Inhelder, B., & Piaget, J. (1964b). *The growth of logical thinking*. New York: Norton.

Inhelder, B., Sinclair, H., & Bovet, M. (1974). *Apprentissage et structures de la connaissance*. Paris: Presses Universitaires de France.

Janet, P. (1928). *L'évolution de la mémoire et de la notion de temps: Vol. II. La mémoire élémentaire*. Paris: A. Chahine.

Janet, P. (1936). *L'intelligence avant le langage*. Paris: Flammarion.

Jardy, Je., Jardy, Jy., & Soumy, J.-G. (1985). *Vivre les mathématiques: Guide pédagogique C.P.* Paris: Colin-Bourrelier.

Johnson-Laird, P. N. (1983). *Mental models*. Cambridge, England: Cambridge University Press.

Kaliski, L. (1962). Arithmetic and the brain-injured child. *Arithmetic Teacher*, *9*, 245–251.

Kamii, C. K. (1985). *Young children reinvent arithmetic*. New York: Teachers College Press.

Kamii, C. K. (1986). Place value: An explanation of its difficulty and educational implications for the primary grades. *Journal of Research in Childhood Education*, *1*(2), 75–85.

Kamii, C. K. (1989). *Young children continue to reinvent arithmetic*. New York: Teachers College Press.

Kamii, M. (1981). Children's ideas about written number. *Topics in Learning and Learning Disabilities*, *1*, 47–59.

Kaufman, E. L., Lord, M. W., Reese, T. W., & Volkmann, J. (1949). The discrimination of visual number. *American Journal of Psychology*, *62*, 498–525.

Kilpatrick, J. (1987). Problem formulation: Where do good problems come from? In A. H. Schoen-feld (Ed.), *Cognitive science and mathematics education* (pp. 123–147). Hillsdale, NJ: Lawrence Erlbaum Associates.

Kintsch, W. (1986). Learning from text. *Cognition and Instruction*, *3*, 87–108.

Kintsch, W. (1988). The role of knowledge in discourse comprehension: A comprehension-integra-tion model. *Psychological Review*, *95*, 163–182.

Kintsch, W., & Greeno, J. G. (1985). Understanding and solving word arithmetic problems. *Psychological Review*, *92*, 109–129.

Kintsch, W., & Van Dijk, T. A. (1978). Toward a model of text comprehension and text production. *Psychological Review*, *85*, 363–394.

Klahr, D. (1984a). Commentary: An embarrassment of number. In C. Sophian (Ed.), *Origins of cognitive skills* (pp. 295–309). Hillsdale, NJ: Lawrence Erlbaum Associates.

Klahr, D. (1984b). Transition processes in quantitative development. In R. Sternberg (Ed.), *Mechanisms of cognitive development* (pp. 112–125). San Francisco: Freeman.

Klahr, D., & Wallace, J. G. (1973). The role of quantification operators in the development of conservation of quantity. *Cognitive Psychology, 4,* 301–327.

Klahr, D., & Wallace, J. G. (1976). *Cognitive development: An information processing view.* Hillsdale: Lawrence Erlbaum Associates.

Klees, M. (1983). *Actes du colloque consacré à la dyscalculie.* Bruxelles: ULB, Centre d'Etudes des Troubles de l'Apprentissage.

Klein, A., & Starkey, P. (1988). Universals in the development of early arithmetic cognition. In G. B. Saxe, & M. Gearhart (Eds.), *Children's mathematics* (pp. 5–26). San Francisco: Jossey-Bass.

Koehler, O. (1950). The ability of birds to "count." *Bulletin of Animal Behavior, 9,* 41–45.

Köhler, W. (1921). *Intelligenzprüfungen an Menschenaffen.* Berlin: Julius Springer. (Original work published 1917).

Köhler, W. (1939). *The place of value in a world of facts.* London: K. Paul, Trench, Trubner.

Kossanyi, P., Waiche, R., & Netchine, S. (1989). L'efficience et l'organisation intellectuelle d'Enfants non-lecteurs analysées à partir du WISC-R. *Revue de Psychologie Appliquée, 39*(1), 23–41.

Kühnel, J. (1921). *Handbuch der Pädagogik für ein Sondergebiet, Neubau des Rechenunterrichts* [Handbook of didactic. A new structure for teaching arithmetic]. (Vol. 6, 3rd ed.). Leipzig: Klinkhardt. (Original work published 1916)

Kwon, Y. (1990). Children's counting and matching in cardinal equivalence situations. (Doctoral dissertation, Northwestern University, Evanston, IL. 1989). *Dissertation Abstracts International, 50,* 2383A.

Labinowicz, E. (1985). *Learning from children: New beginnings for teaching numerical thinking.* Menlo Park, CA: Addison-Wesley.

Lancy, D. F. (1983). *Cross-cultural studies in cognition and mathematics.* New York: Academic.

LaPointe, K., & O'Donnell, J. P. (1974). Number conservation below age six: Its relationship to age, perceptual dimensions, and language comprehension. *Developmental Psychology, 10,* 422–428.

Lautrey, J. (1990). Esquisse d'un modèle pluraliste du développement cognitif. In M. Reuchlin, J. Lautrey, C. Marendaz, & T. Ohlman (Eds.), *Cognition: L'individuel et l'universel* (pp. 185–213). Paris: Presses Universitaires de France.

Lautrey, J., de Ribaupierre, A., & Rieben, L. (1981). Le développement opératoire peut-il prendre des formes différentes chez des enfants différents? *Journal de Psychologie, 4,* 421–443.

Lawler, R. (1985). *Computer experience and cognitive development.* New York: Ellis Horwood.

Lawson, G., Baron, J., & Siegel, L. (1974). The role of number and length cues in children's quantitative judgments. *Child Development, 45,* 731–736.

Lecours, A. R., & Lhermitte, F. (1980). *L'aphasie.* Paris: Flammarion. (Original work published 1979).

Leibnitz, G. W. (1975). *Monadologie.* (Principes de la Philosophie ou Monadologie). Paris: Delagrave.

Lewis, A. B., & Mayer, R. E. (1987). Students' miscomprehension of relational statements in arithmetic word problems. *Journal of Educational Psychology, 79,* 363–371.

Lorenzen, P. (1962). *Metamathematik* [Metamathematics]. Mannheim: Bibliographisches Institut.

Lorenzen, P., & Schwemmer, O. (1975). *Konstruktive Logik, Ethik und Wissenschaftstheorie* [Constructive logic, ethics and scientific theory]. Mannheim: Bibliographisches Institut.

Maertens, N. W., Jones, R. C., & Waite, A. (1977). Elemental groupings help children perceive cardinality: A two-phase research study. *Journal for Research in Mathematics Education, 8,* 181–193.

Mandler, G., & Shebo, B. J. (1982). Subitizing: An analysis of its component processes. *Journal of Experimental Psychology: General, 111,* 1–22.

Markman, E. M. (1973). The facilitation of part–whole comparisons by use of the collective noun "family." *Child Development, 44,* 837–840.

Markman, E. M. (1978). Empirical versus logical solutions to part–whole comparison problems concerning classes and collections. *Child Development, 49,* 168–177.

Markman, E. M. (1979). Classes and collections: Conceptual organization and numerical abilities. *Cognitive Psychology, 11,* 395–411.

Markman, E. M., & Seibert, J. (1976). Classes and collections: Internal organization and resulting holistic properties. *Cognitive Psychology, 8,* 561–577.

Marler, P. (1991). The instinct to learn. In S. Carey & R. Gelman (Eds.), *The epigenesis of mind* (pp. 37–66). Hillsdale, NJ: Lawrence Erlbaum Associates.

Marr, D. (1982). *Vision.* San Francisco: Freeman.

Marton, F., & Neumar, D. (1989, September). *On the perceptibility of numbers and the origin of arithmetic skills.* Paper presented at the third E.A.R.L.I. (European Association for Research on Learning and Instruction) conference, Madrid.

Maurice-Naville, D. (1988). Mise de couvert: Transformations spatiales et coordination des perspectives chez des enfants de quatre à sept ans. *Archives de Psychologie, 56,* 59–77.

McCloskey, M., & Caramazza, A. (1987). Cognitive mechanisms in normal and impaired number processing. In G. Deloche & X. Seron (Eds.), *Mathematical disabilities: A cognitive neuropsychological perspective.* Hillsdale, NJ: Lawrence Erlbaum Associates.

McCulloch, W. S., & Pitts, W. (1943). A logical calculus of the ideas immanent in nervous activity. *Bulletin of Mathematical Biophysics, 9,* 127–147.

McGarrigle, J., & Donaldson, M. (1975). Conservation accidents. *Cognition, 3,* 341–350.

Meljac, C. (1979). *Décrire, agir et compter: L'enfant et le dénombrement spontané.* Paris: Presses Universitaires de France.

Meljac, C. (1980). *Batterie U.D.N. 80 - Manuel d'utilisation et matériel.* Paris: Les Editions du Centre de Psychologie Appliquée.

Meljac, C. (1988). L'activité opératoire des enfants non-lecteurs: Revue du Département des Langues et des Sciences du Langage de L'Université de Lausanne. *Cahier, 6,* 151–177.

Menninger, K. (1969). *Number words and number symbols: A cultural history of numbers.* Cambridge, MA: MIT Press. (Original work published 1958)

Meyer, E. (1935). La représentation des relations spatiales chez l'enfant. *Cahiers de Pédagogie Expérimentale et de Psychologie de l'Enfant* (Monograph 8).

Michie, S. (1984). Why preschoolers are reluctant to count spontaneously. *British Journal of Developmental Psychology, 2,* 347–358.

Miller, G. A. (1956). The magical number seven, plus or minus two: Some limits on our capacity for processing information. *Psychological Review, 63,* 81–97.

Miller, G. A., Galanter, E., & Pribram, K. H. (1970). *Plans and the structure of behavior.* London: Holt, Rinehart & Winston. (Original work published 1960)

Miller, K. F., Paredes, D. R., & Madole, K. L. (1989). *Primed numbers: Developmental changes in number access in the context of subitizing and addition.* Unpublished manuscript, University of Texas, Austin.

Miller, K. F., & Stigler, J. W. (1987). Counting in Chinese: Cultural variation in a basic cognitive skill. *Cognitive Development, 2,* 279–305.

Miura, I. T. (1987). Mathematics achievement as a function of language. *Journal of Educational Psychology, 79,* 79–82.

Miura, I. T., Kim, C. C., Chang, C., & Okamoto, Y. (1988). Effects of language characteristics on children's cognitive representation of number: Cross-national comparisons. *Child Development, 59,* 1445–1450.

Miura, I. T., & Okamoto, Y. (1989). Comparisons of U.S. and Japanese first graders' cognitive representation of number and understanding of place-value. *Journal of Educational Psychology*, *81*, 109–113.

Moore, C., & Frye, D. (1986). The effect of experimenter's intention on the child's understanding of conservation. *Cognition, 22,* 283–298.

Mosimann, O., Bovay, M., Dällenbach, J.-F., & Droz, R. (1982). Les nombres d'Alex: Les comptages d'un enfant de quatre ans. *Archives de Psychologie, 50*(193), 91–164.

Mounoud, P. (1983). L'évolution des conduites de préhension comme illustration d'un modèle de développement. In S. de Schonen (Ed.), *Le développement dans la première année* (pp. 75–106). Paris: Presses Universitaires de France.

Mounoud, P., & Vinter, A. (1985). La notion de représentation en psychologie génétique. *Psychologie Française, 30,* 253–259.

National Assessment of Educational Progress. (1983). *The Third National Mathematics Assessment: Results, trends, and issues.* Princeton, NJ: Educational Testing Service.

Nelson, K. (1985). *Making sense: The acquisition of shared meaning.* New York: Academic.

Nelson, K. (1988). Where do taxonomic categories come from? *Human Development, 31,* 3–10.

Nesher, P., & Katriel, T. (1977). A semantic analysis of addition and subtraction word problems in arithmetic. *Educational Studies in Mathematics, 8,* 251–269.

Neuman, D. (1987). *The origin of arithmetic skills: A phenomenographic approach.* Goteberg, Sweden: ACTA Universitatis Gothoburgensis.

Noelting, G. (1980). The development of proportional reasoning and the ratio concept: Part I. Determination of stages. *Educational Studies in Mathematics, 11,* 217–253.

Oehl, W. (1935). *Psychologogische Untersuchungen über Zahlendenken und Rechnen bei Schulanfängern* [Psychological experiments on numerical thought and computation in first graders]. Leipzig: Barth.

Papert, S. (1990). Preface. In J. Piaget, G. Henriques, & E. Ascher, *Morphismes et Catégories: comparer et transformer* (pp. 7–13). Neuchâtel: Delachaux et Niestlé.

Parrat-Dayan, S. (1980). *Etude génétique de la notion de moitié.* Genève: J. L. de Rougemont.

Parrat-Dayan, S. (1985). A propos de la notion de moitié: Rôle du contexte expérimental. *Archives de Psychologie, 53,* 433–438.

Parrat-Dayan, S., & Bovet, M. (1982). Peut-on parler de précocité et de régression dans la conservation? II. *Archives de Psychologie, 50,* 237–249.

Pascual-Leone, J. (1988). Organismic processes for neo-Piagetian theories: A dialectical causal account of cognitive development. In A. Demetriou (Ed.), *The neo-Piagetian theories of cognitive development: Toward an integration* (pp. 25–64). Amsterdam: Elsevier North Holland.

Peet, E. (1923). *The Rhind mathematical Papyrus (British Museum 10057 and 10058).* London: The University Press of Liverpool.

Peill, E. J. (1975). *Invention and discovery of reality.* London: Wiley.

Perfetti, C. A. (1989). Représentation et prise de conscience au cours de l'apprentissage de la lecture. In L. Rieben & C. Perfetti (Eds.), *L'apprenti-lecteur. Recherches empiriques et applications pédagogiques* (pp. 67–84). Neuchâtel et Paris: Delachaux et Niestlé.

Piaget, J. (1921). Essai sur quelques aspects du développement de la notion de partie chez l'enfant. *Journal de Psychologie Normale et Pathologique, 18,* 449–480.

Piaget, J. (1923). *Le langage et la pensée chez l'enfant.* Neuchâtel: Delachaux et Niestlé.

Piaget, J. (1926). *La représentation du monde chez l'enfant.* Neuchâtel: Delachaux et Niestlé.

Piaget, J. (1927). *La causalité physique chez l'enfant.* Paris: F. Alcan.

Piaget, J. (1929). Les deux directions de la pensée scientifique. *Archives des Sciences physiques et naturelles, 11,* 145–162.

Piaget, J. (1932). *Le jugement moral chez l'enfant.* Paris: F. Alcan.

Piaget, J. (1936). *La naissance de l'intelligence chez l'enfant.* Neuchâtel: Delachaux et Niestlé.

Piaget, J. (1937). *La construction du réel chez l'enfant.* Neuchâtel: Delachaux et Niestlé.

Piaget, J. (1938). La réversibilité des opérations et l'importance de la notion de groupe. In H. Piéron

& I. Meyerson (Eds.), *Rapports et comptes-rendus du Xlème Congrès de psychologie* (pp. 443–446). Agen: Imprimerie Moderne.

Piaget, J. (1939). La contruction psychologique du nombre entier. *Compte-rendu des séances de la Société de physique et d'histoire naturelle de Genève, 56,* 92–94.

Piaget, J. (1942). *Classes, relations, nombres.* Paris: Vrin.

Piaget, J. (1945). *La formation du symbole chez l'enfant.* Neuchâtel: Delachaux et Niestlé.

Piaget, J. (1947). *La psychologie de l'intelligence.* Paris: Armand Colin.

Piaget, J. (1949). *Traité de logique: essai de logistique opératoire.* Paris: Colin. (Nouvelle édition, révisée en collaboration avec J.-B. Grize, 1972, Essai de logistique opératoire. Paris: Dunod)

Piaget, J. (1950/1973) *Introduction à l'épistémologie génétique* (Vol. 1). Paris: Presses Universitaires de France.

Piaget, J. (1952a). *The child's conception of number.* New York: Norton. (Original work published 1941)

Piaget, J. (1952b). *The origins of intelligence in children.* New York: International Universities Press.

Piaget, J. (1959). Les modèles abstraits sont-ils opposés aux interprétations psycho-physiologiques dans l'explication en psychologie: Esquesse de biographie. *Bulletin de Psychologie, 1–2,* 8–13.

Piaget, J. (1964a). Development and learning. In R. E. Ripple & V. N. Rockcastle (Eds.), *Piaget rediscovered* (pp. 7–20). Ithaca, NY: Cornell University.

Piaget, J. (1964b). *Six études de psychologie.* Paris: Ed. Gonthier.

Piaget, J. (1967). La construction du nombre naturel. In J. Piaget (Ed.), *Logique et connaissace scientifique* (pp. 405–412). Paris: Gallimard.

Piaget, J. (1968). *Le structuralisme.* Paris: Presses Universitaires de France.

Piaget, J. (1970a). *Genetic epistemology.* New York: Columbia University Press.

Piaget, J. (1970b). *Psychologie et épistémologie* (The principles of genetic epistemology). Paris: Gonthier.

Piaget, J. (1974). *Réussir et comprendre.* Paris: Presses Universitaires de France.

Piaget, J. (1975). *L'équilibration des structures cognitives: Etudes d'Epistémologie Génétique, Vol. XXXIII.* Paris: Presses Universitaires de France.

Piaget, J. (1976). *Recherches sur l'abstraction réfléchissante. 1 et 2: Etudes d'Epistémologie Génétique Vol. XXXIV et XXXV.* Paris: Presses Universitaires de France.

Piaget, J. (1980). *Adaptation and intelligence: Organic selection and phenocopy.* Chicago: University of Chicago Press.

Piaget, J. (1981). *Le possible et le nécessaire. L'élaboration des possibles chez l'enfant.* Paris: P.U.F.

Piaget, J. (1983). *Le possible et le nécessaire-L'évolution du necessaire chez l'enfant.* Paris: P.U.F.

Piaget, J., Grize, J.-B., Szeminska, A., & Vinh-Bang. (1968). *Epistémologie et psychologie de la fonction: Etudes d'Epistémologie Génétique, Vol. XXIII.* Paris: Presses Universitaires de France.

Piaget, J., Henriques, G., & Ascher, E. (1990). *Morphismes et Categories: comparér et transformer.* Neuchâtel: Delachaux et Niestlé.

Piaget, J., & Inhelder, B. (1941). *Le développement des quantités chez l'enfant.* Neuchâtel: Delachaux et Niestlé.

Piaget, J., & Inhelder, B. (1959). *La genèse des structures logiques élémentaires.* Neuchâtel: Delachaux et Niestlé.

Piaget, J., & Inhelder, B. (1961). *Le développement des quantités physiques chez l'enfant.* Neuchâtel: Delachaux et Niestlé (3d Ed. 1968; 4th Ed. 1978).

Piaget, J., & Inhelder, B. (1966a). *L'image mentale chez l'enfant.* Paris: Presses Universitaires de France.

Piaget, J., & Inhelder, B. (1966b). *La psychologie de l'enfant: Coll. Que sais-je?* Paris: Presses Universitaires de France.

Piaget, J., Inhelder, B., & Szeminska, A. (1948). *La géométrie spontanée de l'enfant.* Paris: Presses Universitaires de France.

Piaget, J., & Szeminska, A. (1941). *La genèse du nombre chez l'enfant.* Neuchâtel: Delachaux et Niestlé.

Piérard, B., & Thuvelle-Delahaye, I. (1985). Les modalités de la compréhension des descripteurs de quantités entre trois et sept ans. *Neuropsychiatrie de l'Enfance, 33,* 393–399.

Power, R. J. D., & Longuet-Higgins, J. C. (1978). Learning to count: A computational model of language acquisition. *Proceedings of the Royal Society of London, 200,* 391–417.

Preneron, C., & Salazar-Orvig, A. (1987). La conduite de récit chez des enfants non-lecteurs. *La Psychanalyse de l'Enfant, 3,* 44–94.

Puche Navarro, R. (1983). Practicas de partir o nocion de particion: Informe de investigacion. *Serie Investigaciones.* Cali, Universidad del Valle.

Rauh, H. (1972). *Entwicklungspsychologische Analyse kognitiver Prozesse* [A developmental psychology analysis of cognitive processes]. Weinheim: Beltz.

Resnick, L. B. (1983). A developmental theory of number understanding. In H. P. Ginsburg (Ed.), *The development of mathematical thinking* (pp. 109–151). New York: Academic Press.

Resnick, L. B. (1984). Beyond error analysis: The role of understanding in elementary school arithmetic. In H. N. Cheek (Ed.), *Diagnostic and prescriptive mathematics: Issues, ideas, and insights.* Kent, OH: Research Council for Diagnostic and Prescriptive Mathematics.

Resnick, L. B. (1986). The development of mathematical intuition. In M. Perlmutter (Ed.), *Perspectives on intellectual development: The Minnesota Symposia on Child Psychology* (Vol. 19, pp. 159–194). Hillsdale, NJ: Lawrence Erlbaum Associates.

Resnick, L. B. (1989). Developing mathematical knowledge. *American Psychologist, 44,* 162–169.

Resnick, L. B., & Ford, W. W. (1981). *The psychology of mathematics for instruction.* Hillsdale, NJ: Lawrence Erlbaum Associates.

Retschitzki, J. (1978). L'évolution des procédures de sériation: Etude génétique et simulation. *Archives de Psychologie, XLVI.*

Reuchlin, M. (1973). Formalisation et réalisation dans la pensée naturelle: Une hypothèse. *Journal de Psychologie Normale et Pathologique, 70,* 389–408.

Reusser, K. (1989, September). *Textual and situational factors in solving mathematical word problems.* Paper presented at the Third E.A.R.L.I. (European Association for Research on Learning and Instruction). Conference, Madrid.

Richard, J.-F. (1990). *Les activités mentales: comprendre, raisonner, trouver des solutions.* Paris: Armand Colin.

Richard, J.-M. (1989). Analyse de protocoles individuels et microgenèse de la représentation d'un problème. *Psychologie Française, 34,* 207–211.

Richard, J.-M., & Poitrenaud, S. (1988). Problématique de l'analyse des protocoles individuels d'observations comportementales. In J.-P. Caverni (Ed.), *Psychologie cognitive: Modèles et méthodes* (pp. 405–426). Grenoble: Presses Universitaires de Grenoble.

Richman, H. B. & Simon, H. A. (1989). Context effects in letter perception: Comparison of two theories. *Psychological Review, 96,* 417–432.

Rieben, L., de Ribaupierre, A., & Lautrey, J. (1983). *Le développement opératoire de l'enfant entre six et douze ans: Elaboration d'un instrument d'évaluation.* Paris: Editions du C.N.R.S.

Rieben, L., & Saada-Robert, M. (1989). Evolution et différences individuelles dans les stratégies de recherche de mots chez les débutants lecteurs. *Maison des Petits, Document interne, 6.*

Rieben, L., & Saada-Robert, M. (1991). Developmental patterns and individual differences in the word-search strategies of beginning readers. *Learning and Instruction, 1,* 67–87.

Riley, M. S., & Greeno, J. G. (1988). Developmental analysis of understanding language about quantities and of solving problems. *Cognition and Instruction, 5,* 49–101.

Riley, M. S., Greeno, J. G., & Heller, J. I. (1983). Development of children's problem-solving ability in arithmetic. In H. Ginsburg (Ed.), *The development of mathematical thinking* (pp. 153–196). New York: Academic Press.

Robert, M., Céllerier, G., & Sinclair, H. (1972). Une observation de la genèse du nombre. *Archives de Psychologie, 41*, 289–301.

Rosenbloom, P., & Newell, A. (1987). Learning by chunking: A production system model of practice. In D. Klahr, P. Langley, & R. Neches (Eds.), *Production system models of learning and development* (pp. 221–286). Cambridge, MA: MIT Press.

Rosenthal, D. J. A., & Resnick, L. B. (1974). Children's solution processes in arithmetic word problems. *Journal of Educational Psychology, 66*, 817–825.

Russel, B. (1903). *The principles of mathematics.* Londres: Allen & Unwin.

Russell, B. (1926). *La méthode scientifique en philosophie.* Paris: Payot.

Russell, B. (1930). *Introduction to mathematical philosophy* (2nd ed.). London: Allen & Unwin.

Saada-Robert, M. (1979). Procédures d'actions et significations fonctionnelles chez des enfants de deux à cinq ans. *Archives de Psychologie, 47*(Monographie), 177–233.

Saada-Robert, M. (1986). Le nombre, significations et pratiques. *Recherches en Didactique des Mathématiques, 7*, 105–148.

Saada-Robert, M. (1989). La microgénèse de la représentation d'un problème. *Psychologie Française, 34*, 193–206.

Saada-Robert, M. (1992). Didier et les poupées russes: Analyse de cas et conceptualisation. In B. Inhelder & G. Cellérier (Eds.), *Le cheminement des découvertes de l'enfant: Etude des microgenèses cognitives* (pp. 139–169). Neuchâtel et Paris: Delachaux et Niestlé.

Sagi, D., & Julesz, B. (1985). Detection versus discrimination of visual orientation. *Perception, 14*, 619–628.

Saussure de, F. (1959). *Course in general linguistics.* New York: The Philosophical Library.

Saxe, G. B. (1977). A developmental analysis of notational counting. *Child Development, 48*, 1512–1520.

Saxe, G. B. (1979). Developmental relations between notational counting and number conservation. *Child Development, 50*, 180–187.

Saxe, G. B. (1981). Body parts as numerals: A developmental analysis of numeration among the Oksapmin in Papua New Guinea. *Child Development, 52*, 306–316.

Saxe, G. B. (1982). Culture and the development of numerical cognition: Studies among the Oksapmin of Papua New Guinea. In C. J. Brainerd (Ed.), *Progress in cognitive development research: Vol 1. Children's logical and mathematical cognition* (pp. 157–176). New York: Springer-Verlag.

Saxe, G. B. (1985). Effects of schooling on arithmetical understandings: Studies with Oksapmin children in Papua New Guinea. *Journal of Educational Psychology, 77*, 503–513.

Saxe, G. B. (1988). Candy selling and math learning. *Educational Research, 17*, 14–21.

Saxe, G. B., Becker, J., Sadeghpour, M., & Sicilian, S. (1989). Developmental differences in children's understanding of number word conventions. *Journal for Research in Mathematics Education, 20*, 468–488.

Schaeffer, B., Eggleston, V. H., & Scott, J. L. (1974). Number development in young children. *Cognitive Psychology, 6*, 357–379.

Schneider, W., & Shiffrin, R. M. (1977). Controlled and automatic human information processing: I. Detection, search and attention. *Psychological Review, 84*, 1–66.

Schoenfeld, A. H. (1988). When good teaching leads to bad results: The disasters of "well-taught" mathematics courses. *Educational Psychologist, 23*, 145–166.

Scupin, E., & Scupin, G. (1910). *Bubi im vierten bis sechsten Lebensjahre* [The 4- to 6-year-old Bubi]. Leipzig: Grieben.

Secada, W. G. (1985). Counting in sign: The number string, accuracy and use. *Dissertation Abstracts International, 45*, 3571A.

Seibel, R. (1963). Discrimination reaction time for a 1023-alternative task. *Journal of Experimental Psychology, 66*, 215–226.

Seron, X., & Deloche, G. (1983). From 4 to four: A supplement to "From three to 3." *Brain, 106*, 735–744.

Seron, X., & Deloche, G. (1984). From 2 to two: An analysis of a transcoding process by means of neuropsychological evidence. *Journal of Psycholinguistic Research, 13*, 215–235.

Shalev, R. S., Weirtman, R., & Amir, A. (1988). Developmental dyscalculia. *Cortex, 24*, 555–561.

Shannon, L. (1978). Spatial strategies in the counting of young children. *Child Development, 49*, 1212–1215.

Shatz, M. (1983). Communication. In J. Flavell & E. M. Markman (Eds.), *Handbook of child psychology: Vol. 3. Cognitive development* (4th ed., pp. 420–494). New York: Wiley.

Shiffrin, R. M., & Schneider, W. (1977). Controlled and automatic human information processing: II. Perceptual learing, automatic attending, and a general theory. *Psychological Review, 84*, 127–190.

Shipley, E. F., & Shepperson, B. (1990a). Countable entities: Developmental change. *Cognition, 34*, 109–136.

Shipley, E. F., & Shepperson, B. (1990b). The what-if of counting. *Cognition, 36*, 285–289.

Siegal, M. (1991). *Appreciating children: Issues, experiments, and challenges.* Hove, England: Lawrence Erlbaum Associates, Ltd.

Siegel, L. S. (1978). The relationship between language and thought in the child: A reconsideration of nonverbal alternatives to Piagetian tasks. In L. S. Siegel & C. J. Brainerd (Eds.), *Alternatives to Piaget: Critical essays on the theory* (pp. 43–67). New York: Academic Press.

Siegler, R. S. (1979). What young children do know. *Contemporary Psychology, 24*, 613–615.

Siegler, R. S. (1981). Developmental sequences within and between concepts. *Monographs of the Society for Research in Child Development, 46*(2, Serial No. 189).

Siegler, R. S. (in press). In young children's counting, procedures precede principles. *European Journal of Psychology and Education.*

Siegler, R. S., & Robinson, M. (1982). The development of numerical understandings. In H. W. Reese & L. P. Lipsitt (Eds.), *Advances in child development and behavior* (Vol. 16, pp. 241–312). New York: Academic Press.

Siegler, R. S., & Shrager, J. (1984). Strategy choices in addition and subtraction: How do children know what to do? In C. Sophian (Ed.), *Origins of cognitive skills* (pp. 229–293). Hillsdale, NJ: Lawrence Erlbaum Associates.

Silverman, I. W., & Briga, J. (1981). By what process do young children solve small number conservation problems? *Journal of Experimental Child Psychology, 32*, 115–126.

Simons, D., & Langheinrich, D. (1982). What is magic about the magical number four? *Psychological Research, 44*, 283–294.

Sinclair, A. (1988). La notation numérique chez l'enfant. In H. Sinclair (Ed.), *La production de notations chez le jeune enfant* (pp. 71–97). Paris: Presses Universitaires de France.

Sinclair, A., Siegrist, F., & Sinclair, H. (1983). Young children's idea about the written system. In D. Rogers & J. Sloboda (Eds.), *The acquisition of symbolic skills.* New York: Plenum.

Song, M. J., & Ginsburg, H. P. (1988). The effect of the Korean number system on young children's counting: A natural experiment in numerical bilingualism. *International Journal of Psychology, 23*, 319–332.

Sophian, C. (1985). Understanding the movements of objects: Early developments in spatial cognition. *British Journal of Developmental Psychology, 3*, 321–333.

Sophian, C. (1987). Early developments in children's use of counting to solve quantitative problems. *Cognition and Instruction, 4*, 61–90.

Sophian, C. (1988). Limitations on children's knowledge about counting: Using counting to compare two sets. *Developmental Psychology, 24*, 634–640.

Sophian, C. (1989). *Making numbers count: The relationships between counting and cardinality in the preschool period.* Unpublished manuscript.

Sophian, C., & Adams, N. (1987). Infants' understanding of numerical transformations. *British Journal of Developmental Psychology, 5,* 257–264.

Sophian, C. & McCorgray, P. (1991, April). *Part-whole knowledge in early arithmetic performance.* Paper presented at the meeting of the Society for Research in Child Development, Seattle, WA.

Spaier, A. (1927). *La pensée et la quantité.* Paris: Alcan.

Spiers, P. A. (1987). Acalculia revisited: Current issues. In G. Deloche & X. Seron (Eds.), *Mathematical disabilities: A cognitive neuropsychological perspective* (pp. 1–25). Hillsdale, NJ: Lawrence Erlbaum Associates.

Spitzer, H. F. (1954). *The teaching of arithmetic* (2nd ed.). Boston: Houghton Mifflin.

Sprenger-Charolles, L., & Khomsi, A. (1989). Les stratégies d'identification de mots dans un contexte-image: Comparaisons entre "bons" et "mauvais" lecteurs. In L. Rieben & C. Perfetti (Eds.), *L'apprenti-lecteur: Recherches empiriques et implications pédagogiques* (pp. 307–325). Neuchâtel et Paris: Delachaux et Niestlé.

Squire, L. R. (1987). *Memory and brain.* New York: Oxford University Press.

Stambak, M., l'Heriteau, D., Auzias, M., Bergès, J., & de Ajuriaguerra, J. (1964). Les dyspraxies chez l'enfant. *La Psychiatrie de l'Enfant, 8,* 381–497.

Starkey, P. (1987, April). *Early arithmetic competencies.* Paper presented at the bienniel meeting of the Society for Research in Child Development. Baltimore, MD.

Starkey, P., & Cooper, R. G., Jr. (1980). Perception of numbers by human infants. *Science, 210,* 1033–1035.

Starkey, P., & Gelman, R. (1982). The development of addition and subtraction abilities prior to formal schooling in arithmetic. In T. P. Carpenter, J. M. Moser, & T. A. Romberg (Eds.), *Addition and subtraction: A cognitive perspective* (pp. 99–116). Hillsdale, NJ: Lawrence Erlbaum Associates.

Starkey, P., Spelke, E. S., & Gelman, R. (1983). Detection of intermodal numerical correspondences by human infants. *Science, 222,* 179–181.

Starkey, P., Spelke, E. S., & Gelman, R. (1990). Numerical abstraction by human infants. *Cognition, 52,* 97–128.

Steffe, L. P. (1990). The learning paradox: A plausible counterexample. In L. P. Steffe (Ed.), *Epistemological foundations of mathematical experience.* New York: Springer-Verlag.

Steffe, L. P. (in press). Children's construction of meaning for arithmetical words. In D. Tirosh (Ed.), *Implicit and explicit knowledge: An educational approach.* Norwood, NJ: Ablex.

Steffe, L. P., & Cobb, P. (1988). *Construction of arithmetical meanings and strategies.* New York: Springer-Verlag.

Steffe, L. P., Hirstein, J. J., & Spikes, W. C. (1976). *Quantitative comparisons and class inclusion as readiness variables for learning first-grade arithmetical content* (Tech. Rep. No. 9). Tallahassee, FL: Project for Mathematical Development of Children. (Eric Document Reproduction Service No. ED 144 808)

Steffe, L. P., Richards, J., & von Glasersfeld, E. (1978). Experimental models for the child's acquisition of counting and of addition and subtraction. In K. C. Fuson & W. E. Geeslin (Eds.), *Explorations in the modeling of the learning of mathematics.* Columbus, OH: ERIC Center for Science, Mathematics, and Environmental Education.

Steffe, L. P., & von Glasersfeld, E. (1985). Helping children to conceive of number. *Recherches en Didactique des Mathématiques, 6,* 269–303.

Steffe, L. P., von Glasersfeld, E., Richards, J., & Cobb, P. (1983). *Children's counting types: Philosophy, theory, and application.* New York: Praeger Scientific.

Steffe, L. P., & Wood, T. (Eds.). (1990). *Transforming children's mathematics education: International perspectives.* Hillsdale, NJ: Lawrence Erlbaum Associates.

Steinberg, R. M. (1984). A teaching experiment of the learning of addition and subtraction facts (Doctoral dissertation, University of Wisconsin-Madison, 1983). *Dissertation Abstracts International, 44,* 3313A.

Stern, C. (1949). *Children discover arithmetic*. New York: Harpers.

Stigler, J. W., Fuson, K. C., Ham, M., & Kim, M. S. (1986). An analysis of addition and subtraction word problems in Soviet and American elementary textbooks. *Cognition and Instruction, 3*, 153–171.

Stigler, J. W., Lee, S. Y., & Stevenson, H. W. (1990). *The mathematical knowledge of Japanese, Chinese and American elementary school children*. Reston, VA: National Council of Teachers of Mathematics.

Stigler, J. W., & Perry, M. (1988). Mathematics learning in Japanese, Chinese and American classrooms. In G. B. Saxe & M. Gearhart (Eds.), *Children's mathematics: New directions for child development* (Vol. 41, pp. 27–54). San Francisco: Jossey-Bass.

Strauss, A. A., & Lehtinen, L. E. (1947). *Psychopathology and education of the brain-injured child*. New York: Grune & Stratton.

Strauss, M. S., & Curtis, L. E. (1981). Infant perception of numerosity. *Child Development, 52*, 1146–1152.

Svenson, O., & Sjöberg, K. (1978). Subitizing and counting processes in young children. *Scandinavian Journal of Psychology, 19*, 247–250.

Svenson, O., & Sjöberg, K. (1983). Speeds of subitizing and counting processes in different age groups. *Journal of Genetic Psychology, 142*, 203–211.

Szeminska, A. (1935). Essai d'analyse psychologique du raisonnement mathématique. *Cahiers de Pédagogie Expérimentale et de Psychologie de l'Enfant* (Monograph 7).

Tardieu, G. (1955). Les infirmités cérébrales de l'enfant. *Revue Belge de Kinésithérapie, XXIII* (2), 47–55.

Taton, R. (1957). *Histoire générale des Sciences*. Paris: Presses Universitaires de France.

Taves, E. H. (1941). Two mechanisms for the perception of visual numerousness. *Archives of Psychology, 265*, 1–47.

Teng, E. L., & Sperry, R. W. (1974). Interhemispheric rivalry during simultaneous bilateral task presentation in commissurotomized patients. *Cortex, 10*, 111–120.

Thérien, L. (1985). *La notion de groupement chez Piaget: Prolongements formels et applications à la psychologie génétique* (Thèse, Faculté des Sciences sociales et politiques, Université de Lausanne). Québec: R. Prince.

Thompson, P. (1982). A theoretical framework for understanding young children's concepts of whole number numeration (Doctoral dissertation, University of Georgia, 1982). *Dissertation Abstracts International, 43*, 1868A.

Thorndike, E. L. (1922). *The psychology of arithmetic*. New York: Macmillan.

Tiberghien, G. (1985). Fragments d'histoire de la psychologie. In J. Mathieu & R. Thomas (Eds.). *Manuel de Psychologie* (pp. 19–37). Paris: Vigot.

Tollefsrud, L. (1981). *Preschoolers' use, understanding, and explanation of the number conservation principle*. Unpublished doctoral dissertation. University of Texas, Austin.

Tollefsrud-Anderson, L., Campbell, R. L., Starkey, P., & Cooper, R. G., Jr. (1986). *Number conservation: Distinguishing quantifier from operator solutions* (IBM Research Report RC 12151). Yorktown Heights, NY: IBM.

Turing, A. (1937). On computable numbers with application to the Entscheidungs problem. *Proceedings of the London Mathematical Society, Ser. 2, 42*, 23–265.

Van den Brink, J., & Streefland, L. (1979). Young children (6–8): Ratio and proportion. *Educational Studies in Mathematics, 10*, 403–420.

Van Engen, H. (1949). An analysis of meaning in arithmetic. *Elementary School Journal, 49*, 321–329, 395–400.

Vergnaud, G. (1981). *L'enfant, la mathématique et la réalité*. Berne: Peter Lang.

Vergnaud, G. (1982). A classification of cognitive tasks and operations of thought involved in addition and subtraction problems. In T. P. Carpenter, J. M. Moser, & T. A. Romberg (Eds.), *Addition and subtraction: A cognitive perspective* (pp. 39–59). Hillsdale, NJ: Lawrence Erlbaum Associates.

Vergnaud, G. (1983). Multiplicative structures. In R. Lesh & M. Landau (Eds.), *Acquisition of mathematics concepts and processes* (pp. 127–174). New York: Academic Press.

Vergnaud, G. (1985). Concepts et schèmes dans une théorie opératoire de la représentation. *Psychologie Française, 30*, 245–252.

Vergnaud, G. (1987). Les fonctions de l'action et de la symbolisation dans la formation des connaissances chez l'enfant. In J. Piaget, P. Mounoud, & J.-P. Bronckart (Eds.), *Psychologie: Encyclopédie de la pléiade* (pp. 821–844). Paris: Gallimard.

Vergnaud, G., & Durand, C. (1976). Structures additives et complexité psychogénétique. *Revue Française de Pédagogie, 36*, 28–43.

Vermersch, P. (1984). L'observation systématique dans l'étude du fonctionnement cognitif. *Psychologie Française, 29*, 297–302.

Vipond, D. (1980). Micro- and macro-processes in text comprehension. *Journal of Verbal Learning and Verbal Behavior, 19*, 276–296.

von Glasersfeld, E. (1981). An attentional model for the conceptual construction of units and number. *Journal for Research in Mathematics Education, 12*, 83–94.

von Glasersfeld, E. (1982). Subitizing: The role of figural patterns in the development of numerical concepts. *Archives de Psychologie, 50*, 191–218.

von Glasersfeld, E., & Richards, J. (1983). The creation of units as a prerequisite for numbers: A philosophical review. In L. P. Steffe, E. von Glasersfeld, J. Richards, & P. Cobb (Eds.), *Children's counting types: Philosophy, theory and application* (pp. 1–20). New York: Praeger Scientific.

von Neumann, J. (1925). Eine Axiomatisierung der Mengenlehre [An axiomatization of the set theory]. *Journal für reine und angewandte Mathematik, 154*, 219–240.

Vonèche, J. (1988). Espace et abstraction. *Archives de Psychologie, 56*, 105–116.

Vygotsky, L. (1962). *Thought and language*. Cambridge, MA: MIT Press.

Wagner, S. H., & Walters, J. (1982). A longitudinal analysis of early number concepts: From numbers to number. In G. Forman (Ed.), *Action and thought. From sensorimotor schemes to symbolic operations* (pp. 137–161). New York: Academic Press.

Weiner, S. L. (1974). On the development of more and less. *Journal of Experimental Child Psychology, 17*, 271–287.

Wertheimer, M. (1912). Experimentelle Studien über das Sehen von Bewegung [Experimental studies on the sight of movement]. *Zeitschrift für Psychologie, LXI*, 161–263.

Weyl, H. (1949). *Philosophy of mathematics and natural science*. New York: Princeton University Press.

Whitehead, A. N., & Russell, B. (1910/1912/1913). *Principia Mathematica*: Vol. 1, 2, & 3. Cambridge, U.K.: University Press.

Wiener, N. (1948). *Cybernetics*. New York: Wiley.

Wilkinson, A. C. (1984). Children's partial knowledge of the cognitive skill of counting. *Cognitive Psychology, 16*, 28–64.

Willis, G. B., & Fuson, K. C. (1988). Teaching children to use schematic drawings to solve addition and subtraction word problems. *Journal of Educational Psychology, 80*, 192–201.

Wittgenstein, L. (1921). *Tractatus logico-philosophicus*. London: Routledge and Kegan Paul.

Wittmann, J. (1929). *Theorie und Praxis eines ganzheitlichen, analytisch-synthetischen Unterrichts in Grundschule, Hilfsschule, Volksschule*. [Theory and practice of a globally, analytic-synthetic teaching in elementary, secondary, and special schools]. Potsdam: Müller & Kiepenheuer.

Wolters, G., van Kempen, H., & Wijlhuizen, G. J. (1987). Quantification of small numbers of dots: Subitizing or pattern recognition. *American Journal of Psychology, 100*, 225–237.

Wynn, K. (1990). Children's understanding of counting. *Cognition, 46*, 155–193.

Wynroth, L. (1986). *Wynroth math program: The natural numbers sequence*. Ithaca, NY: Wynroth Math Program.

Zaslavsky, C. (1973). *Africa counts*. Boston: Prindle, Weber & Schmidt.

Zimiles, H. (1963). A note on Piaget's concept of conservation. *Child Development, 34*, 691–695.

Addendum

Rochel Gelman
Betty Meck
University of California, Los Angeles

Baroody's Chapter 5 in this volume incorporates a variety of responses to our chapter. Although we edited occasionally to clarify what we wrote (see following), our chapter parallels the French version. What follows is neither an inclusive list of pertinent points nor a rebuttal to Baroody. We assume that readers will want to consult original sources on their own. Here, we list some especially salient matters of fact:

1. Contrary to the conjecture in footnote 8 (p. 108), the reversals in the count lists used in the stable-order error-detection conditions for set sizes 5, 7, and 20 were *not* restricted to the first five count words in the Gelman and Meck (1983).

2. Regarding footnote 13 (p. 117), it actually was the normal preschool children, not the school-aged, Down Syndrome (DS) children, who were in the harder condition in Gelman and Cohen (1988). For half of the preschoolers, the position of the item they were to "make the X" varied. In fact, the position of the targeted item for a DS subject varied between but not within subjects. Further, the DS children received intensive training in counting and therefore, if Baroody's account is correct, they should have learned more. Nevertheless, preschoolers outperformed 8 of the 10 DS children on a variety of criteria. For example, they were more inclined to self-correct and/or *self-initiate* a new attempt to solve the novel task. They also were able to benefit from indirect hints, whereas DS children even failed after watching a sample solution.

3. Figure 5.1 (p. 120) is based on a preliminary report to Baroody of the final work published in Gelman and Meck (1986).

4. Regarding footnote 10 (p. 112), children did see *E* point as she counted during the trick trial. Of course, she did not point conspicuously, otherwise she would not have met the design conditions of the trial. Children gave different kinds of explanations on trick trials as opposed to one–one error detection trials, an outcome that mitigates against the suggestion that we have a Clever Hans effect (footnote 11, p. 113).

5. Given Baroody's concerns (p. 113) about S#3, we did a full review of our summary data sheets and found two copying errors: (a) S#3 should have been entered as a 34-mo-old, and (b) the first child (a 29-mo-old) did not meet the spontaneous Card + and Count + criteria. Therefore, the right-most column of Row 1 in Table 8.1 (pp. 184–185) is changed to *No*. The requisite recalculated chi-square value appears on page 183 and is still significant. This analysis is not yoked to the arithmetic reasoning analysis that was published in the original paper. During Phase 2 of the magic experiment, the nonreinforced surprise trial(s) was followed with questions and discussion. The analyses in Table 8.1 are based *only* on the way count words were used after the surprise trial in Phase 2. All counts from this point — be these of each test display, a combination of the items on both plates, or the prizes a child accumulated during Phase 1 — were scored to arrive at the Count and Cardination data shown in Table 8.1.

6. Our adult counting study (pp. 178–179) makes the hypothesis that young children learn a cardinal rule on the basis of opportunities to imitate and be reinforced by their elders less plausible. We find that adults, like young children, do *not* repeat the last tag when answering "How many?" questions. Indeed, they get uncomfortable in a follow-up study that asks the How many? question again, presumably because conversational rules are violated. See Siegal (1991) for further cases of tasks that confound the assessment of interpretative and conceptual competence and excellent discussion of the questions raised by Baroody on pages 123–124.

7. Baroody writes that "learning plays a role in many behaviors that were once thought to be innate" (footnote 18, p. 125) and offers several examples, including bird song. This is true, but it does not follow that terms like *learned* and *innate* are treated as opposites by all modern ethologists and animal learning theorists who study these kinds of complex acts. For example, in his chapter, "The Instinct to Learn," Marler (1991) developed a detailed account of how an innate template helps the immature male white-crowned sparrow attend to and store examples of his adult song, well before he can sing or even enters the extended periods of practice and learning that must follow before he will sing a mature adult song. See Gallistel, Brown, Carey, Gelman, and Keil (1991) for further examples of privileged learnings.

Author Index

Subject Index